One China, Many Paths

V

One China, Many Paths

Edited by

CHAOHUA WANG

VERSO

London • New York

First published by Verso 2003
© in the translations and collection, Verso 2003

10 9 8 7 6 5 4 3 2 1

Verso
UK: 6 Meard Street, London W1F 0EG
USA: 180 Varick Street, New York, NY 10014–4606
www.versobooks.com

Verso is the imprint of New Left Books

ISBN 1–85984–537–1

British Library Cataloguing in Publication Data
A catalogue record for this book is available from the British Library

Library of Congress Cataloging-in-Publication Data
A catalog record for this book is available from the Library of Congress

Typeset in Galliard by SetSystems Ltd, Saffron Walden, Essex
Printed and bound in USA by R.R. Donnelley

To the Memory of Lu Chunlin

(1962–1989)

Contents

MISCELLANIES

Introduction

Minds of the Nineties

Wang Chaohua

For more than a century, Chinese intellectuals have been engaged in translating and introducing Western thought and literature in China. Political developments, including wars and civil wars, and many other upheavals, have interrupted the long flow of this work of learning, but never brought it to a halt. Today, Chinese readers have access in their native language to large areas of Western literature and philosophy, political and economic thought, to classical texts and contemporary ideas of the world. But this process of cultural familiarization has been one-sided. Neither the length and depth of traditional Chinese civilization, nor the importance of China in the modern history of the world, are reflected in a comparable range of Western translations of Chinese thought and culture. Classical poetry and fiction have found skilled and devoted translators, but history and philosophy have been much less well served.

After the establishment of the People's Republic in 1949, the Chinese government set up official translation offices and a foreign-language publishing house, with the intention of correcting the imbalance in the cultural exchanges between China and the West. However, as these institutions became more and more tightly controlled by the ruling power, their selection of works for translation into Western languages became increasingly narrow and arbitrary. In particular, the spectrum of writing from late nineteenth- and twentieth-century China was never adequately represented, since here political criteria determined everything that could be brought to foreign notice. Since the dismantling of most of the cultural apparatus of the Maoist period, such restrictions no longer apply, but the Chinese State has meanwhile ceased to concern itself with large-scale translations. Today it is essentially Western scholars who are gradually starting to cover some of the long-standing deficit in the balance of intellectual payments between China and the West. Major English-language editions of such classics as Sima Qian's *The Grand Scribe's Records* or the *Jin Ping Mei* are cases in point.[1] But the development of modern Chinese culture still remains only dimly visible in foreign mirrors. To take some of the most obvious examples, there are no English translations of the principal works of Hu Shih, the central figure of early Chinese liberalism; of Lu Xun's essays, which have been at least as influential as his fiction; of Wang Guowei's literary and philosophical studies; or of Chen Yinke's historical scholarship.[2]

In the nineties, when China became the world's most dynamic economy – the PRC has overtaken Japan to become the largest exporter to the United States, and is also Japan's major trading partner – coverage of Chinese developments increased enormously in the world's press. Foreign readers are now served by a range of first-rate correspondents reporting on social and cultural life in the mainland, in a way that was not possible before. But while Chinese works of literature have earned growing international recognition since the eighties as deserving translation into other languages in a timely and comprehensive fashion, this has yet to be the case for contemporary intellectual debates, which as a rule remain accessible only through scanty and intermittent coverage by news media. For the most part, all that is available in the West are occasional summaries of particular themes or scattered disputes, with little background explanation. The voices of Chinese thinkers themselves rarely reach the West without much reduction or mediation. In general, coverage of key debates remains thin and patchy, making it difficult even for those highly interested to follow developments in China. Japan, where the range of translations from Chinese is broader and more up-to-date, is better served.

The aim of this volume is to help in a modest way to correct this imbalance, by presenting the diversity of outlook among contemporary Chinese thinkers directly. I believe this is the only way for English-speaking readers to gain a real understanding of the Chinese intellectual scene since the 1990s. Such an understanding is not a mere concern for 'area studies'. In the past decade, debates among Chinese intellectuals have acquired an ever-stronger global colour; they can be seen as attempts to think not just about their own country's problems, but about issues that confront the world as a whole. So a record of their contributions is also a way to provoke and participate in an intellectual engagement across frontiers.

---

[1] See, for these recent efforts, Sima Qian, *The Grand Scribe's Records* (*Shi ji*), William Nienhauser Jr. ed, Bloomington, 1994 onwards; and David Tod Roy's translation of *The Plum in the Golden Vase, or Chin P'ing Mei*, Princeton, 1993 onwards.

[2] Wang Guowei's life and thought have attracted a few research monographs, but there is only one English translation from his writings, by Adele Austin Rickett, *Wang Kuo-wei's Jen-chien Tz'u-hua: A Study in Chinese Literary Criticism*, Hong Kong, 1977. Chen Yinke is quoted extensively in *The Cambridge History of China*, vol. 3, *Sui and T'ang China, 589–906*, Cambridge, 1979, but no English edition of any of his works is available yet.

I

To explain the texts collected below, a brief sketch of the period of Chinese intellectual history they cover may be helpful. This is now sometimes referred to as the 'second reform decade', a term that like many earlier such labels of a semi-official sort conceals as much as it reveals. In this usage the 'first reform decade', or New Era, stretches from 1978, with the 'household responsibility system' emerging in the countryside when the People's Communes were dissolved, to the urban price reforms of 1988. The political crisis of 1989 then marked a sharp divide. After an interval, the 'second reform decade' is generally thought to have begun in early 1992, with Deng Xiaoping's tour of southern China, and continued till the Sixteenth National Congress of the CCP in 2002, which installed a new generation of national leaders in top positions. In a looser sense, we can speak of the two periods simply as 'the eighties' and 'the nineties'.

For Chinese intellectuals, the two 'reform decades' have had sharply contrasting characters, even if there is a wide range of evaluation regarding the nature of the differences between them. The eighties, to which many look back nostalgically, are sometimes compared to the May Fourth period, as a brief time of explosive energies in which new ideas were eagerly explored, in a hopeful and creative climate. If this analogy were valid, the nineties could be seen as something like a counterpart of the years between the late twenties to the eve of the war in summer 1937, in which dreams dissolved and intellectuals came down to earth again under the pressure of major political events that forced them to confront their ideas with the daily life of ordinary people, dividing an intelligentsia that had been hitherto relatively united in a series of splits and disputes. This is a comparison suggested by Wang Hui below, and there is much to be said for it. The parallels between the two historical periods are in many ways quite striking.[3]

Still, such analogies can only go so far, since every intellectual conjuncture has its own specific features. A comparison of the eighties with the May Fourth period may seem flattering. But it also serves to bring out certain limitations of the Open Door climate of the time. The 'emancipation of thought' after the fall of the Gang of Four was real enough, releasing a great burst of cultural energy and enthusiasm, stimulated by new contact with the outside world. The dogmatic shackles of the Mao period were thrown off, and freedom of expression steadily widened. Previously forbidden philosophical or sociological works from the West were eagerly translated and discussed.

---

[3] Xu Jilin has also suggested this comparison; see, 'The Fate of an Enlightenment – Twenty Years in the Chinese Intellectual Sphere (1978–1998)', *East Asian History*, December 2000, pp. 169–186. An earlier version appeared in *Ershi yi shiji* (*Twenty-First Century* – hereafter *TFC*), December 1998, pp. 4–13. Zhu Xueqin, Chen Pingyuan and Qin Hui to various degrees dissent from this comparison in their discussions below.

Experimental forms in poetry, fiction, theatre and the cinema flourished. But amidst all this ferment, public discussions continued to be organized within established frameworks of reference, and were often dominated by leading figures inside the Party and government apparatus, rather than coming from universities or an emergent civil society. Theoretical debates revolved around official slogans like 'practice is the sole test of truth', or problems like 'Marxist humanism'. Even less orthodox themes, like the call for a 'new enlighten-ment', did not stray very far from mainstream discourse. The boundaries of these debates were defined by the suppression of the 'democracy wall' movement in early 1979, at the outset of this period.[4]

Looking back, it is clear that much of the intellectual energy of this period was directed to the effort to re-establish what were felt to be universal values in 'Marxism' that had been trampled on during the era of Mao. However, they suffered from paying insufficient attention to the specific future of the nation, and from lacking much understanding of contemporary developments in the world outside China. The theoretical concerns of the time were closely related to the immediate mentality of the reform process, expressed in the official motto coined by Prime Minister and then Party Secretary Zhao Ziyang that 'the river should be crossed by stepping one stone at a time'. It was generally accepted that there was a river to be crossed, since 'the near bank' (the Maoist experiment) was in hopeless crisis. But there was scarcely any clear idea of what the 'far bank' would look like. The slogan said nothing of what lay on the other side of the water, and intellectual discussion did not make good this shortcoming, typical of the thinking of the eighties.[5]

Instead, there was a widespread belief that if theory just picked its way from one stone to another, policy would follow it. Intellectual explorations seemed to enjoy a rarely seen degree of social influence and authority, which was never really reduced by sporadic official campaigns against the dangers of 'bourgeois liberalism'. Inspired by a feeling they were marching across the river, the intelligentsia spared little time to look back and reflect on the direction its steps were taking it, or whether anyone might fall into the swirling waters. The sudden drowning of its hopes in 1989 came as a tremendous shock. Many of those who had been most active in the eighties

---

[4] The boundaries were broken for the first time in early 1989 with the call by Fang Lizhi for the unconditional release of Wei Jingsheng, symbol of the 'democracy wall' movement. See Jing Wang, *High Cultural Fever*, Berkeley, 1996; Chen Fong-ching and Jin Guantao, *From Youthful Manuscripts to River Elegy*, Hong Kong, 1997; Xudong Zhang, *Chinese Modernism in the Era of Reforms*, Durham, 1997; and Xiaomei Chen, *Occidentalism*, Lanham, 2002.

[5] It is telling that as late as the summer of 2002 Yu Guangyuan – responsible for drafting key Party documents more than twenty years ago – was still defending the direction of the Reform period in terms of breaking old Marxist taboos by introducing the concepts of 'market' and 'commodity economy' into official thinking. Yu, 'Modernization and China's Path', paper at a conference on Globalization, Hangzhou, 2002. For Yu's role in this phase, see Chen and Jin, op. cit., pp. 50–51, 80–81.

were thus ill-prepared to understand and interpret the great socio-economic upheavals of the nineties. Viewed historically, the achievements in literature and the arts of the 'first reform decade' will probably come to be seen as much more striking than its thinking in policy-related fields, and more truly representative of the creative energies of the period. In this sense, the 1980s could be described as a combination of 'high cultural fever' and 'weak (or weaker) intellectual thought'.

The 1990s present a very different picture. The CCP's crackdown on the peaceful demonstrators of Tiananmen Square in June 1989 can indeed be compared to the KMT massacre of workers in Shanghai in 1927, as a traumatic shock inaugurating a new phase of intellectual history. But in other respects the background conditions of the two periods were quite the opposite of each other. Politically, the decade between the formation of the Nanjing regime and the outbreak of war with Japan was one of continuing regional division and a relatively weak central government. Economically, it saw the arrival of the World Depression. In the nineties, on the other hand, the central government was stronger and more united than in the previous decade, and faced no significant threats to its power. Furthermore the economy witnessed an unprecedented boom. The official watchword was to uphold 'stability' at all costs, which ruled out any reversal of the reforms already in place from the 1980s, let alone an internal upheaval within the regime itself. The basic dynamic of Deng's Open Door policy did not stop. While its social contradictions became steadily sharper, politically they were subdued with an iron fist.

Intellectual life reflected this paradoxical development. Though it was temporarily frozen after 1989, it did not suffer thoroughgoing repression, and quite soon picked up again. But its landscape changed significantly in the next decade. Two structural transformations, independent of political conditions, were important here. The first of these was the emergence of an international field of communication and exchange within Chinese culture that now extends from the mainland to Hong Kong, Taiwan and Singapore, the United States and Australia, with outposts in Japan and Europe. This is partly a result of globalization, as ever more Chinese have gone abroad to study, often then settling overseas – they make up far the largest contingent of foreign students in the US. It has also partly been a consequence of the political exile that befell a significant number of intellectuals after 1989. Another factor has been the increasing economic ties, of investment and trade, that the PRC has sought to weave with Taiwan and Singapore, as well as the recovery of Hong Kong by the mainland. Lastly, of course, the Internet has made possible a virtual integration of these different communities that would have been impossible ten years earlier. The consequence is that there is today a Chinese space of discussion across borders that never existed in the same way before, with an ever-growing impact on the production and circulation of ideas within Chinese culture.

The second important change has been the emergence for the first time of modern universities as the primary institutional space for the generation and discussion of ideas. This is a standard feature of Western societies, but it is quite recent in China, where in the eighties academic life was still dominated by the recovering disciplinary traditions of the fifties and sixties, and it was editorial groups and publishing houses that took the lead in intellectual discussions.[6] Today intellectuals in China are much more likely to have university posts, and to fill them in ways resembling their counterparts in the West, than ten or twenty years ago. Chinese universities, in turn, now play a far more significant bridging role to the outside world, organizing exchanges with intellectuals abroad, particularly in the United States, than in the eighties. This change has to some extent reflected greater pressures on the publishing world, from both political controls and commercial forces. But it also corresponds to the influence of the American model of intellectual life, overwhelmingly concentrated in the academy. It may be significant that exchanges between Chinese intellectuals and their counterparts in Japan, South Korea and Europe, where print media seem to play a more active role than universities in stirring up controversies, have grown more slowly and had less domestic impact.[7]

One consequence of this pattern of academic interchange has been an increase in heavily imported discourses of one kind or another in the wake of successive US fashions, by contrast with the direct and highly visible connections between intellectual debates and everyday social life in the 1980s, however simplified the latter might have been. Opportunities for Chinese scholars to go abroad also tend to conform to disciplinary boundaries, since most contacts remain within the field of China-studies, rather than developing intellectual dialogue at more general levels. Notwithstanding such limitations, however, it is clear that Chinese culture has benefited enormously from the deepening of institutional exchanges with the West. If the eighties were principally a time of assimilation, the hallmark of the nineties has been a more sophisticated exploration of a wider range of foreign influences, and a creative tension with them.

II

A decade is a short time in the intellectual life of a country. But in China the dozen years since 1990 divide into three phases, largely determined by political shifts at state level. These do not form watertight compartments.

---

[6] For this pattern, see the excellent discussion in Chen and Jin, op. cit., chapters 3–5.

[7] Quantitatively, institutional exchanges with Japan and South Korea have been growing steadily, but so far these do not seem to have had the same qualitative effects on intellectual debates within China as those with the US.

As one would expect in such a tight time-frame, there was a considerable overlap between them, most intellectual debates initiated in one phase lasting into the next or throughout the whole decade. Nevertheless, it makes sense to distinguish between the interval from the clampdown of June 1989 to the end of 1991; the years extending from Deng Xiaoping's southern tour in 1992 to his incapacitation in 1995; and the period of Jiang Zemin's uncontested leadership that ran till the spring of 2003.

In the first phase public security was the top government priority, in the immediate aftermath of June 4, 1989. The military crackdown was followed by the imposition of much tighter political controls over cultural life. But the intelligentsia as such was not subjected to any wholesale wave of repression. There was no equivalent to the Anti-Rightist campaign organized by Deng Xiaoping in the mid-fifties. The state's objective was more to disperse intellectual opposition than to extinguish it. The various editorial groups and institutes that had been centres of reform ideas in the eighties were suspended or shut down. Intellectuals who were thought to have sympathized too warmly, or participated too openly, in the movement of 1989 were dispatched to the countryside or lost their positions. Quite a few were imprisoned, while others went abroad, voluntarily or involuntarily. Meanwhile economic reforms continued, but party elders were still at loggerheads over future policy, giving little sense of overall direction to the country. Once martial law was lifted in early 1990, rustications were phased out and a semblance of normality returned to cultural life. Henceforward, however, the relationship between state and intellectuals was on a footing very different from in the eighties. The politics of China's ruling party and the thinking of its intelligentsia now took separate courses. The intellectual thought of the nineties lost its earlier function as a weathervane of reform directions that the government would take at the next step. This did not mean that the two necessarily collided. There were, particularly in the early years of the decade, times when official ideology compromised or even cooperated with intelligentsia thinking. But on these occasions the two sides sought to take advantage of each other, unlike the situation in the 1980s when leading intellectuals were closely linked with 'reform-minded' top leaders in public perception. In fact, the terms 'conservative' and 'reformer' that were both popular and quite practical as political distinctions in the eighties now lost most of their relevance.

In this new situation, a key role in the gradual revival of public discussion after 1989 was played by the Hong Kong-based bi-monthly *Ershi yi shiji* (*Twenty-First Century*), founded in 1990 by two leading intellectual activists of the eighties, Liu Qingfeng and Jin Guantao, who had held fellowships in the British colony during the June Fourth Movement, and so were removed from the crisis in the mainland. Setting a high intellectual standard from the start, the journal provided a vital space for theoretical and historical debates relatively free of direct political censorship. Its editor, Liu Qingfeng, passionate and outspoken in her own opinions, maintained an admirable balance and openness regarding even the most diverse viewpoints. Circulating with some difficulty in the PRC, *Twenty-First Century* offered a new kind of bridge between mainland and overseas intellectuals. Many of its contributors were numbered among the former, but many of its debates triggered by the latter.[8]

The first of the issues where intellectuals and power-holders initiated discussions separately, yet converged pragmatically, was the attack on 'radicalism' set off in 1990 by the distinguished overseas historian Yu Ying-Shih, then at Princeton. In a programmatic article in the second issue of *Twenty-First Century* entitled 'Picking up the Pieces for a New Start', Yu deplored what he described as the legacy of Chinese extremism of the twentieth century, rejecting the intellectual radicalism that had been responsible for making an essentially 'marginal class' the rulers of modern China. After a volley of replies, Yu retorted with 'Further Thoughts on Radicalism and Conservatism in Modern Chinese Intellectual History' in early 1992, reaffirming his positions.[9] Three years later, with widespread recognition of the end of the Cold War and the end of 'history', a still more sweeping rejection of the whole course of modern Chinese history came from two exiles of 1989, the philosopher Li Zehou and literary critic Liu Zaifu, in their volume *Farewell to Revolution*, which regretted even the establishment of a republic in 1911 itself.[10] By then, official media and academic spokesmen had for some time also been criticizing the excessive radicalism of the May Fourth outlook, as the ancestor of later aberrations in the Cultural Revolution and Tiananmen Square.

A second debate in these years revolved around the ideas of 'civil society' and the 'public sphere'. Here too the initiative came from overseas, first from exiles looking at the way in which successive regimes were brought down in Eastern Europe, and then from scholars comparing incipient signs of capitalism or modernity in China with those in the West. In early 1992 a conference was held at UCLA devoted to the question whether there had been traditional Chinese counterparts of the Western notions expounded by Habermas, and what the prospects were for their emergence in the mainland

[8] Liu Qingfeng has herself written an informative, though somewhat dejected, account of the recent Chinese intellectual scene; see 'The Topography of Intellectual Culture in 1990s Mainland China: A Survey', in Gloria Davies, ed, *Voicing Concerns*, Lanham, 2001, pp. 47–70, a volume that contains a range of interesting contributions on this period.

[9] Yu Ying-shih, 'Picking up the Pieces for a New Start', *TFC*, December 1990, pp. 5–7; 'Further Thoughts on Radicalism and Conservatism in Modern Chinese Intellectual History', *TFC*, April 1992, pp. 143–149. For an English version, see Yu Ying-shih, 'The Radicalization of China in the Twentieth Century', *Daedalus* (spring 1993), pp. 125–150. Debates around Yu's propositions continued in *TFC* for a few years, with participants including Lin Gang, Jiang Yihua, Xiao Gongqin, Lin Yu-sheng, Chen Lai, and Yan Jiayan.

[10] Li Zehou and Liu Zaifu, *Gaobie geming: Hui wang ershi shiji Zhongguo* (Farewell to Revolution: Looking back at Twentieth-Century China), Hong Kong, 1995.

today.[11] This theme, whose oppositional potential was evident, nevertheless once again found an echo in the ruling discourse, where it took the form of calls for the public to be patient and wait for the growth of a new middle class as a precondition of modernity.[12] Noteworthy in both cases was the official attitude to these discussions, the authorities tolerating all the participants in the debates over 'radicalism versus conservatism' and 'civil society'. Deng Xiaoping's slogan 'Development is the Irrefutable Argument', posted on huge billboards across the country, appeared to promise that once the economy went up and was stabilized, everything would be possible – political improvements would only be a matter of time.

A third example of the same process can be seen with the creation in late 1991 of the independent journal *Xueren* (*The Scholar*), sponsored by a Japanese foundation.[13] The project of its editors – Chen Pingyuan, Wang Hui and Wang Shouchang – was to retrieve the history of modern Chinese scholarship (*xueshu shi*), a tradition they felt was in danger of being obscured or forgotten under the pressure of imported theories. In doing so, they wanted to clarify their own intellectual identity and responsibilities. What was their position in a historical chain of scholarly development? When and how should a scholar speak out on public issues? The result was a pioneering, though eventually short-lived, journal, whose background lay in the self-examination of intellectuals intimately involved in the ferment of the eighties. One of its editors had been a signatory of a famous open letter calling for the unconditional release of Wei Jingsheng in early 1989, another had been exiled to the countryside for participation in the events that followed; the third was a founding member of the recently suspended Academy of Chinese Culture.[14]

Yet here too, with quite different motivations, official ideology developed in a curious parallel, cultivating the spiritual and intellectual resources of

---

[11] See 'Symposium: "Public Sphere"/"Civil Society" in China?', special issue of *Modern China*, April 1993, based on the proceedings of the conference in Los Angeles. In his 1990 article (see note 8 above), Yu Ying-shih had argued that intellectual radicalism was responsible for destroying the potential of civil society in modern China. Also see Wang Shaoguang (Wang Hsiao-guang), 'Reflections on Civil Society', *TFC*, December 1991, pp. 102–114, and Wang Hui, 'Yuci shuli: gonggong lingyu' (Key words: Public sphere), *Dushu*, June 1995, pp. 131–134.

[12] One of the themes of *Farewell to Revolution* was that China needed to go through a four-phase development of 'economic growth → individual freedom → social justice → political democracy' as both logical process and chronological order, an argument criticized by Tsou Tang, 'On *Farewell to Revolution*', and Chang Jiang, 'A Curious Cultural Phenomenon During the Social Transition – On *Farewell to Revolution*', *TFC*, February 1996, pp. 62–67 and pp. 68–71, respectively.

[13] *Xueren* was published in the form of a book series between 1991 and 2000. Approval for books is easier to get than for periodicals, which has encouraged the appearance of irregular journals published as books. Similar cases include *Res Publica* and *Horizons*, discussed below. See Qi Gan, 'Pushing the Limits: The Emergence and Growth of China's Private Book Industry', manuscript, Seattle, 2003.

[14] See Chen and Jin, op. cit., pp. 148 and 154.

tradition for its own purposes. In early 1991, some months before the appearance of *Xueren*, the National Education Commission had held a forum under the theme 'Correctly View Traditional Chinese Culture', intended to help root out the influence of Western theories and the notion of a 'New Enlightenment' that had been popular in the eighties, and to refute the running-down of the Chinese past in the television series *He shang* (*River Elegy*), a propagandist hit produced by circles around Zhao Ziyang in 1988.[15] In 1993 Peking University published *Guoxue yanjiu* (*Research on National Studies*) and *Guguo xin zhi* (*Old Country, New Knowledge*). In August of that year, the *People's Daily* published a long feature report, 'National Studies, Quietly Rising on the Campus of Peking University', stressing in follow-up reports that an important purpose of national studies today must be to arouse patriotic passion among the people.[16] Amid this 'national studies fever' (*guoxue re*), the university started a new 'experimental class in the humanities', dubbed by the news media as a 'class of national studies masters'. What Chen Pingyuan had conceived as the solitary path of the scholar had crossed with the highway of bureaucratic pomp.

A related episode was the rise of Neo-Confucianism as a topic to which mainland intellectuals, overseas scholars and official interests – each with different concerns in mind – contributed. The origins of this trend go back to the eighties, when a group of young philosophy teachers in Beijing set up an independent Academy of Chinese Culture in early 1985, headed by Tang Yijie, holder of a chair in Chinese philosophy at Peking University. At that time renewed interest in Confucianism was part of a wider quest for the cultural resources to assist national modernization. In the crackdown after June Fourth, the Academy was suspended, resuming its activities only in 1993.[17] Meanwhile the recent economic success of the 'Little Dragons' of East Asia had given rise to much overseas discussion of the role of 'Asian values' in fast regional growth. The potential significance of this theme for the PRC was not lost on the authorities in the mainland, and in October 1994 an International Confucian Association was founded in Beijing, at a conference addressed by such prominent dignitaries of the CCP as Li Lanqing and Li Ruihuan – both members of its Central Standing Committee – and graced by the hospitality of President

---

[15] *River Elegy* was a popular television series, offering a melodramatic portrait of the backwardness and tyranny of traditional Chinese civilization, symbolically identified with the Yellow River, while extolling the 'Blue Ocean' of Western civilization into whose liberating waters the PRC should now sail. For a critique of it, see Xiaomei Chen, *Occidentalism*, chapter 1, pp. 23–42.

[16] 'Guoxue, zai yanyuan you qiaoran xingqi', *People's Daily*, August 16, 1993.

[17] The Academy of Chinese Culture is described in Chen and Jin, pp. 129–157. Tu Wei-ming, a scholar teaching at Harvard and involved in the Academy since 1985, had also joined the discussion on radicalism versus conservatism, an example of the intertwining of themes after 1989. See Tu Wei-ming, 'Beyond the Enlightenment Syndrome', *TFC*, December 1990.

Jiang Zemin. With the decay of official Marxism-Leninism-Mao Zedong thought, the potential of Confucian moralism as a substitute code of social discipline was increasingly attractive to the ruling party. In this case, private business showed a keen interest for its own reasons in the promotion of Neo-Confucianism, with various commercial enterprises funding research and symposia along lines similar to those of this gathering. Not a few intellectuals involved in the Academy of the eighties took part in these official activities, making them the most pointed example of convergence in these years.[18]

III

As the ruling party proceeded to rebuild its power, there was a basic change in the way it addressed society. Throughout the late seventies and eighties, the legitimation of the regime had continued to be driven by ideology – no longer Maoism, but the promises of a reformed socialism with 'Chinese characteristics'. After 1989, this discourse experienced continuous metamorphoses, with an ever-growing emphasis on 'Chinese characteristics', while its 'socialist' contents became more and more nominal. Actual legitimation was henceforward driven by interests: that is, the government's ability to satisfy the material demands of enough key groups to give it a basis of passive consent in the population. To achieve this goal, the party turned towards the market. The economic reforms of the eighties had started a process of transforming state-owned enterprises into share-holding companies to improve their management and profitability. The first stocks went on sale in Shenzhen in 1988, getting only a lukewarm public response. But in late 1989, get-rich-quick rumours triggered a sudden frenzy of stock trading in Shenzhen. The government responded by setting up stock exchanges in both Shanghai and Shenzhen by the end of 1990, temporarily stabilizing this mass reaction.

Just over a year later, in January 1992 Deng Xiaoping made his famous southern tour. This marked a clear shift of gear, opening a second phase of the nineties. The high point of Deng's inspection trip was a visit to the Shenzhen Stock Exchange, in which he extolled its innovative 'socialist market' practice and criticized those who dogmatically questioned each reform measure for its legitimacy within China's ideological framework. Deng warned his senior party colleagues that there would be no more

---

[18] See Tang Yijie, 'Some Reflections on New Confucianism in Mainland Chinese Culture of the 1990s' in Davies, *Voicing Concerns*, pp. 123–134; and Jing Wang, *High Cultural Fever*, pp. 64–78. For criticisms of this trend, see, for example, Zhu Xueqin, 'The Illusion that Modernity can be Generated from Traditional Sagehood: On the Political Philosophy of Neo-Confucianists', *TFC*, February 1992, pp. 116–124; and Xia Zhongyi, 'On Confucianism and the Sedimentation Theory of Li Ze-hou', *TFC*, April 1993, pp. 124–132.

debate on 'Surname S or Surname C' – socialism or capitalism (*xing she xing zi*). Obviously, this was a revised version of Deng's remark in earlier years about his indifference to the colour of cats, so long as they caught mice. In the following months, millions of new urban investors rushed to invest, causing a serious riot in Shenzhen in August 1992, which forced a temporary closure of the Exchange. Deng was unmoved and the Fourteenth Party Congress, held in October that year, fully adopted Deng's go-ahead for further marketization.[19] Meanwhile, the print media were set loose to handle their own budget and distribution systems, outside old institutional settings. From 1990 to 1994, investment in advertising rose from 2.5 billion to 20 billion yuan, half of it in the three great metropolitan centres of Beijing, Shanghai and Guangzhou.[20]

Soon a wave of commercial euphoria caught up the big cities, creating a new cultural atmosphere in which market values became increasingly unbridled. In the tidal wave of mass culture unleashed by Deng Xiaoping's guideline of 'To Get Rich is Glorious', the whole nation was called to the task of commercialization. It was in this context that, soon after the party's congress in late 1992, the writer Wang Meng, a former Minister of Culture, published his essay 'Avoiding the Sublime' in *Dushu* (Readings), the leading intellectual monthly in the mainland. In this, he extolled the self-proclaimed 'lout literature' (*wanzhu wenxue*) of Wang Shuo for its 'perfect fit with the Four Cardinal Principles and the market economy'. It is not surprising that this provocation caused a strong reaction.[21] Intellectuals working in the humanities based in Shanghai and Nanjing, where commercialization ran far ahead of other parts of the country, were among the first to see the turn of the party towards garish popular entertainment as a big blow, and a dozen of them struck out against the new trends in *Dushu*.[22] This was the

---

[19] Richard Baum, *Burying Mao: Chinese Politics in the Age of Deng Xiaoping*, Princeton, 1994, pp. 328–368.

[20] Chen Huailin, 'Institutional Changes in Chinese Mass Media in the Nineties', *TFC*, June 1999, pp. 4–14.

[21] Wang Meng, 'Duobi chonggao', *Dushu*, January 1993, pp. 10–16. Chen Pingyuan's article, 'The Decline of High Culture in Modern China', *TFC*, June 1993, pp. 11–22, was the first to criticize this formulation, though it was also a response to one of Yu Ying-Shih's theses that drew reactions in turn from Zhao Yiheng and Xu Jilin. See Yu Ying-Shih, 'The Marginalization of Chinese Intellectuals', *TFC*, August 1991, pp. 15–25; Xu Jilin, 'Can High Culture Redeem Itself?' *TFC*, October 1993, pp. 137–142, and Zhao Yiheng, 'Zouxiang bianyuan' (Marginalization), *Dushu*, January 1994, pp. 36–42.

[22] Wang Xiaoming et al., 'Kuangye shang de feixu: Wenxue yu renwen jingshen de weiji' (Ruin in desolated land: the crisis in literature and in humanistic spirit), *Shanghai wenxue*, June 1993; Lu Shan (Zhu Xueqin), 'Chinese "Lout" Culture: An Uneven Double-Edged Sword', *TFC*, August 1993, pp. 130–133; Zhang Rulun et al., 'Renwen jingshen xunsi lu' (Reflections on humanistic spirit), parts 1–5, *Dushu*, March–July 1994. Lu Shan's article distinguishes between the marginalization of intellectuals by political power and by the market, relating its ongoing forms to the second more than the first. The major contributions to the debate have been collected, with a bibliography, by Wang Xiaoming in *Renwen jingshen xunsi lu* (Reflections on humanistic spirit), Shanghai, 1996.

background for the vigorous defence of the 'humanistic spirit' against the emergent culture industry, mounted by a group of Shanghai intellectuals in 1993, among them Zhu Xueqin and Wang Xiaoming. Neither official ideology nor popular opinion showed any relish for this discussion. In the same year, the literary critic Qian Liqun published a book, *Fengfu de tongku* (Intense Pain) on the trans-cultural reception of images of Quixote and Hamlet. One of the leading themes of this work, the need for intellectuals to accept the challenge of Hamlet in the spirit of Quixote, struck a comparable note of resistance to the new commercial culture.[23]

More or less at the same time, a counter-thrust came from exponents of the 'postmodern' in the journal *Zhongshan*. The notion of postmodernism had been introduced into China by Fredric Jameson in the mid-eighties, when it had fascinated some of the most gifted young graduates at Peking University. When it was taken up and applied to Chinese conditions by Zhang Yiwu, Chen Xiaoming and others a decade later, however, the caustic edge of Jameson's theory, which had described postmodernism as 'the cultural logic of late capitalism', was abandoned for a contented or even enthusiastic endorsement of mass culture, which they saw as a new space of popular freedom. According to these critics, intellectuals, who conceived of themselves as the bearers of modernity, were reacting with shock and anxiety at their loss of control with the arrival of postmodern consumer society, uttering cries of 'quixotic hysteria', panic-stricken by the realization of what they had once called for during the eighties.[24]

These polemics provoked a tart retort from Zhao Yiheng, a leading literary scholar and writer based in London, published in *Twenty-First Century* under the title 'Post-isms and Chinese New Conservatism'. He argued that postmodernism of this sort had a general affinity with the bureaucratic encouragement of intellectual dumbing-down and conformism.[25] In due course this brought a rejoinder from Xu Ben, a comparative literature scholar based in California, contrasting the political urgency of Jameson's theory of the postmodern with Zhang Yiwu's more complicit

---

[23] See the review of it by Wang Qiankun, 'Zhongguo de Tangjikede men' (China's Quixotes), *Dushu*, January 1995, pp. 46–51.

[24] Chen Xiaoming, Zhang Yiwu, Dai Jinhua and Zhu Wei, 'Dongfang zhuyi yu hou zhimin zhuyi' (Orientalism and post-colonialism), and 'Wenhua kongzhi yu wenhua dazhong' (Cultural control and cultural masses), in *Zhongshan*, January, pp. 126–148 and March, pp. 185–203, 1994. Dai Jinhua demurred at her colleagues' ridicule of intellectuals, and said she was herself still in some shock at changes in the cultural scene.

[25] Zhao Yiheng, ' "Post-ism" and China's New Conservatism', *TFC*, February 1995, pp. 4–15. There followed a protracted debate in the journal. For example, Zhang Yiwu, 'The Anxiety of Interpreting China', April 1995, pp. 128–135; Wan Zhi, 'Criticism of the "Post-ism" Criticism', October 1995, pp. 144–146; Zhao Yiheng, 'Cultural Criticism and Post-Modernistic Theories', October 1995, pp. 147–151; special feature on 'Pidgin Scholarship or Epistemological Privilege?', with contributions by Liu Dong, Lei Yi, Cui Zhi-yuan and Gan Yang, December 1995, pp. 4–28.

approach.[26] Debates over 'post-ism' rolled on throughout the nineties, inside and outside the mainland. Towards the end of the decade, Zhang Xudong, a pupil of Jameson based in the US, offered a much more nuanced exposition of the potential relevance of postmodern categories to China. This analysis was closer in spirit to Jameson's Marxist account and pointed out the implications of an uncritical acceptance of the idea of 'modernity' as a codeword for capitalism in China, although still arguing for seeds of cultural democracy in the country's ongoing marketization.[27]

All the debates described so far were of an essentially theoretical nature, revolving around issues of general intellectual or cultural positions, without immediate practical consequences. This was, of course, one of the reasons for the government tolerance of them. But the first half of the nineties also saw a series of policy-oriented discussions, with more directly political implications. In the loosening of media control in 1993, 'cultural workers' quickly discovered that the public retained a considerable appetite for critical social interventions. In both television and newspapers, features of this kind became popular, while private bookstores became centres for intellectual gatherings.[28] Amid the boom in popular culture, two intellectual journals, *Zhanlüe yu guanli* (Strategy and Management), and *Dongfang* (Orient), each of great energy, came into being in November 1993. Both started exploring issues closely related to the direction of China's reforms, including discussions of changes in the countryside, the stock market and the experience of East European countries and Russia since 1990.[29] These periodicals soon joined in the debates originating from intellectuals based overseas that

---

[26] See *TFC* for these sequels, Xu Ben, ' "Third World Criticism" in China Today', February 1995, pp. 16–27; Zhang Yiwu, 'Further Thoughts on the Anxiety of Interpreting China', April 1996, pp. 121–126; Xu Ben, 'What is China's "post-New Era"?', August 1996, pp. 74–83; Zhang Yiwu, 'In Face of the Challenge of Globalization', December 1996, pp. 138–142; Xu Ben, 'Further thoughts on the Political Nature and Historical Context of Chinese "Post-ism" ', February 1997, pp. 132–137.

[27] Zhang Xudong, 'Hou xiandaizhuyi yu Zhongguo xiandai xing' (Postmodernism and China's modernity), *Dushu*, December 1999, pp. 12–20. For the full development of his argument, see 'Postmodernism and Post-Socialist Society: Cultural Politics in China after the "New Era" ', *New Left Review*, I/237, September–October 1999, pp. 77–105.

[28] For example, the Central TV Station started *Dongfang shikong* (*Oriental Time and Space*) in 1993, to be followed by similar programmes at provincial stations. The Guangzhou-based *Southern Weekend* became a leading investigator of corruption and social injustice throughout the country, still active up to the time of writing, though the authorities have repeatedly sought to 'rectify' it. These developments were not, however, registered in the debates around the humanistic spirit or post-ism, in which more theoretically oriented intellectuals engaged. For private bookstores and publishing business, see Qi Gan, op. cit.

[29] For example, *Orient* published special issues on women's questions (August 1995), environmental protection (June 1996) and legal reform (August 1996), before it was closed down by the authorities in 1997. When publication was resumed in late 1998, the journal's earlier openness was all but gone. On the other hand, *Strategy and Management*, aiming at a small but elite readership, has survived by keeping a low profile, while continuing to explore broad social, economic and political issues.

found expression in *Twenty-First Century*. The first such occasion came when Wang Shaoguang and Hu Angang, then working together at Yale, completed a research report entitled 'Strengthening the Guiding Function of the Central Government in Transition to a Market Economy' in May 1993, a shortened version of which was published in *Twenty-First Century* in February 1994, together with three critical responses, to which Wang Shaoguang replied in the next issue.[30]

Wang and Hu warned that the PRC was facing an increasing danger of fiscal starvation. The extractive capacity of the central state, they argued, was declining, while 'hidden wealth' was being cornered by provincial governments and state enterprises, which were running amok with inflationary consumption and investment sprees. If this process was not reversed, the country could eventually suffer a Yugoslav-style disintegration, as the steering capacity and legitimacy of the central government withered away, economic inequality grew between regions and classes, and political unrest escalated. To prevent this disaster, they believed it was time to reconsider the official guideline to 'loosen controls and share profits' (*fang quan rang li*), and introduce a reform that would simultaneously raise and divide tax revenues between the centre and the provinces, with the aim of strengthening the authority of the national government. Most of those who responded in *Twenty-First Century* rejected the idea that the Chinese State could really be as weak as Wang and Hu claimed, and maintained that in any case the government should withdraw from the economy in favour of an unfettered market. The report was dismissed by these critics as exaggerated and moving in the wrong direction. The government, which was better informed, did not treat it so lightly. In the first case in which an intellectual proposal anticipated state policy after 1989, Wang and Hu's report helped to prompt the taxation reform of January 1994, which split revenues and responsibilities between the central and provincial authorities, with major social consequences that are still unfolding.

Among Wang and Hu's interlocutors, only one did not question their account of the fiscal crisis of the central state, but indeed pointed to earlier local resistance to tax reforms as one of the origins of the current situation. This was Cui Zhiyuan, a young intellectual working at MIT, who a few months later caused a much greater controversy in the pages of *Twenty-First Century* with an article entitled 'Institutional Innovation and a Second Liberation of Thought'. In this, Cui drew freely on different bodies of theory from the West, including neo-evolutionism, analytical Marxism and critical legal studies, to call for a further emancipation of Chinese thought,

---

[30] 'Debate on China's "State Capacity"', *TFC*, February 1994, pp. 5–26, with contributions by Wang Shaoguang and Hu Angang, Dali Yang, Cui Zhiyuan, and Rao Yu-qing and Xiao Geng. See also Wang Shaoguang, 'Reply to My Critics: Further Discussion of the Extractive Capacity of the Chinese Government', *TFC*, April 1994, pp. 129–136.

comparable to the explosion of official dogmas in the late seventies, to shake off superstitious fixation on market ideology and the 'institutional fetishism' of seeking to imitate at all costs capitalist models taken from the West. Instead, Cui argued, China should rediscover what was valuable in its socialist experience, and boldly experiment with its own innovations, deepening economic democracy where elements of it could already be found, as in township and village enterprises, or in village elections. Alongside this piece, Cui co-authored an article in the same issue of *Twenty-First Century* with the Brazilian-American thinker Roberto Unger, comparing China and Russia, and arguing that China still had a chance to avoid the Latin American-style fate of the former USSR, with its corruption, polarization and stagnation, and to develop political and economic democracy in a path of sustainable growth.[31]

A variety of critiques and follow-ups poured in over the next few months, many insisting that capitalism was historically imperative for China, and should continue to be the beacon for its reforms, in both general direction and institutional particulars.[32] The most significant response came in early 1996, when the rural sociologist Qin Hui intervened, and a further exchange with Cui ensued. Qin, a staunch foe of peasant exploitation, had been the first intellectual to criticize the share-holding reform and stock frenzy of 1992, when he had pointed to the vast opportunities for corruption they opened up, as those in charge of public assets stole from what they were supposed to be guarding. In the same journal, and two months before Cui and Unger published their articles, Qin had warned that a 'pure market' reform posed both practical and theoretical dangers to China's agriculture, as local governments relinquished their responsibility to aid peasants, which was an indispensable duty of the state to rural development, while obstructing their commercial and social freedoms.[33]

Dismissing Cui's call to move beyond 'Surname S or C', Qin contended

---

[31] Cui Zhiyuan, 'Institutional Innovation and a Second Liberation of Thought', and Roberto Mangabeira Unger and Cui Zhiyuan, 'China in the Russian Mirror', August 1994, pp. 5–16 and 17–28, respectively.

[32] See the feature 'Economic Democracy, Political Democracy and China, II', *TFC*, October 1994, pp. 4–19, in which Ji Weidong and Deng Zhenglai questioned Cui's method of argumentation, while Wang Ying supported Cui. Hayekian responses came from Wang Dingding, ' "Extended Order" and Institutional Innovation', *TFC*, December 1994, pp. 12–20, and 'A Further Response to Cui Zhiyuan and Wang Shaoguang', *TFC*, April 1995, pp. 137–140. Cui replied to the first round of his critics in 'Again on Institutional Innovation and "a Second Liberation of Thought" ', *TFC*, February 1995, pp. 134–145.

[33] See, under his pen-name Bian Wu, 'A Dangerous "Booster Rocket" for Economic Take-off: the Prussian-Tsarist Model is No Answer for China', *TFC*, August 1993, pp. 138–148; and 'The Predicament of Chinese Agricultural Development', *TFC*, June 1994, pp. 4–13. The debate between Qin and Cui on *TFC* included the following: Bian Wu, 'The Amazing Metamorphosis of Neo-Leftism in China', February 1996, pp. 4–17; Cui, 'Yet Again on Institutional Innovation and "A Second Liberation of Thought" ', April 1996, pp. 127–134; Bian Wu, ' "Institutional Innovation" or Institutional Restoration?', August 1996, 128–134.

that Chinese realities had long made these irrelevant anyway. A properly conceived model would not so much replace a planned by a market economy, as a 'command' by a 'planned' market economy based on a modern civil society, capable of helping rather than ordering peasants about. Qin objected to Cui's derivation of the creative potential of rural TVEs from the collective traditions of the People's Communes. For him, the key question in explaining the vitality of TVEs was 'not how far the "collective" is "working", but how far the state is "not working"'. Neither side in the controversy offered a straightforward challenge to official promoters of capitalism with Chinese characteristics, such as Li Yining, although from his standpoint Cui could well have pointed out the negation of any economic democracy in the reform of state-owned enterprises, and Qin could have questioned the direct link between misappropriation of public assets and speculative stock frenzy.[34] But though this debate did not have policy effects, it had far-reaching intellectual consequences, as later became clear.

Before the dispute between Cui and Qin had quieted down, *Twenty-First Century* put together another special feature in the summer of 1996, discussing various approaches to political reform in China. At the head of these was an article on 'Democracy in a Large Country' by Gan Yang, an overseas scholar at the University of Chicago, which began with a criticism of the views of Wu Guoguang and Zheng Yongnian, writers who also contributed to the discussion.[35] Wu had been a senior editorialist at the *People's Daily* in the late eighties and a close aide of Zhao Ziyang, while Zheng was a recently returned overseas student. Together, they had published a book arguing for a more decentralized Chinese State, in which the provinces would enjoy greater autonomy, as an institutional bulwark against potential authoritarian or mass tyranny. In doing so, they appealed to the wisdom of the Founding Fathers of the American Constitution, in designing a federal state built on a division of powers and mediated elections.[36]

In his attack on this position Gan Yang too drew heavily on the Federalist Papers, contending that real state legitimacy could only be based on the direct election of a national government by individual citizens. This was a fundamental requirement if popular sovereignty was to have any meaning. In a large country, any system based essentially on indirect aggregation was a formula for a state that would be both weak and undemocratic. In the

---

[34] A professor of economics at Peking University, Li has been a forceful proponent of marketization since the early eighties. In the mid-eighties, he became a deputy of the National People's Congress and then one of its vice-chairmen. Qin has recently renewed his challenge to both the shareholding reform and stock market manipulation; see 'China's Reform: Is it Successful and How is it Working?', paper at conference on Globalization, Hangzhou, 2002.

[35] Gan Yang, 'Citizen-Centered Politics and Constitutionalism'; Wu Guoguang, 'On Institutionalized Decentralization'; Zheng Yongnian, 'Democracy in Rural Areas and the Political Course of China', *TFC*, June 1996, pp. 4–36.

[36] Wu Guoguang and Zheng Yongnian, *Lun Zhongyang-difang guanxi* (On Central-Local Relations), Hong Kong, 1995.

background of this debate were a number of conflicting developments: the legacy of 'neo-authoritarian' ideas from the late eighties; various 'federal' or 'confederal' proposals from overseas (including exiled) intellectuals, related to Taiwan's position after 1989; concerns over the growing power of local oligarchies and the negative model of Yugoslavia; and desires to maximize local power to weaken control by the central government. Whereas Gan was concerned at the prospect of a potential disintegration of China, Wu was interested in mobilizing provincial autonomy against the national government, arguing that 'liberty must be put before participation', in an indirect system of representation.[37]

In fact, representatives to the various levels of the People's Congress in China have never been directly elected above the rural-township and urban-district level since the establishment of the PRC in 1949.[38] In failing to explain whether they envisaged direct elections even of provincial authorities, Wu and Zheng's positions – although appealing to liberal notions of negative freedom – came much closer to the status quo than Gan's classically 'republican' proposals. Gan, on the other hand, as one critic pointed out, ignored the well-known weakness of the atomized individual citizen, instead moving simply to explain his preference for a two-party over a multi-party system.[39] Even so, while neither side ventured far beyond general constitutional principles, this was an exchange that challenged the definitions of political stabilization, as laid down after 1989, more sharply than any other debate of the period.[40]

IV

Looking back, the debate over 'democracy in a large country' marked the high point of the pioneering role played by *Twenty-First Century* in reviving and developing intellectual life after the watershed of June Fourth. In the second half of the nineties, the scenery changed. By early 1996 Deng Xiaoping was incapacitated, and Jiang Zemin became in fact as well as in theory the political leader of the Chinese Party and State. Economically, the

---

[37] Wu, 'Further Discussion of "The Institutionalization of Division of Power" – A Reply to Gan Yang', *TFC*, October 1996, pp. 123–131.

[38] For the sole experiment of direct election at urban-district (precinct) and rural-county level in the PRC in 1979–1980, see Chen and Jin, pp. 91–92.

[39] Ji Weidong, 'The Importance of Providing a Legal Guarantee of Civil Liberties', *TFC*, August 1996, pp. 126–127. Ji explained the importance of social communities as mediating layers between the state and individuals, but did not extend his challenge to the principle of free associations in forming political parties.

[40] Constitutional reform has since become a focus of discussion in the mainland that is tolerated, or even encouraged, by the authorities. The National People's Congress has authorized several constitutional amendments in recent years, though as yet no further implementation of direct elections.

dangers of renewed inflation had passed. Price stability and fast growth were in place. Arrangements for the handover by the British of Hong Kong to the PRC in 1997 were complete. In this atmosphere, there was a certain political relaxation and the main stage of intellectual debate moved inside the mainland. A critical development here was the appointment of Wang Hui, a founder of *Xueren*, as chief editor of *Dushu*, the leading intellectual monthly of the PRC. He quickly set new agendas for the journal, broadening its horizons and making it the liveliest forum of ideas in the mainland. Articles were shorter and more topical than in *Twenty-First Century*, but the principal difference was now that, whereas the Hong Kong journal published some 3,500 copies of every issue, *Dushu* had a circulation of 80,000, which rapidly increased under its new editor.

Meanwhile, at just the same time in Hainan, the independent-minded writer Han Shaogong was put in charge of the island's literary journal, *Tianya* (Frontiers), and soon made it a wide-ranging and iconoclastic periodical with a national readership, publishing longer essays and enjoying greater political latitude than in Beijing.[41] In the capital itself, *Strategy and Management*, another heterodox journal, was already operating in the field of the social and policy sciences, while three young liberals set up a journal, *Gonggong luncong* (Res Publica), appearing more irregularly.[42] In the south, the monthly *Shuwu* in Hunan, various avant-garde literary journals in the lower Yangzi Delta region, and the hard-hitting and highly popular weekly in Guangzhou, *Nanfang zhoumo* (Southern Weekend), all provided new outlets for expression. Many younger intellectuals eagerly joined in, further integrating the debates into a national grid.

These in turn saw a qualitative jump at the end of the decade, with the Internet boom. Cultural and political debates moved to electronic forums in almost no time, unleashing heated polemics between individuals and groups.[43] Since then, censorship of the Internet has been stepped up considerably, but the space for intellectual exchanges inside the mainland has been shaped by these new technological conditions, which have taken firm root in the past years. On the other hand, easier access to Internet chat-rooms has often introduced strongly personal colours and sectarian tendencies into debates, pushing serious exchanges once again back to printed publications.

---

[41] Han left *Tianya* after his five-year tenure at the position. See Han Shaogong, 'Wo yu *Tianya*' (The Journal *Frontiers* and I), *Shijie* (*Horizons*), no. 3, May 2001, pp. 154–171.

[42] The three are Liu Junning, a political scientist, He Weifang, a legal scholar, and Wang Yan, a veteran cultural activist from the eighties. *Res Publica* has been published in the form of a book series. See note 13 above.

[43] Many intellectual websites have appeared since late 1999. Of these, the most influential include the short-lived *Sixiang de jingji* (Realm of thought); *Shiji Zhongguo* (Century China), co-sponsored by *Twenty-First Century*; and *Tianya shequ* (*Tianya* Community), co-sponsored by the journal *Tianya*.

The second major change that occurred in these years was the increasing differentiation of the Chinese intelligentsia into two political camps, even if the frontiers between them have never been clear-cut. The initial spur to this development was clearly Cui's position on 'institutional innovation', whose repercussions were soon felt in Beijing.[44] Before Qin Hui's criticism of it had appeared, Hong Kong's *Mingpao Monthly* had run a special feature in 1996 on the emergence of a Chinese 'New Left', identified as a group that included Cui, Gan Yang and Wang Shaoguang.[45] These, however, were overseas scholars. The real signal that a new intellectual formation had arisen in the mainland was the appearance of a long essay on Chinese modernity by Wang Hui, which after circulating informally for some months, came out in *Tianya* in October 1997.[46]

Here for the first time was a broad critical reflection on the successive attempts of Chinese society to achieve 'modernization', whether in Marxist or (anti-Marxist) New Enlightenment forms, that offered a survey of recent intellectual developments in the PRC and a diagnosis of where the country was heading – towards a convergence with global capitalism. This trend, Wang argued, was becoming a 'teleology of modernization', and needed to be resisted. The original goal of Chinese reformers at the beginning of the century, to create a society that was not only independent and prosperous, but also just and equal, remained more relevant than ever, even if its forms needed to be rethought. Against a capitalist modernization imported from the West, it was necessary to insist that late-developing countries in an epoch of globalization should seek rather to invent their own 'anti-modern modernity', in the dialectical spirit of Zhang Taiyan and Lu Xun.

This call to arms, challenging much conventional wisdom about the

---

[44] See the criticism by Wang Dingding, 'Huaizhe xiangchou, xunzhao jiayuan' (A Nostalgic Longing for Home), *Dushu*, April 1995, pp. 10–15. Cui Zhiyuan's further proposal, 'An-gang xianfa yu hou Fute zhuyi' (The An-gang programme and post-Fordism) appeared in *Dushu*, March 1996, pp. 11–21, to which Wang Dingding replied conceptually in 'Liangdian chengqing' (Clarify two points), *Dushu* April 1996, pp. 113–117, and Huang Xingang empirically in 'Guanyu An-gang xianfa' (About the An-gang programme), *Dushu*, July 1996, pp. 155–156. At the same time, Cui published 'Meiguo ershijiu zhou gongsifa biange de lilun beijing ji dui woguo de qishi' (The theoretical background of corporate law reform in twenty-nine states of the US and its Relevance for China), *Jingji yanjiu*, April 1996, which was criticized by Zhang Weiying in 'Has Economic Freedom Already Given Way to Democracy?', *Res Publica*, no.3, 1996, pp. 7–16.

[45] *Mingpao Monthly*, January 1996, with a leading report entitled 'Xueshu fenqi haishi zhengjian zhi zheng?' (Scholarly disagreement or political dispute?). In general, Cui did not welcome the label of New Left. See Liu Qingfeng in Davies, p. 51, and Cui's reply to Qin Hui, *TFC*, April 1996, pp. 127–134.

[46] Wang Hui, 'Dangdai Zhongguo de sixiang zhuangkuang yu xiandai xing wenti' (Contemporary Chinese thought and the question of modernity), *Tianya*, October 1997, pp. 133–150. A revised version is collected in Wang Hui, *Sihuo chong wen* (Old ashes rekindled), Beijing, 2000, pp. 42–94. Its English version, translated by Rebecca Karl, can be found in Wang Hui, *China's New Order: Society, Politics, and Economy in Transition*, edited by Theodore Huters, Cambridge, MA, 2003.

Reform Era, came to be considered by people on all sides as a manifesto of the Chinese New Left, in part because it was also the first serious and outspoken publication of its sort inside China. The following year the Shanghai philosopher Zhu Xueqin, himself a leading critic of Yu Ying-shih's condemnation of radicalism and a vocal opponent of commercialized culture, issued a counter-blast in a long essay on 'The Discourse of Liberalism'. This expressed the suspicion and anxiety among a large group of intellectuals at unexpectedly encountering theories of an apparently neo-Marxist or postmodern origin, which, so they felt, had often been rushed back to China from abroad. Against such tendencies, Zhu set out the historical and theoretical reasons why private property, a free market economy, and a negative conception of political liberty were essential to progress in China, which could not be separated from the achievements of the West.[47] More than clarifying his position on liberalism, Zhu singled out a young literary critic, Han Yuhai, as representative of the New Left, and issued his criticism of Han.[48] The curtain had formally gone up on the 'New Left versus Liberal' controversy.

In fact, Chinese intellectuals had for some time been arguing heatedly among themselves about the meaning of liberalism in the pages of *Dushu*, *Tianya*, *Twenty-First Century*, *Strategy and Management* and *Res Publica*.[49] In his intervention, Zhu took care to summarize the main opinions at stake, and indicate where he thought the real oppositions lay, in a relatively thorough investigation of the positions on both sides. In doing so, he was also concerned to dispel misunderstandings and confusions among Chinese liberals themselves, insisting that classical Anglo-Saxon traditions of liberalism were to be preferred, and offering Chen Yinke, Gu Zhun and Wang

---

[47] Zhu Xueqin, '1998: Ziyouzhuyi de xueli yanshuo' (1998: Liberal discourse), part 1 in *Southern Weekend*, December 25, 1998; and part 2 in *Zhongguo tushu shangbao*, January 5, 1999.

[48] Han Yuhai had published some long essays elaborating the New Left positions, among them 'Shichang yishixingtai de xingcheng yu piping de kunjing' (The formation of a market ideology and the predicament of criticism), *Tianya*, April 1998, pp. 20–29; 'Zai ziyouzhuyi zitai de beihou' (Behind the Liberal posture), *Tianya*, August 1998. Zhu and Han disputed each other further on in 1999.

[49] See, for example, in *Dushu*: Liu Junning 'Xinjiapo: Rujiao ziyouzhuyi de tiaozhan' (Singapore: challenge of Confucian Liberalism), February 1993; Su Wen (Qin Hui and Jin Yan), 'Yazhou shi ziyouzhuyi de dianfan ma?' (Is Asia a model of Liberalism?), July 1996; Cai Xiao, 'Yiqu ziyouzhuyi de wange' (An elegy to Liberalism), August 1996; Mao Yushi, 'Shenme shi jingji de ziyouzhuyi?' (What is Economic Liberalism?), December 1996. *Tianya* published both a critique and defence of liberalism: Wang Binbin, 'Dushu zhaji: guanyu ziyou zhuyi' (Reading Notes: on Liberalism), April 1997, and Xu Youyu, 'Ziyouzhuyi, Falankefu xuepai ji qita' (Liberalism, the Frankfurt School and Others), August 1997. *Twenty-First Century*, in which Gan Yang's 'Anti-Democratic Liberalism or Democratic Liberalism?' had appeared in April, ran a feature on the topic in August 1997, which included Wang Hui, 'The Politics of Recognition, the Law of Peoples and the Predicament of Liberalism', Xu Youyu, 'Liberalism Revisited' and Xu Jilin, 'The Liberal Tradition in Modern China'. For its part, *Res Publica* jointly sponsored a conference on 'Economic Democracy and Economic Freedom' in 1996, publishing the papers in its pages.

Xiaobo as pioneers of this line of thought in twentieth-century China.[50] This effort at a systematic clarification of the issues and legacies in dispute was a hallmark of Zhu's contribution to the debate.

As a broad ideological division between New Left and Liberals set in, excessive attacks by each side against the other became common, even affecting the reputation of journals that provided space for both – *Dushu* and *Tianya* were accused of editorial partiality, unjustly.[51] Meanwhile, theoretical discussions of the issue of modernity tended to remain somewhat contemplative.[52] Popular polemical oppositions obscured the reality that many of the most courageous and creative intellectuals of the period could not be easily assigned to one camp or the other, and even when they did so themselves, their work hardly fitted conventional classifications. This can be seen very clearly from the example of the two most explosive books published in the mainland in these years. The background to each was the spread of extreme inequality, rampant corruption, the dismantling of public health and education, and general indifference to social welfare that accompanied the fast-track growth of the nineties.

The first really powerful indictment of these evils came from a writer who for some time now has regarded herself as a liberal. This was He Qinglian's work *China's Pitfall*, based on intensive research, whose manuscript was repeatedly rejected in the mainland, and was eventually published in Hong Kong in 1997. This blistering exposé of the vast opportunities opened up by the reform process for rent-seeking, embezzlement, 'land enclosures', appropriation of public assets, corruption and abuse of power, carried prefaces by Qin Hui and Zhu Xueqin. Each called for economic studies to be informed by both 'mind and heart', reviving the classical tradition of political economy and attacking social injustices directly. *Tianya* had already organized a feature discussing 'national realities' and enquiries into them, with a shortened version of Qin's preface to He's book and an essay by He

---

[50] For Chen Yinke (1890–1969) and Gu Zhun (1920–1974), see notes 11 on p. 111 and 6 on p. 93 below. Wang Xiaobo (1952–1997), after earning his master's degree from Pittsburgh University in 1988, taught in Peking University and the People's University, before quitting teaching to concentrate on writing. His novels and screenplays won many prizes.

[51] For example, under the feature title 'Zhongguo shehui sixiang de shijimo fenhua' (Division in social thought in China at the century's end), *Tianya* published both Wang Hui's 'Guanyu xiandaixing wenti dawen' (Interview on Modernity) and the liberal Ren Jiantao's 'Jiedu "Xinzuopai"' (Interpreting the 'New Left') in its issue of February 1999, while *Dushu* had been publishing authors across the spectrum for years.

[52] See, Liu Xiaofeng's lengthy volume *Xiandaixing shehui lilun xulun* (A Preface to a Social Theory of Modernity), first published in Hong Kong in 1996 and reissued in Shanghai in 1998; Wang Dingding, 'The Enlightenment is Dead, Long Live the Enlightenment! – A Critique of Wang Hui's narrative of the "China Problem"', *Strategy and Management* (hereafter *SM*), no. 32, 1999, pp. 68–83.; Wang Sirui, 'Modernity and the Mainstream of Civilization', *SM*, no. 33, 1999, pp. 1–12; Cao Weidong, 'Fansi "xiandaixing wenti"' (Reflections on the 'Question of Modernity'), *Dushu*, May 2000.

herself.[53] A year later, a mainland version of the book finally appeared, under the title *Modernization's Pitfall*, without the aggressive prefaces. To greet its publication in the mainland, *Tianya* ran another feature, with Zhu's preface included.[54] As an attack on the spread of social injustice and inequality in the PRC, the book was without precedent. The new edition became an instant bestseller, widely pirated by street vendors.

The strong social response to He's book struck a direct blow to public trust in mainstream economic studies, which typically presented the reform process in a bland and euphemistic light. By the late nineties, academic fields in the mainland were by and large aligned with Western academic disciplinary settings, especially with that in the US. Economics, in particular, received unprecedented attention from Chinese policy-makers and international observers, with fierce competition among big Chinese cities to host MBA programmes jointly sponsored by acclaimed foreign institutions. *Modernization's Pitfall* posed a severe challenge to the prestige of the profession, whose initial response was to try to ignore it, while issuing generic attacks on misplaced conceptions of the role of economics as a discipline. Thus in the June 1998 issue of *Dushu* the liberal economist Fan Gang explained to readers that economics was of its nature a 'non-moral' discipline, which did not trade in cheap value judgements, unlike its sloppy or sentimental critics (he had recently been confronted in a public forum on the exploitative practices of the new rich). His essay was an aggressive attempt to rebut the now widespread criticism linking many social disasters caused by the reform process to the work of its apologists.[55]

Eventually another mainstream economist, Zhang Shuguang, was stung into responding to He's book by the questions about it he had to face during an American tour. 'Do we economists have to respond to such a journalistic work?' he complained, before proceeding to dismiss it as an act of self-promotion, offering 'social exposure and outcry for popular effect', rather than 'deep thought appealing to reason and logical analysis'. Indeed, Zhang hinted, He's book amounted to an attempt at thought control, comparable to the incitement of the masses against academic authorities

---

[53] Qin Hui, 'Shehui gongzheng yu xueshu liangxin' (Social fairness and scholarly conscience), and He Qinglian, 'Xueshu paomo yu guoqing yanjiu' (Scholarship bubbles and national studies), *Tianya*, April 1997, pp. 4–13.

[54] He Qinglian, *Zhongguo de xianjing* (China's Pitfall), Hong Kong, 1997; *Xiandaihua de xianjing* (Modernization's Pitfall), Beijing, 1998; Zhu Xueqin, 'Qiaomenzhe de shengyin' (The Sound of Knocks on the Door), *Tianya*, April 1998, pp. 130–133.

[55] Public questioning of the moral responsibilities of their discipline had put pressure on orthodox economists to explain their position. Li Yining had already published *Jingjixue de lunli wenti* (Ethical questions in Economics), Beijing, 1995. For Fan Gang, see ' "Bu daode"de jingjixue' ('Non-moral' Economics), *Dushu*, June 1998, pp. 50–55. In the same issue, Qin Hui praised He's book, 'You le zhen wenti caiyou zhen xuewen' (Only real questions can generate real knowledge), pp. 42–49. He Qinglian's attack on mainstream economics also appeared in *Dushu*: 'Jingjixue lilun he "tu long shu" ' (Economic theories and the 'dragon-taming game'), March 1997, pp. 122–128.

during the Cultural Revolution.[56] To this He Qinglian retorted that it was mainstream economists who, from their positions of official influence, enjoyed an overwhelming advantage in controlling public opinion as well as reform discourse in the late nineties.[57]

The controversy caused by *Modernization's Pitfall* lasted all the way into 2000. Then in March of that year, the Hunan-based journal *Shuwu* published a new research paper by He Qinglian that was the first systematic attempt to map out class stratifications in China in the reform decades.[58] In it she openly contrasted the nominal role of the working class as the 'leading class' in the Constitution of the PRC with its real position in Chinese society today, and sketched a caustic analysis of selection procedures within the latter-day CCP. She ended by calling for 'an entirely new social movement' to solve China's worsening problems. This fearless essay quickly brought down official wrath. The central government, after sending an investigating team to Changsha, suspended *Shuwu*, removed the offending text from its website and banned He from publishing any further writing. Yet her courage in naming the 'new clothes of the emperor' was recognized by society at large, and in December readers of *Dushu* voted her *Pitfall* the book of the year.

Through all this, He Qinglian remained a staunch upholder of the market and of key liberal beliefs, freely citing Hayek in support of her critique of the Reform Era. In fact, both He Qinglian and Qin Hui had been the very first Chinese intellectuals to point out the unfairness and corruption in the initial shareholding reform, at the time of the stock frenzy in Shenzhen.[59] Nor were they exceptional in this stance, making clear how misleading an oversimplified counterposition of Liberal and New Left tendencies would be in the Chinese intelligentsia today. Further striking examples of a similar position came from Sichuan, where the most moving indictment of the national 'industrialization of education' – the official description for com-

---

[56] 'Piping guize, jiaowang lixing he ziyou jingshen' (Rules of criticism, rational communication, and the spirit of liberty), *Dushu*, part 1, Oct. 1999, pp. 83–89, quotations taken from p. 87 and pp. 88–89, and part 2, March 2000, pp. 140–146, reference to pp. 142–143. The same article was also carried by *Jingjixue xiaoxibao*, September 10, 1999, in slightly different form. An electronic version circulated widely before the formal publications of shortened versions. The quotation of his complaint is taken from the electronic version.

[57] He Qinglian, 'Shenme shi zhenzheng de piping guize?' (What are the real rules in criticism?), originally published in *Shuwu*, January 2000, and collected in He Qinglian, *Women rengran zai yangwang xingkong* (We are still watching the starry sky), Guilin, 2001, pp. 275–297.

[58] He Qinglian, 'Dangqian Zhongguo shehui jiegou yanbian de zongtixing fenxi' (An overall analysis on structural changes in contemporary China's society), collected in op. cit., pp. 7–41; an English version under the title 'China's Listing Mansion' was published in *New Left Review*, No 5, September-October 2000, and is included below. A comprehensive project studying the structural transformation of Chinese society, led by Lu Xueyi of the Institute of Sociology at CASS, has generated its first substantial report, *Report on Social Classes in Contemporary China*, Beijing, 2002.

[59] He Qinglian, 'Chinese Stocks: A Socialist Free Lunch', *TFC*, February 1994, pp. 146–154.

modifying schools and colleges, and expelling the poor from them – was the work of an ethics scholar, Xiao Xuehui, of strong liberal attachments. Yet in questions of welfare, few have been more outspoken than she in denouncing social inequality and demanding that the government fulfil its moral responsibilities to all citizens. Likewise, one of the sharpest attacks on the CCP's treatment of the working class has been penned by a young lecturer in law, Wang Yi, a champion of explicitly liberal ideas, also from Sichuan.[60]

The turn towards deepening social criticism at the end of the nineties was not confined to writers at the liberal side of the spectrum. In early 2002, there appeared a book from the left side that caused a sensation comparable only to *Modernization's Pitfall.* Its author, Li Changping, was a rural party cadre from Hubei, who after a long battle against official corruption and exploitation in his locality, had written a letter of detailed protest at the contemporary fate of the peasantry to Premier Zhu Rongji in early 2000. Zhu sent down a team of investigators, who confirmed the accuracy of the charges, in a report which he then merely passed along to Hu Jintao and Wen Jiabao – today's rulers of the PRC – who annotated it, but took no action themselves. Instead, the provincial party apparatus dispatched its own work-team, ostensibly to find out what was going on in Li's area. But before the affair could be stifled by the Hubei officials, the dynamite contained in Li's revelations exploded in the pages of *Southern Weekend,* to the outrage of local authorities, who put an abrupt end to his work in the Party.[61]

Just over a year later, Li's graphic account of the whole story, published under the title *Telling the Prime Minister the Truth* electrified the public. In part, its success was due to the drama of his own experience as an honest official, attempting to struggle against the cynicism and corruption of his superiors. But mainly, it was the book's shocking picture of the extent of rural oppression and misery under layer upon layer of fiscal extortion and usury, in one of China's most fertile rice-growing regions, that shook readers across the nation.[62] Li Changping's burning indignation at the plight of the peasantry was inspired, as he explained, not by dislike of market distortions or residues of collectivism in the countryside, but rather by a conviction of the rightness of the socialist critique of the 'three discrepancies' – between town and country, industry and agriculture, manual and mental labour – he had learnt as a boy during the Maoist years.

---

[60] Both Xiao Xuehui's and Wang Yi's interventions circulated widely on the Internet.

[61] Li Changping, *Wo xiang zongli shuo shihua* (Telling the Prime Minister the Truth), Beijing, 2002, pp. 147–155 and pp. 178–182. Li was subsequently voted one of the ten people of the year 2000 by the readers of *Southern Weekend,* see Li, pp. 260–272.

[62] Ibid, chapters 3, 9 and 26. Li's account is confirmed by many other reports. Studies by the Research Institute of the Finance Ministry have documented the worsening rural debt situation, according to *Caijing Magazine,* January 20, 2003, p. 56. Cao Jinqing's acclaimed field research in Henan, *Huanghe bian shang de Zhongguo* (China by the Yellow River), Shanghai, 2000, exposes similar examples: see pp. 89–97.

Similar notes can be heard in a range of other interventions in this period. Writings on women have often had to reach more complicated judgements about the experience of the Chinese Revolution than purely masculine accounts, since there is little doubt that, in aggregate, the female condition improved more than the male under Mao, if the pre-revolutionary situation of each is taken as a benchmark. This is one of the realities brought home by the *Oral History of Chinese Women in the Twentieth Century*, produced, in four volumes so far, by China's leading feminist, Li Xiaojiang, where PLA veterans still recall with delight their escape from domestic servitude into the disciplines and dangers of war and civil war under the red flag.[63] Such too was the family background of Wang Anyi, China's best-known woman novelist, whose memoir of her mother makes clear the origins of her own independence and loyalty to what was best in the Liberation.[64] The ironic eye she casts on matters of gender and class in the euphoria of the 'second reform period' is conveyed by her dry remark that 'we are rushing towards bourgeois society with all the enthusiasm of a proletarian revolution'.

If a rising tide of social criticism was a common feature of much of the Chinese intelligentsia across the political spectrum in the late nineties, developments in another sphere were to divide it more sharply than ever before. Since the eighties, foreign affairs had been largely ignored by mainland intellectuals. The one forum that was an exception in this respect was the low-profile journal *Strategy and Management*, often incisive in substance, but deliberately drab in appearance, in which area and other specialists could publish articles on international questions and foreign countries that attracted little wider attention. In so far as China's position in the world was at issue in less professional settings, intellectual debates tended to revolve around conflicting views of the role of nationalism in contemporary China. Here the two most significant contributions were, from opposing sides, Qin Hui's article on liberalism and nationalism of 1996 and Zhang Xudong's on theories of nationalism in 1997.[65]

This was the situation when in March 1999 NATO attacked Yugoslavia. The Balkan War was into its sixth week when, on the eightieth anniversary of May 4, Zhu Xueqin published an article entitled 'Two Intellectual

---

[63] Li Xiaojiang ed, *Qinli zhanzheng* (Experiencing wars); *Duli de licheng* (Independent march); *Minzu xushi* (National narrative); *Wenhua xunzong* (Cultural trajectory), Beijing, 2003.

[64] See 'Cong he er lai, xiang he er qu' (Where to come from, where to go to), 'Cheng zhang' (Growing up), 'Fanshen de rizi' (Days of liberation) and 'Guyu qianhou dian gua zhong dou' (Planting seeds in spring), in Wang Anyi, *Qiansha chuang xia* (Under the Rosy-Misted Casement), pp. 201–235. Wang Anyi's mother, Ru Zhijuan (1925–1999), who joined the revolution during wartime and became a self-taught writer, winning many awards for her short stories and novellas in the PRC, was also a fine essayist.

[65] Qin Hui, 'Ziyouzhuyi yu minzuzhuyi de qihedian zai nali?' (Where is the conjunction of liberalism and nationalism?), *Orient*, May 1996, pp 45–48; Zhang Xudong, 'Minzuzhuyi yu dangdai Zhongguo' (Nationalism and Contemporary China), *Dushu*, June 1997, pp. 22–30.

Shortcomings since May Fourth' in the Hong Kong daily *Mingpao*. In this, he roundly condemned populism and nationalism for impeding the modernization of China.[66] Four days later, American bombers struck the Chinese embassy in Belgrade. Mass demonstrations against the US swept the country, with students taking the lead in the popular protests, which the government – highly embarrassed at this turn of events, Premier Zhu having just returned from a fulsome visit to the United States, while the NATO campaign was in full swing – skillfully manipulated and quickly curbed.[67] Under the pressure of student anger, the intelligentsia split from top to bottom over the war, as Zhu Xueqin's article became the target for vehement attacks on the Internet.

Liberals were taken aback by the destruction of the PRC's embassy, which they could scarcely excuse, but nevertheless insisted that the cause of human rights in Kosovo justified NATO's blitz, and attacked the demonstrations against it as Boxer-style xenophobia. The New Left condemned the American campaign against Yugoslavia as an aggression that revealed the role of the United States as the world gendarme, and pointed out the passivity of China towards it. Because of tight censorship, neither side was able to develop its arguments in the print media, but electronic exchanges were numerous and often violent. Reactions to the Balkan War set the pattern for attitudes, broadly speaking, to subsequent Western interventions. Liberal attachment to America intensified with Al-Qaeda's attacks on the WTC and Pentagon. New Left hostility to US military power increased with the invasions of Afghanistan and Iraq. Popular sentiment was mainly aroused by the minor incident of a collision between a PRC fighter and an American spy-plane off the South China Coast.[68] All these events inflamed the intellectual atmosphere, without so far yielding any really striking theoretical or political reflections.[69] One of their effects, however, was to create a more confused scene, as different individuals adopted positions on them that could cross-cut their domestic outlook. In spring 2001, offering to clarify the situation, one electronic wit proposed that any Chinese intellectual's politics could be best determined by 'ranking the battle-order' in which they perceived four possible adversaries – domestic authorities; local capital;

---

[66] '"Wusi" yilai de liangge jingshen "bingzao"' (Two spiritual pathogeneses since the May Fourth Movement), *Mingpao*, May 4, 1999, and *Strategy and Management*, no. 35, 1999, pp. 62–66.

[67] See Jeffrey Wasserstrom, 'The Year of Living Anxiously: China's 1999', in Wasserstrom, ed, *Twenty-Century China: New Approaches*, London, 2003, pp. 256–265.

[68] The Balkan war generated many reactions in *Dushu* and *Strategy and Management* from mid-1999 onwards. Contributors include Cui Zhiyuan, Qin Hui, Wang Xiaodong, Zhang Rulun, He Guanghu, Cao Weidong. For Wang Hui's response to Zhu Xueqin, see 'Wherein Lies the Disagreement: A Preface to Old Ashes Rekindled', *Horizon*, no. 1, 2000, pp. 112–121.

[69] The one exception has been the debate over Chinese entry into the WTO, which the young left economist Han Deqiang has strongly criticized as 'globalization's pitfall', with considerable public echo. See his book *Pengzhuang* (Collision), Beijing, 2000.

foreign authorities; overseas capital – with some lively illustrations of the results of such a taxonomy. These are complications to be kept in mind. But a more general question is posed once more, as leadership of the PRC officially passes to a new generation. The nineties had begun with a curious set of parallels, or partial convergences, between discourses of the intelligentsia and of the state. Where did matters stand at the end of this period?

If we take the two poles of recent debates, it is clear that the great majority of Chinese liberals are united in political opposition to the authoritarian rule of the CCP, and stand firm on the need for human rights and the rule of law. Here there is an abyss between them and the state. On the other hand, they welcome the spread of the market, which has been a fundamental objective of the state – protesting at its distortion and corruption by political power, but not at its social extent. At the neo-liberal edge of the spectrum, of course, any reservations are dropped, corruption and theft of public assets being viewed as an affordable price of necessary privatization. There will thus be a continuing temptation for liberals to accommodate to the state, in so far as it is perceived as 'market-friendly', in the language of the business press; confrontation between liberal and neo-liberal economists has decreased considerably, and not merely because of the absence of He Qinglian.[70] Current discussions of constitutional reform in the mainland, in which all tendencies have participated, suggest that this is a real danger for liberals, some of whom have given top priority to the protection of private property – actually guaranteed in the existing document – rather than to political liberties. The adoption by the CCP of the reality-covering litany of the 'three representatives' has also been greeted by some liberals as if it were a major step forward, regardless of its intellectual merits, simply on the grounds that it paves the way for capitalists to join the party. The risks of a new parallelism along these lines are plain.

In the case of the New Left, on the other hand, it is not the market, but the nation that offers a lure to potential convergence with the state. Here too the picture is a complex one, since New Left intellectuals might have as many criticisms of the defects of official nationalism as liberals have of official versions of market forces. But critical interventions into concrete social ills have often been slowed by misplaced concern at giving comfort to imperialist attacks on the 'socialist' state. Moreover, there are now signs that, rather than conceiving the history of the nation in the tradition of Lu Xun or the early People's Republic, as older intellectuals like Qian Liqun recommend, there is a risk of infection from a strain of academic nativism that embellishes large stretches of the Chinese past in an instrumental spirit,

---

[70] He Qinglian left China in summer 2002. The older liberal economist Wu Jinglian confronted Li Yining in 2001 over stock market corruption. But on the whole, confrontations of this type are in decline.

which does little more than reverse the denigration of it by the *River Elegy* saga of the eighties. Exaggerated claims for pre-modern Chinese economic growth, demographic rationality or imperial tolerance, claiming to dispel the myths of Orientalism, often merely invert them. History is becoming an increasingly important intellectual battleground in China, in which the state has lost no time in rehabilitating some of the worst figures and episodes of the country's past. Almost every single Manchu emperor has been made a historical hero in a string of television series, including the Empress Dowager. More refined versions of these fantasies can be found in university circles. The New Left journal *Horizons*, recently founded by the writer Li Tuo and literary critic Chen Yangu, which publishes longer essays and commentaries than *Dushu*, with a wide range of international reference, covers many sophisticated discussions of these issues. That said, for the first time in many decades, an internationalist protest was attempted in Beijing against the Anglo-American attack on Iraq, a war in which China was not directly involved. Predictably, the authorities suppressed this hopeful sign of another disposition.

The temptations of dancing with power have always been present to Chinese intellectuals, who historically enjoyed greater access to the state, via the civil-examination system, than in most other pre-modern civilizations. This role was eclipsed during the Mao era. Will the deep structures of Chinese culture reassert themselves in the longer-run, and intellectuals regain their political authority, as some believe? In the think-tanks of Beijing, ambitious pollsters and economists offer services of one kind or another to the government in a traditional spirit. But most thoughtful Chinese intellectuals ask themselves the sort of questions that Wang Xiaoming, a veteran of the 'humanistic spirit' debate, poses, not just in front of an authoritarian state, but against the rise of a mass commercial culture that has permanently altered the setting of their work, and to which they must turn a new critical attention. One of the effects of the entertainment industry, and its embeddedness with the state, is a selective filter of what can be remembered of the past. Chinese public life is full of commemorations, and founded on amnesia. Calls to recover the real history of the modern nation, made by thinkers as diverse as Qian Liqun and Zhu Xueqin, are growing, and will form part of any agenda of the Chinese intelligentsia in the new century.[71]

The 'second reform decade' has thus left China with a far more variegated

---

[71] A struggle against political amnesia has been an intellectual strand throughout this period, acquiring greater intensity since the mid-nineties. See, in *Dushu* alone, Zhu Xueqin, 'Sixiang shi shang de shizongzhe' (The missing ones in intellectual history), October 1995, pp. 55–63; Zhang Zhizhong, 'Kangju yiwang' (Resisting amnesia), February 1996, pp. 3–7; Qian Liqun, 'Xiangqi qishiliu nian qian de jinian' (Remembering commemoration seventy-six years ago), May 1998, pp. 3–7, and ' "Yiwang" beihou de lishi guan yu lunli guan' (The historical and ethical outlook sustaining 'amnesia'), August 1998, pp. 99–103.

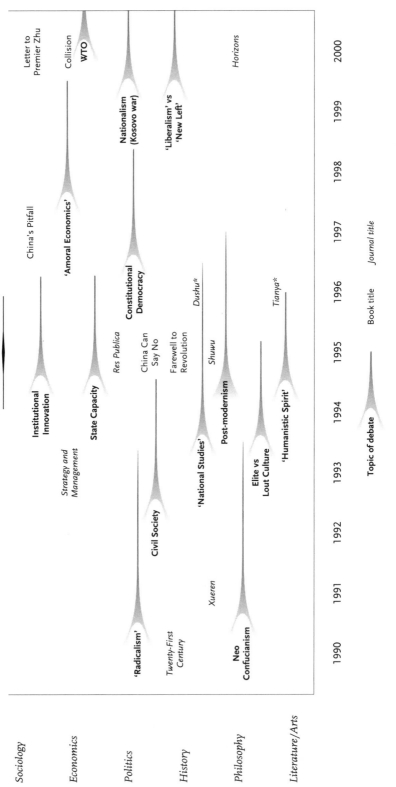

Chinese intellectual debates in the 1990s

Sociology

Economics

Politics

History

Philosophy

Literature/Arts

| | 1990 | 1991 | 1992 | 1993 | 1994 | 1995 | 1996 | 1997 | 1998 | 1999 | 2000 |

Letter to Premier Zhu

China's Pitfall

Collision

WTO

'Amoral Economics'

Institutional Innovation

Strategy and Management

State Capacity

Res Publica

Constitutional Democracy

China Can Say No

Farewell to Revolution

Nationalism (Kosovo war)

'National Studies'

Shuwu

Dushu*

'Liberalism' vs 'New Left'

Horizons

Post-modernism

Civil Society

Xueren

Twenty-First Century

'Radicalism'

Neo Confucianism

Elite vs Lout Culture

'Humanistic Spirit'

Tianya*

Topic of debate

Book title   Journal title

Debates are listed by their initial points; those concerned with literature/arts are covered only selectively.   * Chief editors changed in 1996 and complex scenery of thought than the first. Economic dynamism, political stagnation and deepening social divisions defined this period. But its heritage has also enriched the intellectual life of the country. The space for the discussion of ideas, after starting in unfavourable conditions, has steadily widened. Within it a curve of development can be traced, leading from debates that are primarily located in literature and philosophy, or the humanities more generally, towards social and economic themes with more directly political overtones. The chart opposite, designed as a simplified visual guide to the intellectual history of the nineties, illustrates this diagrammatically, as it moves from the bottom left to the upper right-hand corner of the frame. A fuller account of the period would reveal further complications, and much else of interest, in these years.

V

The selection of thinkers to be included in a survey of any national scene involves difficult issues of judgement. No solution can be altogether satisfactory. Here the organizing decision has been to focus on intellectuals active in the mainland. The only exception is the round-table that concludes the book, where the events of 1989 and their consequences, as viewed by three participants, could not be freely aired within the PRC. Otherwise, all the contributions come from the mainland itself.[72] Direct involvement in the political and economic life of contemporary China is a position that differs from that of intellectuals based overseas, no matter how well informed. It is generally agreed, of course, research and debate should not reproduce the rigid borderlines of states that have often been drawn for contingent historical reasons. That should apply all the more to a cultural community like the Chinese one. Yet to ignore the continuing realities of state frontiers, and the conditions they impose on intellectual life, would be self-deception. I have tried to edit this volume with an awareness of the need both to break out of their mental confinement and to acknowledge their practical impact on our national life.

In composing the mosaic that makes up this book, I have tried to balance two principal considerations, intellectual distinction and political representation. My primary aim has been to give English-speaking readers a sense of how many original and forceful minds now find expression in China. The intellectuals whose texts are included here stand out for the vividness of the

---

[72] Gan Yang, a veteran of mainland cultural activities in the eighties, who spent most of the nineties abroad, and is now based in Hong Kong, could be considered a special case. For collections that include a range of contributors from Australia and America, see Gloria Davies, ed, *Voicing Concerns*, and Xudong Zhang, ed, *Whither China?*, Durham, NC, 2001, each of which contains translated and written-in-English texts.

descriptions they give of different aspects of the mainland scene, the vigour of their definitions of the issues facing the country, and the firmness of their advocacy of solutions to them. In their arguments and opinions, the multiplicity and complexity of China's problems can be seen in a collective magnifying glass. At the same time, their views of the way out of the crisis that underlies the apparent successes of the past decade form a spectrum of the main positions in the Chinese intelligentsia today. Although these can be divided roughly into 'new left' and 'liberal' camps, as indicated above, this is a range that contains many intermediate and overlapping shades of opinion, which reflect the shifts and uncertainties of the period.

The one sector not represented here are those technocrats – most of them economists – who identify more or less completely with government policies, tacitly favouring an authoritarian political system as a condition of an all-out marketization of society. Although an important force behind closed political doors, they cannot articulate their standpoint openly. For to do so would both embarrass officialdom, which does not welcome such frankness, and incur ostracism from the intelligentsia, which is united in its dislike of such kow-towing. For better or worse, Chinese intellectuals today see themselves, virtually without exception, as oppositional. So however close to the 'Washington consensus' the direction of particular state policies may be, there has hitherto been little room for explicitly 'neo-liberal' currents in the intelligentsia itself, as distinct from aides or advisers to power.

Thus of our contributors, Wang Hui, Gan Yang, Wang Xiaoming, Qian Liqun and Li Changping can be situated on the 'left' side of the political spectrum; Zhu Xueqin, Qin Hui, He Qinglian, Xiao Xuehui and Wang Yi on the 'liberal' side; while Chen Pingyuan, Wang Anyi or Hu Angang would probably disavow any leaning to one or the other. The degree of identification of any given individual with either camp, in fact, would be highly variable. What these different intellectuals have in common is a clear generational profile. If we set aside the round-table at the end of this book, out of thirteen contributors, no less than nine were born at the turn of the fifties. In other words, they had not completed middle school when the Cultural Revolution broke out in 1966, dispatching urban teenagers to the countryside and suspending higher education for nearly a decade. The impact of this experience, in which all traditional structures of authority broke down, is recounted here by Qin Hui, Zhu Xueqin and Hu Angang, but can be taken as decisive for all those who lived through it.

Coming back to complete a university education and to a basic accumulation of knowledge in the 1980s, these intellectuals were witnesses or participants in the cultural transformations of the 'New Era', during which they could draw their own political conclusions about their time as sent-down youth. The result was a strong independence of mind, which became widely noticed as a feature of the Cultural Revolution generation. In some cases – of those represented here, Wang Anyi, Gan Yang and (in an older age-group) Qian Liqun – they had already made their mark in the public sphere in the eighties. But for the most part, this cohort entered national debates in the nineties, when it not only had a very strong motivation to speak out, but also the necessary ability to argue and persuade others. No matter what the ideological distance between these figures, they all demonstrated a vigour of thought and a grasp of issues that, while no guarantee of instant support or popularity, proved able to stir up widespread responses and sustain continued debate. In doing so, they have set an example that has been followed by the younger writers in this collection, Li Changping and Wang Yi.

In conceiving this book, I did not deliberately seek any geographical pattern among the contributors, but as it turned out the result is quite satisfying. China is a large country, and it would have been unhappy if there was too great a regional concentration in the volume. Today most of the contributors work in the two big cities of Beijing and Shanghai. But the areas where they were born or spent their formative years cover hugely diverse areas of the country: from Guangdong and Guangxi in the south (Chen Pingyuan, Qin Hui), to Guizhou, Sichuan and Gansu in the west (Qian Liqun, Xiao Xuehui, Wang Yi, Qin Hui), from Heilongjiang in the far north-east (Hu Angang, Gan Yang), to poor villages in the central hinterland of Henan, Hubei and Anhui (Zhu Xueqin, Li Changping, Wang Anyi), as well as cities in Jiangsu and Hunan (Wang Hui, He Qinglian) that have not been political or commercial centres in PRC times. This geographical range informs the breadth of views about Chinese problems expressed here. It also, of course, reflects a long-standing feature of the country's educational tradition – competitive examinations open to the nation as a whole, which were still strong in the eighties, but have since been eroded by localized and marketized settings that attract sharp criticism in more than one contribution below. Occupationally, in keeping with the general institutional change noted above, all the contributors to this volume now have university posts, with the exception of Wang Anyi, a well-known novelist, and Li Changping, till recently a rural party-cadre.

The book that follows is divided into four parts. The first consists of interviews with four leading Chinese intellectuals, Wang Hui, Zhu Xueqin, Chen Pingyuan and Qin Hui, each of whom offers a general overview of the period extending from the crackdown of 1989 to the present, from a distinctive point of view and set of theoretical interests. These interviews serve not only as intellectual portraits of these remarkable figures, but also as contrasting and overlapping maps of the intellectual life of the time, which contest as well as supplement each other on many points. The second part of the book focuses on the character and consequences of the major economic changes in the 1990s. It includes four outstanding examples of a collective effort to understand accurately what is going on in China. These are also among the most critical writings in this collection, exposing to full view the gravity of many of the problems now confronting Chinese society. He Qinglian provides a chilling account of the new social polarization. Wang Yi considers the fate of the working class that was once held to be masters of the country. Li Changping presents a searing picture of crisis in the Chinese countryside. Hu Angang looks at the structural problems and prospects of macro-economic reform.

The third part of the book moves to some of the most sensitive questions thrown up by the transformations of the past decade. Xiao Xuehui analyses the growth of inequality in China's school and university systems, as education is officially 'industrialized'. Wang Anyi offers pithy insights into the position of women and youth. Gan Yang explores the constitutional relations between citizen and state. Wang Xiaoming reflects on the ideology of success that has become a central feature of the contemporary cultural scene. Qian Liqun discusses the historical amnesia that has increasingly accompanied it, threatening loss of memory not merely of the eighties, but of the whole history of China in the twentieth century. These are issues that have given rise to continual debates within the Chinese intelligentsia, and our contributors have been on the frontline of the controversies over them.

The fourth and final part of the book is composed of a dialogue between three participants in the June Fourth Movement of 1989, students in Beijing at the time, Wang Dan, Li Minqi and myself. The crisis of 1989 is universally acknowledged to be the watershed separating two distinct 'epochs of reform', and the necessary starting-point for an understanding of the peculiar character of the nineties as a period. But there is little agreement as to either the course of the political trauma of that year itself, or to its longer-term historical significance. In the candid but comradely exchanges that end the book, monitored by the distinguished literary historian Leo Ou-fan Lee, three different views can be heard. The topics range from a critical consideration of the actions and decisions of the June Fourth Movement itself, to the social and cultural contradictions of the nineties, and the political prospects for a future democracy in China. These are issues that will return in any broader balance-sheet to come, when conditions in China permit them.

In bringing this collection together, I have tried to make it as comprehensive as I could. But although its range of subject-matter is wide, no single volume could cover all major issues of public concern in China's development today. Many important questions await further effort and opportunity. Some omissions here are amply dealt with elsewhere. This is especially true of the cultural field proper. Literature, cinema and the arts have been relatively well served in the West, in a series of lively surveys,[73] although

---

[73] Apart from titles already mentioned, these include Zha Jianying, *China Pop*; Geremie Barmé, *In the Red: On Contemporary Chinese Culture*, New York, 1999; Arif Dirlik and

literary criticism – a field with a long tradition in Chinese intellectual history – has received much less attention. Other gaps are more serious. Among them are the hot debates over 'the rule of law', or the relationship between China's legal system and socio-political establishment, which now attract some of the country's brightest students to its newly remodelled law schools. Such issues have always been hot – in a quite different sense – to ordinary people and their lives, and are perennial topics on popular talk shows on TV and radio. International coverage of them is highly skewed, for the most part concerned with demands that foreign law firms be allowed to operate in China, or that the interests of foreign companies or overseas investors be guaranteed, rather than with the rights of ordinary citizens that need to be legally secured.

A different case is represented by the nationality question. Here there is a marked shortage of discussion within China itself, in part attributable to political controls, but also reflecting cultural blinkers to which Chen Ping-yuan rightly draws attention in this volume. The situation of minority nationalities since the start of Open-Door policy in the late 1970s, and the corresponding ideological transformations in their position, have been largely ignored by mainland intellectuals, surfacing only when tensions threaten official 'stability', as most recently in Xinjiang. Serious discussion, based on careful investigation and independent thinking of these matters is so rare that the one outstanding exception should be signalled here. This is Wang Lixiong's remarkable writing on Tibet, which should be read together with the powerful reply to it from the Tibetan historian Tsering Shakya, and so is not included in this volume.[74] For the most part, however, Chinese intellectuals have so far locked out the nationalities question from their concerns, as if it had no bearing on China's future.

Another fundamental issue that our volume has lacked room to develop is the nature of the Chinese economic boom of the nineties. Alongside the deepening social crisis in the countryside, there has been spectacular growth in the big cities, and a very steep increase of GDP, according to official figures. The sources, substance and sustainability of this urban explosion all remain highly controversial. Explanations for it vary widely. Unlimited supplies of cheap labour; pre-modern commercial traditions; post-revolutionary education and skills; super-exploitation of workers; abundant overseas Chinese and foreign investment; tight currency and capital controls – each hypothesis has had some champion, without any scholarly consensus being reached. The continued viability of the current growth model is in no less dispute,

---

Xudong Zhang, eds, *Postmodernism and China*, Durham 2000; and Claire Huot, *China's New Cultural Scene*, Durham, 2000;

[74] Wang Lixiong, 'Tibet: China's soft belly in the 21st Century', *SM*, no. 32, 1999; 'A Cultural Reflection on Tibetan Affairs', *SM*, no. 36, 1999, pp. 45–52; in English, 'Reflections on Tibet', *New Left Review*, no. 14, March/April 2002, pp. 79–111, to which Tsering Shakya replied with 'Blood in the Snows', *New Left Review*, no. 15, May/June, 2002, pp. 39–60.

with most attention focusing (inconclusively) on the weaknesses of the financial sector, and the puzzle of persisting price deflation amid rapid economic expansion. The PRC's entry into the WTO has raised many of these issues with a new sharpness, and Chinese intellectuals have begun to address them more urgently. But it is still probably true that the main scholarly debate over the performance of the Chinese economy has been conducted by Western specialists rather than in the mainland itself.

Lastly, there is no discussion of China's relations with the outside world in this volume. This is certainly the most significant omission. Foreign policy is, of course, a politically sensitive topic in the PRC, which the authorities wish to keep under political control. But the reasons for the lack of critical spirit of so many Chinese intellectuals in this area seem to lie deeper than simple questions of censorship, which are in any case rarely absolute, since much the same note of apathy can be detected in the diasporas as in the mainland. In general, what few opinions can be found in intellectual circles, within or outside the country, fall into two limited categories, not always distinguished from one another. On the one hand, China's role in the world is conceived of in competitive terms with the United States, and to a much lesser extent Japan, with an occasional glance at South-East or Central Asian countries. Here a narrow and provincial geopolitics is the typical perspective for looking out at the world. On the other hand, in apparent contrast with this nationalism, but actually often not so distant from it, is a dogged attachment to mainstream ideology in the US as a universal value, which has led many Chinese intellectuals inside and outside the PRC to fall in with the international policies of successive American presidents over the past twenty-five years.

These two seemingly antagonistic poles share one thing in common. They lack any sympathetic understanding of other smaller countries, especially those of the Third World, or any critical standpoint on global politics.[75] The legacy of a certain 'Middle Kingdom mentality' can probably be detected in this. Still, the present poverty of thinking about the wider world and the place China should take up in it is not a cultural given. It contrasts not only with the outlook of Chinese intellectuals in the early twentieth century,[76] but also with that of the mid-fifties and early sixties, when the whole nation was concerned with international struggles of the weak and poor. So the current self-absorbed outlook could change again, and in fact there have recently been signs of a more open sensibility, with protests against the Anglo-American invasion of Iraq. But so far no Chinese intellectual of significance has devoted any effort to questioning the

---

[75] Coverage of social movements in the Third World has been a consistent feature of *Dushu* in recent years, but these are not examined in the framework of international relations.

[76] See, for example, Xiaobing Tang's study of Liang Qichao, *Global Space and the Nationalist Discourse of Modernity*, Stanford 1996. Lu Xun, of course, was another outstanding example.

country's external relations that could match the intensity of reflections and debate on its internal problems. Here attempts to locate or commission a contribution to this collection were unsuccessful. The only comfort our reader may take here is from passages that touch on this neglected area in the course of a more general argument.

The nineties were a period of frustration, reorientation and active intervention for Chinese intellectuals. At the beginning of the twenty-first century, in China as in many other poorer countries affected by globalization, regional and social polarization is becoming more pronounced than ever, yet political apathy is spreading among urban youth. It is my hope that this volume will help to give a sense of the country's critical minds, as they reflect not only on their own situation, but on problems that affect the larger part of humanity.

Acknowledgements

In translating and presenting the contributions to this volume, I have tried to make them as accessible as possible to an English-speaking public. This has involved a number of different editing procedures on existing texts, in consultation with the contributors. Listed below are the sources from which the texts in this volume were derived. Unless otherwise indicated, the essays are published here in English for the first time and are translated by myself. All notes are by original authors, except those marked with [tr] to indicate notes by the translator, or with [ed] to indicate notes added by the editor.

Wang Hui, 'The New Criticism': originally an interview given in English, published under the title 'Fire at the Castle Gate: A New Left in China' in *New Left Review*, No. 6, November/December 2000. It appears here with additions translated from Chinese.

Zhu Xueqin, 'For a Chinese Liberalism': drawn from Zhu Xueqin, *Shuzhai li de geming*, Changchun, 1999. Translation by Wu Shengqing.

Chen Pingyuan, 'Scholarship, Ideas, Politics': drawn from Chen Pingyuan, *Xuezhe de renjian qinghuai*, Zhuhai, 1995; *Chen Pingyuan zixuan ji*, Nanning, 1997; and Yang Zao, 'You qinghuai de xueshu yanjiu: Chen Pingyuan jiaoshou fangtan', *Xueshu yuekan*, Shanghai, July 2002.

Qin Hui, 'Dividing the Big Family Assets': drawn from an interview in Beijing, translated by Yao Peng; an interview in Los Angeles; and Qin Hui, *Wenti yu zhuyi*, Changchun, 1999. A slightly shorter English version was published under the title 'The Stolypins of China' in *New Left Review*, No. 20, March/April 2003.

He Qinglian, 'A Listing Social Structure': originally published as 'Dangqian Zhongguo shehui jiegou yanbian de zongti xing fenxi' in *Shuwu* in Hunan

March 2000. English translation first published in *New Left Review*, No. 5, September/October 2000. It appears here with some additions.

Wang Yi, 'From Status to Contract': originally published on-line as 'Beixin-qiyi shi zenyang hefahua de'. For reference, see *Suidao* <http://www.geocities.com/SiliconValley/Bay/5598/> no. 189 (sd0205b) May 2002.

Li Changping, 'The Crisis in the Countryside': drawn from Li Changping, *Wo xiang zongli shuo shihua*, Beijing 2002.

Hu Angang, 'Equity and Efficiency': drawn from *Hu Angang ji*, Ha'erbin 1995, 'Zhongguo fazhan qianjing' and 'Zhongguo zhanlüe gouxiang', manuscript papers.

Xiao Xuehui, 'Industrializing Education?': drawn from Xiao Xuehui, 'Jiaoyu: Biyao de wutuobang', 'Nan ju bei zhi de "jiaoyu chanyehua"' and 'Liang-dian butong kanfa' from 'xuezhe wenji' at <http://www.wtyzy.net>.

Wang Anyi, 'Tales of Gender': 'A Peach was Presented Me/ I Returned a Fine Jade' originally as 'Tou wo yi mutao, Bao zhi yi qiongyao', unpublished essay; and 'For Whom the Bell Tolls' as 'Sangzhong wei shui er ming' in *Qiansha chuang xia*, Shanghai 2002. Translation by Gao Jin.

Gan Yang, 'The Citizen and the Constitution': drawn from 'Gongmin geti wei ben, Tongyi xianzheng liguo' in *Ershi yi shiji*, Hong Kong June 1996; and 'Zhongguo heshi chengwei yige zhengzhi minzu', see *Suidao* <http://www.geocities.com/SiliconValley/Bay/5598> no. 184 (sd0203a) March 2002.

Wang Xiaoming, 'A Manifesto for Cultural Studies': originally as 'Binlin "da shidai" de Zhongguo', unpublished paper in Chinese. An English translation is to be published under the title 'China on the Verge of a "Monumentous Era"' in *Positions*, Vol. II, No. 3, winter 2003. Here it appears in a slightly shortened and modified form. Translation by Robin Visser.

Qian Liqun, 'Refusing to Forget': originally as 'Jujue yiwang: Kexue zongjie ershi shiji Zhongguo jingyan de diyi bu', unpublished paper. Translation by Eileen Cheng.

Wang Dan, Li Minqi and Wang Chaohua, 'A Dialogue on the Future of China': originally published in English in *New Left Review*, I/235, May/June 1999. Translation by Xiaoping Cong, Joel Andreas, Li Minqi, Wang Chaohua.

All editing was checked and approved for accuracy by the individual authors. My thanks therefore go in the first instance to all my Chinese contributors for their patience and generosity in helping to bring this volume into being; and to Leo Ou-fan Lee for kindly agreeing to moderate 'A Dialogue on the Future of China' at Harvard in 1999. I am greatly indebted to Perry Anderson, who carefully read the whole manuscript and spent a great amount of time discussing it in detail with me. I have also benefited from the advice and support at Verso of Tariq Ali, Tim Clark, Jane Hindle and Mark Martin, who have corrected the mistakes in my English and encouraged me throughout the production process; and of Franco Moretti and Jacob Stevens, who helped me design the chart of intellectual developments in the nineties. I remain responsible for all the remaining errors. Last but not least, I owe a great deal to my teachers at UCLA, Leo Ou-fan Lee, Theodore Huters, Pauline Yu, Benjamin Elman and Shu-mei Shih, who have striven to instil in me a sense of scholarship and intellectual curiosity.

*   *   *

I dedicate this book to the memory of Lu Chunlin, a graduate student in the Department of Philosophy at the People's University of China, with whom I made friends in Beijing in the spring of 1989. We promised to discuss questions concerning China's future together later that summer.

W.CH.
June, 2003

Note on Romanization

All Chinese terms cited are in pinyin spelling, except proper names that have been authorized otherwise (e.g., Peking University instead of Beijing University). All Chinese names are presented last name first, except when cited in Western publications (e.g., Xudong Zhang for English publication and Zhang Xudong for Chinese publication). Four journals, the Hong Kong-based *Ershi yi shiji* (Twenty-First Century), Beijing-based *Zhanlüe yu guanli* (Strategy and Management) and *Gonggon luncong* (Res Publica), and Shijiazhuang-based *Shijie* (Horizons), have their table of contents printed in English regularly. Articles quoted from these journals are listed in their English titles only.

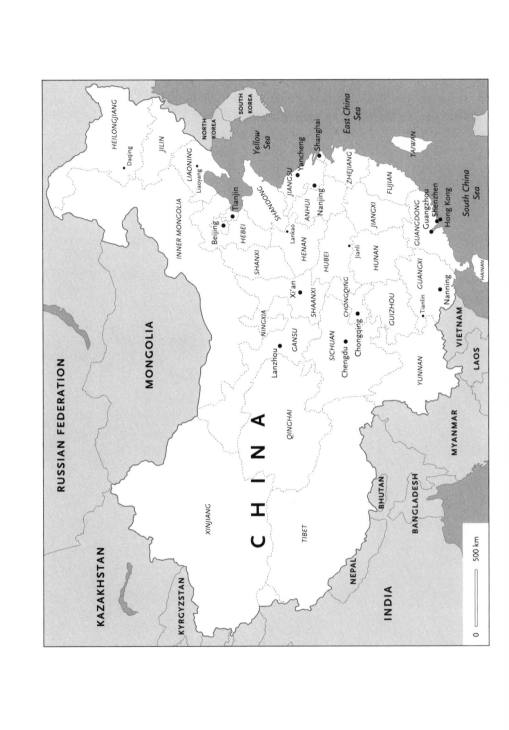

PART I

1

The New Criticism

Wang Hui

What is the role of Dushu *(Readings)* in Chinese intellectual life, and how do you conceive your position in it as editor?

The first issue of *Dushu* was published in April 1979. Its leading article was entitled 'No Forbidden Zone in Reading', and you could say that has been the spirit of the journal from the beginning. This is how we do our editorial job today, and we will never change it in the future. The first editor of *Dushu*, Chen Yuan, a famous social linguist, was a director of the Commercial Publishing House in Beijing, historically the most important imprint in modern China. A year later, Fan Yong – a progressive publisher with close links to the intellectual world since the forties – took over. I think he was one of the most significant figures in the history of the journal, making it a key forum for new ideas and debates in the eighties. From 1979 to 1984, most of these were raised by an older generation of scholars or open-minded official intellectuals, like Li Honglin, Wang Ruoshui and others. It was they, for example, who took up the issue of the relations between Marxism and humanism. Then around 1985 a younger levy of intellectuals took centre stage. Among the most active were the Editorial Committee of *Culture: China and The World*, a series of translations aiming to introduce classics of modern thought from abroad, most of them produced by the Sanlian Press, which is also the publisher of *Dushu*. The journal ran many reviews of these books, which attracted a lot of attention from university students, graduates and fledgling intellectuals. There was an enthusiastic reception of modern Western philosophy, social theory and economic thought. Nietzsche, Heidegger, Cassirer, Marcuse, Sartre and Freud, not to speak of modernization theory and neo-classical economics, were eagerly canvassed in the articles of the time. There was some resistance to all this, since the style in which these notices were written was often criticized as too difficult or obscure. Looking back, one can see that this younger generation was more interested in introducing new theories, without any necessary political bearing, whereas the older generation had a much closer relation to politics. In this phase *Dushu* was not a radical journal – it was relatively detached from the political ferment of the late eighties. But an intellectual space for further discussion was created, which was not without significance in 1989.

That year saw a turning point. Whereas there was a high turnover of editors in other periodicals by late 1989, there was no change at *Dushu*, whose chief editor Shen Changwen carried on till 1996. This was partly just because the journal had played little direct political role in the preceding years. But in the general atmosphere of conservatism and dogmatism after 1989, *Dushu* now stood out as more open-minded. Of course there were pressures on the journal, and after Deng Xiaoping's visit to southern China in 1992, a wave of consumerism and commercialization swept the country. In these conditions, Shen shifted editorial policy towards articles that were easier to read, with less academic discussions, to boost sales. Circulation rose from 50,000 to over 80,000 in five or six years, but while the journal became more popular, it was also criticized for failing to reflect the development of intellectual research in the country. Actually, it was still introducing new themes like Orientalism or post-colonialism, and continued to be widely viewed as a beacon of high culture. But the changes in *Dushu* in the early nineties did herald a new tension between popular culture and high culture in China.

In 1996 I was invited to be a chief editor by Dong Xiuyu, the editorial director of Sanlian Press and one of the most senior editors of *Dushu*. A year later, my colleague Huang Ping joined me as a co-editor. Since then, our policy has been to keep a readable style for the journal, but to move it away from consumerist preoccupations back to real intellectual discussion, and to expand its range beyond literature and the humanities to the social and natural sciences, including subjects never touched on before like archaeology or historical geography. We have launched a series of major debates on the fate of rural society, ethics, Asia, war and revolution, financial crisis, liberalism, law and democracy, nationalism, feminism. Most of these issues – the current crisis of rural society, for example – were raised for the first time in contemporary China in our pages, and other journals then followed. We carry opinions from right across the political spectrum. I should say that, as chief editor, I publish my own articles in other periodicals, to safeguard the impartiality of the journal. Our roster of contributors has expanded substantially, and many of the newer ones have made their names writing for us. All this has made *Dushu* a focus of lively controversy, and increased its readership to between 100,000 and 120,000.

The Internet seems to have exploded since 2000 as a medium of discussion in China. What changes, for good or bad, is this bringing to the exchange of ideas, especially among the younger generation?

Yes, this has been a major development. All kinds of different forces are now finding an outlet on the Net, and even the Chinese government has stepped in with – not very successful – efforts to regulate it. The Internet has brought three significant gains. It creates a space in which direct discussions between mainland and overseas Chinese intellectuals become possible, as a zone beyond the borders of nation-states. Secondly, it allows a lot of directly political issues to be addressed, which the print media in the mainland cannot touch. Thirdly, it spreads information from local levels very quickly across the country, which otherwise would not get national attention. So it offers the possibility of linking local, national and international spaces. But its limitations remain obvious too. The information it purveys is not beyond regulation by various forces. Since much of it is impossible to check, we often have no means of knowing whether something is true or false. The Net is also an ideal medium for intervention without responsibility, encouraging personalized attacks and reckless vituperation under cover of anonymity. At the same time, it does not lend itself easily to theoretical discussions, which are still more or less the preserve of print journals in China, though some are now setting up their websites and we can expect more interaction between the two media. Still, the Internet has certainly played a role in the intensification of polemical exchanges since 2000, with new camps springing to life on the most pressing issues of the day.

In the eighties, the political field in China was conventionally divided into just two categories – Reformers and Conservatives, a dichotomy with its own built-in ideological valuation of the two. At some point in the nineties, the vocabulary changed, and people started to talk about Liberals and then, more recently still, a New Left. What developments lie behind these changes?

Towards the end of the seventies, the terms 'conservatives' and 'reformers' indicated, respectively, holdovers from Mao's last years – also derisively dubbed *fanshipai* or 'Whatevers' – and supporters of Deng's policies. At that time, it was figures like Hua Guofeng or Mao's former security chief Wang Dongxing who were the conservatives, while theoreticians like Deng Liqun or Hu Qiaomu – regarded as conservatives in the eighties – belonged to the reforming wing of the Party.[1] In the late seventies, Deng Liqun was quite radical: while Hua Guofeng was still Chairman of the CCP, he published some lectures in the Central Party School attacking the conservatives very sharply – even criticising Mao himself. But after the 'campaign against spiritual pollution' in 1983, the political map changed. Hu Qiaomu published a famous article about socialist humanism, attacking Zhou Yang,

---

[1] Hua Guofeng was Mao's short-lived official successor as Chairman of the CCP (1976–78). In 1978 Hu Qiaomu – Mao's secretary during the Yan'an period – and Deng Liqun were respectively President and Vice President of the Chinese Academy of Social Sciences [ed].

Wang Ruoshui, Su Shaozhi and other – generally more open-minded – intellectuals within the Party, who had taken up this slogan; and the perception of Deng Liqun changed too.[2] Once Hu Yaobang became General Secretary of the CCP, Hu Qiaomu and Deng Liqun were type-cast as conservatives. But actually they had earlier been regarded as reformers themselves. All these people belonged to Deng Xiaoping's camp. You can see the same kind of shift in categorizations of Li Peng, whom we considered the arch-Conservative in 1989. Known mainly as Zhou En-lai's adopted son, he became Vice Premier in the mid-eighties. His attitude was quite ambiguous at the time – it was not at all clear whether he was a conservative or a radical reformer. The distinction between the two stances was plain for all to see among the older generation of party leaders, but was much more blurred in this generation.

With the crackdown of 1989, it was ostensibly the conservatives who had taken power. But the label did not so easily lend itself to Deng Xiaoping. After June Fourth he held a series of talks with Yao Yilin, Li Peng and others at which he insisted on a continuation of his reform policies, and picked Jiang Zemin to be his successor, as a politician milder than Li Peng but stronger than Zhao Ziyang.[3] So in the nineties, it became very difficult to give any real content to the categories of reformer or conservative. In one sense, the whole 'reform policy' became more radical than in Zhao Ziyang's time, especially the economic field. There were no longer any voices to be heard against it within the power structure. Li Peng himself as Premier carried out many drastic reforms, at Deng's prompting.

It was against this background that a change in Chinese political vocabulary started to occur. We can date its beginnings from around 1993. In the spring of 1992 Deng Xiaoping made a trip to Shenzhen in the South, where he gave the signal for an all-out drive for market-led modernization of the PRC economy. The immediate result was a runaway consumer boom – with high inflation – in Shanghai, Guangdong and even Beijing. This outcome of the southern tour shocked a lot of intellectuals. Most of them had initially welcomed the energetic new burst of reform policies. But when they saw the rampant commercialization of all structures of daily life and culture that followed them, they started to feel a certain disillusion. In the eighties the mainstream outlook of Chinese intellectuals had been – in the phrase of the time – a 'New Enlightenment' very favourable to the Open Door priorities and marketizing thrust of Deng's rule. Two debates now began to alter these parameters. In 1994 the Hong Kong journal *Twenty-First Century*

---

[2] Zhou Yang – once Mao's chief functionary for literature – was a victim of the Cultural Revolution before resuming his position in 1978; Wang Ruoshui was then deputy chief editor of *The People's Daily*, Su Shaozhi director of the Institute for Marxism–Leninism–Mao Zedong Thought in the Chinese Academy of Social Sciences [ed].

[3] Yao Yilin was director of the State Planning Commission in the late eighties; Zhao Ziyang was General Secretary of the CCP from 1987 to 1989 [ed].

published an article by a young Chinese economist at MIT, Cui Zhiyuan, under the title 'A Second Emancipation'.[4] It argued that if the first intellectual emancipation had been from orthodox Marxism, there should now be second one, from the rote assumptions of the New Enlightenment. Cui drew on three different strands of thought: critical legal studies in the US, analytical Marxism in the West, and theories of a New Evolution. For Chinese readers, the startling feature of his essay was its calm reference to analytical Marxism – not that anyone much knew what the term meant: it was just the use of the term 'Marxism' itself, long a virtual taboo for many intellectuals. Cui Zhiyuan went on to collaborate with Roberto Unger in a series of articles on the fate of the Russian reforms, as an admonition to would-be reformers in China. At the same time, another young scholar working in the States, Gan Yang, was publishing articles in *Twenty-First Century* on township and village enterprises, as a form of property neither state nor private, but intermediate between the two, as the distinctive Chinese path to modernity. So the first break with the consensus came from overseas students.

However, the same year saw another important debate, this time in China's leading monthly, *Dushu*, when a number of leading intellectuals attacked the increasing commercialization of life in China as destructive of its 'humanistic spirit'. The topic was launched by scholars from Shanghai, logically enough, since Shanghai is the biggest consumer centre in China and its intellectuals were shocked earlier and more deeply than their counterparts in Beijing by the ruthless wave of commercialization after Deng's Southern tour. Not that these intellectuals were hostile to the market as such. Rather, they lamented that Chinese marketization failed to live up the standards set in Europe and America. Some tried to trace its deficiencies back to the Weber's argument that Protestantism is essential to the true spirit of capitalism. An ideal capitalism should, they felt, be compatible with a humanistic spirit. The underlying attitude was fairly apolitical – behind it lay the offended dignity of scholars in the humanities. But they were now becoming aware that marketization in China relied on a political system that in their eyes remained unchanged.

Independently – actually a little earlier – the group around the journal *Xueren* (The Scholar), with which I was associated, had raised some critical issues, looking back at the June Fourth Movement. They found that the intellectuals of the New Enlightenment, who had exercised a great influence on the June Fourth Movement, in practice knew very little about Chinese history. Rather than studying Chinese realities, they had simply imported Western ideas into the reform process. That was a big mistake. To some extent, Gan Yang and Cui Zhiyuan risked repeating it. We thought it was

---

4 For references to this debate, see Introduction, notes 32–34 above [ed].

essential to reflect very carefully on modern Chinese history, and started to look at the professional scholars who had studied it. Most of their work was quite traditional, and we went on to propose new ways to approach this subject.

This was the context in which talk started of a 'New Left', more critical of capitalism and more aware of the Yeltsin experience than the New Enlightenment. So far as I know, the first appearance of the term was in a short report in *Beijing Youth Weekly*, published after they had interviewed me. I didn't use any such phrase myself, simply stressing the need for critical analysis of Chinese realities. Then I saw the report, which spoke of a new Marxism and the ideas of a New Left, in quite a positive tone. Since, however, the editor of *Beijing Youth Weekly* was a supporter of the theory that China needed a New Authoritarianism, I suspected the term New Left was just being used as a cudgel to belabour liberals.

Was the term 'Liberal' already in widespread usage?

Not yet in its current sense. The government, of course, had waged a campaign against 'bourgeois liberalism' in 1986, not to speak of 1983. But the term was still used much in the way Mao had employed it in Yan'an, to refer to personal misbehaviour and lack of discipline. For its part the New Enlightenment did not take liberalism, understood in a more classical sense, as a model. It tended to appeal to a different kind of socialism. Fang Lizhi, for example, on coming back from a trip to Scandinavia, advocated a Nordic socialism in the tradition of Bernstein for China.[5] The leading philosopher Li Zehou defined himself as a Marxist, not a Liberal. Wang Yuanhua, editor of the journal *New Enlightenment*, claimed to be a Marxist. Su Shaozhi published research on Yugoslav, Polish and Hungarian reforms. At the time, the inspiration of this generation was still socialist rather than liberal. The one significant exception was the political scientist Yan Jiaqi, who did look back to the European Enlightenment, the time of the American Constitution and the early phase of the French Revolution, and was concerned with the division of powers in the liberal tradition of government. But in general, from the end of the seventies to the mid-eighties, the New Enlightenment – most of whose leading intellectuals were very close to the government – still spoke of the merits of socialism. It was in the late eighties that the atmosphere changed. By then Hayek's works were more and more widely read. Friedman was received enthusiastically by Zhao Ziyang. The economists advising the government were pressing for large-scale privatizations.

---

[5] Fang Lizhi: astrophysicist who became Vice President of the new Science and Technology University in Hefei, and leading liberal critic of the government, in the late eighties; now in exile [ed].

So the current self-identification of most Chinese intellectuals as 'liberals' dates from the nineties? In the eighties, no one could openly say: 'Yes, I am a liberal.' But after 1989, the radicalization of official reform policies created a situation where the term could describe a mixture of support and criticism of the government – approval of marketization, but disapproval of censorship or violation of human rights. The basis of this attitude would be: we are liberal because we believe in liberty, and the precondition of liberty is the dominance of private property in society. Would it be correct to think this became a consensus?

Roughly, yes – but with many shades of opinion. Some of the Shanghai liberals were very uneasy about the commercialization of culture, for example – anxieties that came out in the 'humanistic spirit' debate. Others were worried about growing social inequalities. Actually, the self-definition of Chinese liberals didn't crystallize fully until they discovered an intellectual opponent. The first stirrings of a more critical view of official marketization go back to 1993–94, as I've said. But it wasn't till 1997–98 that the label New Left became widely used, to indicate positions outside the consensus. Liberals adopted the term, relying on the negative identification the idea of the 'Left' with late Maoism, to imply that these must be a throw-back to the Cultural Revolution. Up till then, they had more frequently attacked anyone who criticized the rush to marketization as a 'conservative' – this is how Cui Zhiyuan was initially described, for example. From 1997 onwards, this altered. The standard accusatory term became 'New Left'.

What accounts for the change?

It corresponded to a shift in the cultural atmosphere. As the nineties wore on, more and more voices could be heard criticizing the whole direction Chinese society was taking. Even some economists, a very orthodox community, could be heard doubting whether the country was on the right path – scholars like Yang Fan put forward a lot of data that made uncomfortable reading. In 1997 the Hainan journal *Tianya* published an essay I had written four years earlier – at that time no one wanted to risk printing it – on the failure of successive versions of Chinese 'modernization', which ends with a sharp critique of the kind of capitalist modernity the Reform Era had offered the country. At first there was no open reaction, although I was vehemently taken to task in private, and various unflattering descriptions were circulated about me. The public response was silence, but there was a lot of talk about it. Then *Twenty-First Century* in Hong Kong published two or three articles by mainland intellectuals attacking me. This broke the ice, and several liberals followed up with hostile responses in the PRC press, mainly in Guangzhou. Part of the reason for this reaction was that, after a decade as a contributor, I had become editor of *Dushu* in early 1996, and some of its issues had contained material calculated to unsettle conventional wisdom among intellectuals. Circulation went up, though older-generation scholars like Li Shenzhi and others, who were friends of mine, would ask me how I could run such articles. But these provoked a lot of discussion, in which a younger generation became very interested. A collection of essays I published in the same year, mainly concerned with problems of Chinese modernity, sold pretty well. In these new conditions, Gan Yang and Cui Zhiyuan got a real response to their writings in the mainland for the first time. Intellectually, 1997 was a turning-point.

A process of political differentiation has continued since?

In 1998 the Asian financial crisis broke out. Naturally, this shook any blind faith there might have been in the world market. Suddenly capitalism did not seem such a sure-fire guarantee of stability and prosperity after all. Liberals were put on the defensive. But a much worse blow to them came in 1999, with the NATO bombing of the Chinese Embassy in Belgrade. For many Chinese liberals, who are very pro-Western, the approval of almost any American initiative is virtually a reflex. So when there was a wave of indignation among ordinary Chinese and spontaneous demonstrations by students, with the government taking up the rear, they suddenly found themselves isolated. The feeling that they had lost credibility with students was especially painful. Some compared the outburst of popular anger to the Boxer riots, as expressions of an irrational xenophobia, while others blamed the New Left for encouraging a primitive nationalism, that could only strengthen the government. Very little of this found its way into the media, but a fund of suppressed tensions accumulated, which burst into the public domain in 2000, when the 'New Left' became the target for a violent liberal offensive. Actually, people like myself have always been reluctant to accept this label, pinned on us by our adversaries. Partly this is because we have no wish to be associated with the Cultural Revolution, or for that matter with what might be called the 'Old Left' of the Reform-era CCP. But it's also because the term New Left is a Western one, with a very distinct set of connotations – generational and political – in Europe and America. Our historical context is Chinese, not Western, and it is doubtful whether a category imported so explicitly from the West could be helpful in today's China. This feeling was strengthened by the Balkan War. So many Western intellectuals who described themselves as on the 'left' supported the NATO campaign that one couldn't have much wish to borrow the word from them. So rather than a New Left in China, I still prefer to speak of critical intellectuals. But the term has probably come to stay.

Historically, the terms 'Left' and 'Right' have tended to buckle and twist into strange shapes in late communist or post-communist societies. In Gorbachev's

Russia, which had undergone no Cultural Revolution, the term 'Left' was for a time widely used for Friedmanite reformers who wished to push the country rapidly towards capitalism, as against 'conservatives' attached to the old system. It was not until quite late in the Yeltsin period that this reversal of meaning tilted back into a more familiar classification, when Gaidar and his fellow liberals – who freely described themselves as 'lefts' at the turn of the nineties, formed a Union of the Right to contest Duma elections. It seems that today in China, after a long period in which neither term had any currency, the idea of a – New – Left has resurfaced. What about a Centre or Right? Have these terms been reclaimed too, or are they still empty signifiers waiting for the appropriate forces to breathe life into them?

No one has claimed them so far. But that doesn't mean they fail to correspond to actual positions. A good many of our liberals represent a contemporary Chinese Right. This is especially true of the economists who advocate privatization and marketization without any reservations or limits, without the slightest critical distance. They have taken the idea from Hayek that the market is a spontaneous economic order. In China, they maintain, marketization is the only route to prosperity and democracy – not that they care greatly whether there is a democracy or not, but it is required as a rhetorical add-on. Typically, these people work with the big companies and the government. Fan Gang and Zhou Qiren would be representative examples. Other liberals, on the other hand, occupy a Centre position. They have discovered that marketization in China does not generate a spontaneous economic order – since the market is not free, but determined through and by political monopolies and official corruption. So they are highly critical of current realities, and call for social justice along with economic growth. On the other hand, at least until recently, they tended to idealize marketization abroad – not just in Europe or America, but in Eastern Europe and Russia as well – as the 'good' path that China has missed. He Qinglian and Qin Hui represented this position. Qin Hui wrote several articles idealizing the Czech and Russian privatization schemes as the distribution of an equal economic starting-point to all citizens.

How would the Left's position on these economic and social questions be defined?

There are a number of different perspectives. Cui Zhiyuan, for example, emphasizes the need for institutional and theoretical inventiveness, and calls for a 'republican' combination of distinct principles of political order, and diverse systems of economic property. He has written various articles in the Journal of *Strategy and Management* on these themes. His main concern is that a balance should be kept between central and local government, market and planning principles. His basic standpoint does not seem so radical to me. But liberals regard any criticism of the way the central government has ceded so many fiscal and other powers to the provinces – a development that has caused very grave problems – with the greatest alarm. More generally, the characteristic focus of what the liberals call the New Left is the nexus between the market and the state: that is, the relationships between interest groups and power structures, economic forms and political systems. Markets themselves are no novelty in China. Traditional Chinese society had huge regional and inter-regional markets, with a series of distinctive features that have been analysed by historians of the Chinese economy. In the nineteenth century, the process of market formation was for the first time associated with the colonial pressures of world capitalism. That meant the market had to be organized by the state in a new way, with the establishment of a customs organization for the regulation of foreign trade, as a condition of sovereignty. The late twentieth century saw far greater state intervention to mould and create markets, under the pressures of globalization.

But how far does such a focus really differentiate a New Left from a liberal Centre? Many critical liberals insist no less strongly on the power-political determination of markets, and the need to correct the social injustices that flow from it in China.

The difference is quite deep. Liberals of this sort support marketization of the economy as the only correct road for China. In their eyes, it is only the absence of political reform that warps the workings of the market – but if the constitution were revised to protect the rights of the citizen, then we would have a reasonably equal society and a satisfactory degree of social justice. In my view, that is an illusion. Political democracy will not come from a legally impartial market, secured by constitutional amendments, but from the strength of social movements against the existing order. This point is central to the genealogy of the critical intellectual work that is now identified as a New Left. We refuse the implication that all the issues now raised by critical intellectuals come from America or Europe. On the contrary, there is a clear continuity linking these contemporary ideas with the social mobilizations in China during the late eighties. In 1989, why did the citizens of Beijing respond so strongly and actively to the student demonstrations? It was largely because of the adventurist reforms to the price system that Zhao Ziyang had twice imposed, without any benefit to ordinary people. Their earnings suffered from the agreements they were forced to sign by factories, and their jobs were at risk. People felt the inequality created by the reforms: there was real popular anger in the air. That is why the citizenry poured onto the streets in support of the students. The social movement was never simply a demand for political reform, it also sprang from a need for economic justice and social equality. The democracy that people wanted was not just a legal framework, it was a comprehensive social value. It was this great explosion of popular feeling at the end of the eighties that is the historical background to the work of critical intellectuals in the nineties.

You can see the gulf between this way of looking at the market and the liberal view of it. For the liberals, the price system of a free market is the signalling mechanism of a spontaneous order of exchange, as opposed to the distortions of central planning. But the failures of Zhao Ziyang showed that the price system is never a spontaneous order. It is always instituted and managed. People felt that, and revolted against it. But after the armed crackdown on the June Fourth Movement people lost their chance to protest, and price reform introduced at gunpoint became a success. All-out marketization in China did not originate from spontaneous exchange but from acts of violence – state repression of popular protest. We can see the same logic if we look at the foreign side of the picture. For the market as a system has never been just a domestic question within China. The PRC has always been involved in foreign trade: with the USSR and Eastern Europe in the fifties and early sixties, and even during the Cultural Revolution with the outside world through Hong Kong. But the Open Door policies of Deng Xiaoping demanded a much deeper insertion of China into the world market. How did that happen? A key step in the process was China's invasion of Vietnam in 1978 – the first war of aggression by the PRC after 1949. The only reason for this otherwise senseless attack on a small neighbour was Deng's desire for a new relationship with the United States. The invasion was offered as a political gift to Washington, and became China's entrance ticket to the world system. Here too violence was the precondition of a new economic order.

Our liberals never mention the war against Vietnam; and by the mid-nineties they were often criticizing the June Fourth Movement as too radical. They focus on the need for basic political freedoms, and there we can agree. But as soon as one moves from general principles to particular issues, the differences become apparent. They want to separate the political and economic realms, whereas we argue that the problems of each are intertwined – you cannot always distinguish between them, or say which is more decisive. For example, when I published some articles in *Dushu* on the need for factory managers to be elected, liberals attacked the idea. When I argued that it was very important that peasants should become involved in village elections, where official candidates can be defeated, Liu Junning, a young star of our political science, replied 'we don't need that – these elections are totally corrupted; what matters are congressional and judicial reforms'. They don't seem to believe in the participation of the masses in political reform.

Have these differences crystallized into articulated programmes yet?

People often ask us: 'but what is your positive alternative?' The truthful answer is that we have no total project of reform to hand, because we don't believe in trying to work out an ideal order in advance of concrete social demands. What we need are social movements that give rise to specific popular objectives. When such movements do emerge, we should study very closely what sorts of reasons bring ordinary people into them. In 1989, for example, it is clear that socialist values were still alive for many citizens, and formed much more of a driving force than liberal doctrines. So in that case we have to look back at the history of Chinese society since 1949, which is not exhausted by the dictatorship of the CCP or the failures of central planning, but contained other features as well to which people were attached. In the fifties and sixties, for example, there was a system of cooperative medical insurance in rural areas which meant that local people organized themselves to help each other, setting up funds and providing services. Since the state-run health system is now collapsing, why don't we learn some positive lessons from this? There are still some socialist fragments in China today, which few of us have thought seriously about. Cui Zhiyuan once tried to say something about the Anshan experience, but he confused most of his readers and lost the debate that followed.[6] But I think his basic impulse was right. We should look with an open mind at historical practices of the past, without trying to copy them. An unprejudiced intellectual curiosity is something all Chinese intellectuals need today.

What is your view of China's township and village enterprises? Various observers – you mentioned Cui Zhiyuan, but this is a view quite widely shared in the West – have argued that these are the really original institutions to emerge in the reform period, as forms of collective but not state ownership that have proved economically very dynamic. Other scholars in China and abroad believe they are already crypto-capitalist companies, typically controlled by corrupt local bosses, often colluding with foreign investors in throwing environmental concerns to the winds in the search for quick profits. How do you assess them?

Historically the TVEs were a real success for a certain period, and their creation was a great achievement. But we should be sceptical of the larger claim made for them, that they represent a Chinese model of development that offers an alternative to the world market system. They owed much of their success to the dual price structures that came into force with the early reforms. On the one hand, large state enterprises were forced to sell raw materials like iron and steel at low prices. The TVEs, on the other hand, could use these inputs to market goods at higher, uncontrolled prices. Naturally, if they showed any competence, they could prosper; and many proved genuinely able and flexible enterprises. Many also benefited from

---

[6] Anshan: iron-and-steel complex in Liaoning province, whose shop-floor creativity was hailed in the fifties. For references to this debate, see note 44, p. 28 [ed].

effective tax exemption. Whereas state enterprises bore a double burden of tax, as late as 1998 only about a third of TVEs paid any taxes at all. With these advantages, it is not surprising that a good number of them posted an impressive performance. But in recent years, they have entered into a deep crisis. Many have become private firms, others have merged with foreign capital. The ability of village enterprises to absorb labour on the land has declined, leading to greater rural population influx into the cities.

How far is the growing social polarization between rich and poor, and the increase in unemployment, a matter of major public debate today?

For several years now there has been a big debate about social polarization among intellectuals, with many articles in journals and books about it. Some younger generation thinkers have described current trends as a ruthless form of social darwinism. Liberals of an older generation reply that China has unfortunately not known social darwinism, but its opposite – socialism as the survival of the unfittest. So this issue is hotly debated in intellectual circles. In general, however, the mass media refuse to touch it. Unemployment is rather different. There have been quite a lot of articles about factory lay-offs in the newspapers, and what arrangements might be made for workers who lose their jobs; but there is very little discussion of the fate of peasants who drift to the city in search of work, and then become a floating population without employment or rights of residence.

Have there been major changes in the position of women in the labour market?

The basic trend is not unlike that in Eastern Europe and Russia in their reform periods – a reversion to an older division of labour, with a loss of employment and independence by women. But the process has not gone so far. Some corporations publicly refuse to take in female graduates from universities, while others are anxious to maintain a gender balance. There is no doubt that women's social position overall is lower than men's in the PRC, even if there are big differences in the size of the gap that exists in the cities and in the countryside. A significant development is the spread of prostitution once again, which has become a major tax resource for local governments, who give no protection to the women whose earnings they exploit. In cities like Guangzhou, you find a large number of young female workers in factories, paid miserable wages, without any form of public oversight. Still, I doubt whether women have lost as much in China as in Russia under Yeltsin, or East Germany after reunification. Perhaps another fragment of Mao's socialism survives here.

Moving to the political field proper, would it be true to say that one reason for the still blurred boundaries between different intellectual camps in today's

China is that people who disagree sharply about everything else still share at least one aim – they all want greater democracy?

Well, it is true that virtually all intellectuals would like more freedom of expression. The problem is that many of them want it essentially for themselves, without being willing to pay the necessary social price it would involve. It is understandable that intellectuals should care deeply about whether or not they can speak their minds freely. But they should also care about the much larger number of fellow-citizens who have lost their jobs or fallen into sickness or poverty, without anyone to look after them. The issue of democracy is so much broader than just the right of intellectuals not to suffer censorship. After the June Fourth Movement was suppressed, many concluded that radicalism had undone it, and there had to be some other way to democracy. The answer would lie in the gradual emergence of civil society from the development of the market economy. For marketization would produce a new middle-class that could furnish the sturdy basis for civil associations, without directly antagonizing the state. The resulting civil society would then blossom into a democracy. These ideas were actually first developed by Taiwanese liberals in the eighties. My reaction was: 'But what kind of civil society do you want? What sort of social structure do you have in mind?'

After various debates, some liberals decided that China still lacked the social basis for a civil society, and therefore the priority was to unleash the market to create one. Turning to the right, they made it clear their concern was not democracy as such, but the market at whatever cost. A liberal economist once said to me: 'Attacks on corruption are an attack on the market – we have to tolerate the one to develop the other.' In the mid-nineties, the group around Liu Junning argued publicly, claiming that true liberalism is a form of conservatism, because of its belief in order. This is a very revealing shift of terms, since in the eighties and early nineties conservatism was always used as a pejorative term to describe anyone who was regarded as insufficiently enthusiastic about the market, or too willing to envisage a positive role for the state – the label was applied to people like Hu Angang or Cui Zhiyuan. Not all liberals, of course, have made such a sharp right turn. There are much more radical figures like Qin Hui, who continue to insist on the importance of social justice and – still more – political democracy. He argues that the Chinese regime basically remains Mao's old socialist state, which we need to replace with a liberal democracy. To some extent I agree with this, because it is true that we need political democracy to solve virtually all other problems. But I don't believe the current state is just a continuation of the old one. The country cannot be described as socialist any longer, and the state itself has changed a lot. Today the state is itself part of the market system. In some ways it functions very well in that capacity – it makes mistakes, of course, but it is now a key factor in the dynamic of marketization. Qin Hui underestimates this.

Turning to the cultural field, how far have questions of modernism and postmodernism been a focus of interest among Chinese intellectuals, and how far do positions on them correspond to points along the political spectrum?

Postmodernism arrived in China when Fredric Jameson gave a course of lectures at Beida (Peking University) in 1985, which were published as a book a year later under the title of *Cultural Theory and Post Modernism*. That was the beginning. The lectures had a big impact on his students, who included Zhang Yiwu and Zhang Xudong. At the same time another young scholar, Chen Xiaoming, was looking for a dissertation topic and asked for my advice. I lent him the translation a friend in Tianjin had just done of Jonathan Culler's book on deconstruction. He became very interested and decided to write a book applying postmodern categories and deconstructive techniques to the latest generation of semi-avant-garde writers like Yu Hua and Ge Fei. But these were still very small eddies. My generation took no notice.

Then came June Fourth. Afterwards, most intellectuals fell silent for political reasons. But around 1992–94 Zhang Yiwu and Chen Xiaoming became quite active, contributing articles on postmodernism to journals like *The Literary Review*, which had been taken over by real conservatives. They soon became quite influential because at that time very few intellectuals were willing to cooperate with official magazines – *The Literary Review*, for example, after publishing long articles criticizing me very sharply, several times invited me to contribute, but to this day I have refused. That was the atmosphere among the intellectual world of our generation and some of the older generation. But the younger generation was without the same political burdens. They were impressed by the speed of marketization, and made a deduction from it rather like the theorists of civil society. Consumerism could be a kind of freedom: it would undermine dictatorship – which, of course, was partially true. After three years of silence, this caused quite a stir.

My generation found it much more difficult to analyse the new consumerism. They could see it was different from state socialism, and they sensed it was different from the liberalism with which most of them identified. It posed them with a dilemma: if we support market reform, how can we oppose consumerism, however objectionable some of its manifestations? The result was the debate on the 'humanistic spirit'. Hard on its heels came a third discussion. In 1995 *Dushu* started to publish articles by Zhang Kuan, an overseas student, and Shen Changwen on Orientalism. Here was a theme that opened another door to the West, where Said had developed his theory, yet also offered a critique of the West, and so would not offend the official ideology. The liberals were vulnerable on this score, since they could be criticized for accepting quasi-Orientalist premises in taking their model of democracy from the West. My own view differed from both camps, the liberals and their post-colonial critics. The latter were right that we should acquire a more critical understanding of the West, whose colonialist legacies have not disappeared, and which could never just be a model for us. On the other hand, a certain kind of insistence on the dangers of Orientalism could become a covert pretext for nationalism.

Around the same time, Huntington's article 'The Clash of Civilizations' provoked a lot of discussion – both *Twenty-First Century* and *Strategy and Management* devoted special issues to it. Liberal intellectuals criticized it very sharply for implying that conflict was inevitable between the West and China. The followers of Said argued that the extreme Right in the West was just confirming the Orientalist fixation with China as an alien, hostile land. The former rejected Huntington's arguments as a distortion of the real – better – nature of the West, while the latter denounced it as an all too accurate expression of Western colonialism. In the background of these discussions of Said and Huntington was the political context of 1995. In Moscow Yeltsin pounded the Russian Parliament with tank-fire, to the applause of the United States. Naturally, ordinary Chinese asked: why is America's reaction so different to its attitude to June Fourth in China? The hypocrisy of US foreign policy was starkly exposed. Then the West manoeu-vred to ensure that the Olympic Games of 2000 were not held in China. Many intellectuals disliked the PRC's application to stage the games, but it was popular with ordinary people, who were angered by Western obstruc-tion. This was the atmosphere in which Said and Huntington became reference points.

My own view was that, in so far as Orientalism remained a predominantly cultural theory, it couldn't handle a range of problems that were economic-ally and politically pressing in China. It was too soft. In 1995 Li Shenzhi, described as the 'father of Chinese liberalism' by the *New York Times*, published perhaps the first article in the PRC on globalization, which he essentially welcomed.[7] In response I wrote a short piece in *Dushu*, assessing Samir Amin's works – I had heard him talk in Denmark the year before – as a variant of dependency theory, from which we could learn something in China, without accepting his idea of 'delinking' from the world economy, which Mao had in a sense attempted. The article was very sharply criticized by Li Shenzhi, who said: 'That article is so left-wing! How could you talk in that way?' What I was talking about was the power of the world system, as another way of formulating 'globalization', and the need for democracy on a world scale to counter it.

---

[7] Li Shenzhi (1922–2003), former Vice President of the Chinese Academy of Social Sciences [ed].

What about theoretical discussions in the late nineties? Zhang Xudong has recently taken up the theme of postmodernism in a major essay, that develops at least two central arguments.[8] Postmodernism, he maintains, is a theory and practice of what is hybrid and heterogeneous, and as such well suited to the mixed forms and realities of China's economy and society. Where modernity was always conceived as a universal process, moving towards a single end-state, postmodernity does away with this teleology, opening up a horizon of different possible futures. To this intellectual liberation, freeing Chinese mind from preordained norms and goals, there corresponds a popular emancipation in the postmodern culture of mass consumption – which can be seen as an ambiguous form of democratization: the entrance of ordinary people's desires into the space of culture, through the market. What is your view of this argument?

There is an interval between the original introduction of postmodern themes by Zhang Yiwu and Chen Xiaoming – whose influence has declined in the last years, though it was still significant enough to provoke a major debate in *Twenty-First Century* in 1996–97 – and Zhang Xudong's rewriting of these today. His intervention is in part a response to debates over modernity that have divided liberal from critical intellectuals. Whatever the differences between Gan Yang, Zhang Xudong or myself, we share a sceptical attitude to the codified idea of modernity itself. Chinese liberals, on the other hand, tend to accept standard definitions of the Enlightenment uncritically, and take it for granted that modernity is our only possible goal. They refuse any reflection on it. Modernity – naturally, as it has emerged in the West – is simply assumed to be a model for China without frictions or self-contradictions, even as compared with Habermas, who remains attached to the project of modernity, but tries to see the tensions and incompletions in it. My own position has always been Chinese modernity was itself a self-critical project. If you look at the writings of Zhang Taiyan or Lu Xun,[9] who were deeply committed to the modern movement, you find at the same time the resources for a critique of it. Against this background, I can understand why Zhang Xudong wanted to draw a firm line between liberal and critical views of modernity, and to uphold what he sees as the more open-minded standpoint of a postmodernity beyond it.

What is less easy for me to follow is why he should think that the market in China would be a force for democratization, or a check to the homogenizing pressures of the world system. The first part of this argument paradoxically comes close to that of the liberals he criticizes. The second part seems self-contradictory to me. If one is critical of the American-dominated global market, how can one avoid criticism of the Chinese

---

[8] Zhang Xudong, 'Postmodernism and Post-socialist Society: Cultural Politics in China in the 1990s', *New Left Review* I/237, September–October 1999 [ed].

[9] On Zhang Taiyan see note 11 below [ed].

market? Not only is the Chinese market locked into the world market – just as the Chinese State is integrated into the international system, as you can see from its role in the Security Council – but it is not necessarily better than the Western markets, with which it is now interconnected, simply by virtue of being different. In some ways it is even worse. A realistic analysis leaves no room for nationalist self-satisfaction here. Marketization in China is not superior to the market in America. The Chinese State, of course, differs from Western states in a much more significant way, and Zhang Xudong is right to emphasize this. But his tacit suggestion is that it is the socialist past of the state that counts here. What he overlooks is the extent to which the old system rested on monopoly structures that have since changed their form, without losing their role in allowing China to compete as a trading power within the world system.

In this argument about the significance of ideas of postmodernity for China there is more than an echo of the famous Japanese debate, held in Kyoto in the forties, on 'Overcoming Modernity'. The basic terms of the discussion are the same, for both sets of thinkers. Are we forced either to accept Western modernity or to retreat into Eastern tradition, as the only two possible choices? Or can we invent a future that escapes the terms of this dilemma, by creating something at once more rooted in local tradition and more powerfully modern than the modernity imposed on us from outside? This way of looking at the problem poses the question of contemporary uses of tradition very sharply. China has the longest continuous intellectual history of any society in the world. What is the range of attitudes to it in the PRC today – irrelevant? negative? positive? selective? – and how do they relate to the spectrum of political viewpoints?

Mao's Revolution made much more of a clean sweep of traditional culture than anything that ever happened in Japan. So today, knowledge of pre-revolutionary Chinese culture remains comparatively thin among intellectuals – something the overseas diaspora has accentuated. The basic attitude of the liberals to the Chinese past is pretty negative. Their inspiration comes overwhelmingly from the West. This is also true of most of the intellectuals of the New Left, who have done very little research into pre-modern periods. The reference points may differ – the American Constitution or early French Revolution for one camp; American postmodernism or French deconstruction for the other – but the underlying outlook is quite similar. But there are scholars seriously engaged in these questions. It was to explore them in a new spirit that the journal *Xueren*, which I mentioned earlier, was formed. Most of those associated with it were working in the humanities – especially history, philosophy and literature. Many of them became professional historians, concentrated on their field and unwilling to draw wider conclusions from it. Their scholarship is good, even if their methodology may sometimes be old-fashioned: they do hard work on the documents and come up with important results. But of our previous group, there are now perhaps only four or five who are still trying to rethink the modern history of China in a spirit that connects it to contemporary problems.

Would it be right to think there is a particular problem in the appropriation of cultural tradition in China, stemming from the way in which classical Chinese has become a semi-dead language, creating a barrier somewhat like – if less radical than – the switch from Ottoman script to modern Turkish?

That is true. For the newer generations, it is a major obstacle. The very talented levy of young Chinese scholars now working in the States, for example, is largely cut off from the resources of the classical tradition. Most of them were trained in English departments in the PRC, and have little command of classical Chinese. But there is another problem, related to PRC culture itself. I often ask myself why we have no radical historiography of the British sort. Research into working-class or even peasant history is still very limited. The official Marxism of the PRC did talk about modes of production, classes, capitalism and so on, and had some achievements to its credit. But it was so mechanical as a framework that nowadays very few scholars pay much attention to it. So the younger generation is divorced even from a quite recent tradition of writing about the past. The result has been a swing away from social to intellectual history, which is where the best work has been done for some time now.

How would you situate your own work in this context, especially The Rise of Modern Chinese Thought, *whose first two volumes,* Essence and Substance *and* The Making of Chinese Modernity, *running from Song times to the early Republic, have appeared this year? What is most distinctive about it?*

I have great respect for the kind of scholarship represented by Yu Ying-Shih and others, which could be described as a philosophical study of intellectual history, of neo-Confucian inspiration; as I do for the sort of social history practised by American historians like Ben Elman.[10] But my focus differs from either. What I have tried to do is look at the connexions between intellectual history and social history, over quite a long stretch of Chinese history – that is, the way ideas emerged and altered within a fabric of social practices and institutional changes. Without this double focus, taking the ideas and their settings equally seriously, there is the risk of a slide towards a mere account of 'cultural production'. When I first started working on the project, I was interested mainly in thinkers of the late Qing period. I quickly

---

[10] See Yu Ying-Shih, ed, *Intellectual History in Late Imperial China*, Princeton 1984; Benjamin Elman, *From Philosophy to Philology*, Cambridge, MA 1984 and *Classicism, Politics and Kinship*, Berkeley and Oxford 1990 [ed].

realized their conceptions of knowledge, for example, were always intimately related to their occupational practices and to their understanding of the social structure and political order. So when they talk about cognitive issues, they always refer to politics, to ethics, and to their self-identity too. I also found that when they discussed political alternatives – notions of kinship as perhaps an equivalent of civil society in the West, or feudalism, or a new authoritarianism – they always used terms from long-standing intellectual traditions in China to develop or reinforce their current arguments. So I was forced to move back in time to trace the origins and transformations of these terms. In doing so, it became clear that the standard notion that modern times in China started in the Late Qing – only from that period does everything begin to change – is an illusion. A lot of things started much earlier. Tracing them back to Ming or Song times is also a way of criticizing the claims capitalism makes for itself, as if it were the absolute origin of everything new, responsible for inventing the market, social mobility, intellectual curiosity or whatever. That is what explains the first volume, which is devoted to what might be called ideas of Reason, while the principal concern of the second volume is with ideas of Science.

The interweaving of past and present in the thought of even the most radical figures of the late Qing period is striking. Take Zhang Taiyan, for example.[11] He was a first-class classical scholar, who was influenced by Fichte and Nietzsche, although he had difficulty reading them, and at the same time was deeply involved in Buddhism and Taoism. Around 1906 he was the editor of a revolutionary journal, *Min Bao*, the most important periodical produced by the Tongmenghui, the predecessor of the KMT. In it, he published a lot of articles about Buddhism. For a younger generation, this was baffling. What has Buddhism got to do with the revolution? But for Zhang Taiyan, Buddhism was a source for the revolution, and at the time an expression of the revolution, indeed of modern history itself. This was the typical pattern. Yan Fu borrowed from Comte's positivism, and combined it with neo-Confucianism.[12] The choice of sources always had some political or economic implications at the time. So in studying these thinkers, I always tried to find what constituted their basic framework of knowledge – which would include their views of nature, the political structure, the family and their own identity.

The title of the second volume speaks for itself. My focus is on the origins of the Chinese reflections on modernity. If we look at Zhang Taiyan, Liang Qichao, Lu Xun or Yan Fu, we discover in their world of thought and their relations to the surrounding reality, self-ironical, self-contradictory, self-

---

[11] Zhang Taiyan, real name Zhang Binglin (1868–1936): scholar and anti-Manchu revolutionary, prominent in philology and textual criticism from the late Qing to the early Republican period [ed].

[12] Yan Fu (1854–1921): translator, writer and reformer, champion of evolutionary theory [ed].

paradoxical attitudes towards modernity. The sources they drew on were Western and Chinese, and – we should not forget – Japanese too. In the introduction, I suggest that we have to return to that point, the beginning of the modern, if we are to understand our problems today; and that when we do so, it becomes clear how much of what we think we know about the state, the individual, the market of that time – or ours – is a myth. The Chinese intellectuals of the period were facing very complex issues, which they tried to resolve in all kinds of unexpected ways. Lu Xun's attitudes, for example, seem quite paradoxical. He criticized many Chinese traditions savagely; yet he was also an excellent classical scholar, who did fine work on texts from the remote past. He hated reaction, but he was curiously sceptical about progress itself. He became a writer of the Left, but he was always quite critical of the Left. Why? What was the intellectual and political background of these ambivalences? In 1907 Zhang Taiyan became the first person of significance to speak of a Republic of China, and drew a map of the boundaries of the future post-revolutionary state. Yet he also criticized the nationalist project very sharply, even while he was attacking the colonial powers. If his answers were never coherent, the questions he left are in a sense still with us. The questions this generation posed were much more complicated than those that preoccupy contemporary Chinese intellectuals. Why could they do that? It was possible only because they were not pure intellectuals, or scholars isolated in the academy. They were social activists. They sensed problems very acutely – perceiving different dangers, different potentials, different frameworks – even when they couldn't articulate them so well. Because their work was often improvised and rough, it is virtually ignored by our intellectuals today, who are accustomed only to academic theories. But it is full of implications for us.

The project as you describe it sounds – if one wanted a Western analogy – as if it had something in common with Raymond Williams's Culture and Society, *as an exploration of the historically changing meaning of a set of key terms. Of course,* Culture and Society *is a history of ideas in a fairly pure sense – it doesn't say much about social practices or institutions, save at the end, when it suddenly shifts to the labour movement. That conclusion, however, made it an intellectual history with a strong contemporary charge. How do you envisage your project ending?*

The third volume, for which I have started to collect materials, will focus on rebellion and revolution. In China we have no strong tradition of scholarly research on either. What we have is much good research on the literati or scholar-gentry. There are some studies by historians like Qian Mu,[13] highly

---

[13] Qian Mu (1895–1990), historian of Chinese intellectual and political history, moved from the mainland to Hong Kong in 1949, and later to Taiwan where he spent his last years [ed].

conservative in their attitude towards the present, but capable of interesting work on the past – rather like Yu Ying-Shih, whose essays on Ming-Qing intellectual history can be admired even if you think, as I do, that his overall framework is completely misconceived. But there is much less of a canon in the area I want to enter now. The themes of rebellion and revolution remain more delicate topics for scholars.

Would it be wrong to think that the Chinese intellectual scene in the nineties has, despite a more restrictive political context, actually been livelier and more diversified than in the eighties? Could it in some measure be compared – in vigour of discussion, overlapping of positions, absence of rigid labels or definitions – to, say, stretches of the twenties?

Perhaps there is a touch of the late twenties. In the mid-twenties, after May Fourth and before the Northern Expedition, there was a process of differentiation among intellectuals, as some anarchists turned to the right and others to the left, some joined the KMT, others became organizers for the CCP. But there is a big difference. The debates of that time were much more directly political – not so theoretical – because there were powerful social movements, social and national, in the background: in 1923, and on a much bigger scale in 1925, and so on. The issue was no longer the meaning of modernity, or how to relate to tradition. There were new political languages. A closer parallel to today might be with the years just after the establishment of the KMT regime in Nanjing, when a lot of radical overseas students, who had become Marxists in Japan, came back to China and launched various literary movements and cultural watchwords, like the need for a 'Revolutionary Literature', even criticizing Lu Xun and Mao Dun as elitists.[14] Then two years later, in 1930, there was a big debate about the nature of Chinese society, that Arif Dirlik has studied.[15] You could compare that to the questions that confront us today, when people are trying to figure out what is going on in Chinese society now. Is it a socialist country with a capitalist market or a capitalist country? What's the nature of the state? What is the logic of globalization? What will happen to us? The different groups have to work out their own theoretical or political strategy.

One of the themes of your history of modern Chinese thought is the changing organization of knowledge – how it was structured or segmented in different periods. Comparing the period of your second volume with the situation today, what were the disciplines that have dominated the intellectual field?

---

[14] Mao Dun (1896–1981): leading left novelist of the thirties and forties [ed].

[15] Arif Dirlik, *Revolution and History: Origins of Marxist Historiography in China*, Berkeley, CA 1978 [ed].

In the late Qing period, sociology occupied the highest position in the hierarchy of knowledge. Its theorists generally refused to use the term *shehui* (society), preferring *qun* (community or group) instead. But they were sure that sociology was the science of sciences – that is, it arranged the order of the different kinds of knowledge. The kind of order it produced served the state, but in a state-building rather than merely conserving sense: it was linked to various projects of social reform from above. When we move to the May Fourth Movement, however, we see that the main figures wanted to discard any form of social science, and just base themselves on the natural sciences – which would yield a new map of the cosmos, within which social problems could be practically resolved, and whose mastery might offer a kind of moral grace. Individual thinkers could have more complicated positions – Lu Xun never subscribed to this scientism, Liang Qichao gave more importance to literature, and so on.[16] But it is striking that for such a central figure as Hu Shih, even literature itself was modelled on scientific practice – he called a volume of his poems 'A Collection of Experiments'.[17] Later, this produced a vigorous debate between two schools, dubbed 'Mr Science' and 'Mr Metaphysics', or vitalist philosophy, out of which ethics, aesthetics and literature separated out as independent fields, re-mapping the whole taxonomy of knowledge. Overseas students who had been disciples of Irving Babbit's 'new humanism' in America played an important role in this shift. In each episode, you can see how the dominant 'discipline' in a given period is really more than that – its status is closer to a world view. It was just this function that Marxism came to fulfil in the late twenties, even for many natural scientists.

Today, of course, the dominant discipline in China is neo-classical economics. This is a development of the nineties. In the eighties, most of the leading economists like Wu Jinglian were still people who had been trained in the planned economy. They had learnt something from the West, but they were completely at home in the structure of the Communist state, and were quite capable in adapting and reforming it, once the Open Door policy was proclaimed. There were much more radical economists, figures like Li Yining, bent on importing pure free-market doctrines into China, but they were not yet of great use to the state, and had little influence. But after 1990, Hayekian ideas gained real ascendancy. Today economics – understood in its most rigidly liberal acceptation – has acquired the force of an ethics in China. Laissez-faire axioms form a code of conduct, as rules of the commodity

---

[16] Liang Qichao (1873–1929), leading advocate of political reform in the 1890s, exiled in 1898; subsequently intellectual leader and politician in the early Republican years. In the 1920s, he was known as an outstanding scholar of the intellectual history of the Qing era (1644–1911) [ed].

[17] Hu Shih (1891–1962): leading liberal thinker of the May Fourth generation; a disciple of John Dewey who played a key role in introducing Western terms and methods into the study of Chinese thought and literature; Ambassador to the United States in 1938–1942 and President of the Academia Sinica in Taiwan after 1958 [ed].

which no agent may violate. So currently economics is not just a technical discipline, any more than its predecessors: it too is an imperative world view. Of course, no hegemony ever absorbs the whole cultural field. Political science or law are basically tributary to economics, as strongholds of the Right. By contrast critical intellectuals today mostly work in the humanities, although there are also quite a few radicals in the natural sciences.

In the eighties, the West was viewed in a naively enthusiastic way by many Chinese intellectuals. Typical of that time was the television series River Elegy, a hymn to Zhao Ziyang's policies, counterposing the disastrous inland traditions of Chinese autocracy to the dazzling azure of the open sea, symbol of foreign trade and Western freedom. This vision was widely shared at the time. In the nineties, the role of the West has not always appeared in such a flattering light, and Chinese opinion has itself become more diversified. The terms of discussion have also shifted, as 'globalization' has become the current watchword – in theory, a more encompassing category than simply 'the West'. Entry into the WTO, as a practical priority for the CCP, has put the issue of relations between China as a nation-state and the institutions of the world market directly on the political agenda. How far have the pressures and probabilities of globalization been debated within the country, and what would be the main lines of division arising from it?

Issues of globalization were first raised at a conference around 1994, by a number of intellectuals who later described themselves as liberals. One argued that if China did not reform swiftly, it would fail to enter the main trend of globalization. Another spoke of the Enlightenment prospect of a perpetual peace coming true. A year later, *Dushu* published my article on Samir Amin's critical position against globalization. So the debate about it really dates from 1995. At the time, I argued that globalization as such was a misleading abstraction, since it was not a new phenomenon but simply the latest phase of a long history, which could be defined as the whole process of the development of capitalism from the colonial and imperialist epochs onwards. In other words, globalization is not a neutral concept for a natural process. You have to identify the dominant force in its spread around the world.

These early discussions were not very conceptualized, and it was clear that, whatever the differences of opinion between them, feelings about the issue were quite ambivalent on both Right and Left. For there was a general sense that there would be many dangers and risks for China in accepting globalization, but how could we avoid it? Even critics of WTO entry like Cui Zhiyuan and Gan Yang don't say, 'China must never join the WTO'. Their position would be: 'For the moment China should wait. There are a lot of changes we need first'. Most people on the Left believe that the government has been in too much of a hurry to enter the WTO – that a more measured approach would have been more sensible. Liberals on the

Right, of course – economists like Zhou Qiren and Fan Gang in the entourage of Zhu Rongji – have been eager to get the PRC into the WTO as soon as possible. This is a prime minister who has lost confidence in the ability of the government to resolve the problems of state-owned enterprises, and hopes that competition from foreign capitals will take over as the driving force of economic reform. But at the same time, everyone is very aware that the reason why China could avoid the East Asian crisis of 1998 is because it was shielded from financial-market contagion by the strength of the national state. This is something even the enthusiasts for globalization are bound to recall.

The NATO bombing of China's embassy in Belgrade forcibly brought home another reality. The world market, it made plain, is not just an economic space of competition: undergirding it is a powerful set of political and military structures. These make it very difficult to argue that the nation-state, whatever changes it may or may not have undergone, has collapsed. Behind the screens of NATO, the IMF or WTO, American globalism functions as another version of nationalism. After the embassy was destroyed, there was a debate between Zhu Xueqin, the Shanghai philosopher who is perhaps China's leading liberal spokesman today, and myself about the Balkan war and popular reaction to it. Zhu Xueqin maintained that nationalism was the most dangerous force in modern Chinese history. We should enter the world system at top speed, because globalism was much, much better than nationalism. I replied that it was an illusion to think they could be counter-posed so simply. Nationalism as a historical force is not just a subjective sentiment that draws people into the streets, but also a set of social relations on which states essential for the operation of the world market themselves rest. That kind of nationalism is a parallel structure of global capitalism, not its opposite, and we should certainly criticize it.

At the same time, we need to be able to distinguish between the critique of hegemony and nationalism. While national states were passive or silent about NATO's action in Yugoslavia, Chinese people poured into the streets and even threw a few bricks. That was positive. A spontaneous protest of this kind is a social movement that has a democratic potential. It can also be used by the government for official purposes, as the Boxers were – Zhu Xueqin was not wrong in warning of this danger. Every social movement contains different possibilities within it: our job is to analyse their range and support those that move in a democratic direction. For there is a logic here. This is a movement of resistance against imperialism. But if we look at the intellectuals of the early part of the century, we see that when people like Zhang Taiyan or Lu Xun talked about nationalism, they paid attention to the other nations that imperialism had also oppressed: Greece, India, Poland, African countries. They tried to combine nationalism with cosmopolitanism. This tradition contained what I've called a self-negating, or self-transcending logic: embracing modernity as a national project generated a counter-logic that made them also critical of nationalism. They knew that even if they could transform China from an empire into a nation-state, nationalist goals could not be easily achieved within a national framework.

The same kind of dialectic is evident in the revolutionary tradition in China. After the late twenties, the Communist movement changed direction and increasingly set itself the goal of national liberation. Mao said that the national conflict with Japan had become the main social contradiction within China itself. But the revolution could not be compressed into just a nationalist project. Its self-negating logic drove it beyond that limit, to the early forms of internationalism you find in the Bandung Conference or Zhou En-Lai's visit to Yugoslavia. At that stage the CCP tried to help bring Third World countries together in a common struggle for national independence and international equality. Those days are long past. But we should be thinking of these different legacies today, when we reflect on contemporary protests against globalization, in China or elsewhere. They do represent expressions of local protest against outside forces, but their democratic potential will only be truly realized if they can link up with similar protests in other countries, to become a factor for democracy on a global scale. In the world system, as capital moves across borders everywhere, social conflicts should in principle no longer be so easily confined within national structures. But we lack any conceptualisation of such struggles, potential or actual. Internationalism is an old-fashioned term, weighed down by too many connotations dating from the nineteenth or early twentieth centuries. We need to rethink its meanings, or invent new ones, for our contemporary context.

How did liberals – still the great majority of Chinese intellectuals – react to the Balkan War? Presumably the outburst of popular feeling was a discomfiting phenomenon for them, since it was directed against the very Western powers to which many looked with boundless admiration – it must have seemed like an attack on what is in some ways their ideal. But equally it must have been difficult for them to defend the NATO bombing.

The war was a big crisis for them. Whereas we supported the popular movement against the bombing, they opposed it. Their dislike of the demonstrations was not based just on their sympathy – which in the circumstances could not be openly expressed – for the West, or their alarm at the way the government used them, but also on their long-term attitude to the Chinese masses. Most liberals view ordinary Chinese benevolently so long as they are helping to develop the market as consumers. For them the danger of popular nationalism is that the masses may become, not only too critical of the West, but also too mobilized as citizens – veering away from the passive role of consumers to the more active one of militants. They are fearful of popular participation, always remembering its negative examples, and rarely seeing the positive potential of social movements as a condition of democracy. Since civil rights themselves are historically anchored within the structure of the nation-state, the typical narrative of Western liberalism directly connects nationalism and democracy. But Chinese liberals never face these connexions. They only believe in the open door and the global system. All China needs to do is to enter the 'mainstream' – this is the term they use – and then everything will be okay. For them, integration into the world system is the only pass to democracy. This disbelief in the democratic potential of social movements is why more and more of the younger generation are turning away from them. If you log onto the Internet now, you find a lot of criticisms of them. In that sense they have become quite isolated, even while they continue to represent the mainstream in intellectual circles – though even there, an increasing number of people have become more neutral, as between the left and the right. Fewer now define themselves simply as liberals.

What do you think have been the most significant intellectual developments in China since 2000?

The major change has been the emergence of much broader public debates, extending well beyond theoretical discussions among intellectuals, provoked by a wide range of social problems, often brought to the fore by political events. The first of these was China's entry into the WTO, after thirteen years of multilateral negotiations. In 1999, just as NATO's aerial attack on Yugoslavia got under way, Prime Minister Zhu Rongji travelled to the US and President Jiang Zemin to Europe. The main purpose of Zhu's visit was to wrap up an agreement on China's entry into the WTO with the United States. Although Zhu made remarkable concessions, no final accord was signed, and not long after Zhu returned to Beijing, American bombers hit the PRC embassy in Belgrade, and some of the concessions he had made were revealed on the Internet. The result was a noticeable shift in domestic opinion. When the Asian financial crisis broke in 1997, China's economy performed much better than its neighbours, so although the risk that it too might prove vulnerable to the instabilities of neo-liberal globalization was occasionally raised, not only the state but the intelligentsia as a whole remained optimistic about the economic prospects for the country in this new international framework. When China finally joined the WTO in 2000, the Chinese media celebrated the event as a tremendous achievement, offering a golden future to the PRC.

Against this background, *Dushu* and another Beijing-based journal, *International Economic Review*, took the initiative to organize some critical analysis of what the real consequences of WTO entry might be for various sectors of China's economy and society. As early as 1996, *Dushu* had invited a group of sociologists to discuss rural (*nongcun*), peasant (*nongmin*), and agricultural (*nongye*) problems, understood as an inter-related complex (*sannong wenti*). But awareness of the crisis in the countryside only became an acute public issue around the time when the Sino-American agricultural agreement was signed in 2000, when agrarian experts like Wen Tiejun and Lu Xueyi published a series of articles unequivocally exposing conditions in the villages. Not long afterwards, Li Changping published his hugely influential book, *I am Telling the Truth to the Prime Minister*. Wen Tiejun was doing agricultural research under the State Council at the time; Lu Xueyi is the head of the Institute of Sociology at the Chinese Academy of Social Sciences; and Li Changping was party secretary in a local township of Hubei Province. From different perspectives, they all criticized very sharply current agricultural policies and the problems these had created in the countryside.

As a result, both Wen Tiejun and Li Changping were forced out of their jobs, and have since turned to interventions in the intellectual sphere, responding powerfully to ongoing discussions of relations between town and country, of social polarization, ecological crisis and the likely impact of globalization on the peasantry, in ways that have deepened people's understanding of China's agrarian crisis. The Reform Era started with the introduction of the household responsibility system on the land in 1979, linking peasant contracts to output; but once urban reforms took priority in 1985, rural areas fell into a new set of predicaments, the gravity of which China's general high-speed growth had concealed. But now the opening up of China's agricultural market, under the provisions of the WTO agreement, has exposed the scale of the rural crisis, and the lack of any channels for peasants to voice their grievances in a public political sphere.

How do schemes for the privatization of land feature in all this?

For quite some time, proposals for privatization had been floated in government think-tanks and policy-making circles. With the exception of a few critical intellectuals, most economists support land privatization, most local officials have a vested interest in it, and many higher levels of the state apparatus eager to shed their responsibilities for the welfare of the rural population also favour the disposal of public lands. Yet, as Li Changping has insisted, since ordinary peasants, just to maintain production, are now so often heavily in debt to former local officials or rural elites, if land were privatized, many would lose their rights to it overnight. They therefore have no reason to welcome privatization. Analysing the roots of rural crisis, Wen Tiejun, Li Changping and others have highlighted the grim prospect of huge numbers of peasants being expropriated if land is privatized. Their contributions have provided concrete evidence enabling people to reassess the question of private property rights in the Chinese context, which has become a main theme of the media, and a major topic of the National People's Congress.

Meanwhile, in the towns, the privatization of China's state-owned enterprises is proceeding apace. In tandem with this process, and in keeping with official ideology, there has been much discussion of amendments to the Constitution and the passage of a Civil Code to render 'private property rights inviolable'. The National People's Congress has produced a draft to this effect, the ratification of which is imminent. In fact, the first person to raise the theoretical issue of what is actually meant by property was Cui Zhiyuan, as early as 1994 in an article discussing 'savage' privatization in Russia, even if still somewhat abstractly. A decade later, the question of property rights has become the most pivotal social issue in China. The principle that private property should receive protection under the law does not divide intellectuals. The disagreements among them concern more fundamental issues. They include the following: First, should property acquired by abuse of political power or other illegal means be retrospectively legalized? How ought the different forms of private property to be categorized? Second, how can peasants be shielded against another round of unjust land annexations? Third, what kind of property regime is likely to promote – or prevent – an active citizenry and popular democratic life, as opposed to a 'sordid political philistinism'? The latest issue of *Dushu* (April 2003) carries four essays on constitutional and political reforms, posing these questions.

Queries of this kind presumably challenge the existing form of the state?

Certainly. Ever since 1989, the role of the state has implicitly always been at the centre of intellectual debates. I say implicitly, because this is such a sensitive area for officialdom. In 1991 Wang Shaoguang published a long article while he was in the US, discussing state capacities and democracy in China, in which he argued that policies of economic reform designed to devolve power and divide benefits had so weakened the central government's ability to regulate the economy and society that local authorities had often been captured by special interests and become hotbeds of corruption, helping to bring about the crisis of 1989. In different ways both he and Cui Zhiyuan sought political reform that would enable the will of ordinary people to be brought into the policy-making process, as a check on these abuses. However, after 1989 the Chinese State suffered a severe crisis of legitimacy, so any discussion of state capacity tended to be read as if it could be seeking to strengthen the existing unreformed system. In this climate, people naturally asked why – if such social conflicts were caused by the existing state structure – the state shouldn't be thoroughly weakened or completely withdrawn. So why start talking about state capacity? Around 1998 Hayekian theories became highly popular in China. The complete withdrawal of the state from the economy became a major demand of Chinese neo-liberals. Since then, large-scale unemployment, polarization between rich and poor, structural corruption, agrarian crisis and the collapse of the basic social security system have all raised the

question of the state's function in society once again. Increasingly, intellectuals have come to accept that the state must have responsibility for economic regulation and social security. They have also started to ask how far
China's economic achievements since the beginning of the Reform Era can
be attributed to the drive towards neo-liberalism, as opposed to the active
financial, industrial or tariff policies of the state?

For their part, ordinary people have grown sceptical about the myth of the
market as the solution to all problems of political power. But beyond a
general recognition that it is senseless to call for a dismantling of the socio-
economic functions of the state, there is little agreement even among critical
intellectuals over the exact connexions between social processes of corruption
and polarization and the political operations of the state. Adapting Braudel's
historical and theoretical framework, Xu Baoqiang has sought to show the
dependence of an emergent capitalism in China on the state, in particular the
nexus between market monopoly and political structure (in a collection
entitled 'Anti-Market Capitalism' (*Fan shichang de zibenzhuyi*), for which I
wrote an introduction). People like Li Changping, on the other hand, focus
on the ways local governments have propelled the process of rural crisis and
bankruptcy. The CCP, meanwhile, has developed its official doctrine of the
'three representatives' to try to cover the contradictions between a ruling
Communist Party and an increasingly deregulated economy. When in 2001
Jiang Zemin called for capitalists to be welcomed into the Party, and in early
2003 the joint conference of the National People's Congress and National
Political Consultancy Committee dramatically increased the number of deputies representing the New Rich, it became clear how far new economic
interests were now shaping political structures. The state and the business
elite are legitimizing and formalizing their alliance. Against this background,
many intellectuals have again raised the question of political democracy – this
time, however, stressing mass participation and popular control of public
policies, the very opposite of neo-liberal recipes for political reform.

*How far have recent international developments affected the climate of
domestic opinion?*

Considerably. Few had forgotten the bombing of the Chinese embassy in
Belgrade in 1999, when in early 2001 a US spy plane collided with a Chinese
fighter jet over the South China Sea. There followed, in swift succession, the
American attack on Afghanistan in retaliation for September 11, and then the
Anglo-American conquest of Iraq, provoking an unprecedented worldwide
mobilization against the war. The rosy dawn of neo-liberal globalization is
now shadowed by the clouds of the new empire. The result has been that
more and more people have started to make connexions between the
hegemonic structure of the global system and the daily problems of contemporary China – savage privatization, power-steered business, crony capitalism

and ecological crisis. In 2000 a stage play entitled *Che Guevara*, written by Huang Jisu and directed by Zhang Guangtian, caused something of a sensation in Beijing and other cities, where young people flocked to see it. The drama involves only sketchy allusions to the famous guerrilla fighter himself. Its success lay in its combination of a nostalgic tone towards the ideal of a revolution with a stylized form close to the street skits of the years of struggle against the Guomindang, to expose social injustice, class polarization and corruption in contemporary China, and their links to the structure of global hegemony. Summoning up the image of Guevara – by no means a familiar figure in China, having been ignored by Maoism – had the clear meaning of a call: for a combative attack on the social consequences of the open door policy; for a new internationalism capable of resisting American power; and for long-lost forms of popular theatre, in contrast to the elite-oriented stage of the past twenty years.

The play caused a tremendous uproar in intellectual circles, where it was violently attacked by liberals, often discomfited by the quite striking way many of their attitudes were given dramatic expression in the dialectical exchanges on stage, where pro-capitalist arguments were trenchantly expounded, as well as socialist responses. But some left-wing intellectuals also criticized it as overly didactic. Debate about Che had actually originated from two articles published in *Dushu*. The first was a review in 1997 of an American biography of Guevara, by an intellectual on the right of the political spectrum who had little sympathy for Che. The Cuban embassy lodged a protest over its publication. The establishment Chinese newspaper *Guangming Daily*, on the other hand, republished it, and Jiang Zemin is said to have displayed interest in the piece.

The following year, *Dushu* wanted to mark the thirtieth anniversary of the social movements of 1968 – for long an awkward topic in China, as this was also the beginning of the Cultural Revolution: hence official silence. So we carried a number of articles discussing the European and international events of 1968, including a passionate tribute to Che by Suo Sa, a woman researcher in the Institute of Latin American Studies at the Chinese Academy of Social Sciences. Her contribution, written with an ardour intact from the sixties, was a direct rejoinder to the review published the previous year. It soon found its way into other journals, arousing great interest among many young intellectuals. Two years later, the authors of the play invited her to be an adviser in staging their parable. The sarcastic street skit form of the play unequivocally announced that debates among intellectuals are real social struggles too. Whatever one's view of the aesthetic devices of the drama, it presented controversies between 'New Left' and 'Liberal' standpoints in a way accessible to the public.

In general we can say that, since 2000, complex theoretical debates have receded into the background, as the meanings of Left and Right have shifted and been redefined by major political events. Many younger intellectuals, moved by the spectacle of acute social polarization, have veered away from the liberal camp, drawing closer to the New Left. But as debates have become fiercer, divisions have also opened up within the latter, to the point where its boundaries are often unclear. How to accurately summarize and identify ideas critical of contemporary society has always been a difficult task in modern China. Nevertheless, in the three short years since 2000, the change of atmosphere is astonishing. The rapid growth of a 'New Left' is one sign of the times. Ideas that were scattered, extremely marginal notions in the general culture a decade ago, have become voices with a real influence in public life today.

2

For a Chinese Liberalism

Zhu Xueqin

How would you describe your intellectual background?

I completed elementary school in Shanghai in summer 1966, just as the Cultural Revolution broke out. So I couldn't enter middle school, where teaching had been suspended. Instead I attached myself to some high school students from my neighbourhood, who were setting off on a tour of China in accordance with Mao's instruction that youth should 'link up' across the country. I followed them from place to place, greatly broadening my horizons. On getting back to Shanghai, I would wait for a couple of older teenagers to return home at dusk, to inform me about debates in their high school that day or big-character posters that had sparked off thoughts without becoming factional. Those students were very different from the Red Guard stereotypes you see in television series, films or novels today. They did not want to destroy everything. They thought critically, even sceptically, about a series of social and political issues affecting China's future – the kind of thinking that led to the semi-public intellectual debates, which attracted the attention of the authorities of the Cultural Revolution, and was repressed by them.

It was not until the summer of 1967 that my cohorts were enrolled in different middle schools. The one to which I was sent was not a Shanghai key-point school, but since it had been a missionary establishment before 1949, it had over 40,000 books in its library – far more than any normal middle school – and there had not yet been enough time to dissipate all of these. Among them were many old editions, published before 1949, now cast into a rubbish heap. When I accidentally came upon them, finding sets of old books printed vertically and pre-Liberation maps, I was overjoyed and immediately carried a big stack of them home in my arms. It was this forbidden trove that first awoke me intellectually. The volume that left the deepest impression on me was a textbook of world history, translated in the 1940s, whose front and back covers had peeled off. It became my first 'treasured copy'.

Around this time, I developed a habit of 'panning for gold' in the used bookstores on Fuzhou Road, which had lots of old versions of works by Marx, Engels, Lenin and Stalin, the complete works of Lu Xun, and various separate editions. Both the prices and the conditions were good. Unwilling to spend 0.14 yuan to take a bus, I would walk there, acquiring most of the leftist canon on my bookshelves today. In 1968, the movement of urban youth going to the countryside started under Mao's directive, following initial voluntary moves by some former Red Guards. When it was the turn for our grade, I refused to go with my classmates but opted for Lankao County in Henan, where no urban youth was officially required to go. This corner in the south-east of the province, where a shift in the bed of the Yellow River has salinated the soil, is famous for its poverty. There nine students from key-point high schools in Shanghai had voluntarily formed a group working in a village, leading a life of manual labour combined with reading and thinking. Attracted by their spiritual pursuits, I wanted to join them.

Our group in Lankao practised a communal lifestyle, sharing everything among ourselves, reading while working. It was in that environment that I encountered, for the first time, a Chinese translation of Mathiez's *History of the French Revolution*, which kindled my intense interest in that great upheaval. In 1971 the Lin Biao Incident destroyed my belief in the authorities. There followed a general fading of the communal atmosphere in our group. An existing spirit of scepticism from earlier years, mingled with anguish at the disillusioned 'general will' in the revolutionary present. I realized it was not enough to read texts written by Mao in his later years, selections of Marx and Engels, or literary and social criticism from nineteenth-century Russia. I felt that I must learn from other works the political and intellectual history of the West from the very beginning.

In 1972 a chemical factory in Gong County, about a hundred miles away, needed workers, so our group moved there. In this location we merged with another group of youngsters, who had a more rebellious outlook. There a quite unusual atmosphere developed. At that age, we could lug heavy pipes about all day long and still have the energy to study on our own by lamplight in the evening. We were materially very poor, but intellectually very alive, often fiercely debating theoretical or historical issues far into the night, disturbing the adult workers in our dormitory, who would give us strange looks. We were not well informed, or always rational in our arguments, which could easily become too emotional, leading to heated disputes. But we cared about ideas for their own sake, with no thought of personal advantage or career gain – unlike our typical academics today.

Around 1974 Mao gave his approval for the reprinting of 'grey books' published before the Cultural Revolution, and ordered recent novels and political theories from the Soviet Union and the West to be translated. To this day, no one knows exactly why he took this decision. In a period rife with discontent and scepticism, it was tantamount to spreading tinder over dry scrub: who could guarantee the fire would move along the path intended for it? Later, I came to believe that some sparks of the 'New Enlightenment' of the 1980s were secretly ignited by the release of these 'works for internal circulation' of 1974. In my case, I had the great luck of being able to read these two batches of books earlier than others. Here I was truly fortunate. Without them, my personal enlightenment would have been postponed by at least five years.

On the second floor of the Shanghai Bookstore on Fuzhou Road there was a 'counter for books for internal circulation', which could be purchased only with high-level authorization. Wracking my brain as to how to obtain these precious volumes, I used a chain of connexions, from my factory to the county and finally to the provincial authorities, to get the crucial letter I needed from the government of Henan Province. Armed with this imposing document, I travelled to Shanghai and worked out a list of book titles. After the salesman in the store had released them to me, he unexpectedly remarked that there were some good books which were not on the list. I had not heard of these, but, on his warm recommendation, I bought them and they proved to be very useful to me later. What I had purchased were the sixteen volumes of *Selected Research Materials of Western Bourgeois Philosophy and Sociology* and twenty-three volumes of *Selected Materials of Soviet Revisionist Philosophy*.[1] The first set had been produced by the Shanghai People's Publishing House before the Cultural Revolution, and their quality was far superior to the shoddy translations by my peers during the fever for Western culture in the 1980s. Among the works in the collection, Sartre's *Critique of Dialectical Reason* and Sidney Hook's *Ambiguous Legacy* became my favourites.

I remained a factory worker in Gong County for ten years. My experience during these years set the direction for my future thinking. It was not until much later that I realized how fatal the experience of studying on my own was to be. It is very difficult for those who come from this background, even after entering academic life or becoming a university professor, to cast off its undisciplined character, or an 'unofficial aura.' I once labelled this aura 'surplus consciousness' – that is, something that cannot be completely absorbed into academic life. In Liang Shuming's words, the generation of 1968 is 'a problem engaging generation'; it is not 'a scholarship generation'.[2] For those who became intellectuals, the issues posed around 1968

---

[1] *Xifang zichanjieji zhexue shehuixue xueshu ziliao xuan*, and *Sulian xiuzhengzhuyi zhexue ziliao xuan* [ed].

[2] Liang Shuming (1893–1988): taught Indian philosophy at Peking University, the centre of the May Fourth Movement, from 1917 to 1924, and then became a leader of the 'rural reconstruction movement' in the thirties. See Guy Alitto, *The Last Confucian: Liang Shuming and the Chinese Dilemma of Modernity*. Berkeley, 1979.

always shaped their outlook and even determined the outcome of their thought. In my case, among the problems of 1968, the most perplexing was why the French Revolution and the Cultural Revolution should share such striking similarities. That probably complicated and burdened my development. I wanted to continue reflecting on this puzzle, but I had to avoid inappropriate interpretations or farfetched analogies between the two. I endeavoured to sort out the different intellectual currents from the Enlightenment to the French Revolution as objectively as possible, while at the same time laying the groundwork for a future shifting in the focus of my research to China. I held fast to the substantive reason for the French Revolution, and criticized the disasters that ensued when it was taken too far. It was no doubt inevitable that these three oppositions, especially the last, would exact a psychological price on someone like me, whose life was deeply intertwined with that kind of experience.

How did you pursue your studies?

In late 1977 entrance examinations for university were resumed. For various reasons I missed the opportunity to go to college and decided to apply to graduate school directly. It took me four years of repeated attempts. Finally in 1982 I was accepted by the History Department of Shaanxi Normal University in Xi'an, where I majored in the history of political thought in the early modern West. By the time I entered the university, you can image my eagerness to pursue knowledge. In Henan, I had read all the Chinese translations of Rousseau's works published in the mainland, and on arriving in Xi'an I insisted on selecting the French Revolution as my field. I was in a great hurry, and it was not until I immersed myself in a sea of books that I realized that the topic was much too broad, and my intellectual preparation for it quite inadequate. Three years of graduate study was not enough for me to finish reading all the relevant materials. So in the end I concentrated on a much narrower subject, 'Thomas Paine and the French Revolution', touching only marginally on the Revolution itself, to disagree mildly with the long-standing over-valuation of it by official scholarship.

In the early modern history of the West, there were very few people like Paine, who participated in both the American and French Revolutions, worked for a third revolution in Britain, where he was thrown in jail, and wanted to ignite a fourth revolution against established religion. Not many people have put advanced modern political thought into practice and, at the same time, developed it in the process of practising it, as Paine did.

Most Western scholars have declined to consider Paine a major political thinker. A small number have shown sympathy for his tragic life, but still have not sufficiently recognized his contribution to political thought. In my view, Paine made a unique contribution to the history of political thought, in at least six respects. Firstly, he alone took the theory of natural law – the most advanced doctrine of its time – to its limits, interpreting the notion of the inalienable rights of man in a radically democratic way, which included liberation for blacks and women, and the rejection of censitary suffrage based on property qualifications.

Secondly, he combined the concerns of two leading currents of political thought in the West in the eighteenth century, natural law and utopian socialism, in a way that nobody else did. These two strains, in common with the development of early capitalism itself, developed through intense conflict. Roughly speaking, those who benefited from capitalist development proposed or defended theories of natural law, while those who suffered from it conceived utopian socialist ideas – though in the early stages, these had developed from the same premises of natural law and absorbed from it such notions as natural rights or fraternity. The dividing line between the two was their attitude towards property rights. The utopian socialists resisted private ownership of land and other goods. Throughout his life, Paine lived under the banner of natural law. However, he was not limited by its concept of property rights, proposing an agenda of social reform congenial only to utopian socialists. In his important late work *Agrarian Justice* (1796),[3] he started to expose phenomena of class exploitation in the economy, developing ideas about public ownership of land that differed from Locke's. More radically than Locke, Paine believed that uncharted lands are public property and that poverty is the bitter fruit of capitalism, rather than a natural fact.

Paine is also the first thinker to differentiate between society and government. *Common Sense* began with this idea. In his *New Letters* and *Rights of Man*, he developed it.

> Society is produced by our wants and government by our wickedness; the former promotes our happiness *positively* by uniting our affections, the latter *negatively* by restraining our vices. The one encourages intercourse, the other creates distinctions. The first is a patron, the last a punisher. Government is, in short, at best, a necessary evil and, at worst, an intolerable evil. (Italics in original.)[4]

So to rebel against a government is not necessarily to attack society, but may be required in order to save society.

Fourth, Paine was able to combine legacies from Rousseau and Locke in a new synthesis. Agreeing with Rousseau that sovereignty belongs to the people and firmly dismissing the notion that monarchy and parliament could be anything more than its executors, he also absorbed the reasonable core

---

[3] Thomas Paine, *Agrarian Justice, The Complete Writings of Thomas Paine*, collected and edited by Philip S. Foner, New York, 1945 [ed].

[4] Thomas Paine, *Common Sense*, p. 1 [ed].

of Locke's theory, calling for a separation of powers between the legislative, executive, and judiciary. Sovereignty, thus, can and must be divided and be delegated, and there he opened up the practical possibilities of building a republic in a large country. Going a step further, he argued that the revision of any founding contract is the right of each generation, which cannot be bound by its predecessor – and that the government, as the object to be revised, could play no role in the process of revision, same as when it plays no role at all in drawing up the original contract.

Fifth, Paine advocated the construction of a republic in a large nation, helping to destroy the mythology of the British constitutional monarchy. In fact, the slogan he initially launched in the Thirteen Colonies was not 'independence', but 'a republic'. Later linking the two, he projected the struggle in North America beyond its borders to the whole world, letting the Europeans see that the dynamic energy of the new state lay in the combination of a representative system and a mass democracy. This historical achievement was unsurpassed by any thinker of his time.

Finally, Paine's deism tended towards atheism. In *The Age of Reason*, written in 1794 when he was imprisoned in France, he affirmed an episte-mological conception of God as 'the first cause', but deprived this of any ontological substance. His 'God' has a logical status rather than a religious significance. Just as *Common Sense* and *Rights of Man* pushed his theory of natural law to its limits, so *The Age of Reason* put him in the farthest realm of deism.

After completing your thesis at Xi'an, what did you do?

For some years I was teaching in a military college in Shanghai. Then in the autumn of 1989, I registered for a doctorate at Fudan University, also in Shanghai. It was the year of political 'turmoil,' regarding which I had my own position. I was labelled a radical, suspected of heterodoxy, and forced to discontinue my studies for a period. Nevertheless, in the same year, I perceived something in common between the two conflicting sides in the upheaval that shook the nation – a leftist political culture, originating in the French Revolution and taking shape in China since early modern times, that is still active on our streets today. Perceiving such continuity with the past, I was deeply concerned. Not simply to release my own solitary melancholy, or to fulfil my long-standing intellectual interest, but to self-examine the formation of our generation, I felt that I should com-plete the research project of my youth, by tracing the origins of French political culture.

When taking my oral defence in 1992, however, I encountered more trouble. After reading my dissertation draft, some professors refused to participate in the oral defence, characterizing my opinions as 'bourgeois right-wing, conservative historiography.' I was very grateful for Professor

Wang Yuanhua's support at that critical moment.[5] He not only stood up without hesitation to serve as the chair of my committee but, after learning that I aimed to study Rousseau's thought and the French Revolution, gave me the unpublished manuscript of the late Gu Zhun[6] and urged me to draw intellectual nourishment and courage from him. After revising the manuscript in 1994, I had it published under the title of *The Demise of the Republic of Virtue: From Rousseau to Robespierre*.[7]

The central argument of this work is that Rousseau's thought shows the persistence of religious motifs in the history of political thought. Although other factors were of course also at work, Rousseau's enormous impact on the period of the French Revolution was due to the way political and social revolutions were eventually replaced by a moral revolution. So far as Rousseau's own thought is concerned, I focused on three issues. The first of these was the way Rousseau's conception of the General Will swept away two of the foundations of a modern secular society and political system: the private space for individual existence and the aggregated space of the 'collective will' – unofficial schools and parties. Secondly, I considered the danger that his construction of the social contract in practice leads, under normal circumstances, to a moralized omnipotence in which the expansion of the political state takes over civil society and the individual – and, in unusual circumstances, to an anarchy in which political participation is suddenly expanded and no institutional channels within the state can absorb the consequences, setting off a revolution.

The third topic was his linkage of moral intention to political power, and his idea that politics might function as a religion, which transformed concepts of political science into those of political philosophy, and so justified a massive invasion of civil society by the state.

However, from Rousseau's death in poverty and misery in 1778 to his worship by the Revolution twenty years later, many decisive impersonal – in particular, socio-economic – forces must have supervened to give him the authority he acquired. My research is confined to those at work in the history of ideas and political culture. Here I propose three rough explanations. Firstly, a cultural atmosphere had already developed in France that favoured literary and theatrical registers at the expense of philosophical or

---

[5] Wang Yuanhua (1920–): long-time Party member and leading scholar of early Chinese literary theory, who set up a liberal intellectual journal, *New Enlightenment* in the late 1980s, which was banned soon after the crisis of 1989 [ed].

[6] Gu Zhun (1915–1974), a pioneer of modern accounting in China and a Party member since the 1930s, was head of Shanghai's Municipal Finance and Taxation Bureau in 1949–1952, then removed for promoting modern fiscal methods against a commune-style approach. Twice labelled a 'Rightist', he died in isolation while studying the origins of capitalism and modern democracy. His posthumous publications include: *Xila chengbang zhidu* (The Greek City-State System), Beijing 1982; *Gu Zhun wenji* (The Collected Works of Gu Zhun), Guizhou 1994 [ed].

[7] *Daode lixiang guo de fumie – cong Lusuo dao Luobosibier*, Shanghai 1994; Taipei 1997 [ed].

logical forms.[8] Earlier figures in the Enlightenment like Voltaire and Diderot, although also creative writers, concentrated their intellectual attention on British philosophy and the Encyclopaedia. Rousseau by contrast was a rebel within the Enlightenment, whose literary personality transformed his theories to their detriment, yet became the most effective means of their diffusion after his death. In this sense, it is better to state that France needed Rousseau, rather than the other way around.

Secondly, the Enlightenment as a movement lacked a vital foundation: in an epoch of transition towards capitalism, it failed to respond to the discontent of the masses at the bottom levels of society and to shoulder the responsibility of the rising bourgeois class towards them for an all-inclusive reform of values. So in return, they rejected the Enlightenment. In the initial phase of the Revolution, Enlightenment ideas were tolerated; in the next phase, discontinued; and in the final stage they were put on moral trial and pilloried by a mass dictatorship. The ideas of the now deified Rousseau entered the scene in the initial phase, and became the core of revolutionary discourse in the next phase. In the last, his ideas swept all before them, surpassing all the residual effects of Enlightenment thought.

Thirdly, the Enlightenment failed to take up the most important conceptual heritage of the mediaeval period – the idea of salvation. It could marginalize an individual like Rousseau, but it could not fill the vacuum of religious ideas or the hunger for spiritual values in French life. If we say that the French Revolution became increasingly impetuous as it proceeded, this was not the result of extravagant thinking from Rousseau to Robespierre. Various objective factors contributed to the final result. Crises of morality, politics, and society converged. A moral revolution incited political and social revolutions, which offered to assuage the national hunger for a new morality. But first the political revolution was crushed by the social revolution, then the social revolution was crushed by the moral revolution.

Since the 1990s, you have engaged in a series of discussion over various issues in the PRC. What do you regard as the most important?

My participation in the intellectual debates of the last decade can be divided roughly into three stages. The earliest one was a controversy around the humanistic spirit in 1994. Then came the evaluation of the new intellectual trends of the nineties, which lasted for several years. Then, towards the end of the period, there was the debate between Liberals and the New Left.

I was one of the initiators in the first big controversy, over the loss of

---

[8] Tocqueville (1805–1859) discusses this point in his *The Old Regime and the Revolution*. See its Book III, Chapter 1, Chicago, 1998.

a humanistic spirit in China in 1994.[9] In that debate, I already emphasized the practical nature of humanistic spirit. When scholars in the humanities pursue their research, they may adopt the attitude of a technician and remain value-neutral. But this stance should not obscure their duty to be concerned with social problems of the present – the most difficult aspect of their vocation, but an essential one. He who only responds to the past is a scholar, but not a humanist. Only those who persistently respond to contemporary society can be called humanistic scholars. In doing so, they should seek to combine universal principles and individual practice.

In the early nineties, the notion of universal principles faced a crisis. This was precipitated by the incident of Wang Meng's article 'Eluding the Sublime' in *Dushu*,[10] which applauded Wang Shuo's novels celebrating hooliganism. Such indulgence was pervading the intellectual world. What it indicated was a Chinese cultural outlook that, baulked from rising upward, was now seeking to make a breakthrough going downward. This new direction abandoned all claims to spirituality, or responsibility in conduct. The mere fact that in the past hypocritical preaching exalted a fake sublime, does not license us to jettison all notions of nobility or eliminate every belief today. The new ideology suggested that between the hypocrite and the thug, an old Marxist trout and a young slacker yelling 'please don't call me human', no third possibility existed.[11] In fact, aside from hypocritical nobility and real vulgarity, there was a path worth pursuing: we can safeguard our dignity as human beings, accepting neither violent coercion nor hypocritical untruth, and refusing to wallow in the mire with evil. We should be vigilant against the risk of the cult of hooliganism wearing down the humanistic spirit.

At the same time, the universality of humanistic principles should remain a form, not a content. The reason for this formalism lies in the fact that the meaning of 'natural rights' and 'innate understandings', and their expressions, differs from nation to nation. However, their vessels or frames are always communicable between cultures. For example, Kant's first categorical imperative and Confucius's injunction 'do not to others what you would not have them do to you' represent a similar precept in different vocabularies. In that sense, form is superior to content.

Moreover, a universally valid humanistic principle must be individualistic

---

[9] For reference to this controversy, see Introduction, note 22 above [ed].

[10] Wang Meng, 'Duobi chonggao' (Eluding the sublime), *Dushu*, January 1993 [ed].

[11] 'Old Marxist trout' (Malie zhuyi laotaitai): mocking popular stereotype of the early 1980s – an outdated old lady, still repeating Cultural Revolution-style clichés. 'Young slacker' (xiao pizi): generally considered the most representative figure in Wang Shuo's fiction since the late 1980s – a derisive lout making fun of whatever various authorities or older generations might lecture him about. The role had strong subversive implications, though it rarely involved much direct external confrontation or interior contradiction [ed].

in practice, or it risks being dragged towards its very opposite – moral authoritarianism. The result is then Rousseau's formula: 'You lack freedom, so I will force you to be free'. Isaiah Berlin's distinction between positive and negative liberty reminds us of the need to avoid the second being smothered by the first. It warns us against using a universal approach to promote universal principles. Otherwise, the higher our humanistic spirit, the more aggressive our form of life may become, to the point where it could even contain germs of fascism.

Viewed from the standpoint of genuine tolerance, the cultural soil out of which the spiritual life of our generation has sprung – a political culture of saturated ideology – may have incited us to receive and defend the very ideology that was oppressing us. In their spiritual origins, repressor and repressed belong to the same blood type. There were two ways of negating this legacy. One was to break through it downwards, in a dive into the mud of the mundane world, as quite a few people from this generation already have done. This is one type of individual choice, which we can only treat as such and have no reason to exalt. The other is to break through it upwards, by casting off the old self, changing blood type, and adopting other idealistic values. That has appeared too difficult. So far I have seen only a small ray of hope, in the work of one writer – Zhang Chengzhi. I admire his heroic willingness to fight in isolation.[12]

How do you assess the transformation of the intellectual scene from the 1980s to the 1990s?

To start with, one basic fact should not be obscured. In the intellectual history of twentieth-century China, the 1980s were a time when cultural life was reignited after thirty years of repression. Scholars shook off the bonds of ideology and appeared on an empty stage of thought, inheriting nothing and depending on nothing. In Chinese intellectual history, there were few generations as lucky and as unlucky as this one. The May Fourth generation was much more fortunate, because before it rushed into the rapids of the 'new culture', it had many years of training in the old one.

In the Reform Era, the soil of the whole society longed for rain after a long intellectual drought. But much of the intellectual ferment was adolescent in character, and the setting was agitated by internal and external troubles. A few unattractive phenomena, which made contemporaries feel ashamed and latecomers despised, were virtually inevitable. One example was the sort of grand narratives about Chinese culture that fall under the

---

[12] Zhang Chengzhi (1948–), a Muslim writer famous for his stories 'The Black Steed' and 'River of the North' in the 1980s, who took a firm stand against contemporary Han-Chinese ethnocentric ideology [tr].

rubric of 'Jing Ke assassinating Confucius'.[13] Later, what was at first make-believe appeared to become reality, with a flood of reports and discussions. The attribution of particular problems and social ills, rooted in specific historical situations, to a continuous cultural system handed down from the remote past, seemed insightful. But in fact it resembled a grandiose and impractical form of putting Zhang's hat on Li's head (*zhang guan li dai*), or mixing things up.

This milieu fostered a sense of cultural responsibility that could cover everything at the beginning, but nothing at the end. General discussions of cultural history like this, empty at the core and sweeping at the margins, caused specific discussion of reforms to slip through our fingers, ruining the reputation of cultural studies. But what in fact was so strange about these 'strange things witnessed in the new decade'?[14] In my view, with few exceptions, such blemishes were inevitable ills of adolescence in the era of our nation's intellectual liberation. Ills of this kind accompanied the Italian Renaissance, the French Enlightenment, and the German *Sturm und Drang*. Did anybody ever hear those nations deny their adolescence in the name of intellectual cultivation? Instead they are proud of the unsightly, acne-adorned faces of their youth.

Here I would like to make a few points to those friends who have hastened to deny the achievements of the 1980s. First, the backbone of the scholarship of the nineties was not formed by new figures, but by those who were active in the eighties. Their characters were various: there were victims as well as victimizers of that period, benefactors as well as benefici-aries of its intellectual environment. In all fairness, those who remained in China represented the beneficiaries. Without the preparation of the first ten years, there would have been no progress over the next ten years. Even the current scholarly status of those who complain about the eighties would have been difficult to attain without them.

Second, just as the 1980s paid their price, intellectual growth in the 1990s was not without its cost. We lost the precious advantage of a relatively lenient political environment. We had no choice but to shift

---

[13] This refers to a parable written by Qin Hui in the early 1990s, in which Qin depicts Jing Ke, a heroic assassin in historical records of the late Warring States period (third century BC), as a coward, as a way of criticizing the ostensibly 'radical' character of the 'cultural fever' of the 1980s, relating it to the cultural conservatism of the 1990s. Having realized the political might of the First Emperor he is supposed to assassinate, the parable goes, Jing changes his mind and merely stabs a portrait of Confucius, which possesses cultural value only. Even so, the Qin Emperor, vexed by his singing, strikes him and drives him away.When a friend advises Jing to show more deference to Confucius as a cultural figure, he changes course and becomes a scholar of the 'national past' (*guogu*). Qin Hui, *Wenti yu zhuyi* (Problems and Isms), Changchun, 1999, p. 447 [ed].

[14] This phrase alludes to the title *Ershi nian mudu zhi guai xianzhuang* (Strange things witnessed in the past twenty years), a famous novel by Wu Jianren (1866–1910) published in 1909, depicting corrupt official life in late Qing society [tr].

towards more detailed research, without synthesis. This situation closely resembled the substitution of empirical research for neo-Confucian learning in the Ming-Qing intellectual transition of the seventeenth and eighteenth century.[15] Of course, grand narratives always demand detailed, careful evidence, so the values of each are much the same. By its own internal logic, the intellectual world of the 1980s might thus have led to a period that emphasized meticulous documentation. Yet how is our situation today the natural outcome of the immediate past, and how far have non-scholarly factors contributed to it? The logic of intellectual development did not require the nineties to negate the eighties. The intellectual growth of the 1980s was terminated by strong external forces, not by any immanent necessity.

Third, if in comparing the situation of the 1980s with that of the 1990s we contrast our present strengths with past shortcomings, we can no doubt conclude that we have made 'great strides'; but if we contrast our present shortcomings with past strengths, would we still be so satisfied with ourselves? It is unlikely we would feel such over-confidence. A fair comparison would conclude that the two decades had different achievements to their credit, and neither was completely positive. However, if we compare the intellectual atmosphere of the two periods, we should have the courage to acknowledge frankly that the present is inferior to the past and is getting worse.

As a matter of fact, reflection on different modes of work probably began before 1989. Not only middle-aged or youthful, but also senior scholars took part in this. An old scholar told me that as the original intellectual liberation of the eighties sprang largely from the theoretical conference (*lilun wuxu hui*) of the late seventies,[16] which still retained the collective features of old-style mass mobilization, in due course some intellectuals became introspective, separating themselves from the common tide, and deeply examining their own spiritual history. Such reflection, that is individual and not general, self-motivated and not externally forced, serious and not superficial, is to be valued.

The nineties saw a different type of reflection, which had three characteristics. One was a reversal of attitude towards theories of neo-authoritarianism advanced in the late eighties: many who had once opposed them, now –

---

[15] See B. A. Elman, *From Philosophy to Philology: Social and Intellectual Aspects of Change in Late Imperial China*, Cambridge, Mass., 1984 [ed].

[16] *Lilun wuxu hui* was a conference held in 1979 to explore new theoretical directions within the tradition of what was then Chinese Marxism. The conference was presided by Hu Yaobang, the Party's General Secretary in 1982–1987, and lasted for two months. Most participants were ideological cadres within the Party. It followed the discussion on 'criteria for examining truth' (*zhenli biaozhun*) in 1978 and preceded the Third Plenary Session of the Eleventh Central Committee in late 1979, a meeting convened to determine the direction of the Reform Era [ed].

in drastically changed conditions – shifted towards them. Another was a selective – often either instrumental or dogmatic – adoption of foreign discourses, for example, a pragmatic castration of the views of the overseas historian Yu Ying-shih that appropriated one side of his cultural conservatism, and not the other, which has a sharply critical edge. A third characteristic was the discarding of any critical spirit or sense of intellectual responsibility towards contemporary society, in the name of a repudiation of radical excesses since the May Fourth period. Therefore, it is not going too far to understand this recent sort of reflection as a way in which scholarship has sought to ingratiate itself with the tendencies of the time. It is not difficult to see the difference between the two types, if we ask ourselves which maintains critical interventions in current social reality.

You've mentioned Yu Ying-Shih. What is your view of his work?

One of the seminal texts for the change in China's intellectual atmosphere in the 1990s was Yu Ying-Shih's address 'Radicalism and conservatism in early modern Chinese history', given at Hong Kong Chinese University in 1988. Another was his article 'Picking up the Pieces for a New Start', published in the *Twenty-First Century*.[17] In these and other writings, Yu Ying-Shih attributed the social transformation in Mainland China from 1919 to 1949 to the radical trend that originated in the May Fourth Movement. According to him, this trend became more and more extreme, making it difficult for conservatism to survive and resulting in drastic social changes that led to disaster. Yu Ying-Shih's critique focuses on the historical teleology characteristic of much of the May Fourth outlook, which resembled elements in Hegel's philosophy. In this respect, I completely support the project of reflecting critically on the May Fourth era, initiated by Yu Ying-Shih.

The deep-rooted origin of the radical current of May Fourth thought, criticized by Yu Ying-Shih, lay in just this teleological bent. The idea that a few prophets can confidently explain, predict or master human history, and are capable of reorganizing existing society according to a pre-established design, is a teleological belief in the Reason of History, that has been the major single substitute for religious faith since the withdrawal of God in the time of the Enlightenment. It is also the biggest myth that human beings could create – a deified human self. It is only when this myth became widespread that the destruction of traditional society and the establishment of a wholly new type of social order could appear legitimate. Here lay the

---

[17] Yu Ying-Shih: doyen of Chinese intellectual historians, after a long and distinguished career, retired from his final post at Princeton in 2001. For references to this topic, see Introduction, note 9 above [ed].

source of May Fourth radicalism. Circulating in various forms across Eurasia for two hundred years, a certain ideology finally took shape in early modern China, which is the object of Yu Ying-Shih's criticism. In this sense, May Fourth currents of thought did have a spiritual kinship with Hegel's historical teleology. If we ignore vulgar mutations in its lower reaches and focus on certain theories in its upper reaches, then modern ideology can be considered a descendant of the historical rationalism that emerged during the era of the Enlightenment.

However, in thinking along these lines, it is possible to fall victim to historical teleology oneself. The first question I would like to put to Yu Ying-Shih is this: how far can we really attribute the social transformation of mainland China from 1919 to 1949 to shifts in intellectual thought, if we suspend value judgments and look only at the facts? In my view, explaining dramatic social change across a century through the prism of intellectual history can shed some light, but remains a limited approach. I would myself say that the influence of May Fourth trends on modern Chinese society extended roughly to a cut-off date of 1927, or the beginning of the Anti-Japanese war in 1937 at the latest. The subsequent history of China developed more along lines determined by political, military and international relationships.

A second question to Yu Ying-Shih would be this: Was there really an intellectual train that ran directly from the Tiananmen Square of 4 May 1919 to that of 1 October 1949? Chen Duxiu was an important figure in the radical wing of the May Fourth Movement, who indeed changed the whole direction of the New Culture Movement and paved the way for Marxism to enter China.[18] His political experience and intellectual reflection in later years demonstrate that he was perfectly capable of taking responsibility for May Fourth radicalism, as he should have done. But he did not and could not have any responsibility for the party politics developed thereafter. Another example would be Qu Qiubai, whose political career lasted longer than that of Chen Duxiu, and so would appear to have greater responsibility for that kind of party politics. Yet the 'Superfluous Words' that Qu wrote on the eve of his death remind us of the crucial difference between political theory as a conceptual power swaying intellectuals, and a politics involving theories and acting as an organized force competing for state power.[19]

---

[18] Chen Duxiu (1879–1942): best known for being one of the leaders in the May Fourth New Culture Movement from 1917, and the founder and the first General Secretary of the CCP from 1921 to 1927. After being expelled from the CCP in late 1927, he led the main Trotskyist group in China. Jailed by the KMT from 1932 to 1937, he spent his last years near the wartime capital Chongqing reading and writing, without much political activity [ed].

[19] Qu Qiubai (1899–1935): a student of Russian radicalized by the May Fourth Movement, who went to the Soviet Union in 1920, where he joined the CCP, returning to China in early 1923. In 1927 he replaced Chen Duxiu as the CCP's General Secretary for a year. He was

Again, when radical thought and protest revived among intellectuals in the 1940s, were leftist professors direct inheritors of the May Fourth Movement? Take the most famous among them, Wen Yiduo and Li Gongpu.[20] In his early years, after he returned from study abroad, Wen Yiduo supported statism, opposed communism, detested political intervention in scholarship, and believed in the value of research for research's sake. In his early years too, Li Gongpu not only opposed radicalism, but participated in the purge of communists in Shanghai in April 1927.[21] Later both shifted from positions on the right towards the left, from opposing radicalism to supporting it. At the end, both of them were assassinated by the KMT.

There is a logical continuity between the radical thought of the latter half of the 1940s, represented by Wen Yiduo and Li Gongpu, and that of the May Fourth period. But this vertical link is not as significant as the force traversing it horizontally. Among the survivors of the May Fourth generation, the successful were already involved in the party politics of the 1940s. The new levy of radicals in the 1940s had been opposed to the original radicalism of the May Fourth veterans. But the regressive social environment of the time, pressuring them horizontally, stirred them into re-launching radical protests. They were not misled by others, nor did they mistakenly take the wrong train speeding down the line from May Fourth, which actually did not exist. If Russian Bolshevism supplied the backdrop to May Fourth radicalism, the spiritual background of these leftist professors of the 1940s mostly came from the democratic education they received in Britain and America in their early years. This is worth reflecting on.

Exaggeration of the historical effects of the May Fourth Movement, moreover, has an unexpected consequence. It tends to place a weight of responsibility on intellectuals, which they did not seek and should not take. Politicians, generals and diplomats have more of a say in these matters, even when intellectuals play some role in them. Still worse was the variety of reassessments of May Fourth to appear with the changes in intellectual modes in the 1990s. The cultural fever of the eighties may have come to

---

captured by the KMT army while ill in the Communist base in Fujian, and executed soon after. 'Duoyu de hua' (Superfluous words) is an essay he wrote in prison shortly before being shot, in which he regards himself as an ordinary man swept into political events by 'a misunderstanding of history' [ed].

[20] Wen Yiduo (1899–1946): a leading poet in the 1920s and scholar of classical Chinese literature from the 1930s onwards. In earlier years, he believed in cultural nationalism and political statism. During the war, he grew politically concerned and became an outspoken activist in China's Democracy League after the war. He was killed by KMT gunmen on July 15, 1946. Li Gongpu (1900–1946): also an active member of the Democracy League, from the early 1940s onwards. He was assassinated a few days before Wen [ed].

[21] After the Northern Expedition against the assorted warlords achieved initial success, the KMT turned against its ally the CCP, and on April 12, 1927, Chiang Kai-Shek massacred communists and labour activists in Shanghai, with the support of the British community and the Green Gang mafia. On April 18, a new Nationalist government was set up in Nanjing [ed].

an end, but its grand narratives of cultural history have lingered on. Now people are again depicting the history of early modern China as the unfolding evolution of a single strain of thought, and rallying together to attack it. Conservatism is once more in vogue.

How would you explain this?

Although this is an unpleasant point, I think it is necessary to address it. Changes in intellectual atmosphere usually come from two intertwined forces. One is the internal history of ideas, descending vertically from any given generation or period to the next. The other is the social environment outside the world of the intellect, dragging it horizontally this way and that. Sensitive to their professional dignity, intellectuals tend to regard changes in which they themselves are involved as progress in scholarship itself. They are reluctant to acknowledge that their own research may be passively affected by social forces. Such horizontal influences tend to embarrass scholars, who typically 'forget' them – intentionally or unintentionally. I understand this attitude, but I disagree with it.

So if we look back at the dissemination of Yu Ying-Shih's ideas in the PRC, what do we see? They were introduced before 1989. However, it was not until the second half of 1989 and the anniversary of May Fourth in 1990 that his ideas suddenly acquired a pervasive influence. People rose *en masse* to respond to his ideas, as an authoritative source for a conservative turn. Adapting his framework, intellectuals delivered a negative verdict on the eighties, which had just passed, and a less than clear-minded one on the emergent trends of the nineties. To that extent, today's conservatism is a logical upshot of the rejection of May Fourth and of the 1980s.

To grasp the dynamics of this situation, I would like to use a far-fetched analogy. The introduction of Yu's ideas into China bears certain resemblances to those of Marx in an earlier period. Before the October Revolution, Marxism had already been introduced into China by Timothy Richard.[22] However, it failed to gain much attention in the intellectual world. It was not until 'the cannon shot of the October Revolution, sending Marxism to us' that Marx's ideas started to spread in China. When a foreign body of thought takes root in our soil, it does not sprout naturally: it needs 'material' conditions that do not consist of thought. Such conditions always resemble the power of that cannon shot, causing a drastic shift in the selection of interests and ideas in the intellectual world.

Yu Ying-Shih's critical reflections on May Fourth were no exception.

---

[22] Timothy Richard (1845–1919): British missionary, famous for his efforts to marry religious conversion to elite culture in China, who was responsible for many publication projects in Beijing and Shanghai in the late Qing period [ed].

They were disseminated in the PRC after another cannon shot. Of course, the enthusiastic response to them was a tribute to their originality and objective distinction, which answered to a need to replenish intellectual supplies after ten years of cultural fever in China. But it was also prompted by external social forces which had little to do with scholarship. To deny the significance of this factor is as unfair and dishonest as to deny that of scholarship. Changes in critical attitudes towards historical events also serve the purpose of changing attitudes towards current realities.

That is why I am opposed to the contemporary conservative trend. When I was writing my dissertation, the concepts of the conservative and the radical were already extremely popular, which made me feel very uncomfortable. When I delved into the origin of the currents of thought underlying the French Revolution, I realized that the notions of conservative and radical were highly mutable. For instance, the origin of Rousseau's radical conception of overturning the established order was what had once been the medieval world's most conservative concept, the idea of salvation. By contrast, the philosophical origin of Voltaire's conservative ideas was far from the conservative agnosticism of the time. So for the critical framework of my manuscript, I decided against resorting to the analytical concepts of the conservative and the radical, although they were very easy to use.

The frequent use of this pair of terms by mainland academics is not a good sign. It suggests loss of creativity, sense of nuance, or even a kind of necessary patience. It is not, of course, that radicalism in China is beyond criticism. However, the concept of conservatism that functions as its antonym requires very rigorous training in theory and had very specific meanings in the history of China's social transformation. Without clarifying these, the acadamic fashion of using conservatism and radicalism as all-purpose labels is not conducive either to criticizing radicalism or to fostering true conservatism. Rather, in simply recycling foreign concepts, there is a twisted paradox, which is well worth pondering. Those academics who were most voluble in utilizing the terms 'radical' and 'conservative' were also those who most frequently ignored historical facts and exaggerated the responsibilities of intellectuals in history. Yet at the same time they did their best to reduce the responsibilities that intellectuals should take in the present.

On the surface, this might seem coherent. If in the past intellectuals produced a radical strain of thought that perverted the social processes of early modern China, would not contemporary intellectuals have reason to learn the lessons of this history, and withdraw into an academic ivory tower? However, if intellectual thought contains such magical power, why don't they bring this earth-shaking force into full play to speed up social reform of an unsatisfactory present? The sad truth is that the conservative trend in mainland academia can best be understood as an exercise in survival skills under external pressures, a passive spirit in particular circumstances, the articulation of frustration rather than a current of thought.

Do you think grand narratives of Chinese culture are necessarily conservative?

They are the two sides of the same coin. The grand narrative dominant in the 1990s, which used radicalism as a key to interpret the entire history of early modern China in negative terms, was certainly conservative. But we also see a wider vogue for culturalism in the mainland today. In the middle of the decade, there was a debate between the New Left and the postmodernists that exemplified this, when the second group started to use the notion of 'postmodern culture' to interpret the social phenomena of consumerism that developed from the early nineties, and the first group objected. But the debate had yet to fully develop, when the two sides seemed to reunite again in a 'cultural criticism' that became increasingly pretentious and pervasive.

What this illustrated was a situation in which intellectual discussion is confined within certain boundaries defined by censorship. In most cases, within these boundaries, people only talk about issues that have a definite coefficient of safety. The barriers not only sealed off the real problems in the outside world, but also affected the health of discussions inside them. There is also the tendency of our intellectuals to a collective 'Ah Q attitude'.[23] Whenever they are frustrated by reality, and especially if they encounter tragic impediments, they are driven to withdraw into their studies. After a while, they begin to develop profound, self-deceptive interpretations of this limitation, coming to believe that it was their own study desk that decided the direction of the outside world, not that they themselves were forced to return to their studies by it. I have no objection to cultural studies, but I am opposed to the culturalism that ensues from these twisted attitudes.

For in the first place we need to ask whether culture really possesses that kind of determinant power. My answer is no. Economics, politics and culture form a threefold domain, each with their own operating system. If we have to gauge the lay-out of the three, then I think that politics is closer to the economy and farthest from culture. But there is no fixed deterministic set of relations between them. A given culture does not necessarily correspond to only one form of politics or economy. It contains a more open, plural range of possibilities. The idea that once culture takes a particular form, politics and economy must follow suit, is simply wrong.

---

[23] Lu Xun, 'The True Story of Ah Q', *Selected Stories of Lu Hsun*, Beijing, 1960. Lu Xun depicts Ah Q as a figure with a unique capacity to turn any disaster into an imaginary victory [ed].

At the end of 1997, I wrote a preface to He Qinglian's book *China's Pitfall*, which first appeared in Hong Kong, expressly supporting her attack on corruption and denouncing theories that defend corruption as an inevitable phase of progress.[24] In it, I was the first to call social injustice and privatization of public assets 'the cancer of politics'. As a result, the preface could not be published in the subsequent mainland edition. Although I disagree with economic determinism as an approach to history, in that text I argued that, as the problem of social injustice becomes increasingly acute in China today, the theory of political economy remains a powerful tool for analysing social changes and should attract our attention again.

How do you see the recent debates between liberals and the New Left?

At the end of 1998, I published an article arguing that the most important development that year in mainland intellectual life was the emergence of the discourse of liberalism.[25] This article stirred up strong reactions from all sides. In it, I suggested the following description of liberalism. Philosophically it stands for empiricism, in contrast to transcendentalism. Its historical ideas are based on a fallibilistic evolutionary theory, and reject any kind of historical determinism. Its concepts of evolution involve gradual improvement and progress, and a refusal of the voluntarism that is characteristic of radicalism. Its economic theory requires a market system, and rejection of a planned economy. Its political theory requires a representative democracy, a constitutional government and a legal system, proof not only against an individual tyranny or an oligarchy, but also against a mass dictatorship in the name of the 'general will' exercised by a majority. Its ethical code requires the protection of differing values and includes the belief that no individual must be sacrificed as a means to any abstract end.

This set of ideas has now found expression in a whole range of books, magazines, and articles. Liberals too have paid close attention to the increasingly pronounced social divisions and conflicts of interest around us. In a certain sense, it is exactly because they take the full measure of such conflicts, that they call for urgent reform of the political system more vigorously than any other current of opinion. They have taken such a risk, daring to squeeze through a crack in the door, because they perceived that there were two dangerous tendencies in a period when social injustice was becoming increasingly flagrant.

The first of these dangers was the authoritarianism that set in at the end

---

[24] He Qinglian, *Zhongguo de xianjing* (China's Pitfall), Hong Kong 1997; *Xiandaihua de xianjing* (Modernization's pitfall), Beijing 1998.
[25] '1998: ziyouzhuyi xueli de yanshuo' (1998: Discourse of liberal theory), Part I: Guangzhou, *Southern Weekend*, December 25, 1998; Part II: *Zhongguo tushu shangbao*, Book Review Section, January 5, 1999.

of the 1980s. All sorts of vested interests blocked any reform of the power system. The result was not only large-scale structural corruption, but also indifference to the suffering of the disadvantaged classes and stifling of their voice. The second danger is the recent left turn of some thinkers, as the paths of the intelligentsia start to divide. These intellectuals have found a new source of dissatisfaction in market reforms within the country and the world economic system outside it, not only putting the correct course of economic reforms at risk, but also appealing to regressive anti-imperialist and anti-colonialist moods during the opening of China's door to the world. In so doing, they conceal the true origins of social instability in the country.

Liberalism resists both these dangerous tendencies. Economically, liberals press for further market-oriented reforms. At the same time, they not only oppose the plunder of the social wealth that the lower classes had to labour to accumulate in the era of planned economy, but also reject calls for a second land reform at home, in the name of social justice or a fake nationalist stance, Boxer-style, towards the outside world. Twenty years of economic reform have failed to establish the political checks necessary to control and balance it, and so problems of social justice have become steadily worse. These can only be resolved by reform of the political system to establish the rule of law in a constitutional democracy, rather than by returning to the kind of mass mobilization which occurred in the past. Taking their stand on Weber's ethic of responsibility, liberals – although they can understand the social origin of impulses to retrogression – are firmly opposed to any large-scale mobilization of the masses to seek temporary relief, which could only lead us back to the vicious circle of one violence replacing another or stability followed by chaos, that has been the pattern of the last century of Chinese history.

Is there anything against which liberals should be on guard themselves? Yes, of course, there are probably quite a few pitfalls before us. Let me indicate two. Firstly, we should realize that where freedom is long established, negative liberty can have few drawbacks. There Isaiah Berlin was entitled to satisfy himself with a kind of 'static mechanics' of liberalism. However, where liberal values have yet to be realized, insistence on negative liberty can at least in some degree be put to cynical uses. There is a more urgent need for us to create a 'dynamic mechanics' of liberalism. Expressing it cautiously, could we – for the time being – say that we should struggle positively for a guaranteed negative liberty, and look passively forward to positive liberty?

Secondly, when defending the market mechanism, we need to distinguish what a market can legitimately be held responsible for, and what it cannot. Confusion over this question has been introduced by our New Left friends. When they angrily denounced the amount of social injustice they felt the market economy in China has created and attacked what they thought to be the root of the problem – the invasion of multinational corporations and the global capitalist system, they forgot that the market economy here is not the market economy over there. Ours is dragged along by the machinery of power. An all too 'visible foot' is often stamping on the 'invisible hand'. If this hand is dirty, it is not for the reason Marx criticized, that 'every pore is dripping with the dirt of capital', but rather that 'every pore is bleeding from the grip of political power'. On the surface it seems the market is unclean and sinful, when in reality it is the power structure behind it that is practising deception. In China today the social injustices our New Left friends condemn, including the collusion between money and power they pillory, should be attributed more to the violent 'foot' than the dirty 'hand'. When Chinese liberals seek to clarify this confusion and to defend a still very weak market mechanism, however, it is important that they recognize the ugly footmarks on the hand, lest they defend these too as the acceptable attributes of the market.

Thus the difference between liberals and the New Left is not, as many mistakenly believe, that the latter want social justice and the former reject it. It is about the distinction between the 'foot' and the 'hand'. Liberals always target the 'visible foot', even when they too denounce the collusion between power and capital; whereas the New Left, even when most indignant, forever focuses on the 'hand' beneath the forceful 'foot'. We wish our friends on the New Left to keep up their powerful critique, but we also would like them to correct their sights before firing their volleys again.

In resisting authoritarian and New Left tendencies alike, liberals speak out in the narrow space between the two cliffs. They are under frontal pressure from the authorities, and endure misunderstanding and even vehement flanking attacks from friends on the New Left. The principal reason for the divergence between liberals and the New Left is clear: while the latter focus on criticizing the market system, the former call for reform of the political system. This is the root of the difference between the two.

Translated by Shengqing Wu

3

Scholarship, Ideas, Politics

Chen Pingyuan

How would you describe the general focus of your work, since completing your first major research in 1987?

My doctorate, whose title was *The Transformation of the Narrative Pattern in Chinese Fiction*,[1] looked at the period from 1898 to 1927 when classical ways of writing fiction became essentially modern. At that time I adopted certain Western methods of literary study, such as narratology, and emphasized the 'formal revolution' involved in the birth of modern Chinese fiction – not without an intention of reversing an earlier tradition of excessive emphasis on 'content' in literary studies. Taking Chinese classical fiction as its background, the book traced the internal dynamics of the evolution of the genres of the period, with attention on the one hand to the creative native transformation of classical into modern forms, and on the other to the inspiration or influences from the West. This was an approach that reflected the notion of 'twentieth-century Chinese literature' that my cohort had been developing in the eighties,[2] and which has since gained general acceptance, helping to break down the mutual isolation of classical, pre-modern, and modern literary studies in China.

In 1989 I completed a book in a collective project, *A History of Twentieth-century Chinese Fiction: Volume One, 1897–1916*.[3] This too revolved around the formal development of narrative. But it did not confine itself to the study of self-enclosed 'form' along the lines advocated by New Criticism. Instead, it examined formal changes for the hidden ideological elements within them. The most important feature of this book was its

---

[1] *Zhongguo xiaoshuo xushi moshi de zhuanbian*. Shanghai 1988.
[2] First serialized in *Dushu*, October 1985 to March 1986, 'Ershi shiji Zhongguo wenxue san ren tan' (Dialogue on twentieth-century Chinese literature), co-authored by Huang Ziping, Qian Liqun and Chen Pingyuan, was published in Beijing 1988 [ed].
[3] *Ershi shiji Zhongguo xiaoshuo shi*, vol. 1. Beijing 1989. Other volumes in the same project are by different authors [ed].

principle of selection. Centred on the trajectory of fictional narrative forms in modern China, its emphasis was no longer on comprehensive assessment of any single author or work.

My next work was another exploration in the history of fiction, but with a very different focus. *The Chivalric Dreams of the Literati: Narrative Models of Chinese Knight-Errant Literature*[4] is a typological study of martial-art novels that seeks to locate their 'generic elements' and 'basic devices', showing the literary and cultural significance of their narrative syntax. Instead of complaining about the stereotypical features of these novels, my aim was to decipher the 'unconscious' of which these forms were a vector, by looking at the role of 'martial arts' (*xia*) as an expression of folk culture, in order to grasp their dual function – as a way at once of saving others and redeeming oneself. Where previous works on popular culture often look down on their subject, taking narrative forms of the literati as the only yardstick of value, I tried to see what were the specific characteristics of a popular literature that paradoxically was created by literati, withholding judgement on it until I had given as accurate a description as I could of its narrative syntax, to enrich our understanding of 'minor' traditions in our life. My aim was to try to combine a typological study of fiction with an exploration in cultural genealogy.

After a fourth book that addressed most of the practical problems and theoretical considerations I encountered in studying the history of the novel[5] – which remains a long-term interest of my research – my attention shifted to the history of scholarship and education. Of all my works, I found *The Establishment of Modern Scholarship in China: A Case Study Centred on Zhang Taiyan and Hu Shih* the most difficult, taking me more than six years.[6] Briefly, the book examines the two opposite perspectives of 'Western waves lapping the East' (*xi xue dong jian*) and 'old scholarship combining with new knowledge' (*jiu xue xin zhi*) to trace the transformation of research paradigms in humanistic and historical studies in modern China. In so doing, it reverses previous interpretations that placed excessive emphasis on the intrusion of Western learning, while overlooking the dynamics of internal change within native traditions. On this basis, it challenges what has been the dominant approach throughout the twentieth century, which tends to tailor Chinese culture to Western preconceptions. The book covers both empirical work and theoretical reflections of the period, exploring the tremendous tensions that developed between the pursuit of truth and the uses of knowledge, specialists and generalists, official schools and private

---

[4] *Qiangu wenren xiake meng: wuxia xiaoshuo leixing yanjiu*, Beijing 1992; Taipei 1995.

[5] *Xiaoshuo shi: lilun yu shijian* (History of the novel: theory and practice), Beijing 1993.

[6] *Zhongguo xiandai xueshu zhi jianli: yi Zhang Taiyan, Hu Shizhi wei zhongxin*, Beijing 1998. For Zhang Taiyan and Hu Shih, see notes on pp. 74 and 77 above [ed].

academies, as traditional Chinese scholarship negotiated successive adjustments and dilemmas in its march towards 'expertise'.

The focus of my next work, *The Formation and Structure of Literary History*, is the position, function and future of this discipline within the humanities and social sciences as a whole in China.[7] This is a subject that touches on a series of significant questions. It is connected not only to the formation of the modern consciousness of the nation-state, but also to the introduction of Western systems of education, the call for and memory of a literary revolution, the control and utilization by the state of intellectual research, as well as the interaction between Chinese scholarly traditions and Western literary theories. This was a project that combined research on the history of education, of ideas and of scholarship, with broad implications for the development of twentieth-century China. The newly published *Ten Lectures on Chinese Universities* is a follow-up along this line.[8]

The separation between classical, pre-modern, and modern literary studies in the People's Republic is, of course, related to institutional settings of higher education that have enforced narrower and narrower disciplinary boundaries and so divisions of knowledge. However, I have never sought to reject the value of the existing field of 'modern literature', but rather tried to introduce another perspective. When I spoke a few years ago of 'coming out of modern literature', what I had in mind was a way of changing the situation where the moment of May Fourth served both as literary ideal and research topic. Instead, I argued we should view the 'literary revolution' of May Fourth as one step in a developing cultural process (rather than its endpoint), and broaden our research to include the whole development of modern Chinese thought and culture. This temporal and spatial move can be considered the inner thread linking my studies on the history of the novel, of scholarship, and of higher education.

But, research into the history of scholarship is not a development only starting in the early nineties. The intellectual constellations of the 1980s and 1990s are distinct, but also interconnected. The project of a 'scholarly investigation of Chinese literary studies since pre-modern era', headed by my adviser Wang Yao (1914–1989), was formally launched on New Year's Day, 1988. The second collection in *The Modernization of Literary Studies in China* is the continuation of this collective project, which, together with the first volume, covers more than thirty outstanding scholars, examining their experiences and teachings, and assessing their achievements in adopting Western theories and methods while developing Chinese traditions – figures selected not just for their learning, but for the creativity of their ways of conceptualizing literature and designing research, as well as opening up new

---

[7] *Wenxue shi de xingcheng yu jiangou*, Nanning 1999.
[8] *Zhongguo daxue shi jiang*, Shanghai 2002.

fields for study.[9] Our century-old modern scholarship has itself become a sort of tradition, indifference to or misunderstanding of which can easily lead to nihilist attitudes, or radical tendencies to sweep away everything in a fit of enthusiasm.

What have been the differences in the dominant trends of research in the eighties and the nineties?

To imagine that all Chinese scholars were writing versions of the *River Elegy* in the eighties would be over-dramatizing.[10] On the other hand, it is true they became more reflective at the beginning of the 1990s – I wouldn't deny the profound impact of 'political turbulence' on a shift in research paradigms. However, if the Chinese academic world ceased after the summer of 1989 to exhibit the same frequency of 'fevers' and 'centres', falling into relative silence so far as attention in the mass media was concerned, this was not entirely due to political circumstances. It was more a self-imposed exile that scholars needed in order to readjust.

In the years 1990–1991, the questions that concerned Chinese intellectuals inside and outside the country were much the same. First there was the debate over radicalism and conservatism, in which Samuel Huntington's *Political Order in Changing Societies* became required reading. Then the notion of 'civil society' became a focal point of attention, while Havel's essay *The Power of the Powerless* circulated in Beijing. Yet though all were engaged in reconsidering the recent political movement in the light of reason, the different contexts told. It is striking that intellectuals inside China were dissatisfied with merely drawing strategic lessons from the political struggles. They also wanted to reflect on the social role and position of intellectuals. Along with this need came a turn to the history of scholarship. When a group of us young scholars gathered in Peking University in January 1991, we wanted to raise once more the banner of 'independence of spirit and freedom of thought'.[11] This was a stance that naturally implied resistance to cultural conservatism, but also expressed our discontent with the use of research to serve political purposes. In the long-run, to integrate everything into the path of political struggle does far more harm than good.

---

[9] *Zhongguo wenxue yanjiu xiandaihua jincheng*, Beijing 1996; *Zhongguo wenxue yanjiu xiandaihua jincheng*, vol. 2. Beijing, 2002.

[10] Su Xiaokang, et al, *He shang*. See Introduction, note 15 above [ed].

[11] '*Duli zhi jingshen, ziyou zhi sixiang*' – see Chen Yinke, *Jinming guan conggao er bian*, Shanghai 1982, p. 218. Chen Yinke (1890–1969): leading historian of the Chinese imperial past, who spent many years studying abroad. Capable of reading in 13 foreign languages, including Mongolian, Tibetan, Sanskrit, Pali, Persian and Arabic, from the 1920s onwards he published a series of groundbreaking research papers on the Chinese empire and its Central Asian neighbours, combining new methods and theories with great classical erudition [ed].

Putting this positively, to separate scholarship from politics is to safeguard it for general public benefit. For scholarship has an independent value that lasts longer than politics and is worth a life-long commitment. Putting it negatively, scholars should know that they can play little role in real politics and have every reason to lift from their shoulders the heavy burden of the millennial Confucian injunction to 'weave Heaven and Earth together'. In the West, excessive professional stratification can prompt intellectuals to intervene in society and perform a function of cultural critique. In China, where our long tradition of highly politicized literati (*shi dafu*) has not completely disappeared, it is necessary to defend professionalization.

In spring 1991, I wrote in my essay 'The Human Engagement of a Scholar':

> In research, politics and scholarship harm each other when put together and benefit each other when placed separately. If we are talking seriously about scholarly work, the development of arguments can be followed, shared criteria can be applied, and when differences arise it is easy to find a common language. . . . If we have political opinions or grievances, we can write essays or commentaries expressing them; but to give vent to one's anger at the expense of research is too costly. Many scholars from the previous two generations gave up the dignity of scholarly work to follow political authorities: will our generation sacrifice its scholarly independence to rebel against them? If that were the case, it would travel by a different path in the same direction as its predecessors. Our reason for striving to protect the independence and dignity of scholarly work is simply a belief that it will last longer than politics, and transcend popular or party interest, in representing the continuous struggle of human beings to pursue the truth.[12]

In the same spring, Wang Shouchang, Wang Hui and I came together and launched the journal *Xueren* (The Scholar), with support from Japan's International Friendship Research Foundation and the Jiangsu Literature Press. Our aim was to bring together a group of friends who shared similar interests and ideals in the then 'ever-more solitary pursuit of research', in the hope that we could help 'China's learned circles to emerge from their current low ebb.'[13] These formulations expressed the impressions, thoughts and debates of the time. The history of scholarship was the field *The Scholar* chose to concentrate on. At that time I freely admitted that one purpose of taking up this topic was to correct the oscillations in Chinese attitudes of the 1980s. I tend to attribute the 'impetuous' and 'empty' style of much

---

[12] 'Xuezhe de renjian qinghuai', first published in *Dushu*, May 1993.
[13] '"Xueren" de qinghuai yu yuanwang' (Inspirations and expectations of *The Scholar*), *Xuezhe de renjian qinghuai*, Zhuhai 1995.

intellectual life in that period to the loss of old norms and absence of new ones. But if it was a transitional moment full of passion and imagination, in which 'running wild' or 'talking through your hat' could be forgiven, the nineties might need more intellectual self-discipline, and some prosaic procedures for the hard work required to transform the 'sparkling ideas' of the previous decade into solid scholarly achievements.

Chinese intellectual traditions had a strong taxonomic bent. Their cataloguing emphasis had something in common with the history of scholarship at which we aimed. Its principal contribution was not to rank specific scholars or particular works, but rather – by 'differentiating sources and distinguishing tributaries' – to let later generations understand the trajectories of their predecessors. Generally speaking, our aim in studying the history of scholarship was to understand tradition, connect with tradition, and reflect on tradition. This would be a bit better than blindly submitting oneself to some 'isms'. We also had some doubts about approaches that borrowed from Western theories to interpret Chinese culture. Since no better theoretical framework was available, it seemed preferable to resort to an ancient Chinese technique of scholarship: leaving the question answerless (*que yi*).[14] I may not understand, but I'm thinking. For me, research like this was a kind of self-discipline. It was a bannerless 'banner', an attempt to reflect on the methods and foundations of earlier forms of scholarship, and then gradually discover the appropriate path for us to take.

How long did this 'ever-more solitary' situation last? What were the reactions to your stance?

After a year or two, our position somehow became quite well known, and people started asking about the relationship between the history of scholarship and of ideas. In principle, the two ought to have distinct approaches and perspectives. The history of scholarship concentrates more on the process of conceptualization and formulation of ideas, where the history of ideas pays more attention to their content. The former is concerned with how things are said, the latter with what is said. One reason why previous Chinese work on the history of ideas is not very satisfactory is that it tended to focus on philosophical history. By contrast, the history of scholarship explores various fields or disciplines, clarifying the concepts applied in them, reinterpreting intellectual paradigms, and employing cultural contexts to understand the evolution of ideas. The two kinds of history are actually complementary. The history of scholarship considers both ideas and the way they are formulated in learning. This is because for the Chinese, thinking

---

[14] Confucius says, '*duowen queyi*' (listen widely but omit what is doubtful); and '*queru*' (when a gentleman is ignorant, he offers no opinion). *The Analects*, Book II, Entry 18 and Book XIII, Entry 3, London 1979, pp. 65, 118. Translation modified [ed].

and learning are never entirely separate: thinking is embedded in learning.[15] But if learning and thinking cannot be completely independent of each other, the history of scholarship offers an opportunity to assess the relationship between them. For example, Liang Qichao's *Scholarly History of China in the Last Three Hundred Years* and Qian Mu's work of the same title, viewed from today's perspective, are probably histories of ideas or intellectual history.[16] Half these studies are about thinking, half about learning: the two can't be cleanly divided.

Another challenge to us came from those who considered that we were emphasizing learning, while neglecting thinking. Actually, whatever the period, scholars have never received as much attention as thinkers, a situation determined in the first instance by their different audiences. As my discourse is mainly addressed to specialists, how can I expect everyone else to show an interest in it? So in my view this is a false question. It only arose because the mass media for a time took up 'scholarship' as a topic and created the illusion that everybody was turning to scholarship and no one was talking about ideas. Personally, though I accept that learning and thinking may take various forms, I do not believe that scholars with no ideas are capable of producing great scholarship, and do not trust thinkers who spend all their time thinking without learning.

How do you handle the relationship between the two in your own work?

I believe that scholarship should first of all be pursued for its own sake, and then human engagement can be pursued as a citizen, from a scholarly background. These two activities should go hand in hand. There is no conflict between them, but they should also not be confused with each other. Certain conditions are required. (i) In practice, it is possible to let scholarship be scholarship and politics be politics. (ii) A scholar may be allowed to care about politics, or not to care, just as he wishes. (iii) When a scholar does care about politics, that concern will mainly take the form of a human engagement rather than a social responsibility. Though knowledge and understanding based on lived experience can be very precious to a scholar, they cannot be a substitute for serious scholarly thinking. We need to respect scholarly traditions (while allowing revolt against them), to understand the importance of maintaining norms in research (while allowing

---

[15] Of the relationship between thinking (*si*) and learning (*xue*), Confucius says: 'If one learns but does not think, one will be bewildered. If, on the other hand, one thinks but does not learn, one will be in peril.' *The Analects*, Book II, Entry 15, p. 65. Translation modified [ed].

[16] Liang Qichao: *Zhongguo jin sanbai nian xueshu shi*, Taipei 1955; Qian Mu, *Zhongguo jin sanbai nian xueshu shi*, Taipei 1980. '*Xueshu*' literally means 'scholarship' but this is usually rendered in English as *Intellectual History of China in the Past Three Hundred Years* – see, for example, Benjamin Elman, *Classicism, Politics, and Kinship*, 1990, p. 373 [ed].

researchers to rise above them), and to rationalize the practical operations of enquiry.

This double identity of a 'scholar's mode' and a 'citizen's role' is one that I have tried to practise in employing two writing styles. My historical studies are relatively cool in tone, rarely coloured by passion. I keep social intervention or criticism for my cultural commentaries and *causeries* (*xueshu suibi*).[17] I have consciously tried to develop distinctive styles for each. That is to say, while not directly involved in the real politics of the day, I hope that when engaging in academic research I can maintain a compassionate sensibility. This is not to be over-protective of myself, but to acknowledge the complexity of real politics. The principal reason for not giving up occasional interventions is a sense of compassion, based on the need of the self for ethical perfection; it is not a self-righteous attempt to play the role of 'spokesman of the masses' or to 'save the abandoned'. In actual practice, it is never easy to keep scholarly work and political commentary quite separate. Yet firm adherence to the belief that politics and scholarship have different rules for their respective games and should not be mixed (by utilizing scholarship for political ends or vice versa) will aid the healthy development of both. In my case, besides academic research, my cultural commentaries and *causeries* now amount to some eight collections, and the essay on 'A Scholar's Human Engagement' has been selected as reading material in a Chinese high school textbook.

What sort of principles govern your non-academic writing?

In view of the way the mass media operate, I have deliberately spaced my social interventions at considerable intervals. The difference between a scholar and a journalist lies in their different sense of distance from events. Tracing the tide of the time and struggling to speak out constantly carries the risk of being carried away by the tide and losing the conditions of independent thinking. Those who become 'celebrity scholars' find themselves unable to refuse demands from the mass media to speak out on various social problems, on a more or less daily basis. This trend started to appear in the mid-nineties, and has now developed on a major scale. Right after gaining some attention, one would be besieged by requests for opinions on any conceivable topic, and not a few were brave enough to offer answers on everything from astronomy to earth science, from social sciences to humanities – you name it. In cases like these, it becomes very

---

[17] 'To associate the learning of specialists with the taste of the literati, to take into consideration the purse and the knowledge of the reader, and to hope the result will stand frequent revisiting by book-lovers,' are the three criteria for *xueshu suibi* set out by Chen Pingyuan in 'Zongxu (Editor's words)' for *Xunzong congshu* (a series of travelogues in search of historical and cultural traces), Jiangxi 2001 [ed].

difficult to think independently, and the depth of reflection that distinguishes scholars from everyday journalists, based on a richer accumulation
of knowledge and training, is easily lost.

I should also say that my way of looking at the relationship between
thinking and learning comes in part from a belief in the value of 'unofficial
learning' (*xue zai minjian*), which in our case meant a collaboration in
editing a series of research journals, including *The Scholar*. I hope to uphold
my social concerns through these journals, as well as to shoulder some
responsibility for the reconstruction of our culture. In 1991 I wrote:

> According to our understanding of Chinese history and Chinese culture,
> 'unofficial learning' was an important way of maintaining ethical links and
> cultural norms in periods of political upheaval and social transformation.
> Instead of coveting fish from the bank – or complaining of no fish taking
> the bait – it is better to start knitting our own net. Whether or not we
> agree with the value-orientation of those who make cultural policy is one
> thing. It is quite another matter for intellectuals to make their own choice
> and effort. In recent years it has been our shared conviction that we should
> stop complaining about the weak support for scholarly research from the
> government, and start to look for forces among the people, to secure the
> economic and ideological independence of scholarly work.
>
> That these ideas materialized in the launching of the research series of
> *The Scholar* was also due to our belief that scholarship has a longer life
> than politics. So we can spare ourselves thought of temporary gains or
> losses, seeking only to make our small contribution to the prosperity of
> Chinese scholarship and the healthy development of Chinese culture. In
> our work, we aim to purge the old frameworks of historical research, in
> which heroic figures and political events overshadowed all else, and to pay
> more attention to social, economic and cultural settings. In the reality of
> contemporary life, too, we take cultural re-construction to be our main
> purpose.[18]

Furthermore, a scholar's human engagement finds direct expression in
the topics selected for research and the grounds for arguments advanced.
It is a stance that precludes the ventilation of grievances in research, the
bending of enquiries to court social trends, or irresponsible judgements
inspired by political *parti pris*. Scholarly research is by nature individualistic and aristocratic, an invincibly solitary spiritual quest. Of course, any
scholar needs to keep abreast of the work of others. But while participating in the field and responding to trends that seem most promising at the
time, he or she also needs to maintain the independence of their options.
Nowadays, when Chinese academic circles discuss various topics, what is

---

[18] '*Xueren* yu *Wenxueshi*' (*The Scholar* and *Literary History*), *Meiwen*, January 1994. *Literary
History* was another research journal set up in the early 1990s [ed].

often overlooked is the autonomous and individual nature of research decisions. In designing or deciding an academic career, many people tend to adopt a mentality of 'we' or 'ours' – what road 'we' should take, 'we mainlanders' (as in contrast to 'Taiwanese' or 'Hong Kong people'), 'we intellectuals', and so forth. But taking part in debates that range outside of academia should not come at the expense of the individuality of scholarly research. My attitude in this regard can be expressed in Zhang Taiyan's formulation – 'strengthening one's own gate.' He believed that the greatest drawback of the Chinese scholarly tradition was not excessive independence but over-extended connectedness, with no independent voice. Only if one has one's own well-formulated opinions is it possible to have a dialogue between equals, and to talk about competition between a hundred schools.

What is your view of 'Western learning' and Sino-Occidental cultural exchanges?

Ever since the Opium War forced open the door to China, relations between Chinese and Western cultures have been abnormal. In the West no one bothers about Sinocization or Westernization. Yet the same questions have always worried the Chinese. Unconscious fear and defensiveness have made it difficult for them to develop a healthy open-minded outlook. This is what among friends we often talk about as the 'backwardness complex' of twentieth-century Chinese. When they opened their eyes to see the world, they discovered that China was – and is – really backward. The result has been that, prompted by a strong sense of social responsibility, modern Chinese intellectuals have tended to tie their thinking – in philosophy, history, literature and culture – over-tightly to the single drive to make the nation rich and the army strong, to overcome that backwardness. That has obviously restricted the level and depth of their thought. If no one is willing to 'hang in the midair of nowhere,' to engage in some seemingly useless ultra-metaphysical speculation, the absolute value of our thinking, generation after generation, will not be very high. In the end, in terms of theoretical construction, the distance between us and the West will even have increased, and it will be less possible than ever to engage in a dialogue of equals.

As I work on Chinese culture, when I go abroad the people with whom I have most contact are sinologists. There are many great scholars in this field, but sinology – or 'China studies' – does not represent the highest intellectual achievement in Japan, Europe, or the United States. Although as a research subject China is now attracting more and more scholars, we should not deceive ourselves: outside China sinology is a peripheral field. In the past, we tended to compare Chinese studies of Chinese culture with studies of Chinese culture by foreigners, which is extremely unfair. For a true comparison, the achievements of Chinese scholars in the study of Chinese culture should be set beside work on Japanese culture by Japanese scholars, or French culture by French scholars. Then we might get a rough sense of where our shortcomings lie. Generally speaking, every country is more likely to produce better scholarly work in the study of its own culture, and this work provides the best insight into that nations's achievements in research.

So when visiting Japan, I deliberately sought out scholars working on Japanese cultural and intellectual history. In recent decades, one topic that has greatly preoccupied the Japanese is Edo culture, as well as the intellectual and cultural continuities between the Tokugawa and Meiji eras. I myself am very interested in the historical, literary and ideological changes of the late Qing period and early Republican China. Hence, I read quite a few works on the Edo period, trying to understand cultural continuity and mutation, how a nation gained its initial drive towards modernization, and the momentum and direction of its development. In other countries, I have to confine myself to studies on Chinese culture, because of language barriers.

If I have to assess the difference between academic research in Japan with that in Europe or America, I can speak only of the field of sinology, and probably only in general terms at that. In my view, Japanese scholars are to be much admired, for the respect they bring to their subject, for the emotional and intellectual energy that they invest in specific investigations. The research topics they usually choose tend to be relatively small in scale, but their work on them is extremely solid, with a strong commitment to historical accuracy and verification of evidence. All this makes their findings very reliable. American scholars, on the other hand, give more attention to theory, to the observation of contemporary existential conditions, and to the self-conscious analysis of the functions of academic work. Reading their works, you feel they have made a great effort in designing their intellectual framework. A Japanese scholar will tell you what subject they are working on, whereas an American scholar is more likely to explain which theory they are applying in their research project. This is a big difference in approach.

I believe Chinese scholars should be more or less critical towards both positions, as the advantages and shortcomings of each are quite obvious. However, in today's Chinese academic world, we have much more interest in and contact with China studies of the Euro-American theoretical type; and show a lack of sensitivity and patience towards the Japanese style of empirical research and the new issues or approaches emerging from their work. It should have been very important to East Asian countries to pay attention to each other's intellectual and cultural development. Yet both Japanese and Chinese academic worlds share, on the contrary, the common characteristic of according great attention to Euro-America, and not knowing their own neighbours very well. This is quite a serious problem.

For example, since the economic and cultural jump-start of East Asia, many people have begun to write about Eurocentrism. Edward Said's *Orientalism*, Paul Cohen's *Discovering History in China* and other works have been translated into Chinese and Japanese, and had a great impact. Yet they leave many questions unresolved. The Western culture we have accepted for more than a century – from notions of equality or evolution introduced by missionaries, to the advocacy of science and democracy by the May Fourth Movement, or the widespread adoption – and later national implementation – of Marxism, has accumulated so many meanings in our daily life that it has itself become a new cultural tradition. While criticizing Eurocentrism, how should we regard these now inseparable components of our own heritage? Is there not some difference between discussing 'Orientalism' in America and in China? For the American academic world to criticize conceptions of the Orient as the Other, or to accord positive value to what is Eastern, is one thing; the approach of scholars still living in the Orient – China and Japan, for example – is another. If this question is not considered, whatever people in Europe or America are working on, we would follow suit. That way we will end up as we started, doing no more than imitating others.

Do you have any sympathy with trends seeking to revive traditional culture and foster national feeling in China?

Let me clarify this issue at the outset by posing another question. What does it mean to draw on traditional culture in modern society? There are two ways of reviving a traditional culture that present no problems. The first is to appropriate elements of the tradition, separating them from the original macro-system to which they belonged and putting them to work in modern society. Examples would be a connoisseur's appreciation of the brushwork and taste of Chinese ink-paintings, or the personal cultivation of a neo-Confucian outlook. The second is the kind of instrumental exploitation you see in the application of Sun Zi's *Arts of War* to modern business competition. That kind of thing is likely to flourish with social stability and the growth of commerce and tourism: no one need worry about its future. What we are facing is another kind of pitfall. If we can only treat our intellectual and cultural ancestry in the way that a connoisseur appreciates antiques or a consumer accepts Macdonald's, instead of viewing its traditions as a spiritual complex that is still full of vitality, can we say that this is reviving traditional culture? Neo-Confucians know the importance of grasping the essence of things, and correctly stress that inner wisdom lies at the core of Chinese culture. However, they face a fundamental dilemma. How is their inner sagehood to expand outwards to a new external kingship, that comprises democracy, science and a modern economic order?[19]

---

[19] Contemporary Neo-Confucianism was popular in explaining the economic success of the so-called 'four little dragons' of East Asia in the 1980s and early 1990s. Then it was challenged

We also need to be cautious about taking a proprietorial position, as if our traditions belonged only to the Chinese people, instead of seeing in them cultural resources that they have contributed to humanity as a whole. The defect of this attitude is that it cannot maintain a rational critical spirit, let alone accomplish any creative transformation of tradition. Putting aside for a moment the rights and wrongs of the logic behind it, if we simply take its assumption of a 'live or die' antagonism between Chinese and foreign (or Oriental and Occidental) cultures, it is highly problematic. Particularly disquieting is the equation of any revival of traditional culture with an aggressive patriotism, using the banner of 'greater Chinese culture' to cover a Boxer complex. Chinese rarely view other peoples on equal terms or understand and respect another culture. Typically, when China's national power is strong, they scorn other peoples as little better than beasts, and when national strength is weak, they idolize other peoples as their masters. Neither 'idolatry of things foreign' nor 'exclusion of things foreign' are attitudes or feelings appropriate to a modern sensibility.

The rising tide of nationalism is very worrying, especially in East Asia, where economic development is swelling various national egos. The Chinese have long exhibited a Sinocentric mentality. In the twentieth century, economic backwardness mitigated this outlook for a while, but it has never been thoroughly examined with real intellectual vigour. By the 1930s, the kind of criticism made by the May Fourth generation of the 'Boxer complex' had disappeared, and since then we have rarely considered its potential negative impact in our life. When a nation is oppressed, everyone will come forward to affirm the positive value of nationalism. However, if we assume that the Chinese economy will really scale global heights in the twenty-first century, this question will have to be reassessed. Both the blind optimism of intellectuals and the government's blind encouragement of it could bring negative side-effects. On the one hand, we could encounter many problems in international affairs. On the other hand, we must remember that China is a multi-ethnic country. Nationalism is a double-edged sword. When you are a disadvantaged nation and deploy nationalism to fight against a powerful imperialism, nationalism becomes a kind of citizen solidarity. But if you are looking rationally at the formation and features of the 'Chinese nation', can you still take the same view of nationalism? China has fifty-six nationalities: from which national standpoint do you want to talk about your 'national-ism'?[20] We have to consider this question.

---

by writers invoking the Song-Ming (1000–1644) neo-Confucian ideal of 'inner sagehood leading to external kingship' (*nei sheng wai wang*) and its modern applications. For references on this topic, see Introduction, note 18 above [ed].

[20] The figure fifty-six comes from official classifications in the 1950s, after the People's Republic of China was founded, and based on Soviet-inspired criteria for distinguishing between different ethnic groups. See Fei Xiaotong, 'Ethnic Identification in China,' in *Toward a People's Anthropology*, Beijing 1981 [ed].

What problems do you see in today's 'national studies fever'?

The study of the history of scholarship in the early nineties, and the so-called fever for 'national studies' (*guoxue*), are both cases where work within the humanities attracted the attention of the mass media.[21] When this happens, scholars should keep a cool head. As a popular slogan, *guoxue* can circulate in the media; but when academic circles promote it enthusiastically, I am disturbed. Zhang Taiyan emphasized that a 'solitary path is the condition of purity and fidelity.' When you push an idea to the point of becoming an ideological trend in society, it will inevitably become blended with unfiltered elements and produce many problems. Whenever scholarship becomes a hot topic, there will be this kind of negative side-effect. *Guoxue* is a hot topic of this kind, and a sensitive one. Academic circles should be very careful in using this term. From the moment when it came into being, the concept of *guoxue* has essentially been a defensive slogan, designed to aggrandize China's historical culture in order to contest Western learning. In Han, Tang, Ming or Qing times, no such thing as *guoxue* in its current sense existed; it was born out of a contrast to *xixue* (Western learning).

The first problem here is that whenever the term of *guoxue* is mentioned, it now refers to traditional Chinese culture and scholarship, as defined by the cut-off date of the 1911 Revolution. Anything after 1912 is not considered to lie within the realm of *guoxue*. But in the process of its historical development, a national culture will mutate many times: the Song and Yuan dynasties affected the Ming and Qing, the Ming and Qing affected our modern era, and so forth. If we are to understand *guoxue* as the study of Chinese culture, then we should recognize that there is a degree of continuity that was not broken by the 1911 Revolution. If a national culture can be cut off in this way, then it is no more than a museum exhibition without impact upon contemporary social life. That is to deny its vitality.

A second problem lies in the notion of *guoxue* as a pedigreed Chinese scholarship. In fact, the concept of 'China' has itself experienced numerous changes. There is no dynasty in which foreign cultures were not received, whether it was in the spread of Buddhism from the Han to the Tang, or the penetration of Western cultures since the Ming and Qing. So there has never been a pure 'national' scholarship in any dynasty. To imagine a *guoxue* that has never been polluted by external cultures is laughable. Such a fantasy can only cause a cultural crisis, a regression expressing itself in the late Qing gesture of upholding the banner of *guoxue* to resist the influence of *xixue*. I

---

[21] Zhang Taiyan promoted the term *guoxue* when he was in Japan in 1906, as part of his revolutionary activities. By the 1920s, *guoxue* was generally accepted as designating a specialized 'China studies' field incorporated into the imported Western disciplinary structure of the new Chinese higher education system. Prior to this, 'China studies' were mainly treated either as *guogu* (national past) or *jingxue* (classical studies) [ed].

do not believe this is the road we should take. Nor should we equate the promotion of *guoxue* with a simplified patriotism, which would merely convert it into a cheap ideology. In the Republican period, when *guoxue* was also at one time a very hot topic, Hu Shih was invited to praise the national spirit of China. He replied that he was a historian: it was not because the Chinese nation was particularly great that he had started to study Chinese culture. Once you pre-suppose its extreme greatness, your judgements about Chinese culture will obey a particular scheme and method, and will lead you to a predictable conclusion. This adoption of *guoxue* as a tool in the service of ideology is very dangerous, and highly unfavourable to the development of scholarship.

How favourable do you think the present atmosphere is for scholarly research in the humanities in modern China?

In his essay *Two Cultures*, C.P. Snow examined the conflict between the kinds of knowledge represented by science and by literature. In my view, in the China of the 1990s, there has emerged a conflict between social sciences and the humanities. This has been a period of fast commercial growth and of political stability, in which the intelligentsia (*zhishi fenzi*) has been rapidly divided into different professions and interest groups. Not only do there exist great differences between those who have gone into business or politics and those who have stayed on campus, but even among those committed to academic research we find great contrasts, since the various disciplines occupy different positions in market competition. So it has become difficult to find any one stance taken by all sectors of the intelligentsia. Take higher education for example: the more capable of serving the economy a discipline is, the greater the attention it receives from the government and the support it gets from firms. What that means is that in those areas of research funding, professorial salaries, student admissions and graduate job-assignments all benefit.

The least practical of all the disciplines, of course, are none other than the age-old topics of literature, history and philosophy. Their situation is therefore the most precarious. The humanities are less welcome than such social sciences as economics, law or politics. In China this is a new phenomenon. Popular maxims tell their own story: 'honour and insult, after food and clothing'; 'existence determines consciousness'; 'the base commands the superstructure'; 'growth inevitably brings institutional change'; 'economic liberalization must lead to political democratization'. Traumatized by poverty, the Chinese – from the state down to the society – generally believe that so long as the economy continues to develop, every problem will be solved in due course. In an era of economic construction, what could be more natural than to cold-shoulder the humanities? So the different directions taken by the social sciences and the humanities have become an unavoidable issue in discussions of the contemporary structure of knowledge in China. It is probable that every country around the time of its economic take-off witnesses a withering in its humanistic scholarship. Nonetheless, in contemporary China, where economic development has become the central goal of the nation, utilitarian indifference to spiritual, moral and utopian values is now especially pronounced. This is a reality we must face, and a problem we must deal with.

Setting aside the 'great enterprise of managing the country' (*jingguo zhi daye*),[22] the history of specialized research in modern China can be roughly divided into three periods. From the turn of the century to the end of the 1940s was a time of 'individual scholarship'; from the early 1950s to the early 1980s was the period of 'planned scholarship'; and since the late 1980s, what we have seen is the emergence of 'market scholarship'. The economic and political context of each period has affected scholarly attitudes profoundly. During the first phase, though there was an exceptionally difficult spell when academics were starved during the anti-Japanese war (1937–1945), generally speaking the living standard of a university professor was far higher than that of the average citizen. On the one hand the residual authority of traditional literati in Chinese society still held, and on the other Euro-American influences throughout China gave students who had returned from overseas quite some advantage. Take the academic world of the 1920s. In Beijing, many professors enjoyed a monthly salary of 300 or 500 silver dollars, when library clerks had only six to eight each month.[23] If they could spare the energy, scholars might set up their own societies or publish journals and books at their own expense, speaking out with little concern for governmental demands or market sales. Censorship did not yet really threaten the freedom of scholarly research. As late as 1933 Cai Yuanpei could organize a commemoration of the fiftieth anniversary of Marx's death, in the name of 'serious scholarship' and 'freedom of research and freedom of thought', without interference by the authorities.[24]

After the 1950s, along with a planned economy there came planned scholarship. The state handed down topics, funding and frameworks for research. Scholars could exercise their talents only within this structure. They continued to work, as before, to feed themselves and their families, but now they could do so only indirectly, since everything was decided by

---

[22] This is a quotation from 'Dianlun lunwen' (On literature) by Cao Pi (187–226), the first emperor of the Wei Dynasty (220–265), who was also a poet and literary critic. It is the first work in Chinese history to assess contemporary authors systematically [ed].

[23] In 1919, the then President of Peking University, Cai Yuanpei (1867–1942) had a monthly salary of 600 yuan; Chen Duxiu, Dean of the Humanities, 300 yuan; and Mao Zedong, a library clerk, 8 yuan. *Beijing daxue zhiyuan xinjin biao* (Salary chart of Peking University), February, 1919.

[24] 'Ji-nian hui yuanqi' (Explanation on the commemoration activities), *Shenbao*, 13 March 1933.

the government. Since the mid 1980s, the 'employer' of scholars in the humanities has changed again. If salaries still come from the coffers of the government, income from extra-curricular teaching or publications has became a significant economic resource for scholars, weakening the sway of political authority considerably. True, economic independence is not the same as freedom of thought; but without the one, you are unlikely to have the other. On the other hand, under the tidal pressure of the commercial economy, cultural and scholarly endeavours are facing all kinds of crises. The only reason for some relief is that official will and political intervention are much less in evidence than before. However, if the market eases political dependency to a certain degree, the pressure of money can frustrate the independence and dignity of scholarship just the same. What the market wants is for academics to cater to fashion, while a true scholar in the humanities will pursue the 'independence of spirit and freedom of thought' that Chen Yinke held to be disinterested or even critical towards reality. In a sense, it is even more difficult to resist the appeal of money than the dictates of power.

If scholars in the humanities felt a peculiar sense of crisis in the 1990s, did this also reflect some universal problem in cultural development?

It did. Dialogue and interchange between high culture and popular culture has been an important aspect of China's cultural development in the twentieth century. The current rapid reversal of relations between the two is an unavoidable issue. An elite that fought hard to 'reach the popular masses' in the late Qing must now fight hard to defend its own cultural ideals. This general trend can be viewed positively as the rise of popular culture. Or negatively, as the decline of elite culture.

The year 1992 seems to have been a crucial turning point here. The swell of a commercial economy, which had been building up for some time, finally gained political recognition, when the Fourteenth Congress of the CCP formally proclaimed the goal of establishing a socialist market economy in China.[25] The official ideology thereby finally gave a green light to the market as a field of cultural choice. Even the Party's Propaganda Minister now explained that popular music, disco dancing, martial arts novels and other forms of popular culture were worth our attention – something completely unthinkable in the past. In adopting the line of 'heeding, supporting, and guiding' popular culture – 'broadening the horizon of the masses', a faint echo of past 'worker-peasant-soldier arts' – the Party's main concern was to promote the market economy and industriali-

---

[25] The Communist Party of China held its Fourteenth National Congress in October 1992.

zation.[26] With the wind of both market demand and government leadership in its sails, how could popular culture not ride high? Not to speak of economic, political and educational developments over the past century, which had long prepared the external conditions for its take-off.

Thereafter, the cultural elite has had to deal with the rules of the market. For the Don Quixotes of modern China, the worst fate was now not so much to be punished for lack of orthodoxy, as to be abandoned by the market for their 'morality', 'idealism' and 'passion'. Replacing them as a model for the time was the playful trickster of Wang Shuo's *wanzhu* who 'eludes the sublime' and 'resembles the common people'. As Wang Meng put it, this type is 'well adapted to the Four Cardinal Principles and the market economy.'[27]

How has this social change affected the intellegentsia?

The rise of popular culture in recent years is not that much of a surprise, since it continues a century-long trend. What is astonishing is that elite culture, faced with this huge challenge, was so completely at a loss. Though the press is full of reports of writers or professors going into business, the debate around the novel *A Chinese Woman in Manhattan* is probably a more significant indication of elite surrender to commercial culture.[28] A mediocre popular 'memoir' (or so-called reportage fiction), exploiting the money dream of many Chinese today, and enjoying lavish promotion and media coverage, suddenly occupied half of the sky. It is no surprise that such a book could become a bestseller. What should have been inconceivable is that a famous literary critic could announce that 'in a certain sense our future literature should start from this book', or that a well-established academic journal could publish a special feature, arguing that this book's 'pioneering role in contemporary Chinese letters is undeniable'.[29] In general, the opinions of the cultural elite – except those helpful to the sale of this kind of thing – no longer have any weight with the mass of readers. It is not the views of well-trained artists and critics, but the book trade and the media that determine their consumption. The only options left to the cultural elite are either to flirt with the masses or keep quiet. Well aware

---

[26] Xu Weicheng, 'Wei jianli shehuizhuyi shichang jingji de mubiao tigong xinxi fuwu' (Supplying information needed to establish a socialist market economy). *Xinwen chuban bao*, February 12, 1993. Xu was the head of the Propaganda Department of the Beijing Municipal Party Committee.

[27] Wang Meng: 'Duobi chonggao' (Eluding the sublime), *Dushu*, January 1993. A novelist, Wang was Minister of Culture of the PRC for more than three years. He left the post in late 1989.

[28] Zhou Li, *Manhadun de Zhongguo nüren*, Beijing, 1992.

[29] '*Manhadun de Zhongguo nüren* beishou qinglai' (*A Chinese Woman in Manhattan* is extremely popular), *Wenxuebao*, July 16, 1992; and, 'Shengming de huoyan zhengzai chilie di ranshao' (Flame of life burning brightly), *Wenxue pinglun*, No 1, 1993.

that the success of *A Chinese Woman in Manhattan* was an 'insult to the IQ of Chinese readers and critics',[30] the cultural elite could do little but look on.

The issue here is not whether popular culture possesses a progressive historical significance. Nor is it whether elite and popular cultures can help each to create an environment in which both can flourish. The point is the excessive weakness of Chinese elite culture, which has become a potential obstacle to the development of the national culture as a whole. If the burgeoning of a commercial economy is the external cause of its decline, the inner origins of this problem lie in the mistakes of Chinese intellectuals themselves – among them a pan-political outlook, an obsession with revolution, and a misunderstanding of popular literature.

The pan-political outlook came from traditional Chinese culture. The literati of imperial China were at the centre of the whole society, vested with the heavy responsibility of maintaining order for all that lay 'under Heaven'. From late Qing times onwards, this stratum was gradually transformed into a modern intelligentsia with various areas of specialized expertise. To encourage honest intellectuals to enter politics can help to improve the cultural level of politicians, but the running of a modern state has little to do with intellectual ideals, and the domination of politics over everything else has been very damaging. For a whole century Chinese intellectuals never showed any real interest in maxims such as 'scholarship for scholarship's sake' or 'art for art's sake', not because of shortcomings in these slogans, but rather because they escaped any 'practical purpose' (*zhiyong*) and could not satisfy the political passion to 'run the world' (*jingshi*). Amid ceaseless social turmoil, which fed popular expectations that the intellectual was meant to fulfil, the subordination of culture and scholarship to the uses of political reform became the basic trend throughout twentieth-century China. The other side of the coin was a distrust in the independent value of culture and scholarship, which was obviously of little help in building an elite culture without direct political function.

In this context, an obsession with revolution can be seen not only in battles for political power, but also in the cultural tocsin of 'destroying the old and establishing the new.' Culture requires accumulation and an elite requires cultivation. Elite culture on the one hand preserves and amends tradition, and on the other contests existing rules. Neither function can be dismissed. To show continuous energy, an elite culture must be capable of both preserving the old and creating the new. But the modern Chinese obsession with revolution forced intellectuals to keep up with the latest trends and so to cut off themselves from the past. Typically, they feared nothing so much as being behind the times. Such a pressure encourages a

---

[30] Zhao Yiheng, 'Baijin wenxue' (Money-worshipping literature). *Wenyi zhengming*, No 1, 1993.

radically 'critical' outlook, but not a 'constructive' one. No doubt, it is psychologically more attractive to be rebellious than to be 'traditional' or 'conservative'. Wen Yiduo wrote: 'Ours is a time of the overthrow of everything ancient'.[31] To overthrow what is ancient was not to deliberately forget one's ancestors, but rather to pursue a perfected future. Aiming at an illusory cultural utopia, intellectuals time and again denied their own past. A series of dazzling cultural debates and countless emotional slogans form a striking contrast with the rather pallid creative record of elite culture.

Last but not least, much of the celebration of popular culture today appeals for support to the May Fourth notion of a 'commoners' literature' and to Mao Zedong's idea of a worker-peasant-soldier art. This is an interesting misunderstanding. In face of the boom of popular culture since the late 1980s, the elite was powerless. After shouting for more than half a century that the country needed 'what the masses like to see and hear', it discovered that what the masses actually preferred was neither a commoners' literature nor worker-peasant-soldier arts, but a culture driven by the market. Although the pioneers of May Fourth and Mao Zedong's official line differed in their assessment of the outlook and values of the intelligentsia, each in their way sought to raise the cultural level of the masses. Today, however, the new popular culture despises both educational demands by the political authorities and the cultural elite's puritan aversion to the cash nexus. It has no compunction in 'catering to the masses' and never talks windily about raising their standards, in the service of an edifying popularization. Ours is real popularization, it maintains. All that went before was simply the intellectual elite and the political authorities taking turns to cultivate the populace.

The tension between elite and popular cultures has been one of the focuses of my research in recent years. My basic position in such research is that we need to understand popular culture and insist on elite culture. The reason I stress this here is that, as soon as 'civil society' (*minjian shehui*) is mentioned, some of my friends slide to 'folk culture' (*minjian wenhua*), and in no time mix that up with 'popular culture' (*dazhong wenhua*). This is what I cannot accept. If I had to summarize my approach as a research scholar in the humanities since the early 1990s, I would say this: between politics and scholarship, emphasize scholarship; between official learning and civil learning, promote non-official learning; between popular culture and elite culture, insist on elite culture. These three plain sentences cover the hard choices that intellectuals of a whole generation have struggled to make.

---

[31] Wen Yiduo, ' "*Xiandai Yingguo shiren*" xu' (Preface to 'modern British poets') in *Xiandai Yingguo shiren*, Shanghai 1933. For Wen Yiduo , see note 20 on p. 101 above.

4

Dividing the Big Family Assets:
On Liberty and Justice

Qin Hui

Could you say something about your background?

I was born and grew up in Nanning, the capital of Guangxi in south-west China, where my parents worked in the education bureau of the provincial administration. Both had been activists in the student movement against Chiang Kai-Shek's regime in Guilin, where my father was a local student at the Normal College and mother had arrived as a refugee from Zhejiang in 1937, and both were members of the Democratic Alliance, a small party of intellectuals close to the CCP. In the early fifties, they unsuccessfully applied for Party membership, and in 1957 were lucky to escape the Anti-Rightist campaign. Under their influence I became interested in political and intellectual issues early on.

When I was only ten, I can remember listening to broadcasts of the CCP's *Nine Open Letters to the CPSU* in the early 1960s. I could recite by heart the entire text of some of these polemical exchanges of the Sino-Soviet dispute, and even today passages from them are still fresh in my mind. I finished elementary school in 1966, the year the Cultural Revolution broke out. I spent the next three years nominally in middle school, but since teaching was suspended, there were no classes, so I and my class-mates were on the loose. When the first round of Red Guards, controlled by 'red descendants' ready to be 'successors of the Revolution' and targeting – not 'capitalist roaders' – but the 'five black castes (*hei wu lei*)', were formed in our school, I was excluded due to my 'non-red' family background. However, as elsewhere in China, this first rash of Red Guards was soon overtaken by a broader wave of youths responding to Mao's call to rebel, and in the mushrooming of further Red Guard organizations later that year, I quickly joined a dissident group, as one of its youngest members. Initially attracting neither supervision nor attention, a few of us started to run a newsletter that became widely read. This was a very exciting experience for me, increasing my self-confidence. By early 1967, a new phase saw the consolidation of various smaller groups into two big opposing Red Guard organizations. That was the beginning of a conflict that led to some of the bloodiest battles of the Cultural Revolution.

Soon Guangxi became famous throughout China for the violence of the struggles among different factions of its Red Guards, which eventually burst into a full-scale civil war. This was partly because Guangxi was the only region in the country where the provincial party secretary held onto power through the Cultural Revolution – everywhere else they were toppled. But Guangxi controls the supply routes to Vietnam, where the war with America was then at its height, and the local party secretary, Wei Guoqing, enjoyed excellent relations with the Vietnamese Party across the border, so Mao did not want him removed. Our faction battled against Wei in 1967 and 1968. Our base was mainly in a poor district of the city. Here I had eye-opening lessons in sociology. Our supporters were marginalized poor city-dwellers, who did not pay much attention to our ideological rhetoric, but voiced with great energy their accumulated grievances against government officials. Economic activities in our 'liberated areas' were also far from 'planned'. Rather, the ghetto part of the district was full of various stalls and street vendors. When we students were at one point considering surrender after the Central Cultural Revolution Group leadership in Beijing announced unequivocal support for our opponents, the poor wanted to fight on. They included port and ferry workers on the Yong River, whom the faction led by Wei accused of being a *lumpen*-proletariat, closer to a mafia than a modern industrial working class. The contrast between the rhetorical slogans of rival student factions and the actual social divisions between the groups that rallied behind them was striking in Guilin too, where I arrived in the winter of 1967. There, unlike in Nanning, our faction held municipal power, while most of the poor supported Wei's faction, and resisted efforts to bring them to heel. In effect, ordinary people tended to support the weaker side in these conflicts – whoever was out of power – and once they had made their choice were also more resolute than students in fighting to the end.

After a lot of violence in 1967, the final showdown came in the summer of 1968, when Mao launched a campaign to bring a halt to the nationwide chaos before the Ninth Party Congress in early 1969. In Guangxi, Wei and his allies mobilized some 100,000 troops and militants, a much larger force than ours, to crush the opposition. There was heavy fighting in Nanning, where our group was barricaded in an old district of the city, with no more than a hundred rifles among us. Both poor city-dwellers and port workers suffered heavy losses, as did the students who stayed with them. Twenty of my schoolmates were killed in the siege. I was lucky to escape: just before the showdown, I had gone to my mother's home town in Zhejiang, so was away when the attack was launched. When I came back, our middle school, like all other work-units and street committees in Nanning, was consolidating the regime's victory by setting up a new student organization under official control, ostensibly still with the name of Red Guards. The after-effects of the fighting were strong in this new organization and I did not become a member in it. But all students were mobilized to conduct 'voluntary' work to clean up the streets, many of which had been entirely levelled, in scenes reminiscent of *The Defense of Stalingrad*.

Nowadays, officially sanctioned studies of the Cultural Revolution blame the 'rebels' for all the disasters of the time, denying that they might have been fighting against previous oppressions, confusing sociological distinctions between the rebels and the loyalists, and telling of the sufferings of previous power-holders without mentioning the cruelties they inflicted upon the rebels. This is of course wrong. On the other hand, however, when others regard the rebels as an early expression of enlightened resistance to the establishment, they may also go too far. We students were certainly guided ideologically from above and 'rebelled in accordance with the decree'. But even the grassroots city-dwellers, who were of a much lighter ideological colour than we, also lacked enlightenment reason and to a large extent replayed the traditional drama of peasant uprisings – a far cry from the sort of struggle later seen in the Polish Solidarity.

What happened after the repression in Nanning?

A year later, our class was ready to graduate although no real instruction had been offered or taken. Three types of assignments awaited us, based on political performance, family background and age-set – becoming a worker in a factory, a peasant in the countryside, or a student studying in school. There was little chance for members of our faction to get into a factory. But, as I was not yet sixteen, and considered too young to start working, I was given the opportunity of continuing my 'education' for another two years. That I declined, with my parents' support. So I was sent with a mass of other youngsters to be resettled in the countryside. My time of fraught romance in the Red Guards came to an end, and the heavy romantic burden of sent-down youth became my lot. In 1969 I arrived in Tianlin County, to overcome the division between mental and manual labour by working with peasants.

Tianlin County is in the mountainous corner of Guangxi, bordering Yunnan to the west and Guizhou to the north. Its regional capital is Bose, where Deng raised the flag of the Guangxi Soviet in 1930. This is a Zhuang minority area, where the population speaks a language more closely related to Thai than Chinese. Three of us – all boys – were dispatched to a tiny village of eleven families, from which we had to walk a sixty-*li* mountain trail to reach a highway, usually at night in order to avoid paying for boarding, to catch a truck and visit the county town, some 100 kilometres away. Many villagers never got to Tianlin County town in their life. Five years later, I was transferred with a dozen other students to a larger village of seventy households. In Tianlin life was very hard, because of the poverty of the people, even though natural conditions were nothing like as dire as in the barren lands or Gobi desert of north-west China, where so many other students from big cities were sent. Tianlin is in the sub-tropical zone, and the land is so fertile that one should be able to survive from wild fruits and plants, without even working too much. The staple food crop is corn. What poverty meant to the peasants was their virtually complete lack of money. Yet, in this region of natural subsistence the Great Leap Forward had managed to create mass starvation by taking too many people off the land to work at producing steel and not allowing them to return. Around 1959 people had starved to death in every village in our commune. There is no question that the famine was a consequence of the social system rather than a natural disaster.

What were your relations like with the peasants?

I spent five years in the first village and four years in the second. I was the only one among the sent-down youths in our commune to stay for nine years altogether. After almost two decades, when our group went back to visit the villages, I was the only one still able to communicate with the locals in Zhuang. These years in the countryside affected me deeply, but that doesn't mean I had the best relations in my cohort with the villagers. It wasn't that I looked down on them. Rather, I had gone there with the preconception that they would be the ideal teachers to help me to reform my petty bourgeois outlook. However, the peasants in reality were no sages. People who worshipped them would have no more been able to make friends with the villagers than those who discriminated against them. In contrast, some of our group mixed easily with the peasants, swapping dirty jokes or sharing gossip, even if behind their backs they might dismiss the peasants as blinkered or stupid. For me, these were all superficial phenomena: what I was looking for was the 'essence' of poor peasants. Unfortunately, the villagers rarely showed their 'essence', except in organized political study sessions. Years later, I realized that this essentializing attitude towards people and life was no other than the 'alienation' that became a hot topic in the 1980s.

My good relations with the villagers came mainly from my intention to transform myself into a 'real' – and model – peasant. When they were reluctant to be drafted for infrastructural labour away from home, I'd always volunteer to go. Whatever I could do to help them with practical problems, I would. Though I had resolved to be truly independent, declining my parents' offer to send me parcels, I did ask my family many times to get medicine for the village. So the peasants eventually took to me. When I finally left the village – the last sent-down youth to go back to the cities – most families in the village had someone come to see me off. No one wept, but they expressed their respect for me. Frankly speaking, though I worked very hard for nine years, I never became really intimate with poor peasants. Since the late 1970s, there has been abundant literature about the experience of sent-down youth. Most of these works fall into two categories: either lamentations over years wasted in the backlands, or plaintive eulogies for the authenticity of life in the countryside, which is so much in contrast to the desire-saturated cities. I have lost interest in both. Certainly I still preserve a warm feeling for the land where I 'contributed my youth', as the popular saying today would put it, but this is a personal sentiment. I have both positive and negative memories from those years, but they are no reason for me to place those who live in cities higher than those who live in the countryside, or vice versa; or to believe that one should 'educate' the other, as Mao said of both at different stages of his career. I still have many friends in Tianlin County, but these are personal ties – they do not 'represent the peasantry'.

I say this because nowadays people often jump to the conclusion that I study rural society because of my connection to that past. While it is certainly true that first-hand experience of the countryside affected my later research, I believe my studies are inspired by reason rather than sentiment. It is not accurate to say that I am a fighter for peasant interests. As a scholar, I cannot run for a position in a peasant union or a village committee. What I do is merely try to help peasants acquire and exercise the civil rights, such as the right to organize, that would allow them to protect their own interests. The material interest of peasants is not always the same as my own. What we have in common is an interest in civil rights. These are of concern to intellectuals, peasants, workers and others as well. My research area is rural society, but as a social commentator I also care about the rights of workers and other social groups. I don't regard myself just as a spokesman for peasant interests.

What about your intellectual development in these years?

When I was in the countryside, I had something of a reputation as a bookworm among the villagers. My reading was very wide, including practical works on medicine, agricultural machinery, water and electricity supply, and other rural technologies. The knowledge I acquired enabled me to solve many problems in village life and improved my relations with the villagers. In my last three years there, I also did some work for the county cultural bureau. There I developed a keen interest in local Zhuang customs and culture, collected folk songs and improved my knowledge of the Zhuang as a distinctive ethnic group. My interest was anthropological, more prompted by a desire for knowledge than a wish to identify myself with this minority people. More importantly, I kept up my interest in social theories during this period, mainly by reading books published for 'internal circulation' only. Due to the remoteness of our county, no one there cared much what I was reading. There I learnt how to read English on my own, with the help of the Chinese pin-yin system, a deaf and dumb method of learning that stood me in good stead for many years to come. Most of my books I had brought from home, but another major source was the county library in Tianlin. Since not many people were interested in reading at that time, and regulations were few, I could borrow books whenever we got leave to go there. In the 1960s the government had printed a series of titles for 'internal circulation' only, as material for its ideological campaign against Soviet revisionism. Some of these were restricted to the level of county and above. But since no one else was interested in them in Tianlin County, I not only read them carefully but could also take some of these volumes away with me. So I don't regard myself as especially deprived in these years. My copy of *The Socialized Agriculture of the USSR* by American scholar Naum Jasny was printed in August 1965. Other titles included *The New Class* by Djilas. My case was not such a rarity. In the last years of the Cultural Revolution, many Chinese had their eyes opened by works analysing the Soviet system. We could easily relate what we read to what we were experiencing. But these books didn't change my faith in Communism. In fact I became a Party member while in the countryside and remained an ardent Communist, without any doubts about the system, throughout my youth.

What did you do after your time in the villages?

After the fall of the Gang of Four, my parents – who had been sent to the countryside too, in another county – were restored to their posts in Nanning in 1978. There they asked for teaching jobs, and later retired after a few years as academics. The year of 1978 was a significant one for the whole family. Since no open entrance examination was offered for a decade under the Cultural Revolution, universities had to recruit undergraduates and postgraduates from scratch, in a single year. Within a month, my parents came back to Nanning, my sister was admitted to college after passing the newly resumed national college entrance examinations, and I applied – and was accepted – for graduate studies at Lanzhou University in Gansu province, in the far north-west of China. So I went straight from elementary school to postgraduate work, skipping middle school and undergraduate stages – a career made possible, of course, only by the Cultural Revolution. After such a long time in the villages, I had a tremendous drive to study, which absorbed me so completely that I never took a vacation till I got my master's degree three years later and then a job teaching at Sha'anxi Normal University in the venerable city of Xi'an in the early eighties.

What drew you to north-west China?

I chose Lanzhou University to do my graduate study because Professor Zhao Lisheng had been exiled there as a Rightist since the fifties. My reading had convinced me that he was the best historian of land tenure and peasant wars in China. I wanted to work under him and had sent him some try-out essays from my village. Class analysis of land tenure and rent relations, and of social struggles erupting into peasant wars, were the traditional themes of Marxist studies of the peasantry. But Chinese Marxist historians of an earlier generation, such as Guo Moruo and Fan Wenlan, did not concern themselves with the peasantry.[1] Instead, it was actually Chinese Troskyists – who as a school did not have a high regard for peasant movements, in theory or in practice – who published a two-volume *Study of the History of Chinese Peasant War* in the early 1930s, without much response or sequel. After the Liberation Zhao Lisheng had been responsible for laying the foundations of the modern study of peasant wars in China. This was a 'New Historiography' inspired by Marxism, with a great deal of energy and vitality in both empirical research and social criticism. It is very regrettable that it later declined into an ideological instrument of the regime. Yet to retreat from it back to the earlier kind of dynastic history of successive imperial clans was no less tragic. Unfortunately, these were to be the two options most scholars in the field took in the eighties and nineties. At the time, it was mainly old paradigms that rekindled people's interest without provoking much thought. It was concern about these developments in the field since the fifties that drew Zhao and myself together, but after I got to the university we both gave up our interest in the 'theoretical' debates of the time and turned to empirical studies. We wanted to map out the social visions animating peasant rebellions – naturally, neither scientific socialism nor capitalism – and believed our research had to be primarily empirical if we were to judge existing paradigms with the necessary distance.

This preoccupation directed my attention to an area in what is today Yunnan and Sichuan, where during the transition between Ming and Qing rules, a rebel peasant regime set up a militarized system of production that replaced patriarchal social organization with an equal distribution of land and its products. I called this historical model 'agrarian socialism in a patriarchal society based on small peasant production'. The utopian nature of these arrangements was eradicated in subsequent reforms and the system became 'normal' again. Compared to previous studies of the Taiping rebellion, my research relied less on official decrees or programs and more

---

[1] Guo Moruo (1892–1978), Fan Wenlan (1891–1969): leading Chinese Marxist historians, responsible for establishing the CCP's orthodox interpretation of Chinese history from ancient to modern times, before the founding of the People's Republic in 1949 [ed].

on records documenting how economic activities were conducted in this patriarchal version of 'public ownership' in a small-peasant economy. Two long research papers came out of this master's thesis.[2]

On taking up a teaching job in Xi'an, I kept searching for new paradigms to understand the long history of a peasant economy in China, and this led me to broader comparative perspectives. My first focus was on the economic origin of China's recurrent peasant uprisings. The traditional communist explanation of peasant wars in ancient China synthesized them in the formula of 'rent relations→land appropriation→peasant rebellion', in which the emphasis fell on rental and property conflicts between landowners and peasant tenants, conceived as class struggles, and state repression was theorized as an extension of the political power of the landowners. However, what I found on studying the record of peasant uprisings across China, in regions with diverse rent relationships in the late Ming, was the reverse of this sequence. The main body of peasant armies was not made up of tenants but of well-to-do villagers or even small landlords who could not take state exploitation any longer. That is why peasant rebellions occurred mostly in areas where tenancy was rather underdeveloped, while the lower Yangtze Delta – where rent relationships were most advanced – rarely saw such eruptions. In other words, it was not that class struggle intensified to the point where armed conflict finally broke out between peasants and the state. Rather it was conflicts between rulers and ruled which unleashed further clashes between the rich and poor in vast rural areas. The division between the powerful and the powerless was the primary factor, and the distinction between those who owned property and those who did not has been secondary in detonating large-scale peasant wars in Chinese history. Only when pre-modern political privilege and status institutions were dissolved would property distinctions (land included) become dominant as the cause of 'class' divisions as in Chinese Marxist explanations for conflict.

This hypothesis received further support in my research on the rural economy of the Guanzhong plain in central Sha'anxi. There I found a 'landlord-less feudalism' in which renting was much less common than self-sufficient labour and patriarchal forms were much less active than direct interventions by local government. In the absence of intermediate local communities between an authoritarian state and registered peasant households, small peasants were subordinated directly to a traditional power structure and never acquired the characteristics of a petty bourgeois class. The upper class exploited the peasantry, not through its position as proprietors of land or capital, but via the state, which operated as a kind of omni-

---

[2] 'Houqi Daxijun yingzhuang zhidu chutan' (Preliminary study on the camp-production system in the late Great West Army); 'Daxijun zhi dian shiqi de nongye' (Agriculture in Yunnan under the Great West Army). See Qin Hui, *Geng yun zhe yan* (The cultivator speaks), Shandong, 1999.

community ruling the whole population through its tax-registration system (*qiminbianhu*).³ In this model, the connotation of the term 'feudalism' differs from its commonly understood meaning in discussions of West European history or in Chinese Marxist discourse. Yet the term helped me to interact and engage with existing interpretations of the Chinese rural economy. The key point for me was not to dispute over the 'proper' definition of feudalism, but to re-examine the concepts of private landownership and rent relations in the theoretical paradigm that had long dominated our field.

This interest led me towards a comparative study of antiquity. Chinese scholars had worked a lot on comparing the Warring States-Qin-Han period (475 B.C.–220 A.D.) and the Graeco-Roman epoch in the West. Interest in these topics revived in the eighties when works on the Greek city-state and the origins of capitalism by the pioneering communist scholar Gu Zhun were rediscovered.⁴ My essays in this area mostly started from problems in Chinese economic history, and then looked at the way many of our underlying concepts contained assumptions imported from studies of Western Antiquity that did not really fit Chinese evidence. I thought we needed new paradigms that would shift attention from the mode of production to the mode of distribution. But I also assessed new interpretations of the Graeco-Roman economy and proposed alternative models for understanding it. For example, scholars have noticed that in the modern capitalist agriculture of the West today the family farm is the most popular form, which employs a limited number of labourers; whereas in the north China plain of pre-modern times traditional (or 'feudal') agriculture was dependent on large amounts of wage-labour. I pointed out another significant contrast: that rent relations and tenancy were far more highly developed in the Roman Empire than in China under the Han, although the two shared many similarities in credit relations, which were strikingly different from the high-interest loans of Mediaeval Europe or the Tang period. In another paper examining the circulation of gold in the Han and Roman economies, which in both empires stimulated commerce, I argued against the applica-

---

³ Qin Hui and Jin Yan, *Tianyuanshi yu kuangxiangqu: Guanzhong moshi yu qianjindai shehui de zai renshi*, (Pastoral poetry versus rhapsody: the Guanzhong model and the rethinking of pre-modern society), Beijing 1996.

⁴ Gu Zhun (1915–1974), a pioneer of modern accounting in China and a Party member since the 1930s, who was head of Shanghai's Municipal Finance and Taxation Bureau in 1949–1952, before being removed for promoting modern fiscal methods against a commune-style approach. Twice labelled a 'Rightist', in 1957 and 1965, he died in isolation during the Cultural Revolution, while studying the origins of capitalism and modern democracy. He was officially rehabilitated in 1979. Posthumous publication of his writings include: 'Ziben de yuanshi jilei he zibenzhuyi fazhan' (Primitive accumulation and the development of capitalism), *Shehui kexue*, May 1981; *Xila chengbang zhidu* (The Greek City-State System), Beijing 1982; *Gu Zhun wenji* (The Collected Works of Gu Zhun), Guizhou 1994 [ed].

bility of the notion of a 'gold standard' or – later – Gresham's law in either case.[5]

So while trying to follow Western scholarship on Classical Antiquity, I realized the danger of uncritically adopting whatever was the most recent trend in it. My general conclusion was that, ever since the debate between Meyer and Niebuhr in the nineteenth century, modernizing and historicist interpretations of Classical Antiquity had alternated in the West. In the modernizing line of interpretation, from Mommsen to Rostovtsev and early Soviet scholarship, similarities between ancient Greece or Rome and the contemporary West were emphasized. But by the end of the twentieth century, the hot topic in Ancient history was the dissimilarity between the two – that is, the non-capitalist aspects or 'primitive' features of the classical world. In my essays, I made use of many of the new findings of scholars like Moses Finley, Duncan-Jones and others, but personally I lean more to the modernizing side, no doubt determined to a certain extent by my 'modernization complex' as a social being in today's China.

My research on this period provoked some debate among Chinese economic historians. I still think many of my analyses are valid. However, at the time I did not pay enough attention to economic intervention by the autocratic state, exemplified by the extraordinary capacity of the Qin-Han state to mobilize human resources on a huge scale for imperial projects.[6] In this respect, the Han dynasty was closer to the Byzantine than to the Roman empire. The 'de-clanification' unleashed by the Qin and Han did not mean that ties of kinship were eroded by any individual rights of the citizen, but that the autocratic state crushed kinship rights. The process was comparable to the way Byzantine imperial power dismantled Roman lineage rights. The omission of these from Byzantine codes, though apparently quite 'modern' in its purge of the lineage residues of the Roman Republic, actually moved Byzantium farther away from notions of citizenship and closer to the norms of Oriental despotism. The dissolution of local communities under the Qin and Han also took the authoritarian state, not the individual, as its standard. This was a liquidation of patriarchy that led away from a civil society.

Do you feel your intellectual development benefited from the opening up of the 1980s – more generally, what is your view of that period?

Retrospectively, you could say I benefited. My career proceeded quite smoothly, as I climbed the academic ladder from lector to professor, but in

---

[5] 'Gudian zudian zhi chu tan' (Preliminary examination of the tenant-rental system in Antiquity), 'Guanyu gudian jingji zhong de pingdeng lirunlü' (On the average interest rate in the ancient economy), and 'Han jin xinlun' (A new examination of gold in Han times) now collected in Qin Hui, *Shichang de zuotian yu jintian* (Market: Past and Present), Guangdong 1998.

[6] Cf. W.J.F. Jenner, *The Tyranny of History*, London 1992, p. 21 [ed].

terms of intellectual stimulus or inspiration, I was very disenchanted at the time. By the late eighties, interest in peasant history had declined substantially. Conservative scholars were now turning back to traditional dynastic studies – 'the twenty-four lineage histories' of Liang Qichao's phrase[7] – while others were caught up in the ever hotter 'cultural fever' of the time, making all kinds of generic comparisons between China and the West or between 'East and West', in which culture became an index of national character rather than a historical or social phenomenon. Dwelling on the differences between 'China and the West' became a way of minimizing the differences between past and present, elite and masses, power-holders and commoners within China. Of course, I acknowledge that the 'cultural fever' of the 80s, like the May Fourth New Culture Movement of the late 1910s, was a significant moment of intellectual enlightenment. But whereas in the May Fourth period there was a vigorous clash of various 'isms', now all people could talk about was 'culture', to a point where many modern notions like liberal democracy or social democracy were obfuscated by being wrapped into 'Western culture'. Consequently, there was no real debate between opposite positions as occurred in the aftermath of the May Fourth period, particularly between conservative and radical standpoints.

Symptomatic of the emptiness of the period was the substitution in my own field of the 'tenancy-rent relationship' paradigm by visions of a 'harmonious village community', its ethos protected by the resistance of the local gentry to the penetration of the imperial state. Understandably, this paradigmatic shift occurred first of all in academic disciplines – rather than through practical social reform, as with Liang Shu-ming in the 1920s[8] – particularly in sociology and anthropology with their typical interest in small communities and cultural differences. Its drawback lies in the key questions it evades. For example, if the 'traditional' local community was so harmonious, how do we explain the large-scale peasant wars that repeatedly exploded in China and notably disrupted its socio-political and economic life? There was never any real debate about this.

That led me to reconsider my understanding of peasant society in general. I started by looking afresh at Marxist theories of peasant society and their import or transformation in the practice of Russian Social Democrats from Plekhanov to Lenin. Meanwhile I was also surveying the field in the contemporary Anglophone world, studying the work of Teodor Shanin; the debates between James Scott and Samuel Popkin on 'moral' versus 'rational' peasants in Southeast Asia; and works by sinologists like Philip Huang on

---

[7] The phrase refers to the twenty-four dynastic houses in Chinese history. For Liang Qichao see note on p. 77 above [ed].

[8] Liang Shu-ming (1893–1988): thinker and reformer who taught at Beijing University in 1917–24, when his book *Dongxi wenhua jiqi zhexue* (Eastern and Western cultures and their philosophies) sparked a major intellectual controversy; later involved in other debates, while leading the 'rural reconstruction movement' of 1927–1937 [ed].

the involution of the Chinese agrarian economy.[9] Then I moved to the Russian tradition of peasant studies represented by Chayanov, whose theories caught my attention for the first time in 1985, when I collaborated with my wife, Jin Yan, a specialist in the study of Eastern Europe, in research on Russian history. We learned about Chayanov through the writings of Shanin and Daniel Thorner in English, and of earlier Japanese scholars of the 1920s engaged in field-work for the South Manchurian Railway Company – the Japanese and the Germans were the first to make use of Chayanov's ideas. In 1996 we arranged for Chayanov's book *Peasant Economic Organization* to be translated into Chinese.[10] This new direction took me out of narrowly defined peasant studies and provided me with a broader perspective on Chinese history. Before we had the saying 'The Chinese question is essentially the problem of Chinese peasants'. Now we should rather say 'The peasant question is essentially a problem of China's modernization'.

So, even while I was disenchanted by shifts in my own field, not to speak of the cultural scenes of the 1980s, I gained a great deal intellectually in this period. It was after all a very lively time, with an enlightening atmosphere everywhere. Basically I remained in an academic milieu, never joining in intellectual activities outside my – gradually broadening – professional field. Politically, most people were optimistic about the future of reforms, and I myself still believed in the system and its capacity to change itself for the better.

What changed your political outlook?

The social movement of 1989 altered everything. Xi'an was soon affected by the unrest in Beijing. After about a month, as students started their boycott of classes, teachers were drawn into the uproar, and there was increasing commotion everywhere, but I was so intent on my own work that I didn't take much notice. I remember that on May 16, as the wave of protest against the government reached its peak, I went as usual to the classroom with my briefcase on an entirely deserted campus. On May 20 martial law was declared, and a curfew imposed. In the following days, students were extremely disappointed at not being able to locate radical intellectuals who had been active up to May 20. Then the provincial Party committee endorsed martial law and ordered every Party member to express their support of it. There I could no longer be silent. On May 24 I

---

[9] Teodor Shanin, *The Awkward Class: Political Sociology of Peasantry in a Developing Society, Russia 1910–1924*, Oxford 1972; J.C. Scott, *The Moral Economy of the Peasant: Rebellion and Subsistence in Southeast Asia*, New Haven 1976; S. Popkin, *The Rational Peasant: The Political Economy of Rural Society in Vietnam*, Berkeley 1979; Philip Huang, *The Peasant Economy and Social Change in North China*, Stanford 1985.

[10] *Nongmin jingji zuzhi*, Beijing 1996; See A.V.Chayanov, *Peasants and Economic Anthropology*, edited by Paul Durrenberger, New York 1984 [ed].

composed a statement of protest and went with some others in the local branch of the Party, of which I was still a member, to put it up as a big-character-poster, denouncing the imposition of martial law and removal of Zhao Ziyang as Secretary General of the Party, as violations of the CCP's constitution. Reaffirming the democratic rights of Party members, the poster gave the 'Four Cardinal Principles' of the CCP an anti-authoritarian rather than anti-liberal twist, demanding 'insistence on collective leadership against personal totalitarianism; insistence on socialism against feudalism; insistence on Marxism against mediaeval-style Inquisition; and insistence on the people's democratic dictatorship against dictatorship over the people'.

Thus I got involved in a movement that already seemed doomed to defeat. The poster became quite influential in Xi'an at the time. Then came the crackdown of June 4. In Xi'an demonstrations and civil resistance against the repression lasted till June 10. These events were a watershed for me. In a long essay on the social movement of 1989, Wang Hui has recently argued that the movement was attached to the values of the socialist past and opposed to those of liberalism.[11] If the socialism he is talking about is democratic socialism, then this definitely played a part in 1989, but when he claims it was anti-liberal, he is quite wrong. My call to 'insist on the Four Cardinal Principles' was more 'socialist' than the examples Wang Hui gives in his essay, yet it was emphatically not anti-liberal.

This was the first time I became directly involved in current affairs. That doesn't mean I had no sense of contemporary realities in my research. But up to 1989 my main frustration was the crisis in our field – which direction should it take? – while after 1989 my concerns became focused on questions like: Where should Chinese peasants go? Where should a peasant China go? What direction should I myself take? Thus, when most intellectuals were turning away from the grand discourses of the 'cultural fever' to empirical studies of specific questions, I turned from my empirical studies to develop a greater interest in theoretical '-isms' in the early nineties. In 1994, I transferred to work in a Beijing research institute and the next year started teaching in Tsinghua University. In the late nineties, '-isms' came back into fashion again, and I am once more ready to return to empirical studies. In my view, a weakness of the current intellectual scene in China is the separation of debate over '-isms' from examination of 'questions' in social reality. The merit of general '-isms' lies in the universal values that inform them. Yet the specific theory of a given '-ism' is usually constructed in response to particular historical questions, not universal ones. Therefore, when we advocate universal values we should be careful not to confuse them with universal questions. My rule is: '-isms' can be imported; 'questions' must be generated locally; and theories should always be constructed independently.

---

[11] Wang Hui, *China's New Order*, edited and introduced by Theodore Huters, Cambridge, Mass., 2003 [ed].

What were the broader perspectives in your field that you were developing in the nineties?

Actually, already studying problems of the peasantry and comparative Antiquity in Sha'anxi, I had gradually became convinced that what was happening in China should be seen within a much longer-term process of human development. This was the period, of course, when the people's communes were dissolved and the household-responsibility system, which returned economic initiative back to individual farmers, was introduced. That was the key change in the first phase of the Reform Era under Deng Xiaoping. I interpreted it as the latest episode in the millennial struggle of human society to 'cast away the bonds of community in search of individual freedom'. The first stage of this process, I thought, was to advance from the primitive tribal community to the classical society of freemen (I did not believe a 'slave society' was an appropriate definition for Antiquity); the second stage was to move from the feudal patriarchal community to a pre-modern citizen society; and the third was now to advance from our Soviet-style 'iron rice-bowl' community towards a democratic socialism that I believed to be the goal of reform at the time.

After 1989, many people thought that the military crackdown would interrupt the reform process, including economic reforms, and bring a reversion to the old 'iron rice-bowl' system. My wife and I believed the opposite. In our view, after the gunshots of June 4 had torn away the gentle veil of the 'grand patriarchal family', the process of 'dividing up family possessions' would probably speed up. Though the chances of a democratic division had become slim, the 'paramount patriarch', after the showdown with the 'juniors', would have little interest in stitching the previous 'grand clan' together again. More probable was a development resembling Stolypin's suppression of the 1905 revolution, which sped up the dissolution of the Russian *mir*. We already sensed that a Stolypin-style combination of political control and economic 'freedom' was brewing. With Deng's southern tour of 1992, it duly arrived.

Theoretically, our interest in the community and its dissolution came mainly from Tönnies's *Gemeinschaft und Gesellschaft*. Though Tönnies sometimes associated 'community' with circles of acquaintance, by contrast with the 'society' of a nation, the emphasis of his distinction between them did not fall on differences of scale, but of dependence: the members of a *Gemeinschaft* were bound to it, whereas in a modern civil society they were independent agents.[12] Well before Tönnies, the young Marx often used the term *Gemeinwesen*, sometimes interchangeably with *Gemeinschaft*, in his philosophical writings, without assigning specific references in social history

---

[12] Ferdinand Tönnies, *Community and Society*, Ann Arbor 1957 [ed].

to either term. But in his later works of political economy and social history, he uses them in a sociological sense close to that of Tönnies to designate a social ensemble bound by status found in ancient or underdeveloped societies. Marx's conception of the historical movement from 'community' to 'civil society' has the same progressive connotation as its counterpart in Tönnies.

There are differences. Marx not only offers a materialist and voluntarist explanation of this process, but defines community in a far broader way than Tönnies. In a famous dictum he declared that 'the more deeply we go back into history, the more does the individual appear as dependent, as belonging to a greater whole'. In his view the evolution of this 'whole' passed through successive forms, from the single family to the tribe, and then through 'conflict and fusion' into a total unity squatting above all smaller communities, that was the 'Asian state'.[13] In all these types of community, personal character is suppressed, individuals are merely parts attached to the whole as property of the community, and from individual dependence on the community there derives the attachment of all members of the community to the patriarchal figure at the head of it. It is not until the development of a 'civil society' that the individual can break the bonds of the community, by 'the force of exchange', and achieve human independence – and then subsequently overcome the 'alienation' of private property, and advance to an ideal state in which individuals are both free and united. Whereas land and other assets were once distributed according to naturally emergent or politically determined relations between rulers and ruled, they become elements in the private exchange of all products, abilities and activities, before developing further into free exchange between united individuals. Then labour overcomes its own alienation, to become the first need in life and the highest satisfaction of free individuals.[14]

These ideas experienced some minor changes in later Marx, but his basic view of the evolution of members of the community into independent individuals remains the same. Up to the rise of Stolypin, Russian Social Democrats differentiated themselves from Populists by holding to the same position. Plekhanov spoke of the 'exploiting commune and exploited individual'.[15] This tradition shared a common intellectual ground with Tönnies. But where he spoke of the diameter of direct human interaction, in which local knowledge could spread by oral communications, and of 'natural' kin or geographical ties, Marx – who also talked about 'naturally formed' communities – envisaged variations in them, from the clan to the Asiatic state, from primitive tribal systems to mediaeval feudalism.

The appearance of these different types of society did not fall into any

[13] Karl Marx, *Grundrisse*, Penguin/NLR edition, London, 1973, p. 84 [ed].
[14] *Grundrisse*, pp. 18, 104–105, 161–165, 197, 471–515, 493, 496, 517 [ed].
[15] 'Our Differences', *Selected Philosophical Works*, Moscow 1961, vol. 1.

chronological sequence. Forms of social community and the way they changed over time differed widely in China and in the West. From Classical Antiquity to Mediaeval and Early Modern times, European society was more based on small communities, whereas China developed the overriding super-community from the Qin (221–207 B.C.) onwards. Thus, whereas in Europe modernization meant a union of the individual citizen and a supreme community, the monarchical state, against the power of the feudal lord in the small community, in China we may have to consider the possibility of the individual citizen and the small community of villages joining forces against the everlasting supreme power of the huge central state, if the goal of modernization – to make the individual citizen both the foundation and the end of society – is to be realized.

What political conclusions do you draw from this macro-historical outlook?

I believe that, whatever the route to the final break-up of the community, its dissolution always poses three questions. First, to cast off the bonds of the community and to lose the protection of the community are two sides of the same process. The individual is 'freed' of them, in both senses. The gentle veil goes together with the restrictive ties; to break away from patriarchal authority while keeping patriarchal obligations, or to shed patriarchal obligations while keeping patriarchal authority are equally impossible. Nonetheless, the two sides of the process are of different significance for different social classes, whose members typically stand to make distinct, indeed conflicting, gains or losses from them. Therefore each social class will inevitably fight for a 'division of the family assets' that best suits its own interests.

What this means, secondly, is that the question of how to divide up the family assets is more important than whether or not to divide them. The traditional Marxist stress on conflicts of interest and class struggle is reasonable enough, but has its limitations. Besides its tendency to view 'struggle' in absolute terms, denying any possibility of compromise or cooperation between classes, or even lauding 'dictatorship', which people have long noticed, what is more important is that this line emphasizes only disputes over 'whether to divide', assigning reactionary classes to backward society and revolutionary classes to advanced society. In practice, disputes over whether to divide certainly do exist, but often it is a dispute over 'how to divide' that really intensifies a conflict. No one is ever inherently in favour of either the division or preservation of the community. That is also true of a social class. In Ancient Greece and Rome, both aristocrats and commoners betrayed tribal traditions. In early modern France, both royalists and Jacobins destroyed the rural commune. In today's China, the 'big wok community' is being broken up under a dual pressure from the 'uncaring father and disloyal sons'.

Thirdly, disputes over 'how to divide' do not distinguish competing groups as 'radical' or 'conservative', but do involve issues of justice and injustice, with considerable consequences for subsequent historical development. When human society evolves beyond the forms of a tribal community, it makes a difference whether it takes an Athenian or a Macedonian path. Along the former, a lineage polity dominated by elders is transformed into a democratic polity or classical civil society by a commoners' revolution (including the cancellation of debts and the equal distribution of land by Solon and the Leges Liciniae Sextiae, creating private property for commoners). On the alternative route, a lineage polity becomes a strong-man polity, replacing lineage with imperial power (including the formation of vast private domains in the manner of Ptolemy) to establish a despotic royal rule over every subject. Likewise, there are two routes out of a feudal community. One is for 'juniors' to break away from patriarchal control and divide existing assets democratically between them; the other is for the patriarch himself, maybe with some supporting big brothers, to use his iron fist to monopolize the family assets, and drive away or enslave the juniors. Lenin called these two the American and the Prussian roads to capitalism, in the Russian debates over Stolypin's land reforms.[16]

Prior to these reforms, the Tsar was revered by peasants as the 'father of *mir*', which Russian liberals and social democrats alike wanted to abolish to free both peasants and land. That effectively meant privatization of land, along democratic lines. That's why Lenin remarked later that the original agrarian programme of his party had 'been carried out by Stolypin'.[17] The injustice of Stolypin's reforms did not lie in its privatization of land, but in its oppressive expropriation of peasants to do so. At that time the Populists complained bitterly that the dissolution of the *mir* was destroying 'traditional Russian socialism', in much the way some 'leftists' in today's China protest that Deng Xiaoping has destroyed Mao's socialism. On the other hand, as opposed to the Populists, some earlier Russian Liberals became supporters of the oligarchy in the Stolypin period, believing that regardless of the methods by which it was realized, privatization was a boon and people should reflect on the excessive 'radicalism' of 1905, and change their 'signposts' to cooperate with the authorities.[18] Nowadays, this kind of Liberal is also quite numerous in China.

What is your attitude to these positions?

---

[16] 'The Agrarian Programme of Social-Democracy in the First Russian Revolution 1905–1907', Lenin, *Collected Works*, vol. 13, Moscow 1975, pp. 228–242.

[17] Ibid, p. 256.

[18] *Vekhi* (Signposts) was a collection of polemical essays published in 1909 by seven Russian intellectuals, formerly radical liberals, who now called for a more moderate orientation. See M. Bohachevsky-Chomiak and B.G. Rosenthal, eds, *A Revolution of the Spirit: Crisis of Value in Russia, 1890–1918*, Newtonville, Mass. 1982 [ed].

I have criticized both. I am against the praise of traditional socialism by our 'Populists', and also against the support given by our 'oligarchic liberals' to power-elite or police-state privatization along Stolypin lines. In the same spirit as dissident Liberals (like Miliukov) and Social Democrats (like Plekhanov and the early Lenin) in Tsarist Russia, I believe that the issue we confront today is not whether to choose between capitalism or 'socialism' (*mir*-style or Mao-style), as if we have sinned in abandoning the latter; nor between 'feudalism' or capitalism, as if all will be well as long as we reject the former. The real question facing us is which of the only two possible paths rural China should take – the opposite roads to agrarian capitalism that Lenin called Prussian and American: the expropriation of the peasantry from above by big landlords or companies, as in nineteenth-century Prussia, or the emergence of independent small-to-medium modern farmers from below, as in nineteenth-century America. Lenin always attacked the first, and defended the second.

In Stolypin's time, Russia was not yet an industrial society and his programme mainly concerned the privatization of land. That is no longer the case in today's China. In my view, there are two popular myths about the privatization of land today. One says that it will unleash annexation of land by the strongest, social crisis and peasant war; the other says it will automatically optimize distribution of agrarian resources through the market. Firstly, the formula of 'private landownership – free trade in land – economic polarization – social crisis – peasant rebellion', to which the ideological scholarship of the pre-reform era clung, is historically inaccurate. The origins of peasant revolt in China, as I noted earlier, have less to do with tenancy-rental conflicts than with expropriations by the authoritarian state. When there were certain tendencies towards land concentration, they were caused not so much by free trade in land as by political redistribution of land. The Chinese tradition of 'promoting agriculture and demoting commerce' (*zhong nong qing shang*) was the opposite of the physiocratic policies in the West, for its purpose was to 'strengthen the state and weaken the commoners' (*qiang guo ruo min*).[19] Throughout Chinese imperial history, the more the ruling dynasty emphasized agriculture, the heavier the burden that peasants had to bear, and the more likely that a nationwide agrarian uprising would erupt.

On the other hand, I do not believe that under current conditions the privatization of land is the best way of increasing the efficiency of land use or solving peasant problems. My reservations concern mainly two issues: the unalterable features of land that are inseparable from its location; and the

---

[19] See Shang Yang, *Shangjun shu*. Shang Yang (?–338 B.C.), aristocratic politician and Legalist thinker, largely responsible for laying the foundations for the Qin court and thus aiding the unification of the First Emperor in 220 B.C. *Shangjun shu*, compiled by Shang Yang's followers, was a major work in the Legalist tradition.

incompatibility of absolute rights of private landownership with national planning and public welfare. On the whole, I remain convinced by Plekhanov's position that socialists will not favour privatization of land, yet must oppose 'the expropriation of land by a police state that would wipe out all the achievements of modernization and revive an Asiatic autocracy'.[20] So in today's China, what needs to be stopped is not the distribution of land to peasants as private property, but the abuse of existing peasant rights to land by political authorities. In particular, where no issues of specific location or national planning arise, I support giving more rights to peasants and limiting government power. This position is not based on economic considerations – since, as I have explained, I do not think a free market in land would produce 'efficient big farms' – but on the belief that, as a disadvantaged social group vulnerable to abuse, peasants should enjoy greater rights to land as a line of defence against the state. If officials can take away peasants' land at will, what other civic rights would be left to them?

Currently, many peasants living near big cities or along the south-east coast have become landlords leasing land to labourers from provinces in the interior. Elsewhere peasants are abandoning the land altogether, leaving it uncultivated, to escape the fiscal burdens on them. But the great danger facing the population of the countryside is not merger of peasant holdings, but state expropriation of peasant lands for commercial development. This is now a widespread phenomenon in China. In Jiangxi, for example, the local government recently forced peasants off some 8000 acres, capable of supporting 20,000 people, to lease the land to a company supposedly engaged in ecologically enlightened agriculture. The only compensation the peasants received was a tax concession. In the end, the peasants did not get anything from the deal. When they protested, the government ordered the police to quell them. In other words, had the land been private property of the peasants, the company would have found it very difficult to annex an area as large as this by market exchange. The scale of this abuse provoked strong reactions, but it is not an isolated instance. There have been many similar cases, involving smaller amounts of land and attracting less attention, in which the same mechanism has been at work. Thus, many people now hold the view that the only way to protect peasants is to hand land over to them and deprive the authorities of the power to make land deals behind their backs.

So my support for a conditional privatization of land in China is more political than economic. In strictly economic terms, the impact of privatization may be less – leading neither to efficient large farms nor to rural polarization – than is often believed. In point of fact, the notion that Stolypin's reforms ensured the development of a rich peasant economy in

---

[20] *Sochineniya*, Moscow 1925, vol. 15, pp. 19–40.

Russia is itself an exaggeration. The biggest danger comes not from transfers of land between peasants themselves, but from annexations of land by the state machine and bureaucratic officials. This happened repeatedly in China's history, and it is happening again today. By contrast, polarization between capitalist rich peasants and proletarianized poor peasants has never occurred in China before, and is very unlikely to do so in the future. In current Chinese conditions, the most likely outcome of an agrarian crisis is a mass exodus of peasants to the big cities, rather than their reduction to wage-labour for local rich farmers. Agriculture would remain essentially based on family farms. Their size would increase, but the scale would not be very large and nor would it produce a huge demand for hired labour.

Stolypin's 'wager on the strong' failed in large part because he underestimated the moral cohesion of Russian village communities, which resisted individual families 'separating off' from collective ownership practices on the land, and kept a sharp eye out for opportunist conduct by better-off peasants. The Bolsheviks, who had no roots in the countryside, of which they had a very poor understanding, then made the same mistake from the opposite direction. They tried to unleash class war in the Russian villages, by mobilizing 'poor peasants' against 'kulaks'. But the village communities didn't like that either: they had a very strong egalitarian, but also autonomous tradition, which bound all peasants together in a common moral economy. Soviet collectivization proved a disaster. In China, on the other hand, the Party was strongly rooted in the countryside, enjoying widespread respect from the peasants after Liberation, while the villages lacked the sort of collective, autonomous organization that marked the Russian mir *– they were much more like Sun Yat-sen's 'tray of sand'. Doesn't that account for the relative smoothness with which the CCP could initially carry out collectivization in the fifties, by comparison with the cataclysm provoked by the CPSU?*

I more or less agree with this description of Russian and Chinese collectivization, though in China I believe the lack of autonomous village institutions was much more important than the Party's base in the countryside. After all, Stalin defended his policy of rapid collectivization in 1929 by pointing to the communal traditions of the Russian countryside. Along this line, many Soviet experts working in China in the fifties warned the Chinese that collectivization succeeded in Russia because of the background of the *mir*, but would fail in a China full of petty producer traditions. However, history shows that people with autonomous collective institutions can better resist state control than those who lack them; sometimes collectivism is a powerful weapon against statism.

Still, there were also other reasons why China could complete its collectivization so swiftly. A further significant difference between the Soviet and Chinese land reforms was that the Russian version involved a total reversal

of Stolypin's measures, eliminating independent peasants and communaliz-
ing the villages. By contrast, the Chinese land reform eliminated not only
landlords but also what local institutions there were in the Chinese countryside, which had never been very strong. For example, along China's coastline
many rural areas had 'clan land' or 'temple property' (*zu miao gongchan*),
which were all divided and redistributed into individual hands during the
land reform. Thus the Chinese countryside in the fifties was the antithesis of
the Russian countryside of the twenties; the former was unprecedentedly
privatized and atomized, whereas the latter was unprecedentedly communalized. However, just because Chinese peasants lacked common bonds,
they were quite incapable of collective resistance to the will of the state, of
the sort the tradition of the *mir* offered in Russia.[21] So I completely agree
that it is much easier for a strong authoritarian state to control an atomized
countryside than a communalized countryside.

So when I talk about privatization today, I never separate it from
democratization. The one without the other will lead to much suffering and
disaster. In our current conditions, 'no taxation without representation'
would be a very powerful – and though still only hopeful – slogan for
Chinese peasants. In Europe, people assume that if a government does not
protect its farmers, it is not doing its job. There the Right advocates laissez-
faire and the Left a welfare state, while the so-called 'Third Way' rejects
both. But in the situation of Chinese peasants, these are false alternatives.
The majority of the Chinese population – that is, the peasantry – lacks both
freedom and security. It needs at one and the same time both more of a
laissez-faire economy and more of a welfare state.

What sort of services are accessible to them today?

The crisis of welfare services in the countryside is acute. The most publicly
visible disaster – now discussed even in the official media – is in rural
education. Under the 'Law of Compulsory Education', the government
should have the obligation to provide free education to all its citizens. But
in China, this law is now often interpreted just as the duty of peasants to
send their children to school, without any corresponding duty for the state
to provide schooling for them. So in recent years rural authorities have often
arrested peasants who do not want to send their children to school, accusing
them of violating the law – ignoring the fact that they cannot afford to pay
the fees for their children to be educated.

In the Mao years, education was strictly controlled as the 'ideological
frontier' of the state. The masses were required to imbibe a distillation of

---

[21] For this, see Jin Yan and Bian Wu (Qin Hui), *Nongcun gongshe, gaige yu geming: Cunshe chuantong yu Eguo xiandaihua zhilu* (Mir, Reform and Revolution: The mir tradition and Russia's road to modernization), Beijing 1996.

official doctrines. Investment in education was even lower than it is today: rural schools mostly had 'locally sponsored (*min ban jiaoshi*)' and 'substitute' teachers, in effect paid by the peasants themselves. But since the peasant household was not an independent economic entity at the time, and locally sponsored teachers received their wages directly from the production unit, peasant families did not feel educational expenses as an immediate pressure on themselves. This was in line with the general situation in which the state extracted its original accumulation directly from the 'collective economy', rather than by fiscal mechanisms. The Maoist regime did not tax peasant households and so there was no question of 'peasant liability' for fiscal burdens as there is today. But millions of peasants starved to death then, so there is no cause to regret the passing of this system. Those who now point to the absence of school fees in that period are at any rate one-sided. It is not that reforms of the past two decades have destroyed China's compulsory education system. On the contrary, the Chinese state has never fulfilled its duty to provide compulsory education for peasants.

Still, it is true that educational problems in the countryside are different today. Under Mao peasant children were never prevented from attending school because they were unable to pay school fees; but cases where children had no school to attend due to insufficient equipment indeed existed. School conditions were very bad, and for a long time schools taught nothing but Mao's little red book. The system of locally sponsored teachers created opportunities for corruption by local cadres, who had the power to make appointments. On the other hand, things improved at the beginning of the reform era. The amount of political propaganda in schools was reduced and the quality of rural education got better; another big improvement was a change that allowed locally sponsored teachers to transfer to state sponsorship by sitting an exam.

However, the situation has deteriorated significantly in the nineties. On the one hand, school fees shot up in this period, while on the other a new fiscal system has dictated that 'revenues go up and expenditures move down', effectively encouraging villages to collect money from peasants. This practice has not only erased entirely the positive reforms of the early eighties, but has actually turned 'state sponsored' teachers into locally sponsored – i.e.: peasant-supported – teachers as well. Thus we come back to the same question: the crisis in rural education is caused by a state that has too much power and accepts too few responsibilities.

The situation is so bad that private charities now exist everywhere, that try to raise money for village children's education. These, however, are actually controlled, though not funded, by the government. The authorities give no administrative support; nor are there any regulations governing the proportion of donations that may be spent on running costs as opposed to charitable distribution. Naturally, in conditions lacking any transparency or supervision, this leads to embezzlement and corruption. The more closely the charity is linked to the government, the better any irregularity is covered up. The same is true of poverty assistance, where for many years funds were diverted from poor peasants into the pockets of local authorities.

How have peasants reacted to the changes in the countryside since Mao?

In terms of their own rights, peasants need to see both justice and the benefits of reform; in terms of historical development, peasants need to transform themselves from peasants into farmers. This is not a question of public ownership versus private ownership, or 'privatization into big' versus 'privatization into small'. More accurately, it is a process moving from non-freedom to freedom. In Maine's words, it is from 'status' to 'contract'.[22] In Marx's words, it is from the 'dependence' to the 'independence of Man'. If China is to be modernized and its peasants are to become modern citizens, the transformation of peasant into farmer cannot be avoided.

Under the Maoist system Chinese peasants were tightly controlled, and received little protection. Then at the beginning of the Reform Era the People's Communes were dissolved and their main patrimony – land – was redistributed among the peasants relatively fairly, under the 'household responsibility' system (*lianchan chengbao zhi*). So at first peasants were in favour of reform and displayed rather strong 'civic' consciousness. By contrast, the old order afforded more protection to the urban population, so the cost of breaking those bonds was higher. Moreover, the way industrial firms were reformed – the ostensible caretaker bearing away all the valuables of a virtually bankrupt household, while kicking out its members who had an 'iron bowl' in it – was highly unjust. Therefore city dwellers, especially workers of state-owned enterprises, were more resistant to reform and more attached to the previous status system.

But these relationships have altered as the reform process has developed. No class can be forever 'progressive'. In recent years, the continual shift of the transitional costs of reform to the countryside has significantly worsened the situation of the peasantry. Now that China has joined the WTO, its condition will become even more critical. For on the one hand, entry into the WTO will be a big blow to Chinese agriculture, as cheap imports come into the country, lowering peasant incomes. That will be a major challenge to the rural population. On the other hand, the extension of an 'international standard' of civil rights through the WTO will open the door for peasants to move to the cities, gradually cancelling status barriers and yielding them market freedoms, and so once more liberating their potential for development. That will be an opportunity for the rural population. If liberalization both of trade and of residential controls are handled well, WTO will bring

---

[22] Sir Henry Maine (1822–1888), *Ancient Law: Its Connection with the Early History of Society and Its Relation to Modern Ideas*, Oxford 1959.

more benefit than harm to Chinese peasants and so to China. The key issue here will be who is treated as a 'citizen' – that is to enjoy equal rights before the law and to compete on a level playing field. If 'citizen treatment' (or even 'extra-citizen' privilege) is granted only to foreign investors, but not to our own peasants, their situation will deteriorate yet further, and they will resist reform. If 'peasants' are to become 'farmers', they need to move – in Maine's terminology – from status to contract, acquiring the freedoms of a modern citizen. If they are denied these, and see no justice or benefit in the impending reforms, they will be 'forced into reaction', as Russian peasants were in the Stolypin era. In that case, China's future could be doomed.

In Iran, the Shah's 'White Revolution' was an oligarchic capitalist programme of authoritarian modernization, that provoked a strong fundamentalist reaction, eventually unleashing Khomeini's 'Black Revolution'. That looks quite similar to the way Stolypin's reforms met with a strong reaction from the tradition of the *mir*, paving the way for the October Revolution. Yet Russian peasants hated Stolypin's reforms, because it deprived them of land, whereas the attitude of Iranian peasants was just the opposite of that of Russian peasants. When the Islamic Revolution swept through Iran's main cities in 1977–79, Iranian peasants – about half of the population – remained either indifferent or hostile to the uprising against the Shah. They had benefited from his agrarian reform, which had also distributed mosque lands to them, and felt they should be loyal to him – sometimes attacking revolutionary rallies and raiding the houses of landlords and Islamic activists.[23] For the same reasons, Iranian landlords often backed the revolution against the Shah, whereas Russian landlords became the first target of the revolution of 1917. I mention all this to show that no class is inherently 'progressive' in history. We should not be asking ourselves which class can mobilize all others for reform, but what kind of reform would be fair, and benefit the majority of the population, which in China is obviously the peasantry.

What has been the initial impact of China's entry into the WTO?

China's WTO deal includes a ceiling of 8.5 per cent on agricultural subsidies, which is extremely low in the eyes of European and American negotiators,. But what foreigners do not understand is that Chinese peasants have always received zero – if not negative – subsidies from the state. So in practice this is a clause that subsidizes exporters of agricultural produce, and has little to do with peasants. For example, in 2002, the first year of China's WTO membership, China's agricultural trade balance – contrary to general expectations – saw a fall in imports and a sharp rise in exports – all under

---

[23] Farhad Kazemi and John Waterbury, eds, *Peasants and Politics in the Modern Middle East*, Miami 1991, pp. 290–291.

low subsidies and tariffs as agreed, despite US accusations of cheating. As a matter of fact, China's domestic grain market has been stagnant for years, but when grain prices rose in Canada and the US due to natural disasters last year, Chinese exporters seized the opportunity. The subsidies they received from the Chinese state did not exceed WTO dictates, but were enough for them to buy grain from peasants at unprecedentedly low prices and then sell it at a handsome profit on the international market. The official media extolled this achievement as 'transforming a challenge into an opportunity', when in effect it was based on moving the real costs onto the shoulders of the peasantry, in just another example of heavy 'taxation without representation'. Is a practice like this a surrender to America? A surrender to 'globalization'? A surrender to the WTO? Or is it a surrender to the long tradition – stretching from the First Emperor of Qin to Mao Zedong – that does not treat a peasant as a full citizen?

Obviously, in the manufacturing sector no labour force, either under the welfare system of developed countries or backed by trade unions in Third World or East European democracies, can 'compete' with a Chinese working class that has no right to unions or to labour negotiations. So too, Western farmers who rely on state subsidies may find it difficult to compete with Chinese exporters who can rely on peasant producers who have never enjoyed any protection, only strict control – a factor underlying many a 'miracle' in today's China that is often equally baffling to Right and Left alike in the West. In fact, though no one in the contemporary world will say so, such a situation is not without historical precedent. Around the sixteenth century, some East European countries became highly competitive in commercial agriculture by establishing a 'second serfdom'. You can find people in today's Chinese think-tanks who understand this very well. In some internal discussions they bluntly state that as China has no comparative advantages in either resources or technology in today's world, and cannot advance either to a real socialism or a real capitalism, its competitive edge can only come from its unique system of dependent labour – *nu gong zhi* in their own words.

Factually, I admit they are to a great extent right. Without this labour system China wouldn't have been able to pull off the 'miracle of competitiveness', which attracts such interest in the Chinese experience from people all over the world – the West, the former Soviet bloc and many Third World democracies – but which they will never be able to emulate. The question I would ask, however, is whether a 'miracle' of this kind is sustainable? We might want to look at the long-term consequences of 'the second serfdom' in Eastern Europe. Nowadays there is a lot of talk in the US about a 'Chinese threat'. Actually, as no major power emerged out of the sixteenth-century East European experience, it is highly doubtful whether the current Chinese miracle could continue to a point where it really would threaten the West. But even if economic magic of this sort, that does not treat people as human beings, did take China to the top of the world, what would be its value? Such a development would threaten the existence of the Chinese people themselves.

Your focus on agrarian problems has sometimes won you the label of a Chinese Populist. Do you accept it?

No, if the connotation of the term is understood as essentially Russian, I do not. If the term is used in an American sense, then it is more reasonable. I could be considered similar to the American Populists, who were vastly different from the Russian *Narodniks*. I am an opponent of Russian-style Populism, particularly the version represented by figures like Tkachev. That does not mean my opposition is principally to do with *Narodnik* terrorism. Many *Narodniks* were not involved in assassinations, and those who were involved were not always *Narodniks*. My position is that I am for the common people – which is why I share some of the outlook of the American Populists – but against any kind of collectivism that denies personal freedom and suppresses individual rights. Sometimes such collectivism looks popular in character, while in reality it is only a step away from oligarchy. Populism of the sort that allows a consensus of five persons to deprive the sixth of his or her rights to expression easily becomes an oligarchy that then claims to represent everyone. Witte once said that in Russia the Black Hundreds had something in common with the *Nardoniks*: it was just that the latter stood for an innocent, idealist collectivism, and the former for a gangster collectivism. Iskenderov too has commented that in the 1890s the far left and far right in Russia formed an odd unity over the issue of the *mir* versus the individual.[24] In my view, the opposite is also true: in late Tsarist Russia, Social Democrats and Liberals were (not that oddly) united in favour of casting off communal bonds on individual freedom. That was a unity which was both anti-populist and anti-oligarchic.

Originally, the *Narodniks* were famous for their programme of 'advancing from the *mir* to the commune to socialism' – strengthening the existing village communities and opposing the 'individualism' of the independent peasant household. At that time, Social Democrats criticized this as a form of 'popular dictatorship' and 'state socialism' that protected the 'exploitative *mir*' and obstructed peasant freedom. But over time, moderate *Narodniks* grew more tolerant towards independent peasants, whereas the Social Democratic current led by Lenin, in fighting against Stolypin's reforms, changed direction, putting more and more emphasis on land nationalization as if they were extreme *Narodniks*. Many moderate Populists, on the other

---

[24] Akhmed Iskenderov, a Russian historian of the last decade active in rehabilitating Stolypin. See *The Emperors and Empresses of Russia: Rediscovering the Romanovs*, edited by Donald Raleigh and compiled by Iskenderov, Armonk 1996.

hand, had by now become virtual Liberals, and were criticized by Lenin and his followers for favouring petty peasant production rather than the *mir*, and longing for 'bourgeois democracy' rather than 'the people's democratic dictatorship'. The problems in the Soviet system of later years demonstrate that those so accused were more correct than their accusers.

Some time after the October Revolution, Zinoviev pointed out – in 1925 – that what had once been the *Narodnik* charge against the Social Demo-crats (that they were too 'liberal') was now the Bolshevik charge against the *Narodniks*. Zinoviev called this an 'extraordinary historical *bal masqué*',[25] in which after a round of dancing, people finally took off their masks, and discovered that 'you' were 'me' and 'I' was 'you'. I have criticized this mutual transformation as a two-way alienation. What Zinoviev did not say, but which was plain to see, is that what Plekhanov once condemned as the *Narodnik* vista of a populist dictatorship had been transformed into a reality by his students, Lenin and others, who had betrayed him. Plekhanov was a Westernized theorist, very familiar with modern civilization in Europe, and its traditions of socialism and liberalism. But he was not very well informed about Russian society or traditions, about which he knew far less not only than *Narodnik* sociologists but also Lenin.

Yet the irony of history – not just Russian history – is that while Plekhanov, who understood modernization but not Russia, could not realize his programme, those who understood Russia but not modernization, did realize theirs – yet their success led not to the eradication of the traditional evils of Russia but only to their metamorphosis, and to the failure of social democratization. We are facing similar problems in China today. The lesson of the Russian experience, in my view, is that a consistent fight against Stolypin-style policies can only be based on the positions that were originally taken by Liberals and Social Democrats: that is, backing the 'American' against the 'Prussian' road to agrarian capitalism, rather than clinging to any kind of traditional 'socialism'.

How then would you describe the range of prescriptions advocated for China's future in contemporary debates?

Let me put it this way. From the fifties to the seventies, China could be thought of as a great patriarchal family – the state controlled everything, under the rule of the Party. In the eighties, the 'family' could no longer be held together and a division of its patrimony became inevitable. Today, everyone agrees that the 'family' must be split up, but there is hot disagree-ment about how it should be divided. This is the issue that now defines the different camps in China. I would define these like this. Firstly, there are

---

[25] See his *Leninizm: Vvedenie i Izuchenie Leninizma*, Leningrad 1926, chapter 2.

those who want to revive collective traditions to resist the spread of Western-style individualism. They look to what they consider China's socialist legacy as the antidote to the disease of liberalism. This is what I call Chinese Populism. Its intellectual strongholds are mostly in the humanities. A second camp are the Stolypin-style oligarchs. Their outlook is very simple: state assets are booty to be plundered, according to the principle, 'to each according to their power'. Intellectually, they are most strongly represented among economists. People usually term the first group – populists by my definition – the Chinese New Left, and the second group – oligarchs according to my conception – Liberals.

I have been critical of both positions, from a standpoint that is probably strongest in the social sciences, and which might seem disconcerting in a Western intellectual context. For my objections to the so-called New Left in China are mainly based on social-democratic theory, and my objections to the oligarchic programme (or economic libertarianism) are mainly based on liberal theory. Moreover, the social-democratic traditions on which I draw are not those of the contemporary Western parties, which seem to be turning to the right, but rather the classical legacy of the First and Second Internationals, from Marx and Engels to Bernstein and Plekhanov. Similarly, the liberal sources to which I look are not those of the contemporary liberal left, such as the redistributive traditions of Roosevelt or Rawls, but the classical liberalism of Robert Nozick. When I criticize the oligarchic camp, I stand by Nozick's argument that privatization must respect 'integral justice of possession' – that is, principles of just acquisition, just exchange, and just reparation. That means shunning the Stolypin path of robbery in privatizing public assets. That I ignore the tradition of Roosevelt here doesn't mean I'm against it. But how can we talk about a welfare state in China, when we can't even stop the wholesale theft of public property?

In the West, there are conflicts between these two inheritances – classical social-democracy and classical liberalism – over issues like welfare and the regulation of the economy. But these have little bearing in China today. Its situation is much more like that confronting Marx, who preferred the free-market Physiocrats of eighteenth-century France to the state-oriented Mercantilists, and Adam Smith to the German Historical School; or for that matter Plekhanov, who feared the consequences of Stolypin's programme. In fact, when facing a police state, the Left always defended laissez-faire more strongly than the Right.

Historically, the tradition of the Left in the West was socialist, not statist – for a long time statism was regarded as an appendage of the Right. The welfare state defended by the Left today places more responsibilities on the state, but is no Leviathan expanding its own power indefinitely, of the sort liberals have always feared. For their part, liberals have shown time and again how an oversized state may threaten citizens' freedom, but have never argued that the state should have no public responsibilities. So we need to ask: under what conditions do these two traditions enter into contradiction? The answer is that they can do so when the powers and obligations of a state are based on a social contract in which citizens delegate powers to the state and expect in exchange fulfilment of certain duties by it. How much responsibility citizens wish the state to take will then determine how much power they delegate to it. It is in this situation that social democrats demanding that the state assume more responsibilities will come into conflict with Liberals demanding that the state's powers be limited.

In China, however, where the legitimacy of the state is not based on the principle of a social contract, state powers in no way correspond to state responsibilities. Here, on the contrary, the state enjoys enormous powers and accepts few responsibilities. In this situation, the social-democratic demand that the state's responsibilities be increased is in harmony with the liberal demand that the state's powers be limited and reduced. For that would bring the two into greater balance. In China today, we need to restrict the powers of the state, and enlarge its responsibilities. Only democracy will allow us to achieve this twofold change.

How widespread is such a view?

These are positions that should have drawn support from social democrats and Liberals alike, but that is not yet the reality in China today. While holding to my own views, I have friends in both the camps I criticize – what are conventionally called the Chinese New Left and the Chinese liberals. However, though to quite some extent the positions of these two are tolerated by the authorities, mine is not. It seems that in China today, it's alright to be on the left or the right, so long as you don't stick to a firm bottom line. This is a period when the spectres of Stalin and Pol Pot are still floating before us, drowing the 'Havels' as before. Meanwhile, Suharto and Pinochet are riding the tide of the time, killing 'Allendes' no less freely. The first can still rob people's private property for the coffers of the state, while the second can rob the coffers of the state for the private fortunes of power-holders. Where is the bottom line for us, Left or Right, in China? In these conditions why should the Havels of true liberalism and the Allendes of true social-democracy argue with each other?

Looking to the future, do you regard an evolution along Taiwanese lines as a possibility in China – the CCP following the path of the KMT, and gradually relaxing its grip, to allow a peaceful transition to a multi-party democracy?

I very much hope so, since that would be the best outcome for the Chinese people. But it will be much more difficult for the mainland to make the same kind of transition. Some people would say this is because the CCP is even more authoritarian than the KMT used to be. But I don't think that's the fundamental problem. It doesn't matter who was more authoritarian in the past, for any party can change over time – didn't Communist Parties in East Europe do as much as the KMT ever did? The real difficulty is that the PRC could find it hard to reverse direction on the Stolypin road down which it is now driving. Moreover, there are special difficulties in China. In Taiwan, Indonesia or South Africa, political democratization occurred within an economic system that remained the same throughout. Democratization there was mainly a question of political reconciliation: Mandela and De Klerk shaking hands. In Eastern Europe, by contrast, privatization and democratization occurred more or less at the same time. When democratization occurred, publicly owned assets were still relatively intact, so that the division of state assets was accomplished through a bargaining process, which – though people grumbled about it – was perceived as relatively legitimate. Transaction costs were high because of democracy, as some Chinese libertarian economists complain, since sometimes the privatization of a factory met with strong opposition and had to go through a long bargaining process. But the outcome has in the end been accepted by everyone. No one, on the left or right, now seeks to overturn the results. The process acquired procedural legitimacy and credibility, even if people on the left might criticize its lack of 'substantive' justice.

But in China, privatization is occurring *before* democratization. Suppose all our public assets are confiscated by oligarchs. The result will be blatantly piratical and unjust. If democracy is postponed for another 200 years, by then people will have forgotten the huge injustice that is being created today, and will no doubt accept the results. But if democratization comes soon, then there will be no Mandela-style 'political reconciliation', but great popular anger and determination to reverse the injustice. Then the outcome could be like Russia all over again – the new Stolypins in China producing a new Bolshevik revolution, leading to a new despotism once again.

But wouldn't any capable CCP functionary say to you: just so – that is why we need to hold on to power for another couple of centuries, and then you can have democracy without any commotion?

Realistically, another 200 years of CCP rule is not possible. Even if it would be maintained by force, it would still require some sort of political reform – in effect, a new Emperor-system. But look what happened to Yuan Shikai.[26] It would be highly risky and the country wouldn't stand it. I believe most people have some sense of the general direction world history is taking.

---

[26] Yuan Shikai (1859–1916): President of the newly established Republic, who sought to enthrone himself as Emperor on New Year's Day 1916, setting off nationwide protests and military resistance that forced him to retract the title before his sudden death in June [ed].

So I don't think the Chinese political system could remain unaltered for so long.

Well, all the Party would actually need for the amnesia you speak of to work is perhaps fifty years. Is that so inconceivable?

Another fifty years – could the current fast rate of growth be sustained that long? It's easier to build democracy in good times, under conditions of prosperity. But there is a paradox here, for it is just in such times that pressure for democracy tends to be least. It would have been much easier to create democracy in Russia in 1913 (or still more 1905) than it was in 1917. But in bad times, people will cry out – why do we have to accept injustice? – as they did in 1917. On the other hand, such indignation is historically rare. In Indonesia, while people called for the trial of Suharto as an individual, they didn't question the property regime as a whole. But Indonesia was not a transitional society, unlike China where the outcome might be much more chaotic. Still, looking at the comparative historical record, I acknowledge that it is probably a fact of human nature that most people don't have a strong sense of justice.

You say that in Eastern Europe the results of privatization have been accepted. Would you claim the same of Russia, where oligarchic corruption was such that even advocates of privatization have had to excuse today's pillage as the regrettable price of tomorrow's bright future? China's population is ten times larger than that of either Eastern Europe or Russia. Isn't it utopian to imagine a fair privatization among this huge population?

It is true that democratization in Russia was much less advanced than in the Czech Republic or Poland, and so privatization there was far less equitable. Yeltsin's government betrayed its promise to divide and redistribute state assets, putting them directly into the pockets of a new oligarchy. Even Czech-style 'fair redistribution' has in practice had its own drawbacks. But in any case my argument is only that democratization is a necessary condition for a relatively acceptable process of privatization, not that it is a sufficient condition. In a democratic society, privatizations may not be entirely just, but in an undemocratic society they will certainly be unjust. That is the distinction I want to make.

When they consider China, Western economists tend to fall into a number of schools. One is the 'Washington Consensus' of classical liberals, who believe that by avoiding the issue of privatization China is making only temporary gains and will face grave consequences in the future – whereas East European countries that have implemented radical privatization are experiencing temporary pains, but assuring up long-term prosperity for themselves. The other school is more or less Keynesian, thinks China is a 'state-controlled' or 'quasi-welfare economy', and praises it for not rushing into excessive marketization. Both are under the illusion that the Chinese transition is more 'gradual' and 'socialist' than the East European ones. In reality, the process of 'dividing up the big family's assets' has been proceeding as relentlessly in China as in Eastern Europe. What Eastern Europe couldn't match is our Stolypin style of redistribution – Russia is closer to that. What I firmly believe in is an equal, just and open process of privatization, based on democratic participation and public supervision, which is plainly practical. It would be equally practical to sell state-owned assets fairly and use the receipts to fund social security and public welfare. On the other hand, if privatization is an operation performed in the dark under authoritarian rule, whether by 'division' or 'sale', it will inevitably be robbery of the masses.

So far as utopianism is concerned, some Chinese intellectuals have launched the slogan 'farewell to utopia'. I do not agree with it. The 'utopian disasters' of twentieth-century China were caused by coercive experiments in utopia, not utopia itself. For utopia, if we mean by the term 'an ideal that cannot be realized', is first of all not something to which one can simply say 'farewell', since human beings cannot always judge what is feasible and what is not. So there is no way they can just proceed to think within the realm of 'realizable' ideas. In this sense, after a 'farewell' to utopia there will be no more independent free thinkers. Hayek rightly points to the limits of rational thought, urging us to beware of the 'conceit of reason'. But he evades the paradox that just because our reason is limited, we cannot know where its limits may lie. Therefore it is both unnecessary and impossible to 'limit reason', whereas to limit coercion is essential and possible. In other words, no humanistic idea – be it practical or utopian – should be implemented at a destructive cost to either private liberty or public democracy. We must uphold ideals, and resist violence. To imagine a fair privatization in conditions of democracy among our vast population may be utopian, but without such dreams we will open the door on an undemocratic future.

PART II

5

A Listing Social Structure

He Qinglian

The class structure of Chinese society has undergone a profound transformation since the beginnings of the reform-policy period in 1978. The elite, previously selected on a political basis, is now also being recruited on the basis of 'wealth' and 'merit' – profoundly affecting the underlying social structure. These new sections of the elite are now beginning to form their own interest groups, social organizations and lobbying channels, beyond the already established political ones. The working class, hitherto the constitutionally decreed 'leading class', and the peasantry, the 'semi-leading' class, have both been marginalized; intermediate social organizations, although still prone to political control, are developing apace. All these processes have led to thoroughgoing changes in the relations between the state, society and the individual. We have reason to believe that, after China joins the WTO, interest groups will multiply further, and relations between them will undergo yet more complex change.

Before the Reform Era, China was a highly unified, centralized society, in which political, economic and ideological centres largely overlapped. The whole society obeyed a paramount interest – that of the Party – and the value-system appeared to be equally unified. This situation reflected the distribution of essential resources. At that time, the government monopolized not only the basic material resources of society – land, property, income, and so forth – but also the political resources of power and prestige, and the cultural resources of education and information. There were no independent, nongovernmental resources, and no intermediate organizations; an essentially binary structure, 'state vs. people', prevailed. Chinese people at that time had no material goods beyond some simple furniture, clothing, cooking-ware, bedding, and so on. Their incomes, too, were woven into the governmental distribution system. Peasants lived under the rural institutions of the People's Communes, mainly dependent on the labour-point system for their earnings, while urban dwellers relied on the wage scale fixed by the Personnel and Labour Ministries. Under this highly unified, monolithic state, it was impossible to form any social group with independent goals.

Inequality and corruption

The thrust of Chinese reforms has been gradually to reallocate the possession of social resources. However, as this author has repeatedly pointed out, the principal form this has taken has been a process of privatization of juridically public assets by the power-holding stratum. Its most striking feature has therefore been a glaring inequality in the distribution of national resources – an inequality that has been the starting-point of the restructuring of class relations in China in the past twenty years. The way in which current political and economic elites have crystallized has been tellingly described by the sociologist Sun Liping and his colleagues. They write:

> Transferability between political, economic and cultural capitals in China has yielded a type of commutation significantly different from those analysed by Ivan Szelenyi, which we may call 'insider's transfer'. Characteristic of this phenomenon is the pattern of 'missing no chance', whereby inter-generational transfers of various types of capital within interconnected family lineages have reinforced the switchable potentials of the different capitals themselves. In other words, in each upheaval in the distribution of resources, the existing power-holders have never missed out. Some of the high points in this sequence have been: the resumption of nationwide university entrance examinations in the late seventies; the opportunities for study abroad in the eighties; the openings for speculation in the experimental urban reforms of the mid-eighties; the selection of the Third Generation of Leaders in the late eighties; the commercial fever – 'jumping into the sea' – of the early nineties; the trade in diplomas of higher education in the mid-nineties. These were all links in a chain of ubiquitous capital accumulation by this group. If a middle class has had difficulty emerging in China, it is partly because so many of the resources necessary for one have already been cornered.[1]

Though the total size of the elite that now controls a stock of 'all-encompassing capital' is not large, it enjoys commanding power over political, economic and cultural life. Most of its members made their fortunes not through technological innovation or industrial enterprise, but by reproducing and exploiting monolithic positions of power to accumulate personal wealth.

This process of power-generated capitalization was studied in some detail

---

[1] Sun Liping et al, 'Trends and Risks of Changes in China's Social Structure in the Near Future', *Strategy and Management*, no. 5, Beijing 1998.

in my book *The Pitfall of Modernization*, published in 1997. Since then, however, the forms of corruption in China have undergone considerable changes. In the eighties and early nineties, malversation was mainly an individual affair. Typical cases included Yan Jianhong, the former President of the Guizhou International Trust and Investment Company; Gao Senxiang, once head of the Chinese Trust and Industrial Bank in Shenzhen; or Wang Jianye, the former boss of the Shenzhen Planning Office. But by 1995 corruption had developed from an individual to an organizational stage. A number of features distinguished such organized corruption. Often the leaders of social organizations were those most heavily implicated in cases of corruption, utilizing the public authority entrusted to their institution or branch of the state apparatus as the key asset in 'power–money exchanges'. For their part, lower-level social organizations would mobilize the public resources under their control to bribe upper-level organizations, in pursuit of more financial support, better administrative deals or greater business opportunities. The case of Deng Bin in Wuxi City, Jiangsu Province, illustrated these trends. In the corruption scandal in the port of Zhanjiang in Guangdong Province, the Party Secretary, the Mayor and leading figures in other government departments were all involved – and subsequently caught. Revelations of corruption in the Army offer similar examples.

By about 1998 corruption in China had developed further, from an organizational to an institutional or systemic stage. Three features define this new phase. Firstly, corruption has now permeated the bulk of the Party and State apparatus. Secondly, corruption has become an established arrangement within institutions, as official posts are traded as counters in the redistribution of political, economic and cultural power. Qi Huogui, former Party secretary of Dongfang City in Hainan Province; Yang Shanxiu, former mayor and deputy Party secretary of Anyang in Henan Province; Zeng Jincheng, former head and deputy Party secretary of Zhoukou district in Henan; and Zhu Zhenjiang, former mayor and deputy Party secretary of Hebi City in Henan, all sold official posts on a large scale.[2] Thirdly, official campaigns against corruption are often no longer real threats to it, but rather instruments of political leverage and blackmail for personal gain. The case of Rui'an City in Wenzhou District, Zhejiang Province, where a rural hooligan used evidence of local officials' corruption as a lever to gain control over the whole of the political, and part of the economic and personnel, structures of the Rui'an region is indicative.[3] These forms of corruption are rich in 'Chinese characteristics', if we compare them with the scene in developing countries, because of the different social systems. On the other

---

[2] *Southern Weekend*, Guanzhou, April 24, 1998.
[3] Yang Haipeng, 'A Rural Shaman Commanding a Whole Town', *Shenzhen Legal Daily*, December 16, 1999.

hand, their upshot is very similar to patterns in Latin America or South-east Asia. The power and wealth of the few keep them on top, but the crudity of their route to enrichment means that society has no moral respect for them.

Political and economic elites

Chinese society today can now be broadly categorized into a small elite layer, a much larger middle layer, and a burgeoning layer of marginalized groups beneath (although the composition of these layers, and the relations between them, remain fluid). Within the elite itself one can distinguish three distinct groupings, possessed of different types of resources: political, economic and intellectual. We will begin by examining the first two groups, and then go on to discuss the slightly different situation of the intellectual elite in the next section.

Together, China's political and economic elite today comprises about seven million people, or one per cent of the employed population.[4] The political elite proper consists of top state officials, high- and middle-ranking local officials, and functionaries of large state-owned, non-industrial institutions. The composition of this elite shows a high degree of continuity, since many of its members previously held positions within the planned economy system, although others have entered its ranks during the techno-bureaucratization process of the Reform Era. Only a small minority of the old elite has lost social status through retirement or defeat in factional struggles. The majority have been able to use their previous administrative roles to ensure a smooth access to market opportunities – and thus to reconstitute themselves and their families as members of the 'second pillar', the economic elite. This group includes the managers of state banks and large-scale state enterprises – still preponderant within the Chinese economy, dominating steel, cement, mining, engineering, aerospace, oil and petrochemicals, as well as media and telecommunications; the executives of large and medium companies; and the owners of large or medium private firms. The first two of these, at least, can claim to be linked by blood to the ruling political elite for, as we have seen, there has been little substantial change in personnel since before the Reform Era, though there has been a transition from a political elite in a planned economy to an economic elite in a semi-marketized economy. Elite cadres began to 'love the market' in the mid-eighties, and soon understood how to turn the power they wielded into the personal accumulation of wealth, beginning the process of recomposing themselves into a property-holding class.

---

[4] Yang Jisheng, 'An Overall Analysis of Current Social Stratification in China', *Chinese Social Sciences Quarterly*, no. 3, Hong Kong 1999.

The final contingent of the economic elite – the owners of large or medium private companies – can be further divided into three types. One comprises families from an official background, who have been able to acquire wealth most conveniently through a 'one family, two systems' arrangement (husband or parents in government, wife or children doing business). Kin connexions of this kind are ideal for rent-seeking activities. Another group has made its way up from non-official backgrounds, by deft exchange of 'extra-systemic' material assets for 'insider' power resources. It too thrives on rent-seeking operations. Both of these types are linked to the political elite through personal connexions rather than institutional channels, deploying their ties with government officials to maximize their own interests at the expense of the organs of public authority.

By contrast, a third type has achieved success mainly by seizing market opportunities, particularly in the hi-tech sector. The formation of this stratum can be briefly summed up as follows. By the end of the seventies and early eighties, privately run enterprises started to appear in both rural and urban areas, albeit always closely linked to interests in local government. The never-ending changes in official definitions of China's economic system – initially, 'the planned economy leads, the market economy supports', then 'a planned commodity economy', followed by 'a socialist market economy' and now 'a socialist market economic system' – have in part been a reflection of the ailing condition of state-owned enterprises since the mid-eighties. As their deficits have deepened, they have ceased to function as the major tax base of the government – becoming indeed serious fiscal burdens. It is against this background that private firms have acquired greater importance, and their legal position has gradually altered. Accompanying this process, the general quality of this layer of private entrepreneurs has improved: formerly composed mainly of outcasts from the previous employment system, laymen with a barely acceptable education, it is now gradually becoming a stratum whose average educational level is higher than that of the national population. By 1998, the proportion of university graduates in this sector had increased to about 20 per cent.

The lobbying activities of this group in pursuit of their own interests have become stronger and stronger, and their enthusiasm for political participation correspondingly more intense. Persistent efforts have led to the creation of their own organization, the All China Association of Entrepreneurs and Commerce (ACAEC), their own newspaper – the *Chinese Business Times* – and more and more seats in official organizations such as the People's Congress and the Political Consultative Committee (PCC), although these bodies are not at the core of political power in China. According to a 1996 document, more than 5,400 private entrepreneurs were selected or recommended as members of the People's Congress above county level, more than 8,500 as members of the PCC, and close to 1,400 as committee members in the Youth League, not to speak of eight members in the National People's Congress itself. Many businessmen have also entered leading bodies of the ACAEC at national, provincial, municipal or district, and county levels. These figures can only have increased in the past few years.[5] Welcome news for this layer has been the 'constitutional revision' of 1999 to protect private property from infringements, inspired by the conviction that private riches form a legitimate part of the total wealth of society – a discussion that has clarified the logic of free enterprise to policy-makers and public alike. In the year 2000 China's President, Jiang Zemin, proclaimed the theory of the 'three representatives' as the official ideology of the Communist Party, and in a speech on July 1, 2001 declared that the regime was going to absorb private entrepreneurs as Communist Party members.[6] Such actions have simply institutionalized the 'alliance between power and money' of the political and economic elite.

Although the lifestyle of the two major circles of the elite – political/ governmental and economic – may appear slightly different, they share some basic features: fast-lane living, limited spare time, abundant consumption and similar tendencies in their leisure pursuits and sexual proclivities. The reason for the similarity is that the 'cultural consumption' of the political elite – whether sexual consumption or general entertainment – in most cases takes place in the purlieus of the economic elite. As the class consciousness of this elite gradually crystallizes, urban spatial structures are starting to register considerable change. In some of the larger, more economically developed cities, exclusive elite neighbourhoods and mini-urban communities are already beginning to form, responding to the new lifestyle of the ruling group.

An intellectual elite

The intellectual elite is separated from the run of general technical workers by its possession of a commanding social position and its authority over public opinion. This stratum has experienced drastic splits and fractures during the Reform Era, taking a rather different path from that of the political and economic elite, with distinct stages to it. Under the rule of Mao Zedong – who once remarked that the greater one's knowledge, the more reactionary one becomes – intellectuals were dismissed as 'stingy ninth-rankers' (in a nine-rank hierarchy where the working class was formally accorded the first rank, the peasant class the second, and so forth). Policies for intellectual work in the humanities were strictly instrumental, to serve Mao's continuing

---

[5] Hu Yuemin and Zhu Ya, 'The Development of the Private Economy and Structural Changes in Chinese Society', *Changbai Forum*, no. 6, Changchun 1996.

[6] According to the doctrine of the 'three representatives', the CCP represents the most advanced productive forces, the most progressive culture and the interests of the whole nation.

revolution. At the beginning of the Reform Era, however, the publication of an official article under the title 'The Spring of Science' offered an encouraging signal to intellectuals, most of whom identified strongly with the economic and political changes of the time. Intellectuals, in fact, provided the main social support for the reformers of this period within the Party, while conservatives were mainly concentrated within the state bureaucracy. During the nineties, however, the inequalities generated by marketization have triggered increasing strife within the intellectual stratum. Although a segment of the intellectual elite has developed into an interest group tied to the ruling politico-economic bloc, a far greater number have gained very little from the economic reforms; instead, their relative socio-economic position has been irreversibly lowered. The attitude of intellectuals towards the reforms is therefore no longer one of unconditional support, but is now guided by the dictates of self-interest.

A section of the intellectual elite has been a beneficiary of the reforms. Scientific and technological knowledge, as well as certain social sciences such as economics and legal studies, have all become important cultural capital since the Reform Era began. Capable technical experts, lawyers, economists and engineers quickly monopolized high positions in social institutions, with a minority also entering the core of the power elite. This group of experts has been extremely successful in transforming their previous political capital into social capital, the network of social connexions that served them so well under the planned economy era once again playing a significant role in the rent-seeking China of today. Driven by self-interest, some elements have taken up positions that are in direct contrast to their earlier values and beliefs. Their ample cultural capital and money-driven ideology have been put at the service of the economic elite, enabling them to get a handsome share in the first round of wealth accumulation.

This group are important allies of the new economic elite, who need the help and cooperation of economists, legal experts, social scientists, artists and – especially – the media, all those who control social opinion, in order to gain a place within the legitimate ruling order. It became clear some years ago, during official discussions of policy for the property market and for the development of family-car production, that elements of the intellec-tual elite were able to affect government policies both through their influence on public opinion and by their role in advisory bodies. This was clear evidence of their alliance with certain interest groups, and energetic participation in preemptive rent-seeking activities. A vivid saying runs: 'Their left pocket is stuffed with money earned by flattering the regime, and their right pocket with money gained by favouring business profiteers.' At the beginning of the year 2000, articles on the Internet revealed that family members of a well-known economist – who also holds high position in the National People's Congress – were involved in profiteering ventures. The important point here is not so much what commercial activities such relatives get up to, as whether 'theory' joins with money to further particular interest groups, under the guise of serving the welfare of all – abusing social norms and misleading official policy.

The relationship of this sector of the intellectual elite to the political elite is strikingly different from the pattern before the Reform Era. In his essay 'On the Four Social Elites in Today's China', the Chinese-American scholar Cheng Xiaonong divides the intellectual stratum as a whole into a 'commercial group', a 'highbrow group', a 'populist group' and a 'conservative group', according to the affiliation of each with specific interest groups. This is a realistic analysis. Cheng argues that, by reason of their education and social background, the outlook of technocrats within the current political elite is not simply determined by their own institutional interests, but is liable to influence from elements of the intellectual elite.[7] This makes a striking contrast with the disposition of the political elite of the previous generation, who did not doubt that a great ideological gulf separated themselves and the intellectual elite of their time. Today, however, when the latter is deeply divided into different camps, the political elite can borrow or take up ideas from intellectual groups of its choice, causing an acute 'think-tank complex' among some circles.

In reality, intellectuals have never formed a unified interest group, and it is logical that some should have formed linkages to power amid today's rapid social differentiation. The problem for the 'think-tank' sector is its confusion of two sets of essentially different rules: those appropriate to 'politics' and to 'scholarship'. The goal of politics is to maximize rewards with scant concern for means, and to balance between various interest groups. Social conscience is never the starting-point in the thinking of politicians. On the other hand, scholarly pursuits aim at truth, and in seeking it may attain virtue or beauty too. The sector of the intellectual elite with ties to policy-making circles tends to mix the two sets of rules, wrapping up proposals promoting particular interests as a 'new general theory', and so misleading society at large. On the other hand, the 'highbrow' sector suffers from the serious drawback that many of these intellectuals know very little about the actual problems of society. Their social criticism tends to be excessively radical, and lacking focus on empirical issues. Compared to these two types, populist intellectuals have relatively less theoretical training. Many are still confined to an old-fashioned ideology, unable to advance beyond the class-struggle maxims of the Chinese version of Marxism. In this respect, they are close to those categorized as conservatives by Cheng Xiaonong, the traditional 'Left' in China rather than the 'New Left' that has arisen in recent years. As social change accelerates, conflict and regroupment among intellectuals will become more and more

---

[7] See 'On the Four Social Elites in Today's China', *Minzhu Zhougguo*, no. 10, 1999, *www.chinamz.org*.

pronounced. In all probability some old comrades will become opponents of each other in future debates over political and social issues.

The relationship between intellectuals and governments has always been problematic in developing countries. The experience of Latin America and South-east Asia suggests that when intellectuals in these societies forget their conscience and abandon their social responsibilities, the result is a thoroughgoing corruption and complete deterioration of collective life. Nor is national dignity to be restored merely by barking back at the developed countries that 'you too suffer problems of corruption, and are not much better than us'.

An underdeveloped middle class

In the eighties and early nineties, policy loopholes allowed quite a few people from the lower end of society to rise on the economic scale. Occupations traditionally associated with intellectual strata lost prestige, while the standing of government staff, service and commercial workers improved. However, since the mid-nineties some technically advanced enterprises have given rise to a new middle class, assessed by income and status. This group can be envisaged as a ladder with two parts. On the top rungs are well-paid intellectual workers, managers of middling and small enterprises in the state sector, private owners of middling and small firms, white-collar employees of firms with foreign investment and employees of state monopolies – a total of about 29.3 million people, some 4 per cent of the total workforce.

On the lower rungs we find specialized technicians, scientific researchers, lawyers, teachers in higher education and middle schools, rank-and-file employees in the arts or media, average functionaries in government, middle- and lower-level management in state enterprises, upper-level self-employed workers and traders. These groups amount to about 82 million people, or 11.8 per cent of the employed population.[8] With certain exceptions – some private owners of middling and small firms, managers of state equivalents, individual entrepreneurs or traders, and elderly employees in state monopolies – most of this stratum is well educated and progressive in spirit. They are the counterpart of the credentialized middle class in Western countries. But they form a far smaller proportion of the population.

[8] See Yang Jisheng, 'An Overall Analysis of Current Social Stratification in China', for this estimate and that in the next paragraph.

A marginalized working class

Traditionally defined, China's working class consisted principally of employees of state enterprises. Today, however, the Chinese working class comprises two broad sectors. One continues to be those who labour in state-owned or large-scale collectively owned firms; the other is made up of employees working in foreign, joint-venture, or Hong Kong and Taiwanese firms, or in township-and-village enterprises (TVEs). The two sectors are differentiated by distinct types of relationship between the workforce and the state (or managerial agency representing it) on the one hand, and the workforce and capital owners (along with their agents) on the other. At present, with the exception of white-collar employees in Euro-American firms, every part of the Chinese working class is in turmoil.

Before the Reform Era the industrial labour force in China was, much like that in any capitalist economy, divided into core and peripheral sectors. The former were registered employees in state-owned firms; the latter were long-term or temporary workers in collective enterprises in urban or rural areas. The latter represented only a small portion of the total industrial workforce. The relationship between the working class and the state had two main dimensions. There was the balance between management and workers in the sphere of production, where the labour process on the shop-floor and the extent of workers' participation or control over it was determined; and there was the sphere of distribution, where the worker was allocated a given share of the earnings of his work-unit by the state, which set his wages, medical insurance, pension system, and so forth. In those days it was not so much the labour system that generated discontent, as the totalitarian political system. In the production process, managers did not have much real control over their employees, who worked at their own preferred speed – management had to make many compromises to gain their cooperation. The saying 'state-owned firms have no idea of efficiency' pointed to this reality. On the other hand, under the relentless surveillance of the Party branch and Party members, workers had no space for a personal life. Even in very private settings, casual conversation could bring the risk of being labelled counter-revolutionary. As for conflicts in the sphere of distribution, they mainly concerned the fairness with which promotions were made and payment, or housing allowances, were allocated. China did not have a middle class, but workers of state-owned firms could be compared to a 'semi-middle-class' in China at that time. Strict residential controls acted as a social boundary that excluded peasants from coming to the towns, blocking flows between social classes in the interest of urban dwellers. In these conditions, the main body of a 'substitute middle class' was composed of workers of state-owned enterprises and other urban work-units, all of them organized under Party control.

Once the reforms got under way, however, the labour market opened up and state control over private life gradually loosened. Individuals now might criticize the government in private conversations without the fear of being thrown into jail – public spaces remaining another matter. Into what was once a direct link between the state and working class, a series of intermediate agents have now cut in – bureaucrats, local power-holders and capital. With the diversification of production systems, relations between workers and firms now exhibit a range of types.

Collective contracts

The 'collective contract' predominates in state or collectively owned enterprises, which account for about 70 per cent of the industrial labour force, or some 120 million people.[9] In these firms, we find management, party branches, councils of workers' representatives, and trade unions. In theory the coexistence of these bodies is meant to balance power between them, but personnel arrangement procedures have betrayed this purpose. Often a chief manager of a company will concurrently occupy the post of Party secretary, while a powerless but veteran deputy manager might be assigned the presidency of the trade union, and the chairman of a firm would be a representative of the workers' council. The reason is very simple: all management personnel, including the heads of companies, are also nominally employees of the state, and so have the same right as ordinary workers to join the trade union.

Generally speaking, collective contracts have been observed very poorly in recent years. Many firms do not take the documents they sign seriously, some simply going through the motions, others supplying false information, and yet others taking the view that their contracts are non-binding, ignoring

---

[9] Sources for the following section are: Chang Ping and Yu Liuwen, 'Zhou Litai Lodges Law-suits for Contracted Workers – Almost a Hundred Cases of Workplace Injury Go to Court', *Southern Weekend*, Guangzhou, November 26, 1999; Zhao Yunsheng and Liu Rumin, 'The General Situation and Potential Measures against Work-Place Disaster in China', *Labour Safety and Health*, no. 1, 1996; Xiao Xikang, 'A Blood-Tainted Report from a Coal Town on Labour Safety Legal Practice', *Jiangxi Labour*, no. 2, 1995; Ji Wensheng and Li Junchuang, 'A Brief Discussion of the Violations of Employees' Rights in Privately-Owned Firms: Major Manifestations, Causes and Counter-Measures', *Internal Reference on Labour Issues*, no. 4, 1997; 'A Motion to Protect the Labour Safety Rights of Female Employees in Joint Venture, Township-and-Village, and Collective Firms', *Labour Safety*, no. 5, 1997; 'National Production Safety Briefings for 1996', *Labour Safety*, no. 6, 1997; Tang Can, 'The Dual Identity and Discrimination against Female Migrant Workers in the Metropolis', *Sociological Studies*, no. 4, Beijing 1996; Liu Yuanyuan, 'Black Curtains Multiply in Zhanyu factory – Migrant Workers' Crises Multiply', *Yangcheng Evening News – Weekly Supplement*, October 22–28, 1998; 'Seven Female Workers Forced to Strip for Examinations – a Taiwanese-Financed Firm Infringes Employees' Human Rights', *Shanghai Legal News*, July 22, 1998; 'Where are Laws, Where is Justice?', *Newspaper and Periodical Digest*, July 27, 1998.

the articles in them. Sometimes, what happens in practice is the exact opposite of what has been explicitly stipulated in a contract. For instance, in the collective contract signed by a firm in Changchun, the provincial capital of Jilin in the north-east, it is laid down that when a worker is charged with any breach of discipline, the trade union must be a party to the procedure, verifying the facts and signing the verdict, with a final binding power on the decision taken. In reality, when the president of the trade union once differed from the management over the punishment of a worker, not only did the head of the firm pay no attention to his judgement, but the firm removed the dissenter from his post. Cases like this are by no means unusual. The result is that most trade-union leaders have to react 'cautiously' to contractual violations by executives. In their words, 'a collective contract is indeed a legally binding agreement. But who would dare to bring charges against our managers in court? How could we keep our rice-bowl?'[10]

In the initial stages of the Reform Era, it was noticeable that managers of state-owned firms still did not give a high priority to raising productivity or improving the quality of output: they spent most of their energy negotiating with their employees over workers' demands for stable or increased shares of the firm's budget. But under ever increasing market pressures in the nineties, state-owned enterprises – generally outdated in their equipment and short of financial reserves – have fallen into a vicious circle, as markets for their products have contracted, funds have been illicitly diverted to private firms or into the pockets of small managerial cliques, and the central government has tightened its fiscal squeeze on them. In consequence the number of unemployed or 'off-post' workers has steadily increased. By 1999, the shadow of unemployment had fallen over most state-owned firms. Officially published figures put the jobless at 12 million, but the actual number must be far higher than this. In short, workers in state-owned firms have seen their social status sink swiftly and drastically, their once protected positions slipping away day by day. The result has been a major shrinkage in the middle layers of Chinese society, and a rapid expansion of its lower layers, an obvious formula for social instability.

Western investment

The situation is quite different in firms that combine Western capital with Chinese state enterprises, or companies set up in China solely with investment by multinationals. In these, the trade union, Party branch, and Chinese managerial staff typically form a unified front, which takes much the same attitude to foreign investors in their firm as managers in state-owned

---

[10] *Worker's Daily*, Beijing, 24 February 1997.

enterprises do towards the state – that is, treating them as a welfare fund. Most such firms are financially well endowed, pay relatively high wages, offer cleaner, safer and more up-to-date working conditions, and provide better housing and other benefits than even profitable big state enterprises. Their employees thus often attract the envy of other workers. Relations between management and labour-force exhibit no sharp class struggle. Often, in fact, workers' discontent is directed not at the foreign owners but at the Chinese managers, with complaints that they are incompetent, corrupt or nepotistic. In terms of total investment capital and number of firms, this type of company is still quite marginal. American corporations are the third biggest foreign investors in China, but the combined value of European and US investment does not yet amount to even 10 per cent of working capital in the PRC. Of a total of 7 million workers employed by foreign capital, Western firms account for only a small proportion. In the eyes of the media their significance lies in the advanced technology they introduce and the training abroad they can offer Chinese managers. Alternatively, business schools run by foreigners in big cities may disseminate ideas of human resource management, and provide a training ground for modern marketing and managerial skills. In the long term, this could show some results, as Western and Chinese partners come to the conclusion that manpower management by negotiation and consensus creates the best incentives for a loyal workforce.

Asian investment – back to the past

Elsewhere, regression in capital–labour relations is a stark phenomenon in China today. What we are witnessing is a return to conditions common during the Industrial Revolution of the nineteenth century, of which Marx wrote the classic critique in his monumental work *Capital*. In the PRC today, workers employed in firms financed by Asian capital are typically forced to toil continuously for ten or twelve hours every day, with a three- or four-minute trip to the toilet at specified times, and no weekend off. Workers in such firms earn very low wages, in poor and dangerous conditions. Accidents occur frequently. Fires due to the absence of safety measures regularly cause dozens of casualties. Many firms producing toxicants take no safety precautions of any kind, a fact widely reported in the media. Particularly in firms set up by Taiwanese or South Korean capital, struggles between workers and owners frequently erupt. Along the southeast coast, in cities like Shenzhen, Dongguan or Nanhai, the incidence of labour–capital conflict is very high. Though Guangdong Province has issued Labour Protection Acts, the 'East Asian dragons' seldom take them seriously.

This pattern of regression puts the Chinese government in a very awkward position. In name, China is still a 'socialist state where the working class is its own master', and all toilers enjoy basic human rights. In reality, local governments competing to attract overseas capital typically bend to investors' demands. Moreover, many local cadres pursue their own interests in trying to cultivate good relations with foreign owners. Even though they know perfectly well what are the working and living conditions in such factories, they would never intervene to do anything about them. When the more daring media dig out shocking stories, these officials usually refuse to cooperate with reporters, and try to prevent them from pursuing the truth. Whenever major disasters occur, such as the fires that regularly burn workers alive, investigations invariably discover that cadres from the responsible offices of local government never urged the investors to install fire alarms or extinguishers as the Acts dictate. Nevertheless, the enquiry into such incidents is usually concluded in a rush, with the excuse that 'to protect local economic growth, we must not dampen the enthusiasm of investors'. Within the already marginalized mass of workers and peasants, the labourers in this area, overwhelmingly composed of immigrants from the interior, are quite helpless: far away from home and family, without any channel to voice their grievances.

Peasants under pressure

The Chinese peasantry was the beneficiary of the first phase of the reforms. The initial family-contract system did for once give peasants a sense of liberation. However, since the focus of the reforms moved to urban areas, rural regions have experienced increasingly grave problems, which many experts and scholars specializing in village and agricultural research have pointed out in recent years. Wen Tiejun of the Chinese Academy of Social Sciences even claims that China's agriculture has now become an economic sector that runs at pure cost, yielding no net profit. According to the authorities, the fundamental problems facing Chinese peasants are threefold. Firstly, they labour under excessive economic burdens imposed by the state. A series of governmental apparatuses, known as 'the seven institutes and four offices', has been recently created for the administration of rural localities. These heavily expanded bureaucratic settings host an increasing number of functionaries outside the realm of production, on the backs of a decreasing labour force. It is alleged that the agricultural taxes collected by them are often not enough to pay the bureaucrats populating these offices, so that cadres employed by them turn to levying their wages directly from the farmers around them. Another burden on peasant households comes from corruption, as local cadres try to show off their 'achievements' or enrich themselves by launching construction or infrastructural projects, without considering for a moment what it means for a peasant economy to foot the bill for these. Some experts are now suggesting abolition of the monetary tax on agriculture altogether, to lift the weight of the 'seven institutes and four offices' from the shoulders of the peasantry.

Secondly, incomes from farming remain very low, since the huge size of China's rural population makes it impossible to modernize its agriculture by economies of scale, while current backward farming methods have virtually reached the limit of their output capacity. The combination of massive rural over-population and limited arable land is likely to ensure that for a long time it will be all but impossible to increase the income of the peasants, who still make up 70 per cent of China's 1.3 billion people. In these conditions, increasingly serious conflicts are breaking out between peasants and local administrations in rural areas. The bureaucratic tasks assigned to local cadres are in direct conflict with the interests of peasants. Every year, the collection of grain for state granaries, the distribution of tax quotas, and enforcement of the one-child policy lead to a rash of incidents. Peasants have no guaranteed democratic power. In recent years experiments with village elections have sought to meet this problem, but in most cases they have resulted merely in the form, not the substance, of change. Only a minority of villages keep their administrative work open and transparent to the public. Many rural cadres commit fraud or corruption. The worst is that quite a few local administrative powers have fallen into the hands of local bullies. Peasants are harassed by rural hooligans all the time, as I have shown in detail in my book *The Pitfall of Modernization*.

Together the working class, rural-urban migrants and the peasantry comprise some 480 million people, about 69 per cent of the total work-force.[11] Whatever the difficulties of their life, unlike the truly marginalized groups in Chinese society, they are at least employed. Given that their relatively low educational level does not facilitate occupational mobility, to have work at all in a society undergoing rapid structural change is not such a very bad lot. For they could at any moment fall into the ranks of a social group that is much worse off.

A vast marginal population

It is estimated that the 'off-post,' unemployed and pauperized rural popula-tion together make up some 100 million people, about 14 per cent of the total available workforce.[12] In other words, about 80 per cent of the Chinese people live either at the bottom or on the margins of society. Such a distribution is bound to lead to social instability. Since 1988 reported criminal cases have increased year by year and have been at record levels

---

[11] Yang Jisheng, 'An Overall Analysis'.
[12] Ibid.

since 1996.[13] A survey of 197 criminal cases involving 'post-waiting' youth (instead of admitting the existence of unemployment, the PRC has created the terms 'off-post' or 'post-waiting', all too expressive of what are often referred to as 'Chinese characteristics') in northern Jiangsu Province since 1991 shows that they have five major features in common. (i) Overwhelmingly, these are crimes committed for gain. Of the 197 cases, 60 involved theft; 24 burglary; 12 fraud; 9 kidnapping; 5 drug-dealing; 26 extortion; 9 prostitution – for a total of 145, or 70 per cent of the total. It is evident that the penury of the 'off-post' population is a cause of crime. (ii) The first one or two years 'off-post' is the peak period for criminality, especially for workers discharged from poorly managed, very low-wage, heavily loss-making firms. (iii) Young male workers under the age of thirty-five are the principal culprits, accounting for just over 80 per cent of 'off-post' criminals. (iv) The offenders have no special skills before going 'off-post' and, although their educational level is higher than the peasant average, it is still far below the requirements of contemporary society. (v) With a previous experience of collective labour on the shop-floor, 'off-post' workers are recruited to criminal gangs at a higher rate than peasants. Among the accused in the 197 cases, about one-fourth were involved in collaborative crimes, under more than a dozen ringleaders.[14]

Such an analysis has general implications, because the factors causing the discharge of workers from state firms are plain. As the economic system is progressively restructured, those enterprises that use outdated equipment are being gradually eliminated, while the newer industrial sectors require a much more qualified labour-force. The 'off-post' workers from the state-owned firms of today, and the rural workforce that has never received any professional training, will never be able to make their way into these technology intensive sectors. The result is going to be structural unemployment, which a whole generation (mainly those who left high school in the years of the Cultural Revolution) will have to face – a problem closely related to China's demographic profile, and the unlimited supply of unskilled labour in the country. Some people argue that by joining the WTO China will see the creation of ten million jobs, which will ease the current painful levels of unemployment. Such predictions are at best half-truths, since the new employment opportunities will be available only to those with some skills and professional training.

One often reads comments in the media to the effect that the real problem is that off-post workers have been spoilt, and are too choosy about the jobs they will take. This may hold in a few cases, but is certainly not true in general. Others even theorize the situation as the rule in any social

[13] Cao Feng, *The Fifth Peak: China's Criminal Problems*, Beijing 1997.
[14] Liu Zhongfu and Zhang Qinghong, 'A Preliminary Analysis of 197 Criminal Cases Involving "Off-Post" Workers', *Studies of Crime and Re-education*, no. 5, 1997.

transition, which always requires certain social groups to pay more for progress than others. Hence off-post workers must be sacrificed for the good of the nation. If such arguments are not entirely without foundation, they fail to come to terms with the fact that this painful period will not end until a whole generation has disappeared from history, and China's population has reached a zero or negative growth rate. Furthermore there will be an even worse problem in the future, causing yet more social suffering. The increase in school fees will make it very difficult for the parents of children from lower social classes, let alone marginal strata, to pay for their education. Yet these two groups have the highest birthrate. If inequality of educational opportunity is to be reduced in future generations, measures are required now to stop poverty being passed down from generation to generation.

Floating criminals

The large number of wandering peasants in Chinese cities and suburban areas are also a well-spring of various forms of criminal activity in the PRC today. The majority – over 75 per cent – of criminals in big cities such as Beijing, Guangzhou and Shenzhen, are non-resident 'three-have-nots'. Some well-equipped investigators have made local studies of this phenomenon that offer unusually detailed analyses. For example, a cadre at Jurong prison in Jiangsu Province surveyed the 202 prisoners under his supervision. He found that three demographic features defined these peasant offenders. The majority – 64.5 per cent – were unmarried; most – 59 per cent – had criminal skills; and not a few – 16.5 per cent – had been in jail before. Their offences revealed a shift from hidden and individual to open and organized crimes: from thefts to hold-ups, and from isolated action to gang operations, particularly burglaries, heists and hooliganism, involving a large number of people. Such criminal groups will typically have their own organization, plan of action, distribution of tasks and quotas, locations for fencing goods, and rules for dividing swag. A noticeable new feature of this peasant criminality is its use of specialized skills or facilities for breaking the law. Thus bus drivers familiar with neighbourhoods along their routes will help to organize a series of hold-ups on their buses; repair mechanics will steal or alter key parts of other people's motorcycles; locksmiths will open houses for them to be ransacked.

The most important finding of this survey, however, is the changing motivation behind peasant criminality in recent years. Previously, many peasant prisoners displayed clear signs of psychological imbalance, which had led to conflict with the law without any deliberate aim of challenging it. By contrast, the majority of those caught after 1996 had committed crimes with the conscious intention of breaking the law and defying moral prohibitions. 'Since other people are living a highly enjoyable life', one prisoner said, 'I, who am lonely and impoverished, should be able to find some stimulus and relaxation too. Even if this means committing a crime, it is still my only chance of experiencing something different in life.' The author comments:

> Many young people from the countryside, suffering from acute poverty and longing to become rich, have understood the market economy in a very subjective and irrational way, misunderstanding its values and identifying them simply with money and entertainment. Once their view of social values becomes topsy-turvy, their sense of right and wrong quickly follows. Greed becomes 'happiness'; the Mafia boss a 'hero'; lack of taste 'entertainment'. All of these normative inversions are interrelated and interactive, orienting criminal conduct in corresponding directions.[15]

In somewhat different language, a report by Zhang Nanyan of the Prison Bureau in Henan Province reaches similar conclusions about rural criminality.

Black societies

The floating population of migrants in China has given rise to quite a number of underground gangs, of which the principal type is the 'black society' organized on a provincial, city, county, township or village basis. Relatively well-known examples that have attracted legal repression are the Xinjiang Gang in Shanghai, the Beijing and White Shark Gangs in Guangdong, the Ganzhou Gang in Jiangxi, or the Wolf Gang in Shanxi. These black societies, composed of company employees, post-waiting youth or peasants, are bound by ties of personal friendship. Some have well-designed vertical structures, with a formal hierarchy and strict disciplinary rules, often simulating kinship relations to cement the organizational network. Other types are based on real clan ties, or professional connexions.[16] The ever-increasing number of jobless provides a great army-in-waiting for black society recruitment. Such organizations now play an increasing role in Chinese social life, and in some cases even become a kind of local authority as their members work hand in glove with government officials. Historical experience, both in our own country and elsewhere in the world, suggests that the most authoritarian state is likely to be more merciful to ordinary citizens than the most open-minded black society.

---

[15] Shi Xiugui, 'An Investigation of Crimes Committed by Rural Youth Arrested during the Crack-Down Campaign', *Studies of Crime and Re-education*, no. 7, 1997.

[16] Lei Dongwen, 'Organizational Features of Mafia-Style Underground Social Groups', *Zhanjiang Normal College Research Journal in Philosophy and Social Sciences*, no. 4, 1996.

Intermediate associations

Modern societies are generally characterized by multi-layered social participation in the determination of public policies. Each social class will have its
own channels for protecting or expanding its interests. This is particularly
true of the middle classes, which will often mediate or negotiate between
higher and lower classes – a role that depends in turn on the existence of
various intermediate associations. The weakness of the middle strata in
China determines the weakness of such organizations, most of which do
not, in fact, arise out of the interests of upper- or middle-income strata.
Before the Reform Era, all social organizations were under strict state
control. More than a hundred nationwide associations and more than six
thousand local associations existed by the early sixties, until they were
paralysed by the Cultural Revolution. With the onset of the reforms, they
began to revive and by June 1996 there were more than 1,800 such
registered national organizations, and nearly 200,000 local ones.[17] Some
were set up through party or governmental initiatives, to fine-tune control
of a social or economic sector – like the Association of Private Firms, not to
speak of the ACAEC. Others have been formed by enterprises, particularly
professional bodies like the Association of Fashion Design or the Association
for Interior Decoration. Still others are fraternities or alumni associations.

With the exception of the last type, which are definitely unofficial, all of
these organizations operate in a 'semi-official, semi-civil' fashion, under the
watchful eye of the government. The leaders of these intermediate organizations (including the Association of Private Firms and the Association of
the Self-Employed) are all appointed by the state and paid as civil servants.
Functionally, the associations usually have a double face. Towards the
government, they represent their constituents; towards society, they represent the government. One body, in effect, occupies two positions. The state,
for its part, has rationalized its administration of this area. From 1976 to
1988 confusion reigned, as there were no unified procedures for registering
or monitoring social organizations, until the State Council charged the
Ministry of Civil Administration with bringing order into the situation.
After the spring of 1989, the government realized the importance of
controlling this domain closely, and issued new regulations for the registration and administration of social organizations, setting up a double layer of
supervision over it. All social organizations had henceforward to accept a
dual system of control, one from the Registration and Administration Office,
and the other from the occupational Ministry under which the activities of

---

[17] Wu Zhongze and Chen Jinluo, *Managing Social Organizations*, Beijing 1996.

the given association fell. In 1998 the regulations were tightened to eliminate loopholes in them.

Typical of the results are the so-called 'three *shi*': the Accountants' Association, Auditors' Association and Lawyers' Association. Since the professional tasks of accountant and auditor in many respects overlap, the first two merged into a single body in 1997. Theoretically, auditors and accountants are guarantors of public trust in the operations of any enterprise, while lawyers are defenders of the interests of their clients, which are certainly not those of any court. However, the relations between these two big organizations and the government give a fair idea of the situation of intermediate associations in today's China. Lawyers have a very bad reputation in Chinese society. For the outcome of legal cases does not generally depend on the verification or otherwise of violations of the law, but rather on how skilful a lawyer proves to be, and above all how strong his connexions are with the court. There is a saying inside the profession: 'To fight a law suit is to fight for one's connexions'. It is a common occurrence to hear lawyers promoting their services by telling clients how intimate they are with a certain judge. Collusion between lawyers and judges in a law suit is far from unusual in China. There are even cases where the same lawyer will succeed in acting as the representative of both plaintiff and defendant. Public opinion holds the legal profession in very low esteem.

The situation of the Association of Accountants has distinct features of its own. Today, when a Chinese firm prepares annual accounts, or the manager of a factory is about to leave his post, or a state enterprise wants to change its share structure or make a public offer on the stock market, the company or executive in question is required to present a report audited by an officially registered accountant. Typically, the audit is not carried out to improve internal management or optimize capital structure, but to comply with an administrative formality. Thus what the firm or manager will be looking for is not an institutional accounting standard, but an individual flexibility that can set aside professional ethics. If an accounting firm cannot meet the pragmatic demands of its clients, it will lose business. Intense competitive pressures and the absence of disciplinary sanctions within the profession thus ensure the production by some firms of falsified balance-sheets. The results are notorious. In 1998 a nationwide total of 478 accounting associations were warned, fined, had the authorities intervene in their work, had their licences temporarily revoked, illegal earnings confiscated, or were dissolved. No less than 103 firms and nearly 1,000 branch offices were shut down, and over 5,000 personnel discharged.[18] Accountants

---

[18] 'One Hundred Registered Accounting Offices and Nearly a Thousand Branch Offices Closed Nationwide – Bringing the "Economic Police" to Book', *Beijing Youth Daily: Weekend Supplement*, August 14, 1998.

as a profession pay a much higher price than do lawyers for illegal practices – punishment is both more severe and more frequent. Their reputation is now so low that when a domestic company makes a public share-offer on a foreign stock market, a balance-sheet audited by a local accounting firm is considered unacceptable. Under this kind of ill repute, the profession has been forced to do some self-examination. But if the social environment that 'forces ordinary women into prostitution' does not change, such introspection is unlikely to bring much improvement to the professional ethics of Chinese accountancy.

However, although social organizations are generally still unable to defend the interests of those they are supposed to be representing or to participate in the making of public policy, and possess little negotiating power *vis-à-vis* the government, they have created a certain 'overlapping space' in Chinese social life, acknowledged by both society and the state, that is new. If there is not even more political interference with it, the role of this domain in the future development of the country will become increasingly important. For here is the potential for a public sphere, carved out of an iron-block social life, in which citizens can participate in non-obligatory voluntary activities.

The dangers of polarization

At the beginning of the reforms, most Chinese intellectuals imagined that China was entering the path to a middle-class society. This, it was widely believed, would bring social stability. For – so this argument went – middle classes act as a buffer between higher and lower classes, mitigating conflicts between them, and so affording political stability; they diffuse a moderate, conservative outlook inimical to extreme or radical doctrines, facilitating ideological stability; and their lifestyle is dominated by consumption, furnishing – when they become a majority in any society – a vast and steady consumer market, assuring economic stability. The development of private enterprise, the redistribution of state property, and the introduction of share-holding raised high hopes of such an evolution. The fact that today there are members of the intellectual elite who view corruption as a benign phenomenon, helping to wind down the old economy, is testimony to the power of this outlook.

Reality, however, has disappointed these expectations. Since the premise of the reforms always rested on an intrusion of political power into the market, acute social polarization has occurred. Not only has China failed to develop a diamond-shaped distribution of income with a large middle class in the centre, but it has moved towards its very opposite – a pyramidal social structure, akin to that in Latin America or South-east Asian countries like Thailand and the Philippines. A small minority is perched on top of a huge mass of depressed or marginalized strata, comprising more than 80 per cent of the population, with a quantitatively underdeveloped middle class in between. The experience of modernization elsewhere indicates that higher education is the principal machine for producing a middle class, one of its functions being to inculcate mainstream – that is, middle-class – norms. But in China those in receipt of a higher education form a very small portion of the total population. The country still visibly lacks the means to produce a substantial middle class.

Social polarization can be seen in the pattern of urban development. As we have seen, many large or medium-size Chinese cities now have wealthy neighbourhoods, often guarded by state-of-the-art security systems. Consumption too is highly stratified. Specialty stores sell high-fashion items to the rich; street stalls offer cheap wares to the poor. Commercialized political power redistributes wealth to an elite now reproducing itself across generations. Members of the middle or lower classes are acutely aware of the mechanisms of dispossession and exploitation. The most obvious phenomenon is the contrast in the fate of managers and workers when a state enterprise goes bankrupt. Workers are thrown off-post without the slightest compensation, but a former manager or head of a factory never falls into the same pit of poverty. On the contrary, he will often be re-employed by the buyer of the firm's residual assets – not because of his skills as a manager, but for his cooperation in disposing of state property. Such bosses display ever-stronger antisocial tendencies. The result is a rise in terrorist incidents, physical attacks on the rich, stoppages and sabotage in state-owned enterprises – all manifestations of class conflict. The extent of social tension can be measured by the escalating crime rate, including the number of murders.

Cadre selection

The roots of China's problems today lie, among other factors, in the bane of the backward and anachronistic method of selecting cadres. For a long time now there has been no rational basis for the way officials are picked in China. There is no examination system. Nor is there any open democratic mechanism for electing them. Mystery surrounds the whole process in which leaders 'discover' a talent, ministries 'take care' of gifted people, or – still worse – a Party boss picks out a certain 'successor'. Such patterns readily generate corruption, as appointments are based on personal connexions, incompetents cannot be removed from office, and positions are even put up for sale. Not long ago the media exposed the case of a Party secretary at county level who sold more than two hundred posts during his tenure; and this is only one instance. The endless stream of court cases involving corruption and the abuse of power by cadres acting as local bullies are only a small fraction of the problem – many cases never reach the public eye.

Judged by their behaviour, these are power-holders of very low quality. In general, a political elite should not only display competence in social administration, but be capable of considering the interests of classes other than its own, if only to protect its own position in the long run, by allowing them some share in the distribution of common resources. Unfortunately, the current power elite in China is not only incapable of thinking of the interests of other social classes, it cannot even think of the longer-term interest of its own class. Its mentality is expressed rather in the adage: 'Power must be utilized before its expiry date'. Posts freely referred to as having 'gold content' are inseparable from fraud and corruption. These people know as clearly as anyone else that the country will have no future along this path. That is why, while shouting loudly that 'socialist China is the best', they look for various channels to send their children abroad.

Current policy-making reveals a feature that differs from the pattern of the last two decades. More and more economic policies are based not on considerations of any overall national interest, but on a nexus of benefits to a specific social group. Such critical issues for the national economy as the restructuring of lopsided industrial sectors or the cleaning up of bad debts in the banking system remain perpetually unresolved, because tackling them would affect the interests of some elements of the political or economic elite. Production of family cars, far in excess of the traffic that existing infrastructures will bear, continues to 'develop' under the influence of various unscrupulously made deals. Property construction is out of control, paralysing the banks with a huge volume of bad loans, but appears unstoppable. At a time when everyone knows that the purchasing power of the Chinese people in general is still very low, there is only talk of affordable urban housing that is never followed by action, since the building of cheaper flats would hurt the vested interests of sectors of the elite. Measures that would allay social discontent, such as forbidding the use of public vehicles for private purposes, cutting down on official banquets, preventing unauthorized collection of 'fees' from peasants, often have no existence other than as mere paperwork travelling from office to office. By contrast, policies that exploit public authority to further elite interests, like those designed to facilitate lay-offs and cut welfare benefits in a time of economic depression, lessening the burden on the state at the expense of increasing social tensions, are rushed through with rare determination.

Perhaps the best example of this tendency occurred in early 1999, a period when official policies and pronouncements boosted the stock exchange without restraint, helping certain interest groups to lift a bear market with the stimulus of public funds and bank loans. Once the market was artificially inflated, these groups sold off quickly, leaving ordinary small players to take all the losses. Practices like this are plainly incompatible with any long-term stability for the nation, serving only to make quick fortunes for the new-rich. That such suicidal policies could be pursued in China is testimony to the myopia of a political and intellectual elite that has lost confidence in the future of the country that is in its hands. The government of the PRC has made its choice between the elite and the majority of the people. If it has done so, the reason lies not only in the tilting social basis of the ruling party, but in a more general slide towards a 'rent-seeking society'. The ship named China is sinking under the devoted efforts of a power elite that has long prepared a sanctuary for its family members. When it is no longer possible to be a CCP cadre, it will be time for a comfortable retirement abroad.

The media

The Chinese news media have always been under centralized state control. Since the Reform Era, this control has loosened, leaving more room for independent management. But all channels remain ultimately under governmental authority. Private individuals or companies are still not legally allowed to operate in the publishing sector. On the other hand, since the government has asked certain newspapers to find their own financial resources, telling them to 'take their risks in the market economy' – a policy editors have described as 'tying your limbs, then kicking you into the sea' – many publishers have been forced to turn their attention to consumers, while taking care not to offend the government. In consequence there is an economic difference between a party newspaper and a popular newspaper. The former is funded out of government revenues, and cannot afford to be innovative in either editorial direction or reportage: its one duty is to be obedient. The latter, on the other hand, have to survive on sales, which means they must try to be popular and entertaining.

However, while there are publications that occasionally carry relatively daring criticisms of the status quo, they are always being watched by the authorities, and often get 'yellow card' warnings. In recent years, when the economic situation was not very encouraging, the government tightened control over the media. Incongruously, in the same period private companies started to buy up certain newspapers and journals *sub rosa*. Transactions of this kind cannot be officially registered or acknowledged. The deal is usually sealed by a private contract signed by the purchasing company on the one side, and the work-unit in charge of the purchased journal on the other. Both are then bound by the private agreement. The risk falls mainly on the buyer, since if the deal is discovered by the government, or broken by the other side, the company has to write off the loss. The current reorganization of the news media could cause another redistribution of resources in this sector, the results of which may prove quite different from the intended goals. Another challenge to the government, of course, comes from technological progress. The spread of the Internet, now becoming popular with the generation under thirty-five, is an alteration of the means of communication that poses a serious challenge to official controls, and makes it likely that the days when the Chinese media were completely under the thumb of the government will soon be a thing of the past.

Into the WTO

China's entry into the WTO has focused the attention of people all over the world, leading to all kinds of predictions about its impact. Some very influential scholars have expressed an ultra-optimistic view, to the extent of claiming that, after entry, multinational companies will force China to accept the rules of their game and thereby help the country to stamp out corruption. Such a prognosis blindly ignores the lessons of experience. Most Latin American and South-east Asian countries are member states of the WTO, yet suffer from rampant corruption. Particularly in Latin America, the typical regime was for many years a political dictatorship, allied with domestic monopolies and foreign capital. How could it then be that, when the WTO has yet to clear away domestic corruption anywhere else, China alone will enjoy this magical effect upon joining it? For that matter, however strong the US may be, when its multinational companies come to China, they have to follow the local example and play by the Chinese rules of the game, if they want their share of the takings. If we think of the extent to which China has become a 'rent-seeking society', and of the past performance of foreign capital on getting permission to enter China, it should be clear that we have to take up the battle against corruption ourselves.

What we can be sure of is that China's entry into the WTO will accelerate its rapid social polarization. If the knowledge functional for a market economy can be categorized as a sort of capital, and social connexions are a kind of resource, those who possess these assets will be well placed to take full advantage of the opportunities China's membership will provide – far more so than those without them. Euphemistically speaking, the former are prepared and the latter unprepared for the great adventure. The same is true of the gap in regional development within China. The richer provinces will have the resources and the capital to make use of the opportunities afforded by WTO membership; the poorer ones will not. The political elite will soon figure out the best way to cooperate with foreign capital. The intellectual elite will become further divided, as some elements of it update the clients they serve. Today's economic elite will confront a more complicated situation. Sectors with little chance of joint ventures with foreign capital risk being wiped out in an open competition with multinationals (the telecommunications industry has already spoken of this danger). Branches and firms that command a certain market share and an established reputation will most likely opt for collaboration with foreign capital, to cut the costs of competition for market share. Foreign capital will be happy to oblige. On the other hand, small and medium firms, especially those township and village enterprises (TVEs) that can offer technical services only at a low level and have been kept alive mainly by a high level of public commissions, will probably be discarded on China's entry into the WTO. Without policies to counteract these consequences, the result of China's membership will inevitably be to fuel the explosive enrichment of the upper class and further marginalize the middle and lower classes.

China today has developed a social structure quite different from that which existed before the Reform Era. But this has emerged gradually, without a sharp break with the past, as the power-holders of old have been transformed into a new type of elite. The most crucial element missing in this society is any social movements. The only movements in today's China are demographic – migrations. A country which possesses social movements has a mechanism for self-assessment and self-adjustment. For what these represent is always a collective endeavour to find the shapes and norms of a new life. Judged by this criterion, during the two decades of reform in China, it was only in the mid- and late eighties that there were traces of an embryonic social movement. To solve China's problems today, what we need is an entirely new social movement – one capable of a complete reform of both ideas and institutions.

6

From Status to Contract?

Wang Yi

According to a recent report, in a state-owned factory somewhere in Sichuan, a group of female workers, all of whom had been with the enterprise for more than ten or even twenty years, filed a petition in a local court for a 'collective divorce' from their husbands. The reason for their action was that the factory had refused to sign a life-long labour contract with them, to which they were entitled under the relevant articles of China's Labour Code, and a few days later announced that most of the women were now 'off-post'.[1] Since the enterprise has decreed that unmarried workers can keep their posts, the married workers decided to divorce their husbands in a collective 'class action', to be able to keep their jobs amid the local economic recession.

Before this incident, labour unrest in Daqing, Liaoyang and Sichuan had already graphically exposed the fact that the Chinese working class is becoming increasingly disadvantaged, and a whole generation is now facing an unjust future.[2] On the one hand, enterprises need to reduce employees and increase efficiency in order to cope with the harsh necessities of market competition; or else to declare bankruptcy and quit the market, to allow their assets to be restructured. On the other hand, it is 'off-post' workers who shoulder the highest costs of the transition to a market economy, facing job loss in their middle years and a pensionless old age. At the same time, a gigantic number of state assets have shrunk rapidly, having been transferred into the hands of the corrupt.

What off-post workers are now forced to bear is not some normal market risk, but rather the cost of all the accumulated ills of the old institutional

---

[1] 'Off-post,' *xiagang*, means a worker is not required to report to her or his place of employment. In the 1990s, enterprises would often retrench by sending workers home with (or without) some minimum monthly payment, nominally to 'wait' there until further notice [ed].

[2] Daqing is a key oilfield in north-east China. Its residents are mostly oil workers and their families, who migrated to what was then a sparsely populated area at the behest of government directives in the early 1960s. Liaoyang is a town in the rustbelt of Liaoning province, also in the north-east [ed].

setting. They are being forced to pay for a corrupt system. If we consider the fact that, under the system of state-owned enterprises, the mass of off-post workers are actually in part, indeed theoretically, *the* owner of state assets, what we are seeing is nothing less than the majority of owners being fleeced for an extremely small minority of managers. Hitherto, criticisms made by the Chinese New Left have focused on the injustice of a market economy itself. Free-marketeers, on the other hand, speak with great assurance of the situation of off-post workers, whom they treat simply as 'unemployed', emphasizing the legitimate nature of bankruptcy, unemployment and competition in a market economy, and politely criticizing off-post workers for being spoilt by their excessively dependency on the state. For instance, in the discussion about the labour unrest in Daqing, where laid-off workers will on average get a lump sum of 70,000 yuan in lieu of a pension, many expressed concern that this risked creating the expectation that 'a crying baby gets fed'.[3] This figure would indeed set a high standard for areas outside Daqing. To my knowledge, in most counties and cities in Sichuan, for a worker with more than ten years' employment in an enterprise to get a lump sum pension of even 10,000 yuan would be very rare. Old workers in state-owned firms in my hometown on average get considerably less. This has been one reason why the labour movement in Daqing seems unable to arouse extensive domestic sympathy.

However, in my view, an overly dogmatic discourse on the market economy does not shed much light on the significance of this incident. For its logic tends to conceal and erase the issue of social justice it poses. Since we cannot consider workers under the CCP's political system simply as employees, by the same token we cannot view 'off-post' status merely as unemployment. The real question lies in the way that the government, amidst an ongoing social transformation, attempts to utilize a modern legal paradigm to shrug off political debts and moral obligations bequeathed by the previous ideological regime. In consequence a whole generation is being unjustly discarded and sacrificed.

Legitimating Betrayal

The issue at stake here is not that of social justice in a market economy. It is the problem of social justice under the shadow of a pre-market economy

---

[3] Payment of a lump sum to laid-off workers, *mai duan gongling*, is a way of buying off their right to a pension based on the number of years of employment, which has become a widespread practice in recent years. RMB¥10,000 is about US$1,200, and ¥80,000 about US$9,600. The Daqing unrest in early 2002 was in part triggered by the action of the municipal authorities in charging RMB¥3,000–4000 (US$360–480) annual heating fees to retrenched or laid-off workers, in winter. See the report by China Labour Bulletin, *http://www.china-labour.org.hk*, 2002–03–06 [ed].

and rule by ideology. The crux of the question is the betrayal by the CCP of the tens of millions of working-class people who struggled to support it for many years. 'Toiling for decade after decade, overnight it is pre-liberation again' (*xinxinkuku jishi nian, yizhao huidao jiefang qian*) – folksongs like this tell not only of cyclical changes in history, but of the extreme disappointment the working class harbours towards the CCP.

It was Maine's famous argument that progress in human society has basically taken the form of a movement from status to contract. But his vision of this transformation saw it as a millennial process of gradual change in ancient laws and institutions, and consequently he overlooked important questions for us. How is justice to be secured in a transition from status rights and obligations to contractual rights and obligations? How can power-holders be prevented from escaping their historical and moral obligations? How are they to be prevented from utilizing the legitimacy and certainty of written contracts to criticize self-righteously the pleas of the disadvantaged for the few rights and entitlements that have been left to them by a dying status order?

Today, when old status relationships are being rapidly transformed into contractual relationships, we must not allow contracts to be used to legitimize the shameless evasion of status obligations. We should remind ourselves of the striking fact that in the discourse of a contractual world each and every relationship is rootless, starting anew, from zero. Therefore to recover a sense of social justice in China today, it is necessary to put aside modern notions of unemployment, bankruptcy or the wage contract, and go back to the origins of a collective world, when our people were ready to create a utopian society together.

In his introduction to Maine's *Ancient Laws*, Allen raises the question: has there ever been a regression from contract to status?[4] We do not know if that is possible in the spontaneous evolution of human society, which is why Maine is so cautious in his own conclusions. However, we do know for certain that in the course of a violent, programmatic revolution, such a process actually occurred after the establishment of the CCP regime in the mid-twentieth century. In 1952 the two stock exchanges of Tianjin and Beijing formally stopped trading. By 1956 when the nationalization of the economy had basically been completed, contractual labour relationships, together with a modern enterprise system, had vanished from the mainland, to be replaced by a highly status-oriented, bureaucratic personnel system, with hierarchical salaries and retirement structure.

Here all relationships, rights and obligations were tied to status. The working class was described by the Constitution as the ruling class of the

---

[4] Sir Henry Maine (1822–1888), *Ancient Law: Its Connection with the Early History of Society and Its Relation to Modern Ideas*, with an 'Introduction' by Carleton Allen, Oxford 1959 [ed].

state, but we do not know what that might mean. For the working class does not possess any legal privilege to enter the personnel apparatus of the state, though in fact the majority of higher-rank officials did originally come from industrial units. Nor does the working class have any advantage in property rights, since nominally all state-owned firms are 'public property of the whole people' (*quan min suoyou zhi*), so in principle everyone has an equal share in them. The relationship between a worker and a production unit was one of quasi-servitude, under a veil of ideological euphemism ('workers are the master of their production unit' – *gongren shi qiye de zhurenwong*). Workers' salaries were unilaterally set by the state in the name of administrative regulations. More than half of what workers should have received as their basic income was taken away, for investment in industrial construction and rapid accumulation.

In a nominally modern state of the twentieth century, there were basically two reasons why this tremendous exploitation of working people could be legitimitized. One was the imaginary ruling position of the working class itself. The other was that, in exchange for its exactions, the state promised workers a wide range of non-cash benefits, from provision of clothing, food, housing, transportation, to welfare services covering birth, education, health-care, old age, and funeral arrangements, together with jobs. In the words of Wen Tiejun, the famous scholar of China's rural society, by guaranteeing lifelong security to a status-bound urban population, the state could appropriate the bulk of the surplus produced by workers at a very low cost, essentially by 'promising them a future'.

But none of this was stipulated in a written contract. It was simply an oral promise of an extra-legal character made by the revolutionaries. So when this promise is shamelessly betrayed today, you can't go to a court and file a suit with the supporting evidence of the slogan 'workers are the master of their production unit'. The mechanical norms of a legal court cannot handle an ideologized political obligation. Starting from the mid-1980s, when a fully fledged labour contract reform was launched, status began to revert to contract. With this, a process of betrayal set in. The obligations of the government under the previous status system were never converted into contractual labour relations. The state had no intention of reflecting in cash terms its own obligations (i.e. by paying back what it borrowed as investment capital through its exploitation of the working class for several decades) in the new style of contract between itself and the worker. On the contrary, it has continuously sought to evade, under the cover of 'legalization', the historical responsibility it voluntarily assumed on the very first day the CCP raised its revolutionary banner.

There is something akin to slavery in this. A slave is originally the property of a slave-owner. The slave-owner pays no wage to the slave, but allows him a little plot on which to grow food, to keep him alive while he toils on the plantation, and supplies him with a hut, clothing and some medical care. One day the slave-owner suddenly announces 'you are free – we shall contractualize our relationship', cancels all the necessities he has been providing to the slave, and deprives him of his plot of land. If the former slave complains, we criticize his dependence on the slave-owner, and remark that he does not understand the meaning of freedom.

Though I detest moralism, I firmly believe that there can be no worse betrayal than this. Take housing policy as example. In the mid-1990s the government announced a reform to change the almost completely subsidized housing system into a set of monetary arrangements, a proposal which could have effected a transparent and honest transformation from status to contract, replacing a non-monetary status obligation by monetary wage adjustments. However, in the predicament of the late 1990s, when state-owned firms were falling heavily into debt and economic growth was slowing down, the government opted without the slightest hesitation to cancel housing assignment by work-unit (the form in which housing subsidies operated in China), at a time when a distribution system based on rents was far from being in place. This was done simply to promote the real estate sector with the aim of stimulating consumption. In the absence of any democratic rules or controls, or any legal channel for complaint, the rights and interests of tens of millions of people were casually thrown to the winds. Now people must spend their next twenty years working hard and saving cautiously in order to enter a commercial housing unit that was expropriated from them and which, in justice, should have belonged to them in the first instance.

On the one hand, the government pursues legal reform to shed, step by step, its historical responsibilities to workers. On the other, it is also increasing taxation to improve 'profits', further expropriating the working class. In the two years from 2000 to 2001, China's GDP growth was stable at 7 per cent, while the government's fiscal revenues rose almost 50 per cent! During the Ninth Five-year Plan starting in 1996, several tens of millions of workers went off-post and the growth rate of overall employment in towns and cities nationwide was negative, yet tax revenues jumped 108 per cent. In other words, as it shifts from status to contract, the government still keeps to the totalitarian policy of expropriating from labourers as much as possible of their surplus in order to concentrate resources on developing a state-directed economy. In five years of economic difficulties, the government's take from economic development obviously far exceeded that of labour, further depressing the position of the working class.

Has the revenue garnered by the state been redistributed to the labouring masses, or used to discharge its debts to workers? Let's take medical care as an example. The share of health-care in the budget has been falling every year in the 1990s, and is now far below the legislated standard of 8 per cent. During the twenty years of the Reform Era, the ratio of governmental to total medical expenditure has been decreasing at a pace of 1 per cent a year, while personal medical expenses per worker have been increasing at 2 per cent. At present, it is utterly impossible for most retired workers to pay for their own health-care out of their pensions and benefits, let alone that of other members of their family. The Gini coefficient of medical expenditure in China is as high as 0.46 to 0.5, exceeding the Gini coefficient of income itself – far above the critical level of 0.4 according to international standards. The WHO lists China as one of the worst countries in the world – number 188, the fourth from last – in the distribution of health-care.

China had no public pension scheme until as late as 1995. By the end of 2002, the number of retired workers on this programme is expected to reach a mere ten million people. In these years, several tens of millions of workers went 'off-post', most of whom had worked more than a decade or two. In the previous non-contractual relationship, the social-security promised by the government was delivered by the work-unit, and covered old age. Now when workers go off post, they get a few years of subsistence-level dole, after which they receive nothing for the labours of the previous twenty years. Ironically, the overt form of this extreme social injustice is the normal dissolution of a contractual relationship. For the vast majority of these workers signed labour contracts with their work-units that were valid for five to ten years in the early 1990s, during the labour contract reform campaign.

The wave of bankruptcies and closures of state-owned firms has penalized the working masses still further. Long before a state-owned enterprise could be transferred to a legal owner, every work-unit was issued official directives, and was subject to heavy taxation, which could be as high as 50 per cent of its total profits. Up to 1995 the production value of state-owned firms amounted to 47 per cent of total manufacturing output, yet their share of taxable profits was as high as 71 per cent. We have good reason to say that the bulk of today's state-owned assets were accumulated by the blood and sweat of the working class. Now, due to bad management, confusing property rights and rampant corruption, state-owned firms face widespread bankruptcy. At this moment, the state, unabashedly using contractual relationships as its excuse, requires firms to act as independent 'corporate bodies' with limited liability, when their residual assets are far from enough even for the relocation or social insurance of their workers. The declaration of bankruptcy by a state-owned enterprise thus has become not merely a means deployed by the firms and local government to evade bank debts, but a way of legitimizing the liquidation of any historical debts to the working class.

The Fate of Social Justice

Prompted by the political need to maintain 'social stability', the top leadership of the Party and State are not unwilling to spend money to buy off discontent. But in recent years the centre has been under growing financial and economic strains, and has become increasingly pliant to pressure from crony capital and vested interests to get rid of the burdens of the past and enthuse the new managers. Furthermore, under the rubric of 'concentrating the major and dispersing the lesser', an unbalanced allocation of responsibilities between the central and local governments has spurred local authorities into trying to evade their share of them at all costs. The overall result has been that official policy has tended ever more patently to sacrifice the interests of tens of millions of workers in state-owned firms without qualms. A decision-making apparatus lacking in democracy has once more demonstrated its indifference towards the interests of individuals. So long as a market economy with a range of different interests is joined to a political system that does not allow the workers to voice their concerns, China will inevitably ignore the requirements of basic social justice whenever these conflict with the demands of the market or economic difficulties arise.

It is not so much the lack of concern for disadvantaged social groups that really matters, as their lack of means to express themselves and influence policy. How can we prevent a society from disregarding or destroying the vital interests of a given group? Not by placing our hopes in an ideological government singing songs of high-flown sentiment and issuing endless directives. What we need is a democratic system that allows each group with its own social interests to engage in political contest. How did a working class numbering up to tens of millions become a disadvantaged social group? It was because they could not organize their own trade unions or stage strikes, could not create their own news media or political party, could not affect legislation or help to improve the judiciary. In our society which claimed to be ruled by the proletariat, this vast body of workers has no channels to express itself, apart from outbreaks of explosive unrest.

A group that cannot effectively assert its own will is one that will inevitably be scapegoated, discarded or betrayed. In the early nineties, many state-owned firms experimented with single payment buy-outs (*mai duan gongling*) to discharge their pension obligations, but the State Council explicitly forbade this approach as potentially damaging to workers' interests. But since 1996, the central government has shut its eyes to this method, tacitly accepting a price-tag that is extremely unjust to workers, cancelling all past debts to them at one stroke. It is true that the government, facing the bankruptcy of state-owned firms, did sometimes give priority to workers' re-employment and other social issues; while some special directives were occasionally issued to help off-post workers, such as reducing the administrative obligations of firms that re-employed workers for three years. But it was also from the late nineties onwards that, as official emphasis fell ever more strongly on competition and market discipline, state-owned firms started to sell out or go bankrupt in large numbers, and so many off-post workers lost their jobs permanently and virtually all lost their social security.

However, in point of law, no one could say this abrupt cancellation of obligations was illegal or illegitimate. What workers should get but are not getting is something laws today have no way of determining. An epoch of betrayal is the time that lies between the end of ideological rule and the beginning of a constitutional system. Tens of millions of people are struggling in an order that no longer belongs to the one and has not yet arrived at the other. The former has abandoned them, while the latter is not yet even vaguely visible. Thus we really have no way to conceptualize their interests adequately, as they wander – through the ruins of social justice – between two vastly different property and social systems. Their interests seem to be losing any logical foothold in reality.

How could a revolutionary party, which originally disregarded any principle of law and property rights, and rose to power with a promise to assume unlimited social responsibility, now choose to hide behind laws to limit its obligations and consign its voluntary or involuntary followers to the dustbin of history, excluding many millions of people from the fruits of growing social wealth? From status to contract, from revolutionary party to ruling party, from unlimited to limited responsibility: if all these transformations are necessary, how should they be carried out? Under what conditions could we acknowledge that the previous investor with unlimited responsibility may from now onwards take a limited responsibility only?

If a revolutionary party tries to appeal directly to the concept of a legalized society in order to escape its status relationship with the working class, it is committing a terrible betrayal. We ought to reject the application of legal discourse to confer legitimacy on such actions. The procedure that cannot be avoided is none other than a constitutional system – that is, a democratic order where all social interests have an opportunity to vie with each other, in a legislative process protected by the juridical system. This will be the only way by which we can avoid injustices arising from the transformation of status into contract in China. If the CCP on the one hand insists on retaining a highly ideologized political system and a monopoly of public power over institutional changes, while on the other appeals, under the pressure of marketization, to the concepts and logic of a modern legal system in order to evade its moral responsibility towards tens of millions of its 'comrades', tension over issues of social justice will open up a huge fissure in the legitimacy of the Party's rule.

This kind of damage cannot be mended by an ideological myth like the 'three representatives'. If the CCP's totalitarian rule is destined to fade from the historical stage, and if it has to abandon some social groups on its way out, the one it should never betray is the working class. If the Communists have any faint trace of historical conscience left, they should put their own woks on sale.[5] Even if they have to dispose of every last state-owned asset on the stock market, they should have the courage to assume responsibility for the life, ageing, illness and burial of this whole generation, all the way to the end. From another perspective, if historical burdens have to be laid to rest, the only way for the CCP regime to reclaim some legitimacy and contractualize its obligations and responsibilities, would be to institute a constitutional system. Without a constitutional order, laws will command no conviction; 'off-post' will never be the same as unemployment; the relationship between a worker in a state-owned firm and the state will not be that of a labour contract; and the conversion of state-owned firms into corporations with limited liability will continue unabated.

As long as there is a market economy, contracts between members of a society can and should be legitimate. But between a government and its citizens, the relations of a market will never be enough. Without the big contract of a constitutional system, all other contracts become vulnerable. A revolutionary party has no right to sign an economic contract with the people it purports to represent before it signs a political contract with them.

---

[5] 'Put one's own woks on sale' indicates a final desperate decision, since a wok would be the last item for a Chinese family to discard in difficult times [ed].

7

The Crisis in the Countryside

Li Changping

I come from a peasant family in Hubei, where I was born in Jianli County, by the Honghu Lake in the mid-Yangtze tributary area. Life was very hard during my childhood. In 1969, when I was six, the embankments of the Yangtze broke and all the villages nearby were flooded. My parents set out on the road as beggars and took my elder sister and brothers with them. Together with sixteen other children, the eldest eleven and the youngest four, I was sent to a lot less than five-hundred square metres in size, completely surrounded by water. The first night we stayed there, a younger sister had her ears bitten by a rat; soon, her head had swelled so much that she could no longer eat, and she died within a fortnight. No one wept. Our only feeling was fear. There we spent an interminable three months.

When I was fifteen I got the top score in the entrance examinations for the provincial key-point high school in our township Qipan ('Chessboard').[1] Five years later, on graduating from the Hubei College of Electrical Machinery in 1983, I volunteered to go back to my hometown and became a cadre there. Since then I have twice returned to my studies, eventually earning a master's degree at the Agricultural University of Central China. There, I still remember that we once debated the question: what is the mission of a student in an agricultural college? Some believed that it was to promote technology to create agrarian prosperity. Others contended that our mission was modernization of agriculture. My position was attacked by others, but I

---

[1] The administrative structure of Chinese provinces has two main levels. The upper level is either a district (*diqu*) or municipality (*shi*), and the lower level is a county (*xian*). Jianli County is thus under the municipality of Jingzhou City in Hubei Province. Below the county level, rural administrations in China usually have either two or three levels. In Jianli's case, there are now two. The upper one covers both large farming communities (*xiang*) and small towns (*zhen*), and the lower one would be the traditional hamlet or village (*cun*). Both *xiang* and *cun* have been rendered in English as 'village', which does not help Li Changping to explain the rural crisis with clarity. This translation combines *xiang* and *zhen* into 'township' to indicate its administrative level, while keeping *cun* as 'village' throughout. Prior to 2000, a further level existed between the 'township' and 'village' in Jianli County, known as 'managerial district' [ed].

insist on it even today. I argued that our essential mission was to minimize the 'three divisions': between industry and agriculture, between town and countryside, and between mental labour and physical labour. What that means is working hard for a complete 'liberation' of our peasants. This is what I have tried to do, as Party Secretary for four terms in four different townships. I will try to describe the situation, as I discovered it from my own experience, in the Hubei countryside today.

1. Chaos in Chessboard

Towards the end of 1999 I was appointed Party Secretary in the township of Chessboard (Qipan *xiang*), which has a population of 39,000, over 90 per cent of them peasants. At the time, the area was divided into four managerial districts and twenty-five villages, in which some 6,000 peasant households worked 60,000 *mu* – just under 10,000 acres – of rice-paddy, or an average of 10 *mu* or 1.65 acres per household. There I found that the average net income per capita was just over 1,910 yuan ($230) in 1998.[2] In 1999, the average output per *mu* was 450 kg of rice, when its average selling price was 0.2 yuan per kilogram, yielding a gross income of 360 yuan per *mu* ($44). Against this, the average cost of inputs – seeds, fertilizer, etc. – was 170 yuan ($21) per *mu*, while fiscal charges *per mu* amounted to 230 yuan ($28). In other words, there was an average deficit of 40 yuan ($5) per *mu* in household incomes. Up to 80 per cent of the peasant population was losing money in farming. Since farming was unprofitable, land was being abandoned. So fiscal charges shifted to persons. In some villages these amounted to more than 500 yuan per capita ($60), and in addition there were *corvées* for flood-control, disaster relief and irrigation projects. Whether peasants cultivated their land or not, they were liable for capitation taxes (*rentou fei*), ground-rent for housing (*zhaiji fei*), and fees for private allotments (*ziliudi fei*). After discharging the education tax under the total levy, peasants were still asked to pay no less than 600 yuan ($73) for a student to go to elementary school, or 1,200 yuan ($145) for junior high school each year. Even if you were in your eighties and no longer able to work, or if you were born yesterday, certain charges remained the same. I often met elderly people who would hold my hands, weeping and praying for an early death, and little children kneeling down to appeal for a chance to go to school. Heartbreaking scenes.

Nowadays peasants fall into such deep poverty that, to the best of my reckoning, some 70 per cent of the rural population cannot afford to see a doctor and about 25 per cent have no money even to buy seeds and fertilizer

---

[2] The PRC yuan has been at a virtually pegged rate of 8.27 to the US dollar for two decades.

to plant their lands. My own uncle died after a long illness without being able to see a doctor. Many peasant families appealed to our township authorities for a note of guarantee that would allow them to get a loan from the state-run agriculture credit union for some seeds and fertilizers. Usually they would ask for only 300–400 yuan ($36–48). Yet the credit union has to decide loan availability on the basis of savings, and is also obliged to keep funds in reserve for relief of the frequent natural disasters in our region. So it is quite unable to support household needs in agricultural production. Sometimes I had to lend money to peasants from my own pocket.

By the end of March 2000, stock plus sales of major fertilizers and plastic field covers were all down 35–60 per cent, and grain seeds 67 per cent down over the same period in 1999. Right after the Chinese New Year in February, peasants started running away from their homes. For more than twenty days, truckloads of peasants (to save bus fees) streamed out of Chessboard day and night. Of the 39,000 population in Chessboard no less than 25,000 left. After this exodus, out of a total labour-force of 18,000, only 3,000 remained behind. This mass migration had some new features, compared with previous years. Firstly, whereas in the past people usually departed with some definite plan in mind, now most left their villages with no more than the idea of 'taking a chance', or simply out of resentment at being a peasant, thinking 'if I have to die, let me do so in a city and never be a peasant again in the next life'. Secondly, while previously most of those who left for cities were young women or labourers made redundant at home, this year people in every conceivable age group, including many heads of local households, made for the exit. Thirdly, whereas in the past most peasants would arrange to lease their land before leaving for the cities, now they would just abandon their land without so much as making a note of their rights to it.

Jiaohu Village is closest to the township government, with a population of 900, and a cultivated surface of 1800 *mu*. Average fiscal charges on the village in 1999 were 250 yuan per capita, plus 230 yuan per *mu* ($30 and $28). Every household made a loss on the land it tilled. At the beginning of 2000, more than 100 tons of grain were stored in the village, which the state granary did not want to purchase from the peasants even at a much lowered price of 0.19 yuan per kg. The village had collective debts of more than 800,000 yuan ($96,700 dollars). After the Chinese New Year, all rice-paddies were abandoned and people left *en masse*. They said it didn't matter who the next cadres in the village would be – we are leaving. The richest hamlet in Chessboard was in Huangqiao. Of its thirty-five households, seventeen left and of those who remained only nine planned any planting of their lands. Yet, by early April only three families of the nine had prepared seeds and fertilizers – the other six families had no money for fertilizers, and were hoping to borrow from private lenders to be able to plant. The usual rate of interest in the countryside is 3 per cent a month. That means every one hundred yuan that is borrowed costs thirty-six yuan within ten months. Why don't peasants apply for loans from the state-run credit union? Peasants will reply that you would have to provide guarantors and offer gifts in order to be considered by the credit union, so in the end it's not much cheaper than high-interest loans from private lenders.

As estimates of the amount of abandoned land rose to 35,000 *mu* – three-fifths of the entire cultivated surface of Chessboard – the township authorities had to exert every effort to recontract or outsource the land. We mainly took the following measures. First, we leased out abandoned paddy-fields to large aquacultural firms from the south-eastern provinces of Jiangsu, Zhejiang and Shanghai, for breeding shrimp and crab; in this way we distributed 7000 *mu*. Second, we mobilized local cadres to take extra lands on in their annual contracts. Third, we reduced the contract fees to encourage peasants to take over more land. This last measure helped with 17,000 *mu*. Cutting contract fees from around 150 yuan to 50 per *mu* or less is the most effective response so far to the widespread abandonment of land. But since revenue targets handed down to lower from upper levels of government remain unchanged, the gap created by the reduction in contract fees is usually closed up by an increase in capitation charges. In Houwang village, for example, land charges were 370 yuan per *mu* and capitation charges 650 yuan in 1999. Since 90 per cent of its population left the village in early 2000, if it was to meet the revenue targets set by the township government, capitation charges could only escalate.

How and why have fiscal burdens on the peasantry become so crushing? To understand the background to the crisis in the villages, let us look at the finances of township government, taking Chessboard as an example. In 2000 the authorities had 361 persons on their payroll, of whom school teachers numbered 165 and officials 64. This was ten times the size of the township government in the mid-1980s. Each of these people costs some 20,000 yuan a year ($2,400) in salary and supporting expenses, a sum equivalent to the annual taxes on 100 *mu* of paddy-fields. In all, Chessboard was spending some three million yuan ($360,000) a year on salaries and office costs.

Under the current budgetary system, whose calculation is based – with a 10 per cent annual increase – on a balance achieved in 1992, the county assigns a certain revenue target to each township, which it must raise and transfer upwards, and then cover its own costs from the remainder of what it collects. In 1999 Chessboard passed on just over two million yuan to Jianli County government, out of a net revenue of 3.8 million yuan ($460,000) – leaving 1.8 million, plus some transfers from upper-level budgets of the county or Jingzhou City, an income far below the three million yuan it was spending on its staff costs.

However, the overall fiscal burden on the peasant population of Chessboard was as high as 13.8 million yuan ($1,670,000) in 1999, while total agricultural returns were barely 10 million ($1,210,000). In other words, taxes exceeded the entire annual earnings of Chessboard's peasants by a wide margin. The reason for this huge fiscal weight falling on the peasantry is the extraordinary level of indebtedness of each layer of local government. In 1999, interest charges paid out in cash by the three tiers – township, managerial district, and village – of the Chessboard administration amounted to six million yuan ($726,000).

Theoretically, the tri-level administration in Chessboard should have an annual expenditure of nine million yuan. In 2000, peasant taxes were supposed to be just under six million, with another four million coming from township-and-village enterprises, which should roughly have balanced the books. However, every cadre knew that this revenue could not even cover interest payments. The annual expenditure of the tri-level administration in Chessboard in 1997–1999 averaged more than 20 million yuan. So every year, besides extracting taxes from the peasants to the tune of up to 14 million yuan, local government would borrow another 10 million. The result was an astonishing mountain of debt. By the end of 1998 the whole administration was more than 36 million yuan ($4.35 million) in the red. A year later the figure had risen to 47 million ($5.7million) – some 60 per cent of the increase owed at annual interest rates higher than 30 per cent: a veritable time-bomb. As no cadre would like to see the bomb exploding during his own tenure, each would further enlarge it and pass it on to his successors.

This astronomic debt, shaking the economic foundation of all three levels of administration, has created a new class of rentiers. The 47 million yuan debt accumulated in Chessboard is controlled by more than 6,000 creditors – when total peasant households themselves number merely 6,000. Who are these money-lenders? They include county leaders, local gang members, as well as ordinary peasants who have received tokens of credit from state granaries that have not paid for their grain. But the largest group of creditors are local cadres, who have developed into a privileged social class. Cadres don't mind increasing levies on peasants, since these fund the interest they draw from loans to the administration and sustain their levels of consumption. The class that enriched itself in this way is now powerful enough to control political and economic activities in Chessboard. The relationship between these creditors and ordinary peasants is one between exploiters and exploited.

Tonghu managerial district in Chessboard offers a typical example. Its authorized outlays in 1999 were no more than 150,000 yuan ($18,000). Its actual expenditure was 1.4 million yuan ($170,000), of which 500,000 was devoted to interest payments on its debt, at rates that went as high as 40 per cent a year. Not only did cadres profit from the money they lent to the administration. Even when they didn't actually lend any money, they could fabricate records of a high-interest loan and then enjoy the interest. The then Party secretary of Tonghu, a certain Jiang, put his girlfriend's name into the ledger and started withdrawing interest, of up to 20,000 yuan ($2,400) a time, without ever putting any funds into the collective coffer.

The abuses arising from rural debt do not end there. Village authorities that run out of money will contract out to their creditors land abandoned by migrating peasants, illegally promising the new tenants tax exemption for 30–50 years. What then happens if the peasants come back and ask for their land to be returned? Where can other revenues be found to compensate for this loss? In practice, the result is simply to increase capitation taxes. In other cases, local cadres collect special levies for several years from peasants who are told these payments will release them from further charges. The money is used to clear administrative debts before the real beneficiaries disappear to posts somewhere else, leaving the peasants at the mercy of the new authorities, who then refuse to acknowledge the accumulated payments, pressing for annual charges as before. Moreover, since most creditors are cadres, every year during the period of tax-collection they move in to stay overnight in the administrative offices of the township or villages, whose heads – pressured by knife, rope or drug – often dare not go back home.

Are such problems peculiar to Chessboard? By no means. The whole of Jianli County, of which it forms a part, is in acute crisis. Jianli, which contains over twenty township administrations, has a population of 1.4 million and covers a territory of some 1,200 square miles. When the People's Commune system was dissolved in the mid-1980s, its rice yields increased rapidly and the county became a national champion in grain output. Partly because of this success, rice has remained more or less a monoculture, and there is little fish-farming or crop rotation. According to information provided by a deputy to the County's People's Congress, whereas in 1995 the average net income of a peasant in Jianli was between 1,600 and 1,800 yuan a year, it had now sunk to 1,000 yuan ($120). Industry is in still worse condition. As many as 80 per cent of local enterprises have halted production, and about four-fifths of those still in operation are losing money. In 1999 county-wide industrial revenue was a mere 30 per cent of its level in 1995, and the number of workers still employed no more than 20 per cent. On the other hand, service sectors focused on eating, drinking and entertaining have developed disproportionately. An assortment of amusement arcades, restaurants, beauty salons and massage parlours fills every corner of our streets, which are thronged by more and more passenger cars of the latest models, while office buildings become taller and taller, housing for cadres more and more spacious, and their furnishings more and more luxury.

In these conditions, it is no surprise that by 2000 the county was 100 million yuan ($12 million) in the red – nearly double its annual budget. In June of that year the Party's county committee and the county government organized investigation teams to study the rural debt situation, examining twelve managerial districts and twelve villages. The report they produced revealed a series of astounding figures. It emerged that the peasantry had been overcharged more than 200 million yuan in county-wide taxes each year since 1996, to a total of 387 million in 1999. Of this sum, 220 million had been approved by authorities above the county level, a figure that had then ballooned by 85 per cent as it moved down the different administrative levels within the county.

Despite this huge increase in the fiscal burdens of the peasantry, local government at every level was swamped in debt. Throughout the county, 90 per cent of villages owed an average of 500,000 yuan, and the same proportion of townships an average of 10 million. In sum, the 780 villages of Jianli were indebted to the tune of 600 million, the 108 managerial districts of 204 million yuan, the twenty odd townships of 120 million yuan, and the county itself of 150 million yuan. In all the county had piled up public debts of more than one billion yuan ($130 million), or 1,000 yuan per head of the agricultural population in Jianli, an exact equivalent of the average net income for Jianli's peasants in 1999. On this mountain of public debt – which does not include the debts of industrial enterprises – local administrations were paying 200 million interest charges in 1999. About 40 per cent of the total debt had been borrowed at high rates of interest from private lenders, of whom more than 70 per cent were cadres and their family members. By the year 2000, the revenue collection actually authorized by the central government (legitimate annual charges of 170 million yuan) was not enough even to meet the interest charges on the lowest three levels of rural government.

Is the situation in Jianli County exceptional, or typical of the condition of the Chinese countryside today? In Anhui Province, a pilot scheme has experimented with the conversion of all the miscellaneous fees levied on the peasantry into a single annual tax, which was applauded by people from all walks of society and received lavish praise at the double conference of the National People's Congress and the National Political Consultancy Committee in March 2001. But what has been its outcome? In many township governments, revenues have fallen sharply without any visible change in expenditures; high-interest loans have been curbed, leading to intensified pressures for debt recovery. So local cadres, finding it impossible to keep local government running, have often restored fee-collection alongside the lump-sum tax imposed by the provincial government, worsening the plight of the peasants still further.

Commenting on the Anhui project at a press conference, Prime Minister Zhu Rongji offered the following calculation. If the central government raised its agricultural tax rate from 5 to 8.4 per cent, that would increase its revenues from 30 to 50 billion yuan. If, at the same time, it abolished all township and village fees for education, medical care and other welfare services, and other locally added levies, it would spare the peasantry 90 billion yuan, cutting its fiscal burden from a current level of 120 billion yuan nationwide to 50 billion. In that event, to cover the ensuing revenue gap, the central government would have to provide subsidies of 20–30 billion yuan to local governments, who on their side would have to cut personnel and other expenditure by up to 40–50 billion yuan.

Since then, little more has been heard about such a nationwide reform, though experiments in reform at provincial level are officially encouraged. But Premier Zhu's statement raises a basic question. Is the fiscal burden on the Chinese peasantry only some 120 billion yuan? Nationwide, there are more than 2,000 counties with nearly 30,000 administrative offices; almost 50,000 township governments with 700,000 offices. These two levels together employ about 19 million 'cadres'. Below them, there are four million villages with a rural population requiring welfare services of nearly 800 million. The combined cost of all of these layers is in the region of 300 billion yuan. On top of this, nationwide 'compulsory' education employs seven million teachers, costing 80 billion yuan a year in salaries and 50 billion yuan in school maintenance and obligations. Finally, interest charges on the accumulated debts of China's rural administration, which have now reached almost 600 billion yuan, must now be running at some 80 billion a year.

With such a bleak picture in expenditure, where do the revenues to sustain it come from? The answer is that from county level downwards, some 70–80 per cent are extracted from the peasantry. The budget of China's county and township governments comes out of the pocket of Chinese peasants. What this means, as the totals above show only too clearly is that the real size of the fiscal burden weighing on villagers may be as much as 400–500 billion yuan a year. That is the reason why the central government has issued so many instructions to reduce tax pressures on the peasantry in recent years, even as these have continued to increase steadily.

2. Splitting the Kitchen

How did such a disastrous situation ever arise? Its roots lie first of all, I believe, in a misconception of the functions of government, which led to the introduction of 'market' mechanisms in fiscal planning. In the nineties, there was a widespread delusion among cadres at all levels of government, that since China was now on the road to a market economy, rules of the market should guide every area of social life. Imperceptibly, the Party and government relaxed or abandoned essential administrative roles, as what were taken to be market principles started to permeate politics, ideology and propaganda, science and technology, not to speak of health-care and education.

A key development here was the decision taken in the mid-nineties to split fiscal planning into disconnected levels – what was popularly called 'dividing the kitchen to cook meals separately' (*fen zao chifan*). Advocates of this division believed it would encourage local governments to take the initiative in stimulating their economies to increase their revenues, or to cut spending and practise austerity when they could not meet their outlays from local resources. This conception, derived from 'contract' theory in a market economy, urged governments at various levels to 'manage their budgets independently, take sole responsibility for profit and loss, practise self-discipline and plan their own development'. But our political system had no mechanisms of control from below, and mechanisms of supervision from above were now deliberately attenuated.

When there was a planned economy, budgetary balances were controlled from above. Now, with the abandonment of vertical checks, the financial situation at all levels of local government is a tightly guarded secret. The actual situation of indebtedness is known only to the chief of each authority. As not even other cadres know the truth about official finances at their own level, there is no hope of deputies from the People's Congress, or representatives of villagers, learning the real position. For example, after a thorough survey I publicized the statistics of Chessboard's financial situation in early 2000. When investigators were sent down from both Jingzhou City and Jianli County, they studied my figures meticulously in advance, but none of them believed the statistics could be true. A certain Mr He, who was the township head at Chessboard for many years thought I had exaggerated the situation and my figures were 'basically false' (*jiben bu shushi*). My predecessor, a former Party secretary of Chessboard Township, claimed he would put his head on the block as guarantee that my picture of the situation in Chessboard was absolutely wrong. In the event, the investigation teams confirmed that my figures were essentially correct. I have worked as a government and Party official for almost twenty years, but I have never seen the accounting records of a township government investigated by any deputies of the People's Congress. It is even more unthinkable that the accounting records of a county government should be made available to the public.

Dividing up fiscal administration without supervision or transparency has, in effect, led to a vicious growth of short-term calculations and irresponsibility. For when revenues fell short of expenditure, no one would now volunteer to tighten their belts. Instead, large deficits became general, resources were wasted on a major scale, and both enterprises and peasants groaned under ever heavier fiscal burdens. As for development, far from accelerating, it regressed.

Moreover, when governments split their 'kitchens' to 'cook' their own meals separately, the best dishes – levies on enterprises in good financial standing, like industrial companies – were all taken by administrative levels above the county. As a result, not only do townships have to rely entirely on levies extracted from peasants for their fiscal income, but the same holds largely true of counties. The results have been aggravated by the 'great leap forward' mentality that became popular in inland provinces after 1994, in a desire to catch up with coastal regions. Everywhere every sector fought for priority in local investment – education, transport, electricity, telecommunications and so forth. The cost of infrastructures that should have been the responsibility of the state was now extracted by special levies from the peasants. Yet the constructions financed out of their pockets continued to belong to the state, leaving the peasants with no rights whatever to a say in their management. So electricity and telephone services are supplied at much higher prices than in the cities, but village heads still have to bribe power stations to get water pumped out of flooded fields.

Another consequence of 'splitting the kitchen' is that the various administrative offices at an upper level hand down revenue quotas to be collected by the corresponding offices at lower levels. For example, Chessboard shares with two other townships one law court, with just a few judicial personnel. All Chessboard itself possesses is a police station. Yet this station was required to generate 80,000 yuan ($9,700) a year by upper judicial offices, simply adding more charges to local peasants, and burdening the station with the task of raising this cash to the point that it doesn't have much energy left to do its proper job.

Once a peasant woman was arrested in a managerial district under Chessboard for failure to pay levies, and fell ill from her maltreatment. When she appealed to us and we took the matter up, the district claimed it was not liable since it had contracted out its revenue collection to the local enforcement agency (*sifa suo*), and had paid the agency the agreed amount out of the total that had been collected, so any problems arising from the collecting process were not the district's responsibility. But since this office was directly under the control of the county judicial bureau, well beyond the power of the township government, we were helpless. All we could do was express our regret for her sufferings.

Another example of the abuses created by 'splitting the kitchen' is the fate of food grains purchasing. The central state decrees a protective price of 96–110 yuan ($11–13) per hundred kilogram, but in practice the buying price was 76–88 yuan ($9–11). Moreover, grains brought to state granaries would be subject to deductions for impurity and moisture control, lowering prices yet lower. Worse still, granary officials would often keep peasants waiting, sometimes for several days and nights, to extort a bribe from them for the sale of so much as a single sack of grain. Yet even if peasants protested to it, the township government had no power over the granary. But once a heated conflict broke out, it was we who had to rush to quell the peasants.

Or take migration. Some peasants have worked in cities for years. They set up home in the city and apply for residence away from their original village, a demand which should be supported. However, rural cadres usually try very hard to block such moves. Why? Because migration is a matter handled by the Public Security Bureau, whose records are never consulted in order to determine the fiscal obligations of a township. Higher levels of administration simply use population figures from previous years to calculate the revenues to be raised in the current year, so cadres resist the diminution of their tax base.

At the root of this chaos is the fragmenting of any coherent administration by the system of 'kitchen splitting', as control over personnel planning is shifted downwards. At local level you can find a labour office, a personnel office, an organizational office, and a staff control committee all still in place, without any coordination between them. Each work unit enjoys a much greater autonomy in deciding its payroll, and 'consuming an emperor's share (*chi huangliang*)' has got completely out of hand. The reality is all too often that official authority is simply used to exploit ordinary people. Cadres have developed into a special interest that cannot be reconciled with the interest of the great masses.

In the 1980s, Party and State control over organizational expansion and staff structure was extremely strict. Tight restrictions were maintained on promotions, residential status transfer, and recruitment. The opportunities for taking personal advantage of office were limited. The main loophole was the ability of leading cadres to get their children into college, or their relatives into military service, since graduates and veterans could transfer from the countryside to urban resident status. Overall, personnel expansion was quite slow. When the People's Communes still existed in the early 1980s, a county government plus all its annexes would have at most around 400 cadres on its payroll, and a township government with its annexes less than 40 cadres. In 1986 Chessboard had less than fifteen administrative cadres, plus three taxation officials and two policemen. There was no office of industry and commerce, or judicial office, as there is today. Local government was modest, and charges on the peasantry were no more than about a dozen yuan per *mu*. Even as late as 1992, levies did not exceed 30 yuan per *mu*.

Today, things have changed greatly. The total number of cadres employed by Chessboard, plus school teachers and cadres working outside the township but keeping its registration, has swelled to more than 2,000. How has this come about? An example will suffice. The County Educational Office can now appoint graduates directly to posts in schools, and even arrange for the children of retiring teachers to take over their parents' jobs, without getting any approval from the County Staff Control Committee or County Personnel Bureau – forcing the township that hosts the school to revise its budget upwards to add the salaries of the new teachers. In this fashion, county offices can casually distribute titles to people, leaving township governments to foot the bill. This offers huge opportunities for corruption, as the heads of various different offices exchange convenient empty titles for their relatives and friends. In some cases, key leaders, such as a county magistrate or head of a county bureau, will arrange for their spouse or children to draw a salary from a work-unit, without them going to work. As such favours are swapped between cadres without any report to supervisory organs, the number of people 'taking provisions without going to the battlefield' has become a serious problem in many areas of local government.

The central government has tried to reduce the size of local payrolls in the 1990s, but has met with effective resistance. Every year reductions in personnel are reported upwards, while the number of actual personnel continues to expand. For example, since 1995 the *Hubei Daily* has reported annually that the number of staff in Jianli has been cut by more than a thousand people, and the fiscal burden on the peasantry reduced by tens of millions of yuan. In fact, the 1990s was a period when the size of township and – particularly – county government swiftly increased. Central directives that there should be no more than one magistrate plus two, or at most four, deputies per county were regularly flouted – the actual numbers often being six to ten deputies. In the early 1980s, the entire staff of the judicial sector of a county – police, prosecution and court – amounted to no more than 200 people all told. Now the figure is more than 1,500 officials. Efforts to roll back this tide have proved vain.

Since there are no controls from below, and supervision from above relies heavily on reports of official accomplishments, demonstration of such accomplishments becomes the main task of administrative work, and exaggeration and falsification the norm in documents submitted by local governments at all levels. Whenever I went to the county level to attend Party or government meetings, the distance between what was reported or announced as a directive to them, and the actual realities of the countryside was enormous. Take, for example, Jianli's year-end summary for 1999. This report claimed the average income of the rural population had increased by 200 yuan; in fact, it had fallen by 800 yuan. It stated that levies on the rural population had dropped by more than 40 million yuan, while the reality was that they had risen by 200 million. County meetings repeatedly proclaimed that 'agriculture in Jianli has entered a new phase of development', at a time when four-fifths of its peasants were losing money in farming their land, and many could not even afford to plant it. The county reported total revenues of 220 million yuan for 1999, promising an increase to 240 million in 2000, while the actual income was below 180 million.

As government swells in size and fiscal burdens become ever heavier, what was once the grain and payment delivery by peasants to the government has become grain and payment collection by the government from peasants. At the beginning of the Reform Era in early 1980s, levies per *mu* were only about ten yuan and peasants would send in what was due without any need for cadres to collect from them. Now levies have soared to 200–300 yuan per *mu*. Peasants cannot afford to pay them, and cadres rush to their homes demanding cash, often with bullies to coerce them. This phenomenon emerged only after the size of local government had greatly expanded. Of the four parties involved in fiscal transactions – the state, the collective, the creditors and the peasants – the interests of the first three are essentially the same, as cadres representing the state in dealing with peasants are also the creditors. Under the guise of collecting taxes for the state and for rural collectives, they are actually enforcing payment on high-interest loans for themselves.

When officials are faking figures above and peasants are being squeezed below, direct conflict is transferred to the villages. There cadres fall into a working style of offensive bullying and a lifestyle of general corruption. In dealing with ordinary residents under their judicial power, it is commonplace for cadres to arrest and beat peasants or pull down their houses at will. These conditions nurture a mafia mentality, as little teams formed by a cadre or two, leading a group of local toughs, tyrannize the countryside. If peasants voice any protest, they can be locked up in a 'little dark room', enrolled into 'study sessions', or prevented from returning home. If there is resistance, more law-enforcement arrives to suppress 'bad elements' and extract levies, and successful quelling of any disturbance is reported as an administrative accomplishment. If there is a loss of life and higher authorities order an investigation, the common practice at county and township levels is to deal with the crisis by pretending to discipline those responsible, while bribing people to change the official report, and persuading the families of victims to stay in line with the local government. Usually the upper levels of government simply wait for local reports to be sent to it, only rarely conducting a thorough investigation themselves.

Since the Third Plenary Meeting of the Eleventh Central Committee of the Chinese Communist Party in late 1979, rural reforms have great achievements to their credit, which have won the attention of the world. Food grains and other agricultural products are in surplus; township-and-village enterprises have become a cornerstone of the national economy; peasant deliveries have increased sixfold. But the positive results of reform have not been shared by the mass of peasants. In our vast countryside there is still widespread poverty. Many peasants cannot afford to read, see a doctor, or even use electricity. They do not have easy access to reasonable transport, clean water, or films.

Who has consumed the achievements of the structural reform of China's rural economy? The answer is: an infinitely expanding administrative apparatus and a number of officials. At a conservative estimate, I would reckon half of the taxpayers' money is spent on unnecessary staff, and four-fifths of non-production related expenditure goes on personal consumption that should not be in the budget at all. At a county conference in early 2000, I summed up the resulting vicious circle we have been looking at. It can be set out as follows: crippling fiscal burdens on the peasantry → land abandoned without cultivation → loss in land-based levies → increase in capitation charges → peasants fleeing and not returning for long periods → shortfalls in levy collection → local government dependent on high-interest debts to keep running → recruitment of local bullies to collect levies, against promise of commissions → further increase in fiscal burdens for the masses. The essential cause of this desperate situation lies in the delay in the reform of the political system.

3. Unequal Citizens

But if the uncontrollable growth of local officialdom is the first cause of the crisis in the countryside, a second lies in the agricultural policies of the central government. The prices of food grains started to rise in 1992, making farming relatively profitable, and output expanded in response. However, after 1995 grain prices started to decline, and by now have plunged steeply, costing the peasantry dearly. If China's average grain production in this decade was some 500 million tonnes, the average market price of the three principal grains – rice, wheat, and corn – was 2,070 yuan per tonne in November 1996, yielding a nominal peasant income of over 1,035 billion yuan ($125 billion). Three years later, the average market price of the three crops was 1,415 yuan per tonne, in other words, peasant income had dropped by 328 billion yuan ($40 billion) from its level in 1996. Of course, since the larger part of grain output is consumed by the peasants themselves, the actual monetary decline in their earnings was much less. However, if we count in other crops, the figures worsen considerably, and it seems probable the real drop in peasant incomes was of the order of 400 billion yuan. The situation was no better in 2000. In all, from 1997 to 2000, nationwide peasant incomes may have fallen by some 1,600 billion yuan. Between 1978 and 1997, the average incomes of ordinary peasant households – discounting high earners and rural industries – grew by just under 4 per cent a year. Since then, they have fallen sharply and farming has become loss-making. This is what Chinese peasants have contributed to the restructuring of the macro-economy in recent years.

Meanwhile, as we have seen, agricultural taxes have soared. In 1993, nationwide charges on the peasantry authorized by central government amounted to some 12.6 billion yuan ($1.5 billion). By 1998, they had jumped to just under 40 billion ($4.8 billion). The increase in local fees was even higher. Furthermore, since the mid-nineties the trend has been for levies of every variety to be paid in cash rather than kind. So agricultural taxes are often collected long before crops are harvested; corvées for public works like water-control are converted into cash substitutes (*yi zi dai lao*); taxes on special products or slaughtering animals, supposedly specific, are treated as if every household were liable for them. Trying to meet fiscal targets handed down from above, local cadres forced up the monetary component of tax pressures on villagers, which are anyway steadily rising.

Moreover, the central government also passed measures to protect state-owned firms that have forced scores of township-and-village enterprises into bankruptcy. For example, new policies to enforce the monopoly of the state-run Supply and Marketing Cooperative (*gongxiao hezuo she*) ruined a huge number of village-run or private processing firms. Other directives made no economic sense. Thus in the mid-1990s the central government forbade state granaries to re-sell at prices higher than the fixed purchasing price paid to peasants. Yet with more than 10,000 employees in the state-run granaries of Jianli alone, how could this be? The result was simply that from 1995 onwards the official purchasing prices for grain were never respected. But the posted price misled peasants into the overproduction of grain crops – whereupon the local granaries not only ignored the official price, but also limited their purchases or even refused to buy at all. Yet at the same time, they tightly controlled any alternative outlets. In the end, the peasants got the worst of all possible worlds.

A case in point is the history of a former model worker of Hubei Province, and Party secretary of his village for 14 years, Zhang Qiubo from Longwan in Chessboard. When the peasants of his locality had a difficult time selling their grain after a bumper crop in 1992, Zhang set up a Longwan Fine-Rice Processing Plant. Initially, peasants were allowed to fulfil their tax obligations and some of the most common fees by taking their rice to the plant, which would process and sell it on the market as far afield as Guangzhou. The plant handled 2,500 tonnes throughout the year and made a net profit of 150,000 yuan ($18,000). Then Zhang turned it into a share-holding company for the village, whose peasants brought all their harvests to it, for a guaranteed margin of profit above the price of paddy. They could also convert their grain contribution into shares of the company and receive dividends at the end of the year. The upshot was that the villagers gained substantial benefits and the company acquired a large amount of circulating capital. Soon its output reached 10,000 tonnes, and as grain prices rose, its profits increased to over 500,000 yuan ($60,500). Zhang was showered with honours and bouquets, and state banks offered loans to make his story even more glorious.

In 1996, however, disaster struck when the heaviest rains in a century hit eleven townships in south Jianli. All farmlands were flooded and the peasants harvested virtually nothing, so the company had to halt production. Then in 1997 the state government prohibited any grain market outside the monopoly of its own granaries, and the company was forced to shut down completely. Zhang tried setting up companies to process other agricultural products, but he never succeeded again and plunged both himself and the village into heavy debt – whereupon the villagers became so angry they accused him of corruption, and he was imprisoned. When he was taken away by police, his sons could not even go to school, for lack of money to cover the fees.

With no development strategy in sight for agriculture, though the whole nation is supposed to be engaged in 'market reform', local government, especially at township and village levels, is thoroughly disoriented. Worse, when administrative offices are in a direct conflict of interests with the masses, both the government and Party habitually oppress the masses to defend local power-holders. In general, the quality of our cadres is at best flabby. At worst, some are little more than representatives of local clans, while others behave as if natural selection had picked them out as the most ruthless of all local bullies. A cadre like this will be simultaneously an official and a businessman, a political figure and an economic player, with sovereign command of both local Party and government power, and of the local market and public assets. Usually, before peasants can gain any access to the market, cadres are already there, using their power to drive peasants away from it.

One of the reasons they can do so is that peasant organization is at its lowest ebb since the collectivization of the early 1950s. For not only is there a lack of agencies like cooperatives or producer associations to help link peasants to the market, but such collective organizations as do exist are in the hands of Party and governmental officials. Typically they lack even so much as a form for internal activities, and their members have no rights to participate in their decision-making or management. Most fundamentally, peasants lack any organization for the defence of their own interests. Such organizations would help to link not only the peasantry and the market, but peasants and government as well. For they are needed not only to improve peasant capacity to compete on the market, but also to strengthen the position of peasants in negotiating with government. No market agency can be a substitute for this kind of self-organization.

Another major problem of the peasant condition concerns the flow of rural population into the cities. The reforms of the early 1980s that liberated peasants from the 'big collective' of the People's Commune structure and successfully mobilized their energies into increasing output, solved the problem of food supply in China.[3] Then in the late 1980s the policy of encouraging people to 'leave the land without leaving the village' (*li tu bu*

---

[3] The 1979 reform of '*lianchan chengbao zerenzhi*', literally meaning 'accountability in contracted output (on land leasing)', is usually rendered in English as 'household contract system'. Under this system, a contract-signing peasant can retain his output after turning in a portion that is agreed by the contract. Theoretically, however, the land is only leased to a contract-signing peasant and does not belong to the peasant [ed].

li xiang) allowed a part of the peasant population to quit agriculture for township-and-village enterprises (TVEs) in the countryside, once again mobilizing their enthusiasm in productive firms that soon became a pillar of the national economy, opening up new horizons for even state-owned firms.

But the new regulations also meant that a peasant could physically leave both land and village, but could not alter his or her rural registration status. Economically, they ensured a huge supply of cheap labour to developed regions along China's coastline, as some 80 million peasants rushed to its booming cities. Socially, however, the result has been a set of injustices that have got steadily worse. On the one hand, very few employment agencies exist to help an orderly entry of surplus rural workers into domestic or overseas labour markets, while on the other, the state sets up various impediments to such an entry anyway. Thus a peasant who goes to work in a city has to pay all kinds of fees and extra charges for staying there, in addition to the levies of anyone registered as a rural resident. To start with, any peasant who wants to leave the countryside for a spell needs to go through a series of administrative procedures, costing at least a few hundred and possibly several thousand yuan. After moving to a city, the peasant needs to get various identity cards, costing another 600 yuan. Extra 'sponsoring fees', which can run up to tens of thousands of yuan, are necessary to get children into a school in the city. As for securing a transfer from rural to urban residential status, that requires payments anywhere from a few thousand to tens of thousands of yuan. In effect, the state utilizes non-economic restrictions to impede peasant migration into cities, while extracting up to a 100 billion yuan a year in extra charges from those who do manage to get there. When they get there, many of them fall into modern urban misery: they have to work twelve to fifteen hours each day, often be abused verbally, physically, and economically. In Houwang Village 90 per cent of the labour-force left for the cities in 2000. Its Party secretary, Hou Mengxuan, a veteran, depended upon the 300 yuan ($36) that his wife sent back each month, to keep their children in school and to buy fertilizer for the land he was planting. What was she doing? Shoe-shining on city streets, staying with another seven women from Houwan in a small room of nine square metres. Unable to afford a bed, all eight women were sleeping on the floor, and keeping themselves alive with leftovers from restaurants in exchange for cleaning tables and dishes for their proprietors.

The root fact is that peasants do not have equal citizen status. Discrepancies between cities and countryside, between industry and agriculture, and between mental and physical labour, have not been reduced at all. Instead, they are increasing. Mental workers and urban residents only pay income tax after their salaries reach a certain level, whereas peasants must pay taxes and fees when they are farming at a loss. When urban workers lose their jobs, they are eligible for unemployment benefit, while peasants who lose their land still have to pay rural fees. City dwellers can apply for consumer loans at very low rates of interest and long repayment schedules, whereas in the countryside peasants often can't even get a small loan to plant their crops, and when they do the interest charged on it is very high, and the term is one year. In the cities water and electricity supplies, together with roads and other facilities, are covered by the state, while in the countryside all infrastructural works must be paid for by peasants themselves.

4. An Agenda of Reform

What are the prospects for reform? Our experience in Chessboard in the year 2000 shows that there are solutions. To reduce the burdens on the masses, after all, means to reduce the privileges enjoyed by cadres. So a key task was to reduce the size of local government and cut the number of staff on its payroll. My target was to bring the 360 people living on fiscal revenues in Chessboard to around 250, and all those living on peasant fees from 1000 to 600. That summer we removed the whole managerial district level in Chessboard, sparing villagers the equivalent of up to 130 yuan per capita in levies and 650 yuan in household charges.

The other key task of reform was debt reduction. We took three months to sort out and put in order all accounting records of high-interest loans since 1996, checking them line by line to establish a comprehensive picture of the way they had originated and how they had developed. The most common methods of extortion were these: extending the length of debts to generate higher yields; drawing multiple interest from small debts; creating debts without lending any money; collecting compound interest; converting legitimate fee payments into high-interest debts, and eligibility for bank loans into private high-interest loans. With clear accounting records in hand, I was able to target the beneficiaries of these malpractices and carry out debt and interest cancellation work. Seventy-nine cadres were either disciplined within the Party and the government system or prosecuted in court for corruption. All high-interest debts were lowered from above 30 to below 8.3 per cent (later Jingzhou City issued a regulation stipulating that all interest rates should be held below 3 per cent and Party members should set an example by giving interest-free loans). With these measures, we were able to cut the outstanding total of 47 million yuan by some 10 million.

At the same time, we set up a democratic managing group in each village to control spending. By the end of the summer, overall expenditure had been reduced by 3.5 million yuan township-wide. Of that amount, living expenses alone were cut by 800,000 yuan compared with 1999, and interest payments by 2.2 million. Some creditors, when they realized their traditional game was up, volunteered to convert their claims into shares in the township's fish-farming company, to gain management rights and chances of profit there. Others resorted to telephone threats or even rushed into our offices. We stood firm. Nevertheless, I calculate that to liquidate the whole debt burden of the township would take ten to fifteen years of austerity, without any major natural disasters.

What then is ultimately the solution to the problem of rural indebtedness in China's inland provinces? I would suggest the following measures:

1. Put accounting records in order, as we did in Chessboard, to sort out the various kinds of loan and lower the interest rates on them, phasing out old agreements with new ones starting from fresh bases of calculation.
2. Pay off part of the existing debts by leasing or selling abandoned lands, hillsides, and water surfaces.
3. Transfer debts of village and township governments into shares of TVEs.
4. Liquidate part of local government obligations by shifting debts and credits to exchanges among peasants.
5. Issue 500 billion yuan in state bonds over five years to help county and township authorities settle existing debts, with an obligation on them to repay each tranche over ten years; and perhaps also allow each province to issue its own bonds for the same purpose.

Think about it carefully: issuing a 100 billion yuan bond each year to support the countryside will be well worth doing. For in the past few years, China has been suffering from a creeping deflation, which the government has tried to combat in vain. Yet this is a country where peasants make up the majority of the population, peasants have the strongest need to consume, and the rural market has the greatest potential – but peasants have no money to buy goods. According to official statistics, the peasants' share of national purchasing power fell from over 53 per cent in the mid 1980s to 38 per cent in late 2000. In other words, the total consumption of the peasantry – who make up more than 70 per cent of China's population – is now below that of urban residents, who represent less than 30 per cent of the population.

According to some surveys, China has a rural population of nearly 870 million, or about 230 million households. A simple calculation tells us that a one per cent increase in the spread of any consumer good amounts to a demand for two million units. According to the latest input–output information, if final consumption in the countryside were to the value of 100 billion yuan, that would create 236 billion worth of demand in the economy as a whole. Since 1996 grain prices have fallen every year, and as the cash income of ordinary peasants has declined, rural purchasing power has dropped sharply. But if we look back to earlier years, the market was also very weak in 1991 – yet when grain prices picked up at the end of 1992, increasing peasant incomes, consumption soon warmed up. Indeed it rose so quickly that inflation appeared. From this example we can see the extent to which the ups and downs of peasant income determine the movements of the market. If we can ensure an improvement in the cash income of ordinary peasants, I believe we can walk swiftly out of the whirlwind of deflation.

Yet truly to overcome the rural crisis in China, our long-term goal must be to diminish the three great social discrepancies. The relationship between urban and rural worlds needs to be changed. It is now time to liberate peasants with a third reform: they should be allowed to 'leave both land and village'. That means allowing rights to land to circulate, by helping peasants to exit or re-enter agriculture in a free and orderly way. That alone will enable us to 'transfer peasants, reduce the village population, and enrich those who remain', assisting urban development and the transition of the rural economy to large-scale, professional farming and commercial enterprise.

Institutionally, in the process of establishing a socialist market economy, the central government has transferred many powers downwards to provincial and local authorities. However, lower levels of government have since kept powers that ought to be transferred directly to enterprises or to workers and peasants. Excessive concentration of power without effective democratic supervision is the root cause of corruption. The biggest frustration, in my experience, of attempting local reforms in 2000 was that, when I was certain of the support of the masses and even of the deputies to the People's Congress, I could not locate the lever by which it could be given material effect. Democratic supervision should not be mere lip-service: the mandate of the people's will must be guaranteed by the processes of government. The first remedy is to re-establish the authority of deputies to the People's Congress over public finances, official appointments, administrative oversight and other important issues.

When there is no supervising authority in the People's Congress, correction of malpractices by the central government will prove very difficult, for they can always spread more rapidly than it can intervene. Before excessive use of luxury cars by local officials can be corrected, excessive construction of luxury housing develops, then excessive acquisition of luxury cell-phones, computers, and so on. There is no efficiency at all in long-distance superintendance by the central government. The most efficient way of countering corruption is to entrust authority to the people. It is democratic supervision and administration that can exercise effective control over the power of officials.

The key to securing the political leadership of our Party today is to make sure the masses are in charge and to start reorganizing the structure of government. The aim of political reform is to make certain our government remains loyal to the people, and acts according to its will. There is no need to fear the consequences – as if once peasants emerge from their current condition as a 'tray of sand', and acquire a certain organizational cohesion and the collective ability to defend their rights, society will be destabilized. That's wrong. We should trust peasants, advance their consciousness, mobilize and rely on them to lend wings to the political construction of democracy in the countryside.

8

Equity and Efficiency

Hu Angang

China is currently undergoing two profound transformations. The first is changing the country from a predominantly agrarian into a predominantly industrial and service-based economy – and therewith a traditional, mainly rural society into a modern, mainly urban one. In the past twenty-three years (1978–2001), China averaged an economic growth rate of 9.4 per cent, while GDP increased almost eight times. Over the same period, the total Chinese population rose by 310 million, while the urban population grew at the same rate, or some 13.5 million a year. The net increase in the employable non-agricultural population was 247 million.

The second transformation is changing an economy based on imperative planning into a modern market system, and moving a highly centralized political order towards a socialist democracy. This is typically a very difficult and painful process, rife with unpredictable developments and steep challenges. Among the latter may be numbered sudden drops in the growth rate or in the improvement of labour productivity, high inflation, explosive levels of unemployment, unyielding budgetary deficits, serious balance of payments problems, heavy foreign debts, and so forth. This is not to speak of elements of social instability that could cause serious political crises.

Chinese Realities

The outcome of the various changes now under way is much more complicated than we tend to imagine. Modern China is best described by a trio of contrasts. The first of these is between institutional systems. The inhabitants of town and countryside respectively are governed by two quite different sets of regulations – dealing with residential registration, education, employment, public services, financial transfers, and elections. For example, the Fourth Session of the Ninth National People's Congress in 2002 stipulated that every 960,000 rural adults would elect one representative to the Tenth

National People's Congress to be held in March 2003, whereas the same number of urban adults would elect four representatives. The design of the 'two systems', illustrated by this disparity, is such that the gap in per capita income and public services between the cities and the countryside keeps widening. Currently China's rural population is about two-thirds of its total population, but no more than a tenth to a seventh of the national budget is directly allocated to it. This inequality in the distribution of public expenditure is a critical factor in the huge abyss that separates the cities and the countryside. If the historical origin of the 'two systems' goes back a long way, there is also an immediate political reason for their existence today. While the peasantry makes up the majority of China's population, when it comes to budgetary transfers, distribution of investment or provision of public services, it lacks a voice of its own in society – having neither real political representation in the decision-making process, nor institutional channels to affect policy-making.

The second contrast is regional. Within China, if we adopt the World Bank's method of classifying regions by per capita purchasing power (PPP), there are virtually four worlds. The 'First World', which has entered the Bank's high income group, comprises the three municipalities of Shanghai, Beijing and Shenzhen – amounting to about 2.2 per cent of the whole population. The 'Second World' is made up of those regions with a PPP equivalent to its middle-income standard: they include the cities of Tianjin and Guangdong, and Zhejiang, Jiangsu and other provinces along China's south-east coastline, with about 22 per cent of China's population. The 'Third World' are those regions whose PPP corresponds to the lower-middle income level, with some 26 per cent of the population. Finally the 'Fourth World', located mainly in the impoverished central and western parts of China, with about half of China's population, are regions whose PPP is the equivalent to the World Bank's low-income countries. According to our comparative study, China has the greatest regional development disparities in the world. Even within a province, the income differentials are typically enormous.

The final contrast is sociological. China remains a predominantly agrarian society. Half its labour force is still employed in agriculture, a level comparable to that of France, Germany or the United States in the 1870s. Labour productivity on the land is incredibly low, and so too is the proportion of grains and other crops that is marketed. But China also contains an industrial society that, if we include construction, now accounts for nearly a quarter – 23 per cent – of its labour force. Alongside it there is a service society that employs another 22 per cent. Lastly, there is the sphere of what we may call educated society – the intelligentsia understood in a broad sense, including sectors of education, health-care, culture, science and technology, finance and insurance, and government. That can be computed at about 5 per cent of the employable population.

These structural divisions correspond fairly closely to the opposition between cities and countryside. In rural China, agriculture absorbs nearly two-thirds of the population, industry some 14 per cent, services 17 per cent, and intellectual occupations less than 2 per cent. In urban China, 27 per cent of the population works in industry, 23 per cent in services, 21 per cent in intellectual occupations, and there are estimated to be from 70 to 100 million migrant workers of rural origin, or more than another 20 per cent of the urban labour force.

Major Challenges

Against this background, China is entering a period of many interconnected challenges. After almost two decades of fast economic growth when demand exceeded supply, the wheel is turning, and in many sectors supply now exceeds demand. Deflation appeared for the first time in 1997, and since then has become steadily more acute. In the past six years, agricultural prices have plummeted; and the price of producer goods has also fallen, if more unevenly. Traditional industrial sectors like timber, textiles, iron and steel, coal and machinery, having ceased to expand, are being forced to restructure; while rising sectors like electronics, telecommunications, computers, ecological protection, biotechnology, finance and insurance are all growing rapidly, but do not yet form pillars of the Chinese economy. Employment in manufacturing and mining is dwindling; in services it is increasing. Global financial crisis is accompanied by worldwide overproduction, as international competition intensifies, hitting Chinese exports.

Meanwhile, China is experiencing unprecedentedly high unemployment. On the one hand the country has an enormous army of surplus labour on the land. The United States has 1.4 times as much acreage under cultivation as China, yet the labour force in Chinese agriculture is 100 times larger than its American equivalent. By my conservative estimate, the number of surplus rural labourers in China was about 200 million people in 1990, dropping to 160 million in 1996. On the other hand, urban unemployment shot up from 1993 onwards. The majority of the jobless – at least among those officially registered – are young, but there has also been a huge increase in laid-off workers who are mainly middle-aged. By the end of 2001, the real rate of unemployment was running at 8–9 per cent, much higher than the official figure of 3.6 per cent, and the total number of unemployed nationwide – i.e. those officially registered as jobless + laid-off workers who had not found new jobs + migrant workers who had lost their jobs in urban areas + job-awaiting graduates of colleges and professional schools – was 18 to 19 million people, more than the combined unemployment – 17 to 18 million – of the eleven states of the European Union.

At the same time, income differentials of every kind are steadily increasing.

In 1997 the World Bank's report *China's Income Distribution Gap* noted that the Gini coefficient in the mainland had risen from 0.281 in 1981 to 0.388 in 1995.[1] Today the situation is much graver. Overall, income inequality in China is now comparable to that in the United States, and somewhat higher than in Eastern Europe. From the early 1980s through the 1990s, the Gini of East European countries rose 10 per cent; there was almost no change in developed countries; while in China it jumped by 38 per cent, the fastest increase in any country. According to the first survey of the assets of urban households in China, the top 10 per cent own 45 per cent of total urban residential wealth, while the bottom 10 per cent own a mere 1.4 per cent. The Gini coefficient of urban wealth is 0.51, far above that of urban income.[2]

The major discrepancy in material well-being between cities and country-side is also widening. The per capita income of urban residents was 1.72 times that of rural residents in 1985; it was 2.47 times in 1997. Possession of colour televisions and washing machines was then about four times as high in towns as in villages. In 1996 rural areas had a switchboard availability of 2.7 per hundred people, each of which would have access to 1.7 telephones; the comparable figures for urban areas were 19.3 and 15.4. In 1995, there was an average of 0.95 hospital beds for every thousand people in the countryside, as against 5.8 in the cities. As the World Bank has noted, changes in health-care funding have intensified the inequalities of access to medical treatment. Insurance cover mostly benefits city dwellers and government officials, leaving the rural population to bear all the costs of their medical care themselves.

Regional disparities have moved in the same direction. In 1991 per capita income in Shanghai was 11.6 times that of Guizhou; four years later it had increased to 15.1, and the figures for domestic investment followed in step, rising from 18.6 to 24 times those of Guizhou. Social indices of education, health-care, technology, cultural facilities, infrastructure projects and environmental protection are no less splayed. According to the World Bank's human development index, China belongs to an intermediate group of countries in the world. But Shanghai and Beijing are among its most highly developed regions, ranking thirty-third in an international league table, while Qinghai and Tibet are among its least developed, ranking 121st and 131st on the same scale.

China has, moreover, entered a period of widespread environmental danger. The largest national population in the world is still growing; industrialization is advancing rapidly; while vast areas are dominated by a backward traditional agriculture. In these conditions, the nation is suffering

---

[1] World Bank, *China's Income Distribution Gap*, 1997.
[2] The National Statistics Bureau conducted the survey of 3,997 households in big, medium and small cities in seven provinces, plus the metropolis Tianjin, in July 2002.

from extensive ecological damage. World Bank experts reckon that current pollution of air and water costs China an annual equivalent of between 3.5 and 7.7 per cent of GNP. If pollution of the atmosphere could be brought down to officially sanctioned levels, some 300,000 lives would be saved each year. Natural disasters provoked by destruction of the environment regularly inflict heavy losses on the economy, varying between perhaps 3 and 5 per cent of GDP each year. In 1998 the flooding of the Yangtze, and of the Songhua and Nen River region in the far north-east, cost the country some 250 to 300 billion yuan. The bill for other kinds of ecological damage – deforestation, soil erosion, desertification of grasslands, shrinking of rivers and lakes – is harder to estimate. But it is clear that much cultivated land is dwindling, mineral reserves are being depleted, and many resources wasted (recycling rates are very low). If all these costs were put together, it is possible they would amount to as much as a tenth of China's GDP – that is, more than its recent annual increase in value. Economic growth is being undermined by environmental damage.

Another scourge of the time is rampant corruption. While no country has been able to stamp out corruption completely, it is clear that the degree of this ill varies widely according to the institutional setting. In China today, it represents a very serious problem. A conspicuous example is furnished by the PLA, and the military police and law-enforcement agencies themselves. These institutions, often described as a 'great wall of iron and steel' or 'solid pillars' of the nation, are all involved in commercial activities, that may include smuggling or its protection. Elsewhere 'bureaucratic privatization' is occurring, as power-holders under the old system (and their social nexus) employ legal or illegal means to steal, annex and divide public assets, and with this primitive accumulation of capital become *nouveaux riches* over-night – all in the name of reform. Then too an underground economy is flourishing, which in some areas along the coastline has given 'black societies' (mafias) virtual control of the local scene. Here criminal groups practise smuggling on a huge scale, manufacture fake or pirated products, launder foreign currency, evade tariffs and taxes, and openly bribe local Party, government and law enforcement agencies to ensure political protection.

In a research project published in September 2000, I have analysed the four major types of corruption plaguing China's economic transition: rent-seeking; underground activities; tax evasion; and embezzlement of public expenditure.[3] I have since collected further information published by various official sources during anti-corruption campaigns, providing information on the economic losses caused by the cases they document and categorizing these into ten different kinds of loss. There I define 'systemic corruption' as

---

[3] 'Fangzhi fubai de zonghe zhanlüe yu zhongda jucuo' (A comprehensive strategy and key measures for preventing corruption), Beijing 2002.

the abuse by governmental organs or public institutions of the power which is entrusted to them, to benefit officials in these departments. My research concluded that the economic damage such corruption inflicted may have averaged as much as 14.5–14.9 per cent of GDP in the years 1999–2001.

Finally, China faces growing risks of social instability. Different groups and classes are splitting away from each other, conflicts of interest are intensifying, and social order is threatened with significant disruption. A high proportion of China's enterprises – not only state-owned or collective enterprises, but township-and-village enterprises and private firms – are in operational difficulties today. Together with this, corruption and abuse of power are seriously harming the masses. Consequently, the incidence of all sorts of symptoms of social instability is on the rise, indeed increasing at a pace that is outstripping the growth of the economy itself. Between 1996 and 2000, China's GDP grew by over a third – 35.8 per cent. In the same years, however, the number of labour disputes accepted by the courts, criminal cases investigated by police, transport and other accidents, multiplied yet more rapidly. Labour relations are often very tense, and conflicts with management are increasing fast. Crime and insecurity are becoming a more and more conspicuous problem. Innumerable transport and industrial accidents are reported. Levels of corruption are rising, involving ever greater sums of money and higher-ranking officials. All kinds of gang-controlled organizations are emerging and growing in number, engaging in criminal and black-economy activities. In China, these different ingredients of social instability are rapidly expanding in number, affecting ever wider spheres of the population. This is grave cause for alarm.

If such are the major challenges facing China, how are the four goals that lie before us – 'strengthening the nation (to become a world-ranking power), enriching the people (to raise the standard of living of the whole population), promoting democracy (to establish a socialist political system), and securing stability (to ensure enduring security of the nation)' (*qiangguo, fumin, minzhu, wending*) – to be realized? Below I will offer some political, economic and social proposals that have grown out of my own thinking on these problems. I should first say something briefly about the provenance of these ideas.

Background

I belong to the intermediate generation of the People's Republic. I had just completed elementary school in June 1966 when the Cultural Revolution broke out, and at the age of sixteen was sent along with another 100,000 youths from Beijing to a military farm in Heilongjiang, in frontier conditions on the Siberian border. There I spent seven years, before being transferred to a geological survey unit in North China, where I worked as a driller in a prospecting team, often travelling to desolate locations in remote mountains or valleys, staying in the homes of villagers. Witnessing their absolute poverty, I became acutely conscious of the degree of China's backwardness, and was stirred to try to understand and help overcome it. After a day of heavy physical labour, at night I would study whatever I could get hold of, from official texts to the natural sciences, by gaslight, using my bed as a writing desk – determined to follow Gorky's example of attending the 'university of life'.

When nationwide examinations were restored by Deng Xiaoping in 1978, I got into Tangshan Technology College, and went on to do a Ph.D. at the Institute of Automation of the Chinese Academy of Sciences. The subject of my doctorate was China's demographic problem. At that time – 1984 – the strict controls on population growth that had been put in place after the Cultural Revolution were being questioned, and a fierce scholarly debate broke out about the wisdom of continuing to enforce them. Based on long-term demographic projections, my dissertation came down firmly in favour of tight controls. By that time I was part of the Research Group for the Analysis of National Reality set up by Zhou Lisan at CAS. In 1988, I completed the first report published by the Group, under the title *Survival and Development*.[4]

This work sought to look systematically at four major historical factors conditioning China's path to modernity: the continuing population growth, with its attendant problems of employment; increasingly scarce agricultural resources; worsening environmental damage; and expanding demand for food grains. Warning against 'impatience for success', it insisted that the modernization of China would be a protracted battle, in which there was no possibility of repeating the path taken by the West. What was needed was a model of growth adapted to China's unique set of liabilities and endowments, capable of ensuring a secure existence and sustainable development for those living today, without damaging the chances of survival or well-being of posterity. Deng Xiaoping read *Survival and Development* and his daughter Deng Nan invited me and a colleague to turn it into a television series, which was eventually aired in four instalments under the title 'Unsettling Reverberation' (*Zhenhan de huisheng*) in 1991.

Soon afterwards, arriving in Yale for a postdoctoral programme, I started to collaborate with Wang Shaoguang of the Political Science Department there, on the question of central–local government relations since the beginning of the Reform Era. Our research showed that the fiscal system of 'contracted taxation' was tending to produce a weak centre and strong provinces, seriously damaging the capacity of the state to manage the transition from a planned to a socialist market economy. To remedy this

---

[4] Zhongguo kexueyuan guoqing fenxi xiaozu, *Shengcun yu fazhan: Zhongguo changqi fazhan de jige wenti*, Beijing 1989.

disquieting trend, we proposed a unified system of modern taxation, separating national and local taxes, with stable relations between central and provincial authorities. In May 1993, our report was published by the Xinhua News Agency, for internal circulation, and drew the attention of political leaders. On reading it, Jiang Zemin asked our age, and on being told we were in our forties, remarked: 'youngsters – that's terrific.' Two months later, the government announced that from 1994 China would separate central and local taxes, in a unified fiscal system.

In 1998 I set up a series of 'Research Reports for the Analysis of China's National Reality', designed to provide reference materials for central and provincial leaderships. This periodical had published some 500 issues by late 2002, and has prompted numerous instructions from the State Council. It is the most effective channel I have found for helping to shape policy. But though I believe that where possible it is the duty of a scholar to provide responsible and original suggestions to policy-makers, the first requirement for being able to do so is scientific research conducted with an independent outlook – 'seeking truth from facts' (*shishiqiushi*), not from prevailing opinions. This is what I have tried to do in my writings in the nineties, and in the Centre for China Studies at Tsinghua University that I direct today. The propositions advanced below are made in that spirit.

Politics

If China is to become a modern country, the first task is to modernize its state structure. That means establishing a socialist democracy, in a society based on law. What should be the role of the state in such a democracy? A market economy is the most efficient system so far discovered by the human race for the allocation of resources. But the market mechanism is not omnipotent. In a market economy, state intervention remains a basic condition for economic development. The duties of the state include provision of public goods, direction of public investment, redistribution of income and wealth, stabilization of macro-economic balances, and implementation of industrial policies. The market cannot perform these essential functions. To acquit itself of them successfully, the state must have the necessary means of fiscal extraction, and power to intervene in fields outside the market. In a socialist market economy, the following should be the goals of the state: a reduction in its own functions in the field of competitive production and investment; an increase in its function as the provider of public goods; a continuous increase in its function of supplying social services; and a consolidation of its function as the guarantor of social security.

In the constitutional balance between national and provincial authorities, the central government should be responsible for overall supervision and take major policy decisions, while the power of local governments to express their views and participate in the policy-making process should be enhanced. China is the most populous country in the world, with a vast territory and complex domestic problems, which make it impossible for the central government to administer everything. At the same time, China's regional development is highly unbalanced, and there are fifty-six ethnic groups nationwide, which make it equally unimaginable to let provincial governments make their own decisions over every local issue. It is impossible for China either to concentrate all power in the centre or divide it among the provinces: a mixed system of authority, in which central government is dominant, is indispensable. Therefore the basic principle in handling central–local relations must be to combine unity and diversity.

The cement that will unite this system is the role of the central government in adjusting macro-economic balances, setting monetary policy, supporting social security, addressing unfair income distribution, reducing economic disparities between regions and between the cities and the countryside, establishing a national taxation system, enforcing fair market competition and determining the minimum level of public services provided to all citizens. Diversity will stem from the rights of every province to make local laws and regulations, so long as they are not in contradiction with national legislation, without arbitrary interference from central government. In practice that means redistributing the relative administrative powers of the centre and the provinces in accordance with the principles of a modern market economy, to ensure that all the regions have an equal say in the distribution of public expenditure and investment of nationwide importance. Whether big or small, rich or poor, all provinces should enjoy equal rights of participation in the central policy-making process. The current preferential treatment of the Special Economic Zones should be terminated, and every region guaranteed equality before the laws and institutions of the land, without exception.

At the same time, there needs to be a horizontal division of power, and central policy-makers have to be made accountable for their decisions. According to the Constitution, the State Council is responsible to the National People's Congress (NPC) and its Standing Committee. Certain powers currently in the hands of the State Council – for example, concerning public finance and investment – should therefore be gradually returned to the NPC and its Standing Committee, while the State Council should be put under the authority of the Prime Minister, as the Constitution stipulates. At the national level, the government needs to re-centralize its own budgetary planning, and allow the State Council and its Finance Ministry to concentrate on funding a few big national projects. The state should also set up a National Security Committee to handle major crises or sudden incidents that threaten the country's interests, and coordinate action between the various departments involved in them.

To avoid major policy errors, a decision-making process has to meet certain conditions: so far as possible, it must be democratic, transparent and professional. To that end, the government should set up an advisory committee or think-tank to provide it with in-depth research on issues of strategic importance, and foster the creation of independent, unofficial institutions for the analysis of public policies. So too, it ought to stimulate – wherever they do not infringe state secrets or state security – both internal and public debates over issues that affect the interests of a broad range of social groups. Finally, it should encourage news media to cover promptly and truthfully events that affect ordinary people's livelihood – such as natural disasters, job lay-offs, price changes, environmental dangers, serious accidents – and in general to mirror the interests and demands of the masses.

Another urgent task is to stem the growth of official institutions. It should be strictly forbidden for party organizations or government agencies to engage in business or run companies. The government should be financed by ordinary taxation. China has the largest state apparatus in the world. Though market reforms have made substantial progress, they have never seriously touched the massive and inefficient administrative structures created by and for China's planned economy. Tackling these is very much in the interest of less-developed regions. Local governments need to close down all their production bureaux and keep a minimal staff to synthesize economic policies and to improve the delivery of public services. They should have the power to determine both the size and pattern of their own institutions, which do not have to correspond to the arrangements of the central government. The different layers of administration need to be compressed, and office personnel reduced by at least a third. Officials in general should receive substantial salaries, and the average income of government workers be set somewhat above the middle level of the whole society, while every variety of secret bonus or perquisite should be revoked. The income and assets of all government officials must become completely transparent to the public.

Lastly, the army must be strictly banned from engaging in commercial activities. All companies run or co-run by the military must be closed down, without exception. The PLA should not be permitted to take part in any kind of profitable enterprise. Its units must also be forbidden to accept presents, donations or expenses from local authorities where they are stationed. On the other hand, the military budget should be significantly increased, to a level where it accounts for at least 2 per cent of GDP. The state needs to redefine the tasks of the armed forces to reduce their non-military expenditure, and to purchase equipment other than arms on the market, while contracting arms production to specialized companies. It should also reimburse the army for its contributions to the relief of natural disasters.

Economy

Moving to the economy, it is my conviction that China should turn from mere pursuit of GDP growth to goals of human development. The two are by no means synonymous. Economic growth is a means for realizing human development: it is not an end in itself. If growth is to serve people, rather than the other way around, it must improve not only their living standards, but also their chances of education and training, health-care and job openings, and their social security. Development here means enhancing people's capacity to secure competitive employment, move their income level upward, protect themselves against risk, and participate in democratic life. The government has to set a given economic growth rate as a national objective; but ordinary folk care more about the tangible benefits they may – or may not – derive from increases in GNP, and the responsibility of a government is to solve problems in their livelihood. If inventories rise steeply, while firms incur heavy losses, then no matter how high the growth rate, it will not mean much to the people.

Considering these principles, China should take full advantage of its size as a nation to expand domestic demand. When the Asian financial crisis broke out in July 1997, setting off shock waves in financial markets across the world, dozens of newly developing countries were plunged into a serious recession, and the growth rate of the world economy, and of international trade and investment, fell sharply. The result was a big drop in the growth of Chinese exports and a slowdown in direct foreign investment in China. Moreover, the global overproduction of energy, minerals and other raw materials, and their consquent fall in price, has combined with rampant smuggling to strike hard blows at extractive industries in China. The consequence has been a decline in growth that has brought it below its trend line of 8–9 per cent. Effective demand is weak, overproduction is extensive, deflationary pressures are strong. So it is no surprise that inventories are high, increasing numbers of workers are being laid off by former state-owned or collective enterprises, and the real rate of unemployment is rising sharply.

In these conditions, 'moderate growth and demand expansion' should be the main goal for China's macro-economic policies. China has the advantage of being a big economy. If it is forced to restructure and adjust, China has greater room for movement: its domestic market is relatively large, and its regional differences are remarkable. Expansion of domestic demand is in any case not merely a short-term remedy for current difficulties, but a long-term strategic priority. Here the tertiary sector has the greatest potential for development, since service industries have the greatest capacity for job-creation and is the most likely to attract foreign investment. State monopolies in education, health-care, culture and sports need to be broken up, opening up – but also regulating – a market in these activities. Likewise the banking and insurance sectors, domestic and international trading, transportation, storage, air and sea cargo, communications, scientific research and technical services should all be opened up to competition.

Infrastructural projects offer a second set of opportunities. If in the past infrastructure has always been a bottle-neck in China's economic growth, it could in future furnish one of its most powerful motors. World Bank studies have shown that for every percentage increase in the infrastructural stock of developing countries, there is a comparable rise in the growth rate, and the next decade should be a golden age of labour-intensive public works in China. Many of these will be located in cities, where accelerating urbanization will stimulate demand for construction of all kinds. If China's urban population were to rise from its current 30 per cent to the world average of 45 per cent, at least 300 million peasants would become city-dwellers, creating an enormous demand for public facilities and residential housing. For that to happen, the government will have to loosen its controls over migration from the countryside, and abolish the present residential registration system, replacing it with individual identity cards of the kind that exist elsewhere.

At the same time infrastructural investment is no less needed in the countryside itself, where rural industrialization should be pressed forward and local markets vigorously expanded, to raise peasant incomes and lift the 50 million worst-off in the population out of absolute poverty. There too environmental protection will require the mobilization of a massive labour force, capable of absorbing laid-off workers from the cities as well as surplus labour in the countryside, to carry out forestation of abandoned or uncultivated land, water and desert control, road and rail works, and fructification of arable land.

In all this, the guideline should be to maximize purposeful employment by 'saving capital and using surplus labour', except in the case of selected capital-, resource- or technology-intensive industries. Movement of workers from state-owned firms, or of graduates and veterans, into the private sector or self-employment should be encouraged. Export of labour should be increased by bidding for international construction projects. Enterprises should provide regular holidays and flexible hours. Jobless youth should be helped to find contractual employment on a hourly or piece-work basis. Training and information should be available to job-seekers, and the constitutional rights of employees protected. Creation of job opportunities and the real rate of unemployment should become important criteria of government performance at all levels.

On the international front, China must make the best use of its comparative advantages, in speeding up liberalization of trade and investment, while cautiously experimenting with financial liberalization and lifting of capital controls. The market in domestic services must be opened up and foreign firms offered 'citizen treatment' on a par with native enterprises. Trade policy should aim to increase the number and quality of labour-intensive exports and raw materials with abundant reserves and selectively promote the export of capital-intensive products. China should import moderate amounts of grain, and actively seek energy resources like oil and natural gas abroad, either through imports or acquisition of foreign resources by domestic firms, to assure the nation stable bases of supply.

Finally, China needs to promote a new model of consumption that is discriminating, equitable, and sustainable. That means it should discourage or curtail the luxury consumption and wasteful expenditure of a wealthy minority, and encourage instead habits of moderation. The state should turn away from its policy of boosting the prestige of rapid fortunes – 'to get rich is glorious' – and seek rather to guarantee a minimum standard of consumption for each and every citizen. It must show responsibility for a rational utilization of resources, making use wherever possible of market mechanisms to eliminate subsidies, and promote clean technology. Overall, the focus of government should shift from producer to consumer protection, ensuring accurate information about commercial goods and services and safety codes for them, and encouraging market competition to lower the price and raise the quality of products for sale. That requires a more open-minded attitude to the international market, to reap the benefits of free trade and the possibilities of common consumption created by economic globalization.

Society

In promoting economic growth and market mechanisms, China should follow the principle that 'efficiency is the priority, but equity should not be forgotten'. On the other hand, when it comes to the provision of public services, the principle should be 'equity is the priority, but efficiency should not be forgotten'. Under socialism, efficiency and equity are not necessarily in conflict or exclusive of each other; the two play differing complementary roles in different fields. Reliance on market mechanisms to liberate and develop the forces of production, and on principles of justice to achieve well-being for all, is a hallmark of the superiority of socialism. We should not merely emphasize the 'efficiency goals' of the present period. Reform of the economic system can take many paths, and restructuring can produce a variety of options. From among these, it should be after all possible to devise a scheme that will compensate those injured by the changes under way, and materially benefit the most vulnerable groups in society, such as the unemployed, the discharged, the poor, the disabled, or low-income pensioners and women. The state should spare no effort to minimize the damage inflicted on those who are disadvantaged in the process of transition.

For that, China needs to set up a modern social security system. In the United States Roosevelt considered the Social Security Act of 1935 the cornerstone of his New Deal. It linked, for the first time in American history, the personal interest of the citizen to the interests of the nation. Since then legal statutes of this kind have reduced social conflicts and stabilized social order in the US. In China, with few exceptions – the 'Labour Security Code' published by the State Council in 1951 was one – there is no formal legislation in this area. Instead of setting up individual accounts for retired employees, the government passes responsibility for pensions to their previous work unit, whatever its degree of solvency, and the laid-off or unemployed get no dole. In the absence of any comprehensive social security system, a large number of citizens face a wide variety of risks. There is therefore an urgent need to set up a benefits system appropriate to Chinese conditions, covering pensions, unemployment insurance, health-care, housing loans, work injury compensation, and life insurance.

The right to survive and the right to develop are the most basic human rights. The Constitution of the People's Republic promises every citizen education, employment, access to medical care and social security. To make sure these services are equally available to every Chinese citizen means to specify a minimum national standard, which will be lower than the average standard nationwide, but should serve a threefold purpose: to assure basic elements of social justice, to develop human resources, and to raise future productivity. Equal opportunities for development, however, also require the state to 'send charcoal in snowy weather' – that is, to provide timely help to impoverished regions and populations. Generally speaking, China has by now reached a phase of lower-middle income development: most of its people live above the line of absolute poverty; a significant number – especially in the cities, and parts of the countryside along the coast – enjoy a 'decent' (*xiaokang*) living standard; while a minority are relatively well-off.

But when the poor fall below 10 per cent of the population in China, economic growth will not immediately lift them out of their misery. That will require the state to mobilize its resources to eliminate absolute poverty in the country. The fight against poverty, however, needs to change in three major respects: it should be institutional rather than charitable; it should aim less at relief only, and more at development; and it should try to help people who are poor, rather than provinces or counties that are poor. In other words, the direct beneficiaries of poverty-assistance programmes should not be the various levels of government in an impoverished region, but instead the poor who live in it. To achieve better results in our anti-poverty action, we need to target the remote hamlets and villages where most destitute peasant households are located.

Lastly, we must deepen ongoing educational reforms. China is running the largest school system in the world on a budget of less than 3 per cent of the world's total public expenditure on education. This basic fact means that we must insist on effective use of what resources are available for Chinese education. Public expenditure should be devoted mainly to its compulsory stage, in elementary and junior high schools. For subsequent stages, market mechanisms need to be introduced, moderately increasing the fees to be paid by individuals, and encouraging unofficial funding, including private or foreign investment to speed up the industrialization of education. College degrees are one of the new hot spots in domestic consumption, and will be an important area of increased domestic investment in future. The existing educational system artificially inhibits demand by the broad masses – urban or rural alike – especially consumer demand for higher education. The authorities should open up the market here, breaking up the current state monopoly in higher education, and allowing different kinds of modern college to develop – some owned and run by the state; others owned by the state and run by local collectives or private firms; others owned and run privately; or owned and run jointly.

While promoting this diversification, the state should also promote work-study programmes among students, and offer financial aid to students from low-income families, scholarships to outstanding students, educational loans to all students, and teaching or research assistant fellowships to graduate students. It should also make full use of foreign sources of funding, actively applying for hard loans from international financial institutions to develop China's higher education industry. Domestically, it should create either a Higher Education Bank, or a special fund for higher education within a national development bank, to extend loans on a rolling basis. The political sphere must be separated from university administration. Institutions of higher education should become corporate bodies enjoying full autonomy in policy-making, management, self-discipline, and responsibility for profit and loss. They should each have a president answerable to a committee of trustees. China also needs to develop adult professional education, aiming to create a mature student body two or three times the size of its undergraduate enrolment.

The political, economic and social proposals set out here reflect not only my own experience, but the general attitude of Chinese scholars of my generation.

PART III

9

Industrializing Education?

Xiao Xuehui

Injustice in Compulsory Education

China's education is afflicted with a multitude of acute problems today. The most serious are the following. First and foremost, access to schooling is utterly unequal. Nominally, there is compulsory education for all children for nine years. In reality, a vast number are excluded from it. This injustice is compounded by the enormous differences in the quality of teaching and school conditions from region to region, or between urban and rural areas. Per capita investment in education in Beijing, Tianjin and Shanghai is several times higher than in remote, backward provinces, and in poor rural areas of the hinterland is virtually nil. Many areas struggle to maintain schools at all. In the big cities themselves, key-point schools and classes enjoy privileges denied to normal schools and classes, giving a minority of children an elite education while a majority receive a substandard one.

As early as the late 1980s, it became clear that many Chinese children either had no schools to which they could go, or were dropping out of schools to which they did go. From my own personal experience, I know how expensive it is for even a college teacher in a city to get an only child through elementary and secondary education – let alone for peasants in the countryside or urban workers without stable employment. The government has talked for years about solving this problem. But year after year, there is no improvement. Instead, the situation is getting steadily worse, as reports that a million children have either abandoned their schools, or have no school to go to, reappear annually in the press. At stake here is a basic requirement of social justice.

Compulsory schooling is the basis of an education. Nobody can afford to miss this very first link in a long chain. Without the knowledge and culture nurtured by it, an individual will find it difficult to function as a responsible member of society, and will face a blocked future. Therefore everyone has a basic right to education, above all to the first years of compulsory schooling.

Society has a duty to provide a minimum schooling for all its children, to equip them with the literacy necessary to lead a normal life, find a job, pursue their education and act as a citizen. Compulsory education can be described, in the words of a recent report to UNESCO, as a 'passport to life'. That is why it is a responsibility that must be shouldered by the government, and be free of charge.

It is only after discharging this responsibility to them that a society is entitled to make demands of individuals, and to enjoy their trust. Since every country has its own gap between rich and poor, it is only if basic education is provided free of charge that everyone can enjoy it, regardless of class. In China, there are two further reasons why parents should not have to pay for their children's schooling. The first is that average incomes remain low, even in the Reform Era. The wages of state employees are heavily taxed at source, while other members of society are afflicted by endless chaotic fees and charges extracted by various governmental offices. An education tax is deducted monthly from the salary of each urban state-employee, while the rural population has to pay an additional tax for its schools on a yearly basis. In these conditions, to oblige families to pay for their children's schooling is to charge them twice over.

The second reason is that there are tens of millions of people in China classified as living below an official 'subsistence level' that is miserably harsh, while worsening corruption and expropriation of public assets is forcing more and more people into a huge army of the poor. In this situation, if parents are made to pay out of their own pocket for the schooling of their children, universal education becomes so much empty talk to families that have to struggle even to buy food and clothing. They simply lack the means to send their children to school. Without a necessary minimum of education, adolescents are ill-prepared on all fronts of life, or not prepared at all. Not only do they have no chance of sharing in the intellectual and cultural resources of the society, but even in a basic struggle for survival they are at a disadvantage. Citizens' rights are little more than empty words for them. Untrained and unequipped, they will often have difficulty in behaving in normal civilized ways. To them, stupidity, humiliation, failure, defeat, poverty, crime, and punishment are shadows following them wherever they go. The large number of people now falling into this condition represents a shameful dereliction of duty by society. Every year more children join the growing army of those who cannot, or can barely, read and write. A hereditary class of the illiterate and poor is being created, the most striking of all injustices in a society that is already full of them.

The illiterate population produces more criminals than any other social group. This is an indisputable truth. Yet in meting out punishments, the legal system rarely considers another factor of great injustice. In crimes disrupting social order, there is a significant distinction between those with an education and those who lack one. What the former know how to avoid, the latter do not. Neglected by society, illiterates have missed the opportunity to gain any proper comprehension of social rules and legal regulations, but this is never taken into consideration in reducing or averting their punishment. In practice, sentences generally move in the opposite direction, inflicting heavier penalties on the disadvantaged than on anyone else. For they possess no power, no money, no ability to defend themselves. This is the social group with the least means of self-protection.

In recent years, it has become more and more obvious how vulnerable these people are. Migrant workers are a case in point. This is a social group that is young, poorly educated, and which frequently changes job and changes location. Clustered in big cities, migrant workers earn the lowest wages, do the heaviest labour, and live in the worst conditions, and are given no respect or protection. When there is any police sweep (*yan da*) in the cities, as often happens before significant political events, they are the first to be targeted. In Shenzhen alone, there were more than ten thousand injuries and eighty deaths among migrant workers in 1998.[1] Those responsible are rarely brought to court. But when migrants themselves break the law, punishments are savage. The *Southern Weekend* reported two cases on July 2, 1999. In Beijing's version of Silicon Valley, the Zhongguancun area, a migrant worker from Inner Mongolia got drunk and stole a mini van in 1998. He was caught the next day, while driving the van back to his hometown. On June 23, 1999, the district court held a hearing on the case. The worker obviously had no idea of how to defend himself in legal terms. All he said was that he had 'stolen the car to go back home and would have returned the car once he got back'. The judge replied: 'Are you crazy?' The hearing lasted for less than an hour: he was sentenced to ten years' imprisonment.

In Hangzhou, a law student from Peking University witnessed a trial, at which the accused was sentenced to several years in prison for thefts amounting to just over 600 yuan ($70), not enough to cover a single meal consumed by some of our officials at public expense. The law is so harsh on people from the bottom layers of society that it is like a sword hanging over them. It is more than often powerless in dealing with those who abuse their position to make off with huge amounts of taxpayers' money.

The multiple injustices that befall those with little literacy derive in large measure from the original, primary injustice at the beginning of their lives: they did not receive an equal basic education. That is where the chain of consequences started, which all too often ends with certain government officials regarding those at the bottom of society as mere social trash, and treating them in advance as criminals. Young people falling into this class have a very dark future.

---

[1] *Zhongguo hezuo xinbao*, June 21, 1999.

Misplaced Values

A second problem is the political utilitarianism that threads its way through educational guidelines, goals of training, curricular schemes and contents of textbooks. Children's personalities and wishes get absolutely no respect at all. They are treated as shapeless clay to be manipulated according to specific political needs. Pounding set ideas into the mind becomes the most essential part of education. This is much more damaging than the 'exam mentality' (*ying shi jiaoyu*) that has recently drawn indignant criticism, which may not have much direct connexion with the content of what is taught, whereas political utilitarianism directly affects what is learnt in the classroom. Any political pressure on education, even if not self-interested, tends to lead to conformism and short-term calculation of advantage, discouraging broader horizons, greater ambitions, and more critical intellectual life, putting disinterested curiosity, and a spirit of exploration and adventure at a discount; and if it is self-interested, then a blinkered outlook and misinformation of every kind inevitably follow. The 'knowledge' drilled into children by text-books becomes from the start a kind of anti-knowledge.

[Education can serve different ends – nurturing a strong nation, an equal and peaceful society, the self-development of individuals, international competition or cooperation, and so forth. If an educational system fails to reflect this range, it falls into a morbid state] We should be cautious about collective entities interposing themselves between humanity as a whole and the independent individual. At present, we are witnessing an irreversible ongoing movement from monism to pluralism in modern ethics, which combines a respect for universal values and universal laws to protect them with a tolerance and acceptance of diverse ideals, faiths, standards and codes of conduct. Such a contemporary morality answers not only to the universal need for self-preservation, but also to the eternal human search for self-realization and personal dignity. This is a much more inclusive conception of ethics than the rational-interest versions of morality that are now widely influential in both intellectual circles and governmental policy-making in China. Personally, I have defended the somewhat concrete morality of rational self-interest, but also dared to defend an idealism that is generally ridiculed and abandoned nowadays. That is why I contend that current principles of mere 'practical interest' have monstrously distorted the purpose of education. Against them, we must insist on the idealistic dimension of any education worthy of the name.

In China today, an extremely narrow understanding of education prevails, that sees only its uses to the nation and society, ignoring its significance for the individual and humanity. Even compulsory schooling is not universal; there is little care for the individual, or conception that education is a basic right. At best, people are viewed instrumentally as a 'precious resource' or 'human capital', not as ends in themselves. Building the nation is posited as the ultimate objective of education, dissociated from the fate of humanity as a whole, whose unity students are rarely taught to understand or respect. Rather than encouraging curiosity and mutual exchange between different cultures, current Chinese education instils – involuntarily or intentionally – unhealthy arrogance and chauvinism.

This is a utilitarian outlook that trains its subjects to fulfil pre-set social objectives, emphasizing practical skills and knowledge at the expense of the development of personality or exploration of human potential. Our middle schools impose disciplinary divisions unnecessarily early on teenagers, with a heavy imbalance between sciences and humanities. The latest reforms in higher education point in the same direction. When this utilitarian conception of education converges with market fundamentalism in society at large, amidst a consumer euphoria fanned by the mass media, the result is an extremely debased social atmosphere.

Education in China has long been a vassal of politics. What its reform requires, at the most fundamental level, is another set of institutional arrangements. The priority is to withdraw all political and ideological interference from the whole system. In elementary and middle schools current political classes should be replaced by courses in citizenry. In colleges and universities, academic autonomy should be restored, political criteria in appointments and curricula abandoned, and control of campuses transferred from administrative offices to academic senates.

The Ills of Higher Learning

A further problem is the state of higher education. There lack of freedom in research and teaching is compromising the position of universities as centres of autonomous scholarship. Extreme utilitarianism of purpose and separation of disciplines are leading to a decline in standards, as the role of the university in preserving and creating a common culture has been reduced to its lowest point. The humanities and social sciences increasingly become mere annotators of current government policy, while the natural and applied sciences value practical technology at the expense of basic theory. Meanwhile, rampant corruption in the award of degrees and titles has caused inextricable confusion on the ladders of academic promotion, creating a more and more incongruous and ironic situation in our universities. All this has led to the deterioration of any potential for the pursuit of truth in China's institutions of higher learning.

In my view, higher education in China after 1978 experienced a short-lived golden age. The resumption of national college entrance examinations that year replaced the system of recommendation institutionalized in the latter half of the Cultural Revolution, when students were recruited according to purportedly political criteria. In practice, since the power to recommend candidates was controlled by local cadres, offering hefty opportunities for abuse of power, an already absurd system became a way to drop a curtain across many cases of corruption. With the abolition of this system, national examinations restored the traditional right of colleges to judge candidates, however imperfectly, on the basis of their knowledge, encouraging a passion for learning in our elementary and middle schools. At that time, the newly reinstituted national exams had not yet gone to extremes in forcing middle and even elementary school pupils to cram for the sole purpose of passing them.

Secondly, there was a short-lived movement for intellectual liberation following 1978. In many a ground-breaking debate, college faculty and students demonstrated unusual courage and enthusiasm in exploring the historical and socio-political problems facing our nation. This was a time when we saw an eagerness to learn, a thirst for truth, and demonstrated a capacity to invent and create. I believe it was exactly this energy that brought a long-lost honour and prestige back to our campuses, though after a decade in which research had been completely stalled, the levels of instruction were not yet very high.

Thirdly, higher education during that period broke out of its stupid state of self-imposed confinement. Vigorous intellectual exchanges not only sprang up between universities inside China, but broad connexions were established with the academic world abroad. Chinese universities started to appreciate research criteria commonly accepted internationally. These contacts made scholars aware of the huge gap in standards between Chinese and international practice. Faculty, students and administrators were all inspired to press ahead with reforms, independently of official directives, and to explore hitherto forbidden areas of knowledge. Had this *élan* been preserved, our higher education system might have subsequently taken fewer detours. There are those who believe that in leaving their seclusion our academies were asking for trouble. But Chinese education in closed conditions had been thoroughly instrumental in nature and narrow-minded in outlook. Since it left no room for independent development, it brought no trouble, and offered no hope. Our troubles today come not from opening our doors then, but from the continuing political resistance to this, which has entrenched the double standards of an open policy limited by heavy regulations.

Unlike the early 1980s, reforms in higher education since the late eighties have been driven by short-sighted utilitarianism – ever-narrower curricular divisions, and a more and more unbalanced preference for the sciences over the humanities. Actually, what replaced the humanities courses is not always science per se, but sometimes courses that can be translated into 'cash' instantly – or can be advertised so. In rushing to set up new 'empirical' courses, teachers would cut-'n'-paste to throw together something on a subject that they might not have really understood in the first place. Corrupt reform like this will not teach students even basic skills in their field.

Education as an Industry

In June 1999, after a National Education Working Session, the news spread that colleges should both expand admission (*kuozhao*) and raise tuition fees. By late summer, in rapid succession many provincial and municipal governments had hiked fees by huge amounts, and schools fell into a frenzy announcing their new 'standards', with all possible justifications for increased fees. For example, in Shanxi, a mountainous province with a relatively underdeveloped economy, new regulations stipulated that students at senior high school should each semester pay registration fees of 800, 700, 600, and 400 yuan according to the ranking of the school. In other words, the annual cost would amount to 1,600 yuan for a good school, and 800 yuan for a bad one. Furthermore in practice, as every parent knows, there will be books, lecture notes and all other kinds of expenses throughout an academic year, amounting to a total cost equivalent to a couple of months' wages for a middle-income worker, earning say 800 yuan a month. As for colleges, take Chengdu – the provincial capital of Sichuan – where I live: an otherwise obscure college announced that it would now charge freshmen average annual fees of 2,600 to 5,000 yuan, according to how 'hot' a major is considered in society. If we add the usual miscellaneous expenses that can be up to 2,000 yuan, the total cost for a new student ranges from 4,500 to 7,000 yuan. This is low for Chengdu. Some colleges sent out bills for tuition fees of more than 4,000 yuan, and collected more than 6,000 merely for admission.

Moreover, both senior high and college levels quickly seized the opportunity to demarcate their 'official quota' from 'expanded admission' students, charging the latter exorbitant special fees. In Shanxi again, an 'expanded admission' student at senior high school was required to pay 10,000 yuan each year for registration alone. This is more than an entire year's wages of a middle-income worker. Greed was even more unbridled at college level, where 'expanded admission' students were charged tens of thousands of yuan merely for being admitted, in some cases even up to 100,000 yuan.[2] In Deyang, a small city near Chengdu, there were twenty students facing painful decisions after receiving admission notices, conditional on their families paying huge fees they could not afford. Deyang is not a remote town and not poor either. Imagine what such charges mean to families living in impoverished villages, dreaming of getting their children

---

[2] The uproar over the sudden escalation of fees was so great that the Ministry of Education decided to call a halt to them in September 1999. However, its decree specified only that increases were to be 'stopped in future (*xia bu wei li*)' – fees already collected would not be returned. Nor did it say anything about the different charges for 'official quota' and 'expanded admission' students.

into senior high school or college. In fact, as we have seen, even the nominally compulsory education at elementary and secondary (junior high) level is now often too expensive for many rural families.

What we are witnessing is a Pandora's box that, once opened, releases incurable greed and bottomless corruption, of a kind probably without precedent in the history of world education. If test scores fall short, money can make good the numbers, in the shape of so-called 'score deduction fees' (*jiangfen fei*) of tens of thousands of yuan, or 'sponsoring fees' (*zanzhu fei*) to secure priority entry into 'hot', highly competitive majors. Every imaginable type of corruption has sprung up virtually overnight. All of this forms part of the so-called 'industrialization of education' (*jiaoyu chanyehua*) that has been one of the most striking expressions of market fundamentalism in recent years. Why should education be industrialized? Supporters argue that senior high schools and colleges do not form part of compulsory education. A Senator of the Chinese Academy of Sciences, whose name enjoys nationwide recognition, says in stern tones: 'It must be made crystal-clear that higher education is not part of compulsory education, and so in principle expenditure on it must come from the broad masses, the people themselves'[3] – as if state revenues didn't come from 'the broad masses, the people themselves', but were gold eggs laid by the government itself!

The advocates of 'industrialization' reveal their view of education in the kind of calculations they make about its effects. According to them, the current deflation is caused by lack of consumer enthusiasm for purchasing goods, so expanding college admissions and jacking up student fees is a constructive way of forcing people to loosen their purses. Whether the results of 'industrialization' will be in line with the predictions of these prophets is another matter. But the term 'consumer' is explicit enough in letting people know that to get an education is no different from going to a shopping mall: you get what you pay for.

Among those who share this premise, some talk bluntly, others approach the subject more obliquely. The straightforward ones declare that higher learning is a 'luxury good' in the consumption of education that does not belong within the category of products whose price is protected by the state, but should be marketed at prices reflecting changing relations between supply and demand. Since college capacity is limited and population is continuing to grow – however many fall under the poverty line – the upshot is, of course, patently an absolute 'seller's market': whatever hardships parents may suffer are what you deserve if you decide to send your children to college. The more indirect apologists explain that higher education is, after all, an investment in one's future, and therefore the future beneficiary must bear the cost. Whether higher education is not part of the investment

---

[3] He Zuoxiu, quoted in *Gaojing – Zhongguo kejide weiji yu tiaozhan* (Warning: crisis and challenge in Chinese sciences and technology), Tianjin 1998, p. 40.

the state must make for the future of the country is never considered. Others argue, in more accounting spirit, that as the average cost of an undergraduate student in China is about 20,000 yuan per year, the 3,000–5,000 yuan registration fee after the recent hikes has not yet matched outlays, on a principled basis of 'best price for best quality'. Obviously, the implication is that the fees need to be raised further.

In the vision of these champions of the 'industrialization' of education, the function of institutions of higher learning is not even to serve a social purpose or promote economic development (by, for example, creating job opportunities for graduates in the private sector). Its aim appears to be simply to make higher education a scarce – therefore hot – consumer good, and to extract more and more money from the pockets of student families. They ignore both the level of most people's actual incomes, and the redundant personnel and squandered resources that inflate the budget of Chinese universities. Today higher education in China typically suffers from an excessive administrative apparatus, lack of any serious audit of expenditures, astonishing waste of resources, and a doubtful quality of instruction.[4] The 'industrializers' could not care less about these problems, or the need to catch up with international standards of teaching and research.

In this atmosphere, we often hear dignitaries – especially officials in charge of local educational affairs – explaining that 'the development of education should not aim one-sidedly at social justice', since 'its supply is not essentially different from that of other commodities', or that 'educational equality is an issue so remote from the present reality of economic inequality in China that it could be considered a practical issue only after another century or two', so to speak of it is 'to lag behind the market economy, remaining stuck in utopian nostalgia for the planned economy'.[5] The logic of such arguments is characteristically perverse. Since there is such economic inequality, China cannot afford educational equality. Commercialization of education is the only way forward, under the slogan: *no cash, no classes*! Far from becoming a driving force for social justice, education along this line would only entrench and deepen the surrounding inequality, so that in 'a century or two' educational equality will be even more unthinkable than today.

Even worse, some economists who are baffled by prolonged deflation think they have the answers for education, while knowing virtually nothing about it. According to their logic, if education is not compulsory, then it ought to be a commodity, tradable at a profit at appropriate prices in the

---

[4] For example, the *Guangming Daily*, a leading official paper covering intellectual and cultural life, ran a long feature on January 31, 1997, entitled 'Jichu xueke boshisheng zhiliang bu rong leguan' (Little reason to be optimistic about the quality of Ph.D. students in basic scientific theories). Faculty, students and parents have all expressed concern about standards of training in recent years.

[5] Quoted in *Shanxi fazhan daobao*, July 13 and 10, 1999, respectively.

short run, without any regard for the uneconomic loss of intellectual potential in the population as a whole, and the resultant waste of what is actually the country's greatest 'wealth'. Higher education is an undertaking that requires a huge budget to support it, and in most countries it faces financial difficulties. To resolve these, alongside government expenditure and philanthropic assistance, students may also need to pay certain fees. But as higher education is a public benefit that should be as available to every citizen as possible, fee levels should always be related to the ability of the average citizen to pay them, rather than trying to extract from students their training costs, let alone to profiteer from them under the guise of fee-collection.

In Italy, a college freshman needs to pay nearly 300,000 lira a year, part at the beginning of registration and part before the end of March each year. But students who can demonstrate either financial need or an outstanding performance can secure waivers of part or whole of that sum. What is considered as financial need? By an Italian law of 1986, when the annual fee amounts to between 5.5 and 10.2 per cent of the income of the poorest families in the country, according to the number of members in their household. This kind of levy can be universally accepted. In the United States, where fees are at the high end among developed countries, in recent years fees for higher education have run at 11.8 per cent of average per capita income for four-year public universities, 5.2 per cent for two-year public colleges, and 50.6 per cent for four-year private universities. In other words, school fees in the public sector are manageable for ordinary families.

If we look at China, on the other hand, in 1998 – before the fee-increase mania – the cheapest college in the south-west city where I live and teach charged between 1,700 and 4,000 yuan a year, according to discipline, amounting to 40–85 per cent of average per capita income in urban areas. This was already a figure beyond the means of most families. After the hikes of 1999, college fees ranged from 5,000 to 8,000 yuan, or well above 90 per cent of average urban incomes in 1998, and 250–300 per cent of rural incomes. Even this represents only official fees, and does not take into consideration the epidemic of extra charges rampant in our colleges and universities.

Some economists close to policy-makers, ignoring the basic facts of low incomes and lack of social security in China in their search for ways to ease deflation, have exclaimed that private savings in China have 'reached 5,000 billion yuan'. Actually, they are less than 4,000 yuan per capita, and needless to say, the overwhelming bulk of it belongs to a tiny minority of the wealthy. Ordinary people have few savings. As health-care, pension and other social security problems deepen, families with limited incomes, if they want to send their children to college, will have to tighten their belts still further as education is 'industrialized'.

It is plain that higher education in China has more and more become a specially arranged banquet for rich people only. The direction it has been taking is more and more the opposite of the international trend towards democratizing schools and universalizing higher education. From elementary schools to universities, Chinese education is now unmistakably tending to exclude lower social strata and to enlarge the gulf between classes. Such is the undeniable reality.

A Necessary Utopia

Utopia is a design or dream of the future, usually of a wishful or idealistic cast. Milan Kundera has a famous aphorism that can be paraphrased roughly as follows: captivated by utopian ideas, people fight hard to force their way into Heaven, only to find that – when the gates have shut behind them – they are actually in Hell. The image can be especially appreciated by Chinese who believe that they have been recklessly fooled by a fake idealism in the twentieth century. When they started to reflect on their own experience, the very idea of 'utopia' became an object of condemnation, equated with a hypocritical ideology, naivety and mendacious promises. I believe this negative judgement has gone too far and the case has been somewhat simplified.

If we set aside cases of deliberate deception, the reason people distrust utopias is that they seem unrealistic. But dreams that are unrealistic are not necessarily futile, or harmful. A report by the International Committee on Educational Development remarks that any cause which aims at changing the basic conditions of human life will inevitably contain some utopian elements.[6] What is taxed as utopian are frequently just visions. Dreams themselves simply express discontent with current realities and the status quo. People without dreams are wanting in youthful vigour and liable to conformism. But human beings will always retain some ability to dream, and so construct one utopia after another. Some of these may express the last yearnings for an outdated ideal; others display an acute understanding of real social ills. Some can induce human beings to sacrifice the present to a supposedly glorious future, victimizing people here and now for a wonder world in the beyond; others can be a tremendous force for progress, inspiring creative passions and a direct intervention in public affairs. Some may be arrogantly confident of their own superiority, ruthlessly crushing all other dreams, and putting to death those with different ideas or ideals; others may be protective or tolerant of alternative visions. In short, apart from the common feature of their contrast with established reality, utopias may differ vastly from each other.

---

[6] *Learning to Be: The World of Education Today and Tomorrow*, UNESCO Publishing, 1982.

In the West, the later Renaissance saw a range of utopian proposals, of which the most famous are More's original *Utopia* and Campanella's *City of the Sun*. Today we may well criticize these as so over-detailed that they left almost no room for further initiatives or rational reflection, and by neglecting the value of freedom lent inspiration to modern authoritarian regimes. However, the authors of these proposals were honest thinkers, and even with their share of serious mistakes, their ideas still express a belief that is true and valuable: namely that human beings can work to further the happiness and harmony of mankind. The critical charge of these conceptions was sufficiently powerful to yield practical results where least expected: More's *Utopia* was to affect British pension laws.

Such visions of the future offer people lasting ideals that may wait centuries to be realized. Huang Zongxi (1610–1695) imagined a state where schools were the arbiter of all social rights and wrongs, with powers of supervision and impeachment comparable to those of a parliament in a modern political order, principals and teachers openly elected – rather than appointed – and students able to exile any who were corrupt.[7] Huang's conception still seems dream-like in today's China, but versions of it have come into being elsewhere in the world. In his *Commonwealth of Oceana*, James Harrington (1611–1677) imagined a republic of equals with a written constitution, elected officials, secret ballot, separation of powers, the rule of law – and freedom of religion and universal public education. Although such a republic was a pure utopia in the seventeenth century, many of its features came to pass in modern democracies that emerged hundreds of years later. In 1941 Roosevelt and Churchill promised to establish a world based on freedom of speech, freedom of religion, freedom from want and freedom from fear. No country has yet fully embodied this ideal, which we could therefore call utopian. Yet this was a great dream that inspired many human beings, and remains dear to the heart of many. Orwell said somewhere that the Western ideals of liberty and equality may be contradicted by the realities of injustice, cruelty and deceit, but that such ideals mean that not many people can now view these iniquities with complete indifference. A state where the mind is occupied by concepts of liberty and equality and the heart is not indifferent to social evils is *the* force to change reality.

The history of human development is one of continuous struggles to transform ideals into reality. In those struggles, education has played a crucial role. In the contemporary world, the ideals of democracy, freedom, peace and human rights are universal, but their realization is very partial, and depends to a significant extent on the kind of education each country possesses. If freedom is shackled, segregation or hatred encouraged, popular will ignored, social hierarchy imposed, and cynicism encouraged, then

---

[7] See *Hu Shih xueshu wenji: Jiaoyu* (Scholarly Works of Hu Shih: On Education). Beijing 1998, p. 270.

education can either arouse a reforming critical spirit or train people to conform to the status quo. If it does the latter, it loses its essential function, and inevitably becomes complicit with the darkest forces of society. For its proper vocation lies in the opposite direction. When economic growth is pursued at the expense of the natural environment, war and dictatorship still flourish, and social exclusion and injustice abound, education is needed not only to provide every individual child with a better future, but to raise people's sights to a world in which such evils are not accepted.

These are the reasons why, I believe, UNESCO's Education Committee for the Twenty-First Century defined the common need for education as 'a necessary utopia'.[8] In other words, education is only true to itself when it is capable of looking to the future. This idea has been expressed in the saying that education should always instil the belief that present conditions are not the sum of what is possible. This conception of the role of education is particularly needed in China. It is unfortunately a fact that we tend to be straightforwardly utilitarian as a people. More generally, ours is anyway a time when we are beguiled by material consumption. It would be better to start thinking carefully, and take seriously the principle that the end of education is to develop the potential of all human beings, rather than to reproduce the inequalities that divide them.

Of its nature, education can never be entirely industrialized. The functions of its higher reaches include the preservation of basic social values, the cultivation of minds and the accumulation of knowledge, and these duties can never be replaced or performed competently by any other kind of institution. A society is without hope without the contributions made to it by learning, and these cannot be calculated in monetary terms. Not only the traditional vocation of higher education, but the newer tasks that have fallen to it since the Second World War, as humanity faces more and more serious ecological, demographic and military threats to a common life, are beyond any simple economic calculus. When every nation is confronted with continuous challenges of all kinds, what essentially determines its ability to meet them is its educational level, of which the extent and quality of its higher learning ought to be the most important marker.

---

[8] *Learning: The Treasure Within*, a report to UNESCO by the International Commission on Education for the Twenty-First Century, UNESCO Publishing, 1998.

10

Tales of Gender

Wang Anyi

A peach was presented me
I returned a fine jade

I consider myself fortunate. From the time I was born, equality between the sexes was always regarded as normal and desirable, even something protected by law. My grandmothers sit stiffly and solemnly in their photographs, their misshapen feet so remote from me they seem unreal: I can hardly believe we belong to the same century. I once asked, with some curiosity, an old teacher who remained single all her life: was celibacy also fashionable in your day? She looked at me kindly and replied: that didn't occur to me; I simply realized that most of the married women around me were unhappy. Even this scene is now so eroded by time that its memory is blurred. In her article 'Thoughts on March 8', Ding Ling once argued for improving the social position of women, warning against the persistence of male domination in the early years of a proletarian regime.[1] Those disputes have since melted away. It was on the ground prepared by the submission, sacrifice and struggle of several generations of women that we grew up.

I lived in this society of gender equality in innocence, and even ignorance. In the classroom we drew '38th Parallels'[2] on our desks to mark a clear boundary with the boys who shared them with us. That was how the buds of adolescence swelled. At work, women performed the same tasks and received the same wages as men; they were proud they were not judged inferior. In the family, because they were economically independent, they

---

[1] Ding Ling (1904–1985), leading woman novelist from the late 1920s onwards, who put gender questions at the centre of her writing. 'Thoughts on March 8' (*Sanbajie you gan*) was written when she was a CCP cadre in Yan'an in 1941. See *I Myself Am a Woman: Selected Writings of Ding Ling*, Tani Barlow with Gary Bjorge, eds, Boston 1989, pp. 316–321 [ed].

[2] A term popular among pupils of elementary school in the fifties and early sixties. It refers to the demilitarization line between the two Koreas at 38 degrees of north latitude, indicating a determination to brook no reconciliation [ed].

were on an equal footing with men. Where I live, in Shanghai, husbands are affectionately regarded as henpecked. An equality attained so easily brings its own illusions, obscuring the reality of women's lives in a relatively backward economic setting. Women paid a double price for their external equality: they were overworked in their manual labour, and obliged to repress their identities as women. In the absence of any challenge in this placid environment, gender equality – won by the tenacious struggle of several generations of women – gradually became deformed, tending to suppress gender difference. I, however, was in luck again.

With the eighties came an ideological emancipation that brought various philosophical trends to us, bearing the fruits of centuries of thought. Starting as a writer at that time, I was lucky enough to benefit from them. I had the chance and means to reconsider gender relations. Many new issues perplexed me. Are there natural differences between the sexes? If they exist, to what extent has society modified them? Is respect for such differences, or elimination of them, more in keeping with our humanity? All these questions and more were endlessly debated over the next twenty years, and conclusions were hard to reach. But doors and windows were opened on ideas that had long been imprisoned, and fresh air flowed in, giving them new energy. Thinking was restored to health. That was a more dynamic period, the vigour of which resonated with my desire for freedom and growth. For a woman writer, it was especially favourable. I was not only able to observe the world as any man might; I had a further perspective on it, as a woman, from an angle that made it clear men and women were not yet truly equal. To some measure, women were still dissociated from the centre of society, wandering in its margins.

This was a time when we joined the worldwide revolutionary community of women. That was like a great festival. In 1994, I went to Melbourne for the Sixth World Exhibition of Women's Books. It was a female carnival. At the opening ceremony, a male Australian official was allowed to give a speech by the organizing committee, as a financial sponsor of the occasion. He was barely able to finish his first sentence before he was shushed and driven away by hoots from the audience, who stared at each other with surprise: what was he there for? That was a merry scene, but there was something bathetic about it. Women were to celebrate their sweeping successes at an evening party where no man could be present. But after the party, wouldn't we have to return to our respective lives and face the world together with men again?

At such international conferences, the relationship between the sexes is detached from its social and historical contexts. Its forms become abstract, its circumstances vague, the understanding of it parochial. The inequality in gender relations is abstracted from them, and then reinforced as a simplified confrontation, expanding and submerging every aspect of existence. But my luck still held good.

This time I should particularly thank the world around me. Resisting radical change, reality enjoins us to wise up and face our circumstances. Time flies, and a new century has started. All we see around us is new. Women who used to be plain and modest are now radiant and enchanting. The rediscovery of gender has enriched human nature and confirmed the values of the individual. Onto this lovely stage, women step forth with grace and confidence – a splendid scene indeed. But trouble is where fortune prospers, and fortune where trouble prospers.[3] Making themselves so spirited and vivacious, women slip into the era of the market economy unawares. The fruits of their new-found theory and practice are traded more or less as objects of consumption. Advertisements for every kind of commodity restore the tradition that 'women make themselves pretty for those who love them'. Newspaper supplements and columnists expose their private lives to the public. With skilful strokes, women writers too, create apparitions of their sex that can also be enjoyed by men. Above and beyond this market, there is a further consumer power – the world's hegemonic culture. As China is gradually globalized, the inequality its women suffer is redoubled.

As a woman writer from the Third World, I cannot escape what I hear, see and experience. Circumstances, ever more pressing, drive my thoughts forward, never letting them stop or idle. New topics stir my emotions and force me to learn and to understand. They save me from the callousness of this materialistic time and its quiet paralysis. I can remain anxious and ardent, maintaining my writerly energies. I feel grateful to have lived through a half century that allowed me to grow up freely and happily, then opened my mind, and finally forced me to face our present difficulties. I try to express that gratitude in my work as a writer, searching for the words, at least, of a better world. The title of my essay comes from *The Odes*: 'A peach was presented me / I returned a fine jade'. The poem has three stanzas, each ending with the same refrain: 'Not in exchange / but that our friendship might last'. That conveys something of my hope for this existence.

Shanghai, November 9, 2002

---

[3] Lao Tse, *Tao Te Ching*, Hong Kong 1989, p. 85: translation modified [ed].

For Whom the Bell Tolls

When TV news reports that another criminal gang has been sentenced, when the camera scans one young, indifferent face after another, how often do we think about the circumstances in which they lived, and or where they came from?

A reportage, 'Youth: The Proximity of Heaven and Hell', published in four instalments in the Shanghai magazine *Shoots*, reveals some of these people's hidden stories.

Its principal figure was born in 1973 and lived in Panhuang, a rural town in Yancheng County, Jiangsu Province. Although the town apparently has a long history, it has been in gradual decline, perhaps since the economic centre of the area moved to Yancheng. Its main street is some 500 yards long, running from east to west, connecting at its western end with a road, regarded as a new street, running from north to south. A national highway passes the town's perimeter at a tangent. Yet this ancient, decaying town has more than twenty dance halls. We learn that the drying-ground of the Staple Foods Control Office may serve as an outdoor dance-floor, kindergartens become ballrooms in the evening, and the dining halls of certain work-units can also be converted into dance halls. Evening after evening would seem to be filled with revelry, yet this is also a lonely place. One might think of Macondo, and the tumult in its seclusion. Modernity hovers over the town like an iridescent cloud, but its life remains unaltered.

Young people here belong to a generation that has grown up since the Open Door policy came into effect. The consequences of a laissez-faire economy are all around them: small factories, started in haste, swallow up farmland; surplus labour streams from the countryside into the cities; the urban population increases; the job market becomes more and more competitive. In a letter to a girlfriend, the central character of the story described his future perilously: 'There is no need to say anything. Now I only want to come top in the High School Entrance Exams. If I don't get good grades, I won't be able to go to a good college. If I don't have a college degree, I won't find a good job.'

Prospects are limited; for a young man from the rural interior, especially so. But now human nature is to an unprecedented degree liberated, and personal desire upheld by opportune theories of individualism, spurning traditional morality. In his diary, the protagonist noted his principle for choosing a wife: 'I need another kind of woman – the sort that can support Julien's attempts to enter politics financially, and help a husband to meteoric success and fame.' This lad of little experience and meagre knowledge may not have actually read *Le Rouge et le Noir*, or had much notion of what individualism was, but he had no difficulty setting himself this goal all the same.[4] A youth caught in a contradiction of this sort – engrossed by fantasies of freedom, and trapped by limitations of choice – is at serious risk.

Such situations have a deceptive sheen of modernity. The shrinkage of farmland, expansion of cities, bustle and disorder of markets, create a mirage of metropolitan life. When the protagonist failed the college entrance exam, he gave up his original ambition and entered society. Unexpectedly, he found he could dabble in different kinds of jobs. Each lasted only a short time, but when he lost one, he readily found another. Life was hard and insecure, yet he assumed great airs. He wrote to his girlfriend: 'Although the world is wide, there is no niche for me . . . I need to wait, and until the right opportunity comes, grin and bear it . . . I have always wanted to recover my self, and to pursue my own positive way of life.' How would such an opportunity come? People no longer believe in low-efficiency labour based on the notion, 'no pain, no gain'. Everyone feels pressed by time. Though he said he had to, he was too impatient to wait. Drinking with his companions, he told them: 'There's something I can't understand. Those who live in villas, own cars, and dally with women aren't smarter than us. If we're not inferior to them, why shouldn't we rise high too?' They replied: 'Why not? If we had money, we could buy anything'. Question and answer were equally stupid and conceited. They decided to go south, saying: 'People below the Yangtze live happily, and are afraid to die. We can use this weakness to get money from them'. This plan was also stupid and conceited, and sounds like a dream. But when myths of the upstart abound, any dream may pass for reality to anyone who has the bravery to act on it. Matter of means would be ignored. There were no longer any moral codes to bind them.

This ancient town turned out to be rather open in personal matters. The impact of the Reform Era seems to have broken through many a fortress of private life, where individuals had the most independence to operate. Production might be backward, people still at the mercy of the elements, life impoverished, education scant, competition fierce, and basic gender relations fixed by tradition: when they grow up, all men and women should marry – but sexual conventions had shaken off the old shackles, advancing ahead of all other matters. Such a situation was very dangerous, especially for girls, who lost their customary protection and now had to wrestle with their fate unaided. Often they staked everything on a single throw – sex. But they dressed up their gambles with a shimmering rhetoric of modernity. They were adept at turning expressions of sentimental longing, in letters worthy of any soap-opera heroine. Calling our hero 'prince', in a highly westernized

---

[4] Both Stendhal's novel and – especially – a French film version of it became popular in China in the mid-1980s. When commercialization brought many changes to society, the story and its protagonists became frequent metaphors for writers and columnists throughout the 1990s. Hence the boy may not really have read the novel itself [ed].

style, they wrote of sexual intercourse as 'stealing the forbidden fruit'. But behind such flights of fancy, reminiscent of campus romances from Hong Kong and Taiwan, lay the relentless demands of their actual lives.

Between the lines of these dreamy incessant whispers of love, the existential realities of these girls peep through. Yuting, probably the most rational among them, withdrew from the battlefield of competition for the prince, consoling herself with the role of a 'spiritual lover'. Expressing her feelings in the idiom of a pop song, she wrote: 'I so want to be your good girl, forever, and you to be my big tall brother'. But in another letter, she describes the flooding of her home village in plain language. All the cotton fields were swamped, houses were collapsing, chickens at risk, and though her father was ageing, her second elder brother still lacked the money to marry. The anxiety she betrays is more authentic than her love.

Even love had its practical side. We read that 'in places like Yancheng County High, while students were surreptitiously exchanging notes or dating "underground", their parents were openly visiting each other to make new connexions ahead of the marriage of their children'. Once mentalities had adjusted, peasant families could derive tangible benefits from freer love among adolescents. The boys' families could perhaps save the cost of betrothal gifts; the girls' families could hope for the addition of another labourer, or half of one, to the household. It is unlikely the young were completely unaware of such calculations. They naturally welcomed this new version of old customs, which lent a fashionable aura to their youth. But they would have sensed the pragmatic significance of the romantic forms. Zhou Li, for example, unlike other girls who indulged in daydreaming, made up her mind early on to settle the main affair of life – getting married. She had precise goals and was decisive in action. When the moment of crisis arrived, she revealed her uncommon potential. Adopting a severe tone and a stern expression, she reported the 'prince' to the school authorities, and he was expelled.

The boy had grown up in this ancient rural town filled with illusions of modernity. He was one of the numerous children of an ill-starred, unstable, destitute family. We are told that his parents were sent to border regions when they were young, and only moved back to their home county when he was five. By then they would have been regarded at least in part, if not wholly, as outsiders. Their social status must have been low, their financial resources few. When he boarded in high school, he was almost always starving. In these difficulties, the affections of girls would have seemed a luxury. He regarded a college education as the key to escaping from his plight, so he studied hard and got excellent grades. To his satisfaction, he was admitted by Geling High School, which is regarded as inferior only to the key-point schools at provincial level. Even after he was expelled from it, he made earnest the plans to complete the rest of the high school curriculum by himself and pass the college entrance exam.

He knew, of course, that he now had to concentrate on improving his situation, but that did not deter him from continuing to accept feminine attentions. Like a stranded fish thrown back into the water, he readily flirted with girls, enjoyed their romantic affections, and accepted their presents with good measure. What is most surprising was his ability to keep his head through all this, like a man whose shoes are never damp, however often he walks along a riverbank. He never let himself be trapped. In his diary, he wrote that his way of attracting girls was 'to show affection to many, but never focus on one'. Of course, he wished to find a wife who could help him rocket to success and fame. But a wish is only a wish. It must have taken quite some effort and skill to remain so nonchalant. A boy making his debut in society, he acted more like an experienced swindler, impervious to any emotional attack.

When he failed to get into college, he started to drift. The jobs he found he soon lost, partly because times were hard, but also because he was wilful, lazy and undisciplined. But in his eyes the fault lay with others, and he had a thousand resounding reasons to denounce society. Pouring out his grievances in a letter to a girlfriend, he wrote: 'Many people take me for a gullible weakling and treat me roughly'. He also noted indignantly in his diary: 'Girls possess a treasure. It is neither a permit nor cash, but with it they can go anywhere they want. Eating, drinking, playing, they make merry and sleep with pleasure. But what do men have?' To make their mark, he and his companions went south of the Yangtze River in search of money. During the time of their assaults, only one among them could not endure what they were doing and quit. The others never wavered. They were tidy, and made quite careful plans. Not even once did they fail. After they had killed eleven people, they were sent to the guillotine.

Illusions of modernity created excessive expectations; cruel realities constrained the actual existence of these young men; their unrestrained imaginations gave birth to egotism. The three forces were expanding into each other. Unchecked, they eventually led to tragedy. They, who came from an isolated interior, could not see their part in the bigger picture. We remain a developing country in a global economic system. Surplus capital has flowed into China from all over the world, disturbing a land that for two thousand years relied on sowing and harvesting once a year. Young people assumed that this new development in the economy would bring them progress and happiness.

Shanghai, July 1, 1998

Translated by Gao Jin

11

The Citizen and the Constitution

Gan Yang

Throughout the twentieth century, it might be said that the Chinese people have time and again placed greater value on collective goals, such as national liberation and state independence, than on personal independence and individual freedom. The question I want to ask in this essay is whether we have not, in recent years, been witnessing a repetition of this pattern, in which the collective once again risks overshadowing the individual, but this time in the form of the 'province' or 'region'? Contemporary discussions revolve heatedly around the relative merits of federation or confederation, central and provincial governments. But I fear that we are in danger of confusing the most important issues at stake here by our paradoxical way of proposing questions and providing answers, so that instead of coming closer we have been drifting farther away from the goal of constitutional democracy.

Centre and Provinces

Let me take as an example the book *On the Relations between the Centre and the Provinces*, co-authored by Wu Guoguang and Zheng Yongnian.[1] This work is one of the most serious contributions to the debate. Unlike much fashionable writing on the subject, it correctly emphasizes the need for China to escape from the vicious cycle of the 'concentration – fragmentation – concentration' of power that has dominated so much of our history, and argues that, while a great deal of authority should be devolved to provincial governments today, it is also essential to 'construct a strong, powerful central government capable of coherent, purposeful administration' (p. 137). But how do the authors propose to combine these

---

[1] Wu Guoguang and Zheng Yongnian, *Lun zhongyang-difang guanxi*, Hong Kong 1995, page numbers are given in the text.

principles? They call for 'the development of regional democracy'. This is a solution which, in my view, could only lead in a direction opposite to their ostensible intention. What it would produce is not a strong or powerful centre, but one that lacked any independent foundation for its own authority, and so would be highly dependent on provinces that must increasingly constrain it.

The belief here seems to be that the way to bolster central authority is to build up local authority, as if a strong centre must rest on a base of strong provinces. In this model, the centre strengthens its own power by absorbing influential local cliques, and exercises its function of national integration through the web of provincial governments. As the authors put it: 'For the localities, this is the way to consolidate provincial power and participate in central politics; for the centre, this is the way to integrate local powers and strengthen a national authority' (p. 153). It is no surprise, then, that they end by arguing that 'the political agenda for a reform of the central government' must be 'to institutionalize the regular recruitment of regional elites' into it (p. 161).

Plainly, this is a political structure whose axis lies in the provincial authorities. Under such an arrangement, the relationship between the individual citizen and the central government is mediated through the power of local governments. Between the central authority and the individual citizen, political relations are indirect, a system that logically then leads to indirect elections too. This is, in fact, exactly the position taken by Wu and Zheng, who contend that nationwide direct election 'even if put into practice, would come at too high a cost for too small a benefit' (p. 142). Their concern, by contrast, is to found political society on local authority, and thereby – as they put it – 'to translate the legitimacy of provincial governments into the bases of a legitimate central government' (p. 161).

How, then, could the central government still muster a political will of its own, independent of local governments? If local governments decided to withdraw their support from the centre on the grounds that it did not answer to their needs, what sort of a response could the centre make? One way of clarifying these questions is to look at the historical example these authors invoke, in making their case for 'regional democracy' (*diyu minzhu*). They cite the United States as their model, confident that the constitutional arrangements of the Founders of the US support their argument. Indeed, they write: 'In the thought of the inaugural period of US history, particularly that of the Founding Father of the American Constitution, James Madison, "regional power" is strongly emphasized and systematically elucidated . . . The ideas of Madison and his colleagues found expression in the Constitution of the United States, which sets out very clearly the distribution of powers between the federal government and the states. In America at that time, power was primarily located in the states, rather than in a capital city

or the nation. As a country of settlers, the US had never invested independent power in a capital' (p. 140).

The American Federalists

Now it is true that Madison offered a 'systematic elucidation' of 'local
power', from which we can learn today. But should we not ask what sort of
elucidation this was, historically? The answer, as we shall see, is far from the
scheme now so often suggested in China. A year before the Constitutional
Convention in Philadelphia, Madison had started to study the history of
political systems based on provincial power in the West, taking notes and
writing commentaries on them. His basic conclusion was that none had
achieved long-term stability, all without exception collapsing under pressure
from internal strife or external disaster. A month before the Convention,
Madison produced a working document, 'Vices of the Political System of
the United States', whose central theme was that the defects of the original
Articles of Confederation stemmed from their 'mistaken confidence' in the
authority of the states, which had led to a situation where the central
government was at the mercy of local powers, unable to contain or discipline
them.[2] In Madison's view, this meant the US still lacked the most significant
condition for any constitutional system to survive, namely the power of the
central government to curb local authorities. It can be said that the
overriding aim of Madison and his Federalist colleagues was to establish a
powerful 'national' government, in lieu of a political system based on the
principle that power is primordially local, of the kind that had existed in
the US up to that time.

In this context, it is enlightening to recall the debate between the
Federalists and Anti-Federalists, for the situation of the United States in
the late eighteenth century bears some resemblance to that of China today.
The reasons why the Federalists were so anxious to create a powerful central
government in America lay in the daunting circumstances of the time. There
was a serious financial and fiscal crisis, since the Congress of the Confederation had no authority in this field, and could not secure the cooperation of
the states. Nor did the Congress have sufficient power to adjudicate or
temper commercial disputes between the various states, which were escalating. At the same time, the large volume of internal migration after Independence had provoked territorial disputes and secessionist movements.
Nowadays we tend to think only of the splitting up of former Yugoslavia,
without registering that similar tendencies were a serious problem facing the
newly independent United States two centuries ago. For instance, today's

[2] James Madison, 'Vices of the Political System of the United States', *Papers of James Madison* (eds W.T. Hutchinson, et al) Chicago, 1962–91, vol. IX, pp. 3–24; 345–57.

Vermont is a breakaway from what was then the state of New York. The Federalists believed that these territorial conflicts would lead to bloodshed in North America if there were no powerful national government to control them.

Finally and the most importantly, separatist pressures within the country prevented the US from acting as a unitary nation in the diplomatic arena, exposing it to ready defeat by European powers. As a matter of fact, one important precipitant of the Philadelphia Convention was a diplomatic issue. Spain was blockading the Mississippi River at the time, causing a serious dispute between northern and southern states over whether or not a compromise with Spain should be reached. In the *Federalist Papers* published after the Constitutional Convention, the first seven essays are mainly concerned with this grave situation.[3] They warn the American people of the danger that they could be repartitioned by European powers and lose all the gains of the War of Independence, should the US maintain a political structure in which power was primarily local and not create a unified nation-state represented by a firm central government.

The eleventh essay of the collection is a particularly plangent appeal. It complains that Europe has for a long time been so dominant in Asia, Africa, and Americas that it is used to regarding itself as the Mistress of the World, to the extent that even dogs become inferior by living in America. Thus 'it belongs to us to vindicate the honour of the human race, and to teach that assuming brother [Europe] moderation' (p 133). To that end, instead of being mere pets of the European powers, Americans should unite into a strong and integrated nation, and forge a future where Americans could not only avoid manipulation by Europe, but eventually force European powers to deal with America on American terms as well. It was the acute concern of the Federalists at the fissiparous tendencies of the US after Independence, and the extent to which the Confederate Congress was a name without substance, lacking any of the authority of a central government, that spurred them to the revolutionary step of scrapping the Articles of Confederation at the Philadelphia Convention (1787).

The US Constitution

In framing a completely new Constitution, the Federalists laid the legal basis for establishing a central government in the US capable of overriding each and every local power. In practice, however, to create an authoritative government in the US of that epoch was vastly more difficult than for the national government in Beijing to engineer a restructuring of the Chinese

---

[3] James Madison, Alexander Hamilton and John Jay, *The Federalist Papers*, edited by Isaac Kramnick, Penguin Classics, 1987. Page numbers are given in the text.

political system today. The Philadelphia Convention itself was composed of deputies from the states who had not been entrusted with drawing up a new Constitution, but merely with revising the Articles of Confederation. So the new text could not simply be approved by the old Congress. It required a higher sanction. That, the Federalists argued, would have to be the people of the United States.

In the ensuing debate over ratification of the new Charter, the Anti-Federalists attacked it as an annexation of the sovereign power of the thirteen states by a menacing central government, fighting to keep the old Constitution as a loose coalition of the former colonies. In reply, Madison and his colleagues produced the famous refutation collected in the *Federalist Papers*. Their central argument was that the Anti-Federalists 'seem to cherish with blind devotion the political monster of an *imperium in imperio*' (p. 147), or a structure in which local governments blocked direct connexions between the central government and individual citizens, or what Madison described as 'a sovereignty over sovereigns, a government over governments, a legislation for communities as contradistinguished from individuals' (p. 172). Against this conception, Madison pitted the principle of popular sovereignty. As he put it,

> the adversaries of the Constitution seem to have lost sight of the people altogether in their reasonings on this subject; and to have viewed these different establishments not only as mutual rivals and enemies, but as uncontrolled by any common superior in their efforts to usurp the authorities of each other. These gentlemen must here be reminded of their error. They must be told that the ultimate authority, wherever the derivative may be found, resides in the people alone [p. 297].

There is no need to idealize the American Federalists. Most were first of all American nationalists, keen to strengthen the competitive power of the United States. But their great achievement was to lay the foundations for a modern central government, and cohesive national identity. That is why, although the central government's authority over the states was not really consolidated until the Civil War and the Fourteenth Amendment passed after it, the Federalists were revered by later generations as architects of lasting peace and stability in America. For it was they who first argued that the sovereignty of a democratic country must spring directly from its individual citizens, rather than emerging from any local community, whether state, province, city, township or village. Where the old charter was based on local sovereigns, the new constitution was founded on popular sovereignty. The Articles of Confederation define the United States as a 'perpetual Union between the States'. The US Constitution today opens with the famous words: 'We the People of the United States'.

Reform in China

I believe that this legacy of the Federalists has a direct bearing on contemporary debates in China. For in our country too the question is posed: what should be the foundation or basic unit of a modern political society? Is it the relationship between provincial and central authorities, or is it the individual citizen? Looked at like this, it quickly becomes clear how closely many recent arguments repeat the original contentions of the Anti-Federalists in the history of the early United States. For the thrust of these is to restrict or replace central power by provincial power, instead of showing that central power must be rooted in popular sovereignty as a direct authorization by citizens. Here the local community rather than the individual citizen again becomes the basic unit of political society, and central government derives its legitimacy from provincial power.

In my view, by contrast, the principle of a constitutional democracy is that the individual citizen should be the foundation and a unitary constitution should be the framework of the nation. Moreover, I believe that not only is this dual axiom generally appropriate for China, but that it is especially pertinent in Chinese conditions. For the reason why traditional Chinese politics could never escape a perpetual pendulum swing between centrally concentrated and locally oligarchic power structures was precisely that the individual citizen never became the legitimate basis of political authority. In this sense, we may say that the fundamental task of Chinese politics today is to overcome, once and for all, this historical vicious circle.

It is true, of course, that a rising tide of new ideas and movements in the West, associated with communitarianism, have mounted a considerable challenge to individualist conceptions of politics, and that feminist theories have pointed out, even more sharply, that Western constitutional democracy has never truly rested on individual but rather on 'patriarchal' foundations. However, I believe the value of such criticism is to deepen our understanding of the democratic principle we need, rather than prompt us to discard it. Actually, today's Chinese discussions focus not on the family or neighbourhood level, but as Anti-Federalists once did, on the political level next only to central power – that is provinces or autonomous municipalities.

So it is even more necessary for us to emphasize that a constitutional democracy does not allow the presence of any *imperium in imperio*. The principle that the basic unit of modern political society can only be the individual citizen means that there must be a direct political connexion between the citizen and the central state, which no regional community may obstruct or sever. Indeed, in its original sense, the very concept of a 'citizen' presupposes the idea of a 'state': there can be no citizen of a province or a region. Therefore, the goal of political reform in China must absolutely not be to impede or break – in the name of 'provincial or regional power' – the political connexion between the individual citizen and the central state, but to make it highly democratic.

To avoid any confusion here, I should make it clear that I am not contesting that Chinese provinces should have their own authority (certainly they should), nor that they should develop their own democracy (of course they should vigorously do so). I sympathize with the good intentions of many who advocate devolving central power to the localities or building a confederate or federal structure in China, and can understand their fear that a concentrated central power will inevitably lead to authoritarianism. Historically, however, centralized power has not invariably been authoritarian, and provincially divided power has by no means always been democratic. A famous remark by Tocqueville comes to mind: 'For my part, I cannot conceive that a nation can live or above all prosper without strong governmental centralization'.[4]

The Problem of Size

These issues acquire a special edge in China, because the country is extremely large. They pose the general question: how is a democracy to be built in an enormous nation? Recent approaches, however, not only avoid but cancel this issue, by breaking a 'big' country down into a series of 'smaller' ones, before talking about democratic possibilities at all. Theoretically, this is a reversion to the long outdated view that democracy is only possible in small countries. In my view, the way to build a democracy in a big country is not to divide the large into small, but on the contrary to place value on the large as such. This cannot be done by putting some smaller democratic entities together; it depends on setting up an internal democratic mechanism appropriate to the large country itself. This is where the legacy of the American Federalists is of particular relevance to China, with its gigantic population. For their greatest contribution to political thought lies in the way they put to rest the traditional Western view that democracy is possible only in small societies, proving for the first time in Western – indeed all human – history the opposite: that, correctly understood, it is easier to realize democracy in a large society.

Robert Dahl once remarked that this was the greatest development in democratic theory since the time of the city-states of Ancient Greece.[5] It emerged from reflection on the failure of attempts to build a democracy in a large country on the basis of provincial decentralization. From this experience, the Federalists drew the lesson that the creation of a republic in such a setting would encounter the same problem as the establishment of a

4 *Democracy in America*, Chicago 2000, p. 83.
5 *Democracy and its Critics*, New Haven 1989, chapter 15.

monarchy: how was the danger of an *imperium in imperio* – that is, provincial powers waxing and central power waning to mere figurehead status – to be averted? In a large republican country, indeed, central authority required a more secure foundation than in a monarchy, where it could rely on dynastic legitimacy. In their foresight, the Federalists saw that the only way to solve the problem was to erect central power directly on a foundation of popular sovereignty, putting it beyond challenge from the provinces. In doing so, they solved a problem that had haunted the West since the time of Machiavelli: how could a republican system be made stable and durable? The solution they found is the fundamental reason why the United States was able to break with the Western tradition that a 'large country can only be ruled by a monarchy' and become the first example in history of a large country without a monarchy, but with a lasting and stable polity.

This American experience should help to persuade us that the Chinese tradition of 'the four corners of the earth under heaven's roof', handed down since Qin and Han times, is not necessarily an obstacle in China's path towards democracy. On the contrary, once the individual citizen is taken as the basis of political sovereignty, China's unitary tradition could be of great benefit to it, as the country develops into a modern state in which a legitimate central authority 'covers all that is under heaven'. The recent fashion for discussions of confederation, federation or provincial decentralization in a sense reflect a bafflement at China's size, leading to a conviction that the country must be divided into autonomous regional entities before it can become really democratic. Such proposals in effect revert to the old Chinese opposition pitting feudatories against bureaucrats, and if put into practice, their most probable result would be to plunge the country back into the traditional cycle of Chinese history, continually swinging between central autocracies and provincial oligarchies.

We are all familiar with the tales in Chinese history in which chaos spreads once the throne is shaken. We also know the high value set on lasting stability by Confucian literati, ever since Jia Yi wrote his essay on the mistakes of the First Emperor.[6] Moved by this concern, the mainstream Confucian tradition always felt an obligation to maintain the overall unity of China. But since the 1911 Revolution ended the last imperial dynasty and established a Republic, we have never yet succeeded in creating a political system that is stable and durable, and in truth have not given much serious thought to how this huge country could become a genuine, lasting republican state. Recent trends among Chinese intellectuals tend to belittle the Confucian tradition of safeguarding China's unity unduly, in a self-congratulatory way, as if this concern itself was wrong.

---

[6] Jia Yi (Chia Yi) (200–168 B.C.), 'Guo qin lun' (The faults of Ch'in). See Cyril Birch, ed, *Anthology of Chinese Literature*, New York, Grove Press, 1965, p. 46 [ed].

This neither does justice to Confucianism nor addresses the root of the problem. Long ago in the West, Aristotle realized that the problem of the 'throne' was inherent in every political system. For what it essentially amounted to was the question – how is central authority to be enforced? We probably should recognize that our ancient Confucian scholars had a profound understanding of this issue. Their historical limitation lay not in their concern for China's grand unity, but in an inability to imagine that the stable and durable rule of a large country was possible without a monarchy. This was a belief they shared with thinkers in the West: Dante's *De Monarchia* is an exemplary case in point. By the same token, we should not be opposing the tradition of grand unity in the name of a new 'feudal' devolution, but taking up the Confucian concern with a lasting and stable rule, to explore how to re-establish a legitimate foundation for central authority in a society with our enormous population. The Federalists were the first to realize that the most powerful centralization is possible only in a political society where central authority comes directly from citizens. In doing so, they paved the way for the expansion of mass democracy. Later on, Weber shared exactly this view with the Federalists.

Weber's Concerns

A century ago, Max Weber was deeply preoccupied by the swift rise of his fatherland, Germany, long a weak and backward part of Europe, to the rank of an economic superpower. He feared that this sudden ascent brought with it life-threatening dangers, as economic success exposed the political immaturity characteristic of a retarded nation. Throughout his life, Weber was always anxious that Germany would not achieve 'political maturity'.[7] His fears were confirmed by the development of German history after his death. The Weimar Republic became a virtual byword for lack of political maturity. It was succeeded by Nazism and the Second World War, with all their disastrous consequences. After the war the country was divided, the East becoming dependent on the Soviet Union and the West on the United States. It was only when the Cold War ended that the German people finally regained an opportunity to become a unified political nation – nearly a century later.

Weber's basic idea was this. Modern economic development determines a high degree of social differentiation. As society becomes increasingly diversified and centrifugal, the basic task of modern politics is to establish a structure capable of integrating it into a national whole equipped with a political resolve and centripetal power. Thus an important issue in the rise

---

[7] See Max Weber (1864–1920), 'Suffrage and Democracy in Germany', *Political Writings*, edited and translated by Peter Lassman and Ronald Speirs, Cambridge 1994.

of any backward nation is whether or not its leading forces have enough vision and resolve to create new political machinery to match its tremendous changes in social structure. As the basic trend of modern economic development is to incorporate the total population of a society into a unified process of economic exchange, Weber argued the political mechanism that corresponded to this mass economy could only be a mass democracy. Those who had been integrated into a unified economic system must at the same time be able to participate in a unified political process. A people that forged its identity through such broad political participation was a modern 'political nation'.

Here, in Weber's view, lay a crucial difference between a backward and a developed society. In the former, 'unpolitical nation', the majority of the population, lacking any channels of participation, live outside the national polity. The condition of such exclusion is slow economic development and a low degree of social differentiation. In backward nations, social integration depends mainly on traditional religion and morality, while politics is a matter of the balance of forces among an elite minority of power-holders. However, when a modern economy picks up pace and society becomes highly differentiated, a political system of this sort ceases to be viable. Accordingly, Weber believed that not only the political system of Wilhelmine Germany, with its feudal ranks, but the old European liberal order exemplified by aristocratic parliamentarism in England, was doomed, since both confined political life to a restricted social group and could not integrate the masses, who had entered the stage of history, into it (Britain's transition from liberal to democratic politics started with the reform bill of 1867).

It was at this point, Weber emphasized, that an economically developed nation must generate a modern political system, which can only be a democracy based on mass parties and universal suffrage. The distinctive feature of mass parties is that their political activities extend beyond specific social groups, linking together the local interests of various forces, strata and regions to create a wider common vision of the national interest. On the other hand, regular national elections provide opportunities for negotiating compromises and reaching mutual understanding between social groups that are otherwise at loggerheads with each other, helping society to reach a contingent consensus. For Weber the most significant feature of a fully developed electoral polity was that it diffused a universal political education, giving social groups or regions with differing interests a basic awareness of national politics, and citizens a habit of sharing responsibility.

Thus, in Weber's view, the fundamental contrast between a developed and a backward nation lay not in mere 'external success' in market or military competition, but rather in the 'internal success' of a centripetal political system based on a high degree of consensus over long-term national interests, formed among citizens through their participation in public life. This is why Weber was worried about Germany. Though Germany had risen swiftly to economic primacy in Europe, it was at the same time, in his view, 'a nation entirely lacking in any kind of political education'. Economic growth alone did not guarantee political maturity. In fact, the 'political immaturity' of a backward nation often suppressed internal accomplishments in favour of external kinds of success – dominant political forces and newly rising economic classes embracing what Weber calls 'myopic law-and-order philistinism': that is, one-sidedly emphasizing stability and repeatedly missing opportunities for political reform. Weber strongly attacked the German bourgeoisie's 'phobia about democracy', and refusal to accept the entry of the German working class and Social Democrats onto the national political stage. He thought this phobia a sign of its immaturity, and inability to become the leading political class in Germany. (In the event, the German bourgeoisie's long-standing rejection of the working class became an important factor in Hitler's rise to power.) Weber argued that such 'political philistinism' involved a self-deception tantamount to a slow political suicide. For its practical consequence could only be that while the old political order withered away, a new one could not emerge in its place. To remain in such a limbo for long would eventually lead to a collapse of law and order itself.

After two decades of Open Door reform, social differentiation has reached a relatively high level in China, giving our country certain basic features of a modern society. Today, the interests of diverse social groups, regions, or even work-units within the same region, are widely divergent, giving rise to many conflicts between them. So the question is now posed for us too: by what political mechanisms can China achieve modern social integration? Here Weber's conclusions have lost none of their relevance: the more differentiated economic development in a society becomes, the more necessary it is that central power be rooted in direct national elections. In other words, the best way to strengthen central authority is to expand mass democracy. We might say that in a modern political system the nameless masses become the 'Son of Heaven', and expanding mass democracy is the contemporary version of 'holding up the Son of Heaven to counter the feudal lords'.

Popular Sovereignty

In China today, the 'centre' has increasingly felt under pressure from clashes between divergent social interests and lacks a firmly grounded authority to encompass these conflicts. The reason is that it has not yet founded its legitimacy fully on the basis of popular sovereignty. In the absence of a national political process requiring universal participation by the masses, China's central political power does not have a foundation for its own independent authority. What political arrangements would secure one? In my view, provincial authorities should on the one hand retain a high degree of autonomy: they should not be formed by appointments handed down from the centre, but by elections in the localities. On the other hand, and no less importantly, the central authority must retain its own high degree of independence from provincial authorities. Since regular national elections aggregating the political will of the whole population are the index of the political maturity of a nation, we need to explore the practical possibility of directly electing the National People's Congress in China.

A major defect of China's current political system is its multiple layers of indirect election: deputies to the NPC are elected indirectly by the People's Congress of each province, just as the deputies to each provincial People's Congress are elected indirectly by the People's Congress of each county. The result is an immense distance between the central authority and the mass of the population. On the one hand, the majority of citizens live to all intents and purposes outside the political process, and on the other the authority of the centre trickles away through successive layers of government, losing any channel by which it might gain direct popular support. China's 'centre' now negotiates in solitary splendour with various provincial or other cliques and is increasingly dragged this way and that by external forces that sap its strength and resources.

Actually, the best way for developed countries to bolster the authority of central government is to keep indirect elections to a minimum and to expand direct elections, to guarantee that the topmost central power possesses greater popular legitimacy than each and every provincial power or group of influence. In the United States, the House of Representatives and the Senate are directly elected. Even more importantly, after deliberating over the matter for a long time at the Constitutional Convention in Philadelphia, the Federalists concluded that the President should not be chosen indirectly by the House of Representatives, but be directly elected by the American people through another group of deputies, the Electoral College. The purpose of these dispositions was to transform the United States from a loosely confederated country into a mature and unified 'political nation'. Though parliamentary systems differ in other respects from presidential models, they too rely on direct elections to guarantee the legitimacy of the central power. As a matter of fact, the most frequently adopted method for parliamentary countries to solve a crisis of governmental authority is to call early national elections, for the winner can gain a renewed political legitimacy from the direct support of the masses.

The Chinese Communist Party still remains fearful of electoral politics, so there is no prospect of China seeing comprehensive national elections in the near future. However, as Weber forcefully pointed out to his compatriots, it is not an accident that all developed nations have adopted the electoral politics of a mass democracy as the only effective method for aggregating different social interests, in times when traditional religion and morality are no longer strong enough to ensure national cohesion, and the price of a narrow-minded nationalism is a retreat from social differentiation. In the absence of such an arrangement, the Chinese political system is finding it increasingly hard to tackle the problems of our society. The 'Ten Thousand Word Letter' attributed to Deng Liqun correctly points out that the social base of the CCP at grassroots level is shrinking rapidly, and the Party is ceasing to be an organization rooted in the masses.[8] On the other hand, the Letter's call for the CCP to return to its traditional political path is neither feasible nor desirable. The right way for the CCP to re-establish itself as a mass party is to take the initiative to expand electoral politics. Exploiting the advantages of being a ruling party, it could then use the electoral lever to expand its social bases.

The Role of Mass Parties

Nowadays the issue of direct elections to the National People's Congress can be discussed inside China, even if steps in this direction are unlikely to be taken soon. The theoretical urgency of the question is plain. In regard to direct election, our current Election Law speaks only about deputies below county level. Institutional arrangements for a national direct election remain virtually a blank sheet. I once imagined that the introduction of balloting in millions of Chinese villages could become a starting-point for China's electoral politics. Now I would like to emphasize the opposite. Direct elections below the county level have little relevance to the designing of an institutional arrangement for direct elections to the NPC, since these will face problems of an entirely different order – for example, the question: how many electoral districts should there be nationwide?

To answer this question we need to determine, first, which electoral system is most appropriate to China, and second, how many representatives the NPC should have in total. The current consensus, inside and outside China, is that the present 3,000 deputies of the NPC are too many for an efficient legislative body. Yet there is no agreement as to how many would be appropriate; some suggest 400 and others 2,500, plucking such numbers more or less out of the air. I would prefer to follow the preliminary conclusion of various electoral studies, that the number of national representatives should be the cube root of the national population. With our population of 1.2 billion, that gives a National People's Congress of around 1,000 deputies.

---

[8] Not long after the CCP's then Secretary-General Jiang Zemin gave a key speech on July 1, 2001, on the anniversary of the Party's founding, to redefine the Party's nature and tasks, a 'Ten-Thousand-Word Letter' (*Wan yan shu*) was circulated on the Internet under the name of Deng Liqun, a Party elder who was the head of the Propaganda Ministry in the early 1980s, criticizing the speech for its abandonment of Marxist positions [ed].

But there is a more fundamental issue at stake here. The choice of an electoral system inevitably involves questions to do with political parties. The former cannot be designed without considering the latter. So far most scholars inside and outside China still envisage reform of the NPC along the line of 'separating the Party from politics' (*dang zheng fenli*). I am sympathetic to their good intentions, but believe the formula is theoretically absurd. Modern parliaments are without exception dominated by political parties. A parliament without political parties usually indicates that the country is under military rule or still a traditional monarchy. Therefore political scientists like Sartori have repeatedly pointed out that to understand the workings of a country's parliament is to understand the structure of its party system, and to understand the difference in the parliamentary arrangements of two countries means to understand the difference in their party systems. Likewise, the selection and design of electoral methods will vary according to the party system. For example, 'simple plurality' elections protect a two-party system by excluding third parties; likewise, in a system of proportional representation, threshold criteria are designed to limit the multiplication of political parties.

In short, parliament, election and political parties form an interconnected chain. Without the link constituted by political parties, how can we select or design arrangements for national direct elections or an effective parliament? The interrelations between the three have been invisible in China only because we have never had any nationwide direct elections. But once such elections to the NPC are on the agenda, they will immediately become inescapable. By the same token, conceptions of political reform along the lines of 'separating the Party from politics' will come to an end. For we obviously cannot imagine that a future NPC in China would be a parliament without parties. Moreover, everyone certainly knows that the present NPC has always had a very powerful party running it, which is none other than the CCP. Without the CCP, the NPC would not function at all.

Thus reform of the National People's Congress is essentially a question of the reform of the Chinese Communist Party. How to select and design an election system for China is a question about how the CCP will position itself in a national direct election. In fact, whether the NPC can become a directly elected body is, in the last analysis, a question of whether the CCP will become an electoral party. Therefore, the guiding line or basic principle in reforming the People's Congress system should not be impractical or deluded talk of 'separating the Party and politics'. Its central task should be to spare no effort in pushing the CCP towards becoming an electoral party. Far from separating the two, reform should work towards 'combining the Party and politics', by making the ruling party a parliamentary party.

In fact, the current system of 'democratic centralism' in the decision-making of the NPC, though very different from the workings of Congress in the Presidential system of the United States, has some resemblances to the way European parliaments in practice operate. If the ruling party could be transformed into an electoral and parliamentary organization, it is not impossible that the NPC might gradually develop into the highest organ of central authority in China, acquiring full 'parliamentary sovereignty'. Reform of the People's Congress system should therefore focus on fundamental issues rather than on details (for example, it is not really necessary to create two chambers in the national parliament). That means concentration on helping to change the CCP into an electoral and parliamentary party.

Transition to a Predominant-Party System?

To this end, we need to remember that the main difference between what are usually regarded as two-party and multi-party systems is that the former – Westminster or British – model is designed to form a 'single party government' after the elections, whereas the latter usually gives rise to coalition governments. A special variety of the Westminster model is one in which a single party is continuously in power over a long period, winning repeated elections at regular intervals. This model is often described as a 'predominant-party polity'. It constitutes, we may say, a peculiar form of one-party rule. The United States offers an important example of this system. From 1870 to 1950, in twenty-seven American states the same party was in power for as long as 80 years. Other versions of a 'predominant-party polity' have included Sweden, Norway, Japan and India. Countries like Singapore can also be categorized into this group. In my view, this is the destination towards which political reform in China should tend. To borrow Giovanni Sartori's terminology,[9] China's gradual transition towards democracy could be envisaged in the following stages:

1. The change in China from the era of Mao Zedong to that of Deng Xiaoping can be considered as a transition from a totalitarian one-party polity to a pragmatic one-party polity.
2. The current system of 'multi-party cooperation and consultation under the leadership of the CCP', as China's Constitution terms it, can be regarded as a pragmatic-hegemonic party polity.
3. A relatively feasible aim as the next step in China's political reform would be to transform this pragmatic-hegemonic party polity into a predominant-party polity.
4. In the longer term, if the predominant-party polity gradually fades, I would personally still prefer to see a single-party government along Westminster lines, rather than multi-party coalition rule, as a future polity for China.

---

[9] *Parties and Party Systems*, Cambridge 1976, pp. 131–85.

This last may, of course, prove wishful thinking on my part, as there are actually fewer than ten two-party systems in the world and most Western political scientists consider them less democratic than multi-party systems. But looking at the political transformations in the former Soviet Union and East Europe since 1990, I have come to the conclusion that the key issue for us will be the creation of a 'governable democracy'. In Eastern Europe a common phenomenon has been the mushrooming of small parties, which block the emergence of any big ruling party capable of controlling a majority in the parliament. For example, in the 1991 elections to the Polish Seym, 29 parties gained representation in the lower house, and the largest eight parties held between 6 and 19.6 per cent of seats in the chamber. A parliament of this sort, where no political force is dominant, usually creates a president eager to dominate by himself, unleashing in turn a vicious power struggle between president and parliament. Polish politics were virtually paralysed as a result. No doubt in reaction, Russia then went to the other extreme. The new Constitution passed by a referendum in December 1993, tailored entirely to suit the personal needs of Yeltsin, created a distribution of power designed to ensure that the President would win in all circumstances. A structure like this is probably too far away from the concept of a constitutional democracy not to bear bitter fruit in the future.

At any rate, for the moment the key step towards democracy in China would be a transformation of our current pragmatic-hegemonic party polity into a predominant-party polity. For a hegemonic party is one that takes its rule for granted, whereas a predominant party has to win dominance at the polls. Though a predominant-party polity is not perfect, no one can deny it is one variety of democracy. At the same time, progress towards democracy in mainland China can only be realized within the existing framework of a unitary state. Federal or confederate proposals will harm China's democratization, which must not to be entangled with the issue of unification of the country across the Taiwan Straits. The two issues are unrelated. To confuse them will neither help China's unification, nor encourage its democratization.

At stake here is a basic constitutional issue that has drawn renewed interest in the West. This is the principle that a constitutional democracy is possible only when the extent of a political community has been determined beforehand. For questions concerning the frontiers of a political community cannot be decided democratically. Such problems are beyond the remit of a constitutional polity. For just this reason, a mature democracy does not usually acknowledge a right to secession in its national constitution – that is, does not grant any part of the country's territory a licence to exit from it. The United States is a case in point. In its ruling on the case of Texas versus White (1869), the Supreme Court explicitly condemned the demand made by Texas that it be allowed to secede from the United States as unconstitutional.

In fact, as the American jurist Cass Sunstein points out, the very concept of a constitution is in conflict with the right to secede.[10] For the essential premise of a constitution is that within its structure peaceful solutions are possible for every conflict, whereas the premise of the right to secede is a denial of any such basic structure. In that sense, a constitution which includes the right to secede is one that can be cancelled at any moment. Accordingly, Sunstein recommends that East European countries drafting new constitutions should not include the right to secede, as the former Soviet Union had done. Generally speaking, if the extent of a political community is not yet resolved, it is better not to draft a constitution in a hurry. Otherwise it risks becoming useless, since a constitutional democracy is impossible if its boundaries are in dispute.

Precisely for this reason, I believe that there is no possibility yet of a common constitution for both sides of the Taiwan Straits. By the same token, to imagine changing the national structure of China from a unitary to a confederate or federal state, merely out of a good intention to solve the problem of unification, would be recklessly light-minded. The result could only be the opposite of what is intended – not only failing to assist unification, but also slowing down its democratization. There is no reason whatsoever for us to push China into a Balkan situation before designing a viable democratic system for the nation. On the contrary, in order to democratize our country, we must block any move that might Balkanize it.

Of course, our entire discussion could be regarded as having no practical relevance. Yet in discussing the political future of China at this turn of the century, we cannot only consider a short-term agenda. We must develop a longer-term perspective grounded in basic political principles. Even if we cannot yet reach our goal, we should at least know clearly what we want to pursue.

---

[10] 'Constitutionalism and Secession', *University of Chicago Law Review*, no. 58, 1991, p. 633.

12

A Manifesto for Cultural Studies

Wang Xiaoming

In the winter of 1927 Lu Xun wrote: 'China is on the brink of a momentous era. But that does not necessarily mean a time that will give life. It could also bring death'.[1] In terms Lu Xun used later, this was an era akin to the 'critical period' in medicine, when life is in the balance.[2] One could scarcely have thought that, seventy years later, this would still be the most accurate description of contemporary life. Since Lu Xun, people have so often believed that China was on a new path, leaving behind the uncanny sensations of upheaval, collapse and uncertainty. In the late seventies I felt such optimism myself. Today, however, after two decades of twists and turns in the 'Reform Era', sentiments all too familiar to Chinese in the past – a sense that society has been corrupted, that the daily scene is conflicting and ambiguous, that the fate of the nation and the self are impenetrable; even an unpleasant premonition that a massive upheaval is approaching – have returned. Where is China going? The question, which seemed so academic not seven or eight years ago, has suddenly become real again. It cascades into a series of more detailed questions. What kind of society is China today anyway? Is it still a socialist country? What is the relationship between China's modernization and capitalism? What changes have been occurring in the state, its system of organization, social order, totalitarian ideology? Who are the major beneficiaries of these changes, and who are its principal victims? Is society in the midst of a crisis – if so, what sort of crisis? What are the forces that could mitigate or worsen our problems? If there were to be a sudden storm, would it be followed by sunshine, or a long period of haze? Those whose eyes are open to the reality of their own lives are likely to ask themselves many questions such as these, and to feel their

---

[1] Lu Xun, 'Chenying tici' (Forward to *Shadows of Dust*), in *Lu Xun quanji* (Complete Works of Lu Xun), Beijing 1981, vol. 3, p. 547.

[2] Lu Xun, 'Xiaopin wenxue de weiji' (The Crisis of the Essay Form), ibid, vol. 4, p. 576.

pressing weight. I believe Chinese intellectuals must offer some clear answers to them.[3]

That is not easy. The continual changes of the past twenty years have transformed the face of Chinese society, especially in the coastal regions of the south-east, now altered beyond recognition. The gulf between different parts of China today is so great it is almost shocking.[4] There are even tremendous differences among cities – between the silent rust-belt of the recession-stricken north-east and the crackling consumer culture of cities like Hangzhou and Wenzhou, or among major centres like Guangzhou and Tianjin, or Shanghai and Beijing – not to mention the extreme contrasts beween the coastline of the south-east and interior of the north-west. These differences are not only economic and ecological, they are also cultural and political. Deng Lijun's gentle music still fills dance halls in Taiyuan, while nearly every high school student in Shanghai owns the latest Westlife CD. A touring group of county officials from Ningxia will still be debating whether it is politically incorrect to visit Chiang Kai-Shek's birthplace near Ningbo, while the 'professional achievement' of officials in Xiamen, long allied with criminal gangs, is to milk the public of billions of yuan. On the same day that a party newspaper in Chengdu publishes a social commentary sharply criticizing the corrosive effects of capitalism, a government representative in Shanghai will be hosting the CEO of a multinational corporation. A book censored in Beijing can be placed in full view on the shelves of a private bookshop in Foshan, where no one even asks about it.

Thus almost every generalization about China – that it is a communist-led socialist society as before, that at its core it is a society of traditionally centralized power, that it has virtually become capitalist, that it is a fully-fledged consumer society, or even that it is already postmodern – can be supported with examples, as can its opposite. This causes people to reflect. Could it be that the long-standing query 'Whither China?' lacks a purchase on the complexity of contemporary society? Perhaps all that we can grasp are several, or even only one, of the many dissimilar 'Chinas' that now exist. Of course, any country with so vast a territory and long a history is bound to contain a multitude of internal differences. Normally, such differences do

---

[3] It is my firm conviction that, in China today, those who combine a warm concern for society, independence of mind and basic (often university) training in ideas and theory, continue to make up a group of 'intellectuals' (*zhishi fenzi*) who continue to exert influence in society, even though this influence has waned in the past decade. This is the community best equipped to address the questions raised above. I have never agreed with the view that has become popular since the 1990s, that intellectuals should 'step down'. Rather, I believe that self-reflection by intellectuals, far from withdrawing them from social responsibility, is now the condition of renewing it.

[4] This gulf has not just appeared in the past twenty years. The priority given heavy industry by the state in the 1950s exacerbated rather than reduced the inherited disparities between the cities and the countryside. But it is only since the mid-1980s, the widening of this gap has become truly shocking.

not mean that other commonalities and unifying characteristics are so absent as to prevent more than a limited glimpse of the whole – it could even be argued that they make an overview of it all the more necessary. But in our circumstances today, I am more inclined to urge that we give our full attention to the internal differences within our society. We need to pay closer attention to the details of daily life, not only because every level of society is already divided into many disparate parts, but also because comprehensive theories fail to convey the textures of current experience. The most pressing task for intellectuals is to reconstruct a broad understanding of contemporary China that acknowledges the extent of its structural discrepancies. The first step in this direction can only be a sober realization that the social system established in the fifties and sixties is collapsing, so that it is now extremely difficult to give any general answer to the question of where China is heading.

If we consider the new divisions in society, someone like myself, accustomed from youth to terms like 'class', 'exploitation' and 'economic structure', thinks first of the tremendous changes in social class in the past ten years. Indeed, the most obvious result of market economic reform is the complete breakdown of thirty continuous years of socialist class formation. On the one hand, original classes such as workers, peasants, government cadres, soldiers and intellectuals[5] still exist, although each has undergone changes. On the other hand, many new social classes, first springing up in coastal areas and large and mid-sized cities, have proliferated so fast that society has yet to find any consistent names for them. Take Shanghai. In the past fifteen years or so of market reforms at least four new classes have already emerged: the new rich with average personal assets of ten million yuan ($1.25 million); hard-working white-collar strata hunched in their cubicles; the unemployed, laid-off, and early retirement class of former workers now living at home; and the migrant workers from the countryside who perform the bulk of Shanghai's unskilled manual labour.

All of these continue to multiply and alter Shanghai's economic, political, and cultural landscape. For example, advertising and the media present white-collar workers as emblems of China's modernization and vectors of its new purchasing power. So Shanghai's consumer goods, fashion and real-estate sectors target this class as their key market, without registering what it really is: exhausted young or middle-aged men and women who make up only a fraction of the population, by contrast with European or American middle classes. The situation of migrant workers is just the opposite. They

---

5 In the official classification, the term 'intellectual' refers to those who received an education in or above the middle-level technical or professional schools, and entered government service, without administrative power. From the 1950s to the 1980s they were often referred to as 'intellectuals,' and some still persist in calling them such out of habit. Needless to say, the connotation of this usage is virtually the opposite of that intended in this essay, as set out in note 3 above.

do not have Shanghai residence cards, so according to government statistics they are not part of the city's population. Planners of Shanghai's municipal development often ignore them as if they did not exist. Yet migrant workers, a class that already exceeds two million in Shanghai, are clearly frequent customers in its video and movie theatres. At the bookstands their preference for martial arts novels and romances, and low-brow popular magazines, influences many publishers. In these ways migrant workers are quietly shaping, among other things, a significant portion of the city's cultural output.

On the broad streets and narrow alleys of Shanghai, these new classes live and mix with the old ones. Often they share the same apartment complexes. While a father worries about not being able to make ends meet on the meagre wage he earns from a state-owned factory, his son is secretly scheming to save for a new car, as he returns from his job at a foreign-owned enterprise. From this family's window, they can see the makeshift shacks of migrant workers, and beyond them opulent villas protected by high walls. Anyone who sees these great disparities in social orders, legal regulations, moral codes, and economic interests that coexist in a single small area is bound to react strongly to them.

Consider, for example, the way the wealth of the economy is distributed. If one merely observes people riding their bicycles to work each day, it would seem that the 'second distribution' system of socialism is still operating smoothly.[6] In fact, when a laid-off worker applies for relief from the social security office, he can still grumble confidently that 'at least the Communist Party ought to give me a bite to eat', in the belief that he has the right to a 'second distribution' even though he has now lost his qualifications for receiving a 'first distribution'. But if we consider the continual increases in the cost of public services (transportation, utilities, medical cover, telecommunications, housing), the gradual 'marketization' of education from senior high school upwards,[7] the expanding range of taxes and charges at every level of government,[8] not to mention the large

---

[6] This term refers to the historic system in the PRC whereby the government instituted a low-wage structure – the 'first distribution' – to guarantee full employment, and then provided free health-care and education, and inexpensive housing, transport, utilities, consumer goods, and cultural activities – the 'second distribution' – to return the wealth produced by the people to the people. Currently, the relevant legal provisions of the Constitution and labour laws of the People's Republic of China still take the 'second distribution' as one of the legitimating bases of the state.

[7] Since the spring of 1999 the government has openly used education to 'create needs' (i.e. stimulate spending), by ordering every college to increase enrolments and strongly pushing the marketization of education. By September 2000, most universities in China were charging between four and six thousand yuan per semester.

[8] Prior to the 'market economic reform', individual citizens were not generally required to pay taxes. In the mid-1980s, the government imposed proportional income taxes on individuals, gradually increasing their share of total revenue over the years. In many places, especially in the countryside, where the rates are high relative to low farming incomes, the result can only be

numbers of defunct government enterprises that have laid off tens of millions of workers in the first place, it becomes clear that several completely different types of economic system are replacing the 'second distribution' economy.

Suppose we then stroll along the stretch of exclusive clubs on Huaihai and Hengshan Roads in Shanghai, and observe their ostentation. What we can observe here are the results of the operations of the new rich, as they deploy 'red' (political), 'yellow' (sexual), and 'black' (criminal) methods to accumulate capital, in the firm conviction that they are helping to craft a superbly efficient new order. The extent to which the social wealth that was to fund the 'second distribution' has found its way into the pockets of these new rich becomes clear.

In this complex situation virtually any political programme, theoretical agenda or even administrative measure can be circumstantially exploited, and deviate so far from its original goals that it yields results diametrically opposite to those intended. The 'institutional reform' of state-owned enterprises has frequently evolved into a violent tide swallowing up public assets altogether. The Ministry of Education calls for an easing of student work-loads, yet helps teachers to tutor privately on the side – the corruption of a whole professional sector. Appeals for 'modernization' swept the nation in the mid-1980s[9] – anyone over thirty today will remember the slogans of that time: 'separate politics and business', 'stop price-fixing', 'destroy the common pot', 'smash the iron rice-bowl', and the posters declaring 'efficiency is money'. Scholars were especially keen on the maxims 'change systems of ownership', 'the market economy is the height of efficiency', and 'the market economy is modernization'. The model of modernity, naturally, was Western Europe and America. The logic that informed these appeals seemed rational to all, for there was a deep historical basis for the consensus they achieved. The twenty years of economic stagnation after the Great Leap Forward had indeed oppressed people far too long. The implications seemed obvious: to liberate social forces of production, the bloated and inefficient planned economy had to be eliminated. Economic reform would be the first step in reforming the entire system of centralized political power.

Who could have imagined that a decade later all of these rousing slogans would lose virtually all their revolutionary charge, and become mere grandiloquent excuses for those in power to pillage society? The government

---

described as an exorbitant fiscal burden. Total tax revenues were 900 billion yuan in 1998, and one trillion in 1999.

[9] In the course of the 1980s, there was a marked shift in emphasis in the quest for reform and modernization among intellectuals. In the first half of the decade, they focused primarily on ideas, politics and culture, and rarely considered economics or everyday life. It was only after this original agenda suffered repeated setbacks, while the government's agricultural reforms registered initial success, that the academic community, eager to gain a foothold for comprehensive societal reform, gradually placed its hopes in a market economy.

uses them to rid itself of the responsibility of carrying out any 'second distribution',[10] while many officials are freely embezzling public funds. In the name of marketization, the state continues to reduce its investment in education,[11] while public utilities boldly continue to raise prices. In the name of efficiency, large numbers of workers can be sent packing, and residents in Beijing, Shanghai, and other city centres are forced to relocate to the suburbs. Nearly every such change is for the worse, and they are decided upon as if every social ill were due to the government affording the people too much 'welfare', or simply the fact the Chinese population is too large.

In the face of these absurd, bitter realities, I am ashamed to recall the enthusiastic clamour of intellectuals in the eighties. How could we have engaged in such wishful thinking – imagining that our idealized market economy was the only one possible, and that once a market economy was in place, the whole society would gradually be emancipated? Why did we fail to foresee that an arbitrary and corrupt power could create a completely different kind of market economy and use it to perpetuate even greater deceit and more ramified sorts of exploitation? It is difficult not to feel that if the intellectual community had been less naïve in the first place, and emphasized justice and democracy as much as competition and efficiency – giving proper attention to social goals like ecological balance, public probity, cultural vitality and overall quality of life – we would not be in our present situation. Had we taken a different course in the eighties, perhaps Chinese society would not have been so lacking in resistance, so easy to toy with, in the nineties.

Of course, regrets like these overstate the influence of intellectuals. In the face of such complex social developments, the capacity of scholars to intervene truly appears weak: their naïvete and confusion was certainly not the primary reason for the panorama we witness today. If we want to unlock the door to the confused reality of present-day China, it is perhaps to the emergent class of the new rich that we should look for the key. The history of their rise is very brief, less than two decades, and very rapid. From the 'ten thousand yuan' household of the early eighties, their standard of wealth had exploded to ten million and even a hundred million yuan by the late nineties. Today you see the presence of the new rich in all the coastal areas

---

[10] In the past few years, some have started to criticize this. See, for example, Pei Jianguo, 'Ye tan woguo xiaofei buzu de chengyin' (Reasons for our nation's insatiable consumption), *Hainan shifan xueyuan xuebao*, No 1, Haikou 2000.

[11] In the 1990s nominal government investment in education, expressed in yuan, has not visibly decreased and sometimes even increased. But if one considers rising prices, personnel increases, and the actual amount spent on opening new schools, building libraries or laboratories, repairing facilities, providing research stipends, and so on, real investment has actually declined. The lack of educational resources in the countryside, interior provinces and border regions became especially marked in the late 1990s, after the government poured funds into a few top schools in Beijing, Shanghai, and coastal regions.

and large- and mid-sized cities is betrayed not only by every conceivable luxury automobile and four- or five-star hotels, not only by golf courses and exclusive gyms and clubs, but in many places such as Shanghai by luxury complexes surrounded by forbidding gates that keep out ordinary society from homes that rival the residences of top government officials. This class makes up less than one per cent of the population, but controls half or more of the gross national income![12]

Along with its rapid increase in wealth, the composition of the new rich has changed. Its earliest members were marginals, rejected by society for lacking any respectable background, who had nothing to lose by risky business ventures,[13] and most quickly went under. But they were gradually replaced by recruits from the middle and upper strata, and even government officials themselves, who had access to all kinds of social resources. Since the mid-1990s this type of replacement has accelerated. Although a few of the original marginals managed to survive, they could no longer distance themselves from those with power. A few young entrepreneurs in information technology have also entered the ranks of the new rich by virtue of their talent and energy.[14] But as a whole, the close ties between this class and the operations of the bureaucracy are now ever more clearly exposed. The rich no longer even use the back door to gain access to official circles; they directly occupy the front stage of political power. In the smaller cities and countryside, the mutual support and cooperation between the new rich and officials has reached such an extreme that they do not even bother to conceal it. How could people devoid of any special intelligence or knowledge acquire so much money overnight, if they were not backed by corrupt power? [15]

The most important secret of contemporary China lies in the rise of the new rich. Since that October day in 1976 when crowds poured onto the streets to celebrate the destruction of the Gang of Four, Chinese people had

---

[12] See Li Peilin, ed, *Zhongguo xinshiqi jieji jieceng baogao* [Report on Social Classes in China in the New Era], Liaoning 1995, especially 221–291, 334–374; Sun Liping et al, 'Zhongguo shehui jiegou zhuanxing de zhongjinqi qushi yu yinhuan' (Recent Trends and Latent Dangers in the Transformation of China's Social Structure), *Zhanlue yu guanli*, No 5, 1998; Li Qiang, 'Shichang zhuanxing yu Zhongguo zhongjian jieceng de daiji gengti' (Market Changes and the Generational Replacement of the Chinese Middle Class), *Zhanlue yu guanli*, No 3, 1999.

[13] For example, poor farmers, urban unemployed (including some who lost their jobs due to punishment or incarceration), and needy clerks. Those who went into private business in the early 1980s and struck it rich as a 'ten thousand yuan household' include many in these categories.

[14] As with the stock market or real estate a decade ago, as soon as the Internet was seen as a honey-pot, officials immediately got involved, so that by the year 2000 many branches of the central and local government had started Internet companies, both openly and secretly, to monopolize the market. Obviously, once this happened, the space for young people without powerful backgrounds to start up enterprises shrank.

[15] There are, of course, a few genuinely talented figures among the new rich, but as a class they are far from exceptional.

sensed that their society was changing. In time those changes affected nearly everyone's life. In the mid-eighties the extremely optimistic outlook of the academic community was widely diffused through society. The history of feudal authority had come to an end: China had moved from a closed to an open, a traditional to a modern society. China's long and distinctive historical legacy would no longer hamper its progress; even if people wanted to shift into reverse, nothing could now ultimately thwart the dynamic of modernization, as we were finally leaping into the new world of telephones, refrigerators, cars, and skyscrapers.

Such beliefs were very widespread and deeply held, and no matter how many immediate difficulties presented themselves, many preferred to look away. Even after the terrible, bloody shock of June 1989, as soon as the top leaders proclaimed that economic reform would continue, people quickly recovered from their depression, as if nothing much had happened, at worst a slight detour. The tune of 'modernization' struck up again, and the rhythm of 'reform' beat even faster, as if China had more hope than ever. Even today I can clearly remember how loud the clamour for modernization was in 1992, when the slogan was launched once again, drowning out all other sounds, filling everyone's ears with one ringing call: 'This is modernization – hurry up and hop on the bandwagon or you'll miss it!'

In some ways, the cacophony was not unpersuasive. In the past twenty years, Chinese society has become much more open and the economy very robust. In Shanghai, so many tall buildings have gone up, so many gleaming stores have opened, so many Westerners can be seen, that walking down Huaihai Road feels not that different from being in Tokyo or Hong Kong. In comparison with the seventies, personal space has also grown considerably. The woman from the Street Committee no longer comes to your door to ask for the name of your guests, and you are unlikely to worry that a friend will report you, if you grumble while drinking tea with him. Residence certificates, government quotas, official permits: these once inescapable features of daily life have all been de-emphasized – if you ignore one or two of them, you can now survive. The government has signed the Universal Declaration on Human Rights and entered the World Trade Organization, and 'unofficial' voices call for a constitutional amendment to guarantee that 'private property may under no circumstances be infringed'. Thus the theoretical framework underlying the popularity of modernization would actually seem to explain the social reality of contemporary China – at least one part of it.

Unaccounted for, however, is the sudden ascent of the new rich. The intimidating arrogance of this class, high above the poor, confused and angry crowds who emerged at the same time, is ground for suspecting that the modernization paradigm contains serious flaws. When a traditional society moves towards modernity, its original class structure will naturally undergo changes, as wealth and privilege are redistributed. However, when a country like China seems to be breeding out of the existing system a completely new class that instantly becomes rich, it is bound to seem strange. It might be thought that a new social class that gains power as a result of a modernizing transition should be eager to continue reforms. However, this is not the case with the new rich in China today. They appear unwilling to see society reformed in any profound way; instead they prefer the status quo. Are they at least those most confident in the future? Just the opposite. The new rich are for the most part very pessimistic about China's future.[16] Almost every one of them has a foreign passport in his or her pocket, as if preparing to escape a dangerous situation.[17]

Why is the class that has profited the most from the Reform Era so pessimistic about its future? Unlike those scholars who sit in their studies, humming the high-pitched tune of 'modernization', the new rich understand the new reality. They know what they have done, know what results from their kind of activity, and are extremely clear about what it is that allows them to do such things. The pessimism of these people thus has especially profound implications. In my opinion, it is precisely the strange existence of this new rich class – its miraculously rapid ascent, its stark contrast with other social classes, its characteristic short-term psychology – that should prompt us to put aside the modernization paradigm and look at the past twenty years of social change from another perspective.

Looking back, the impetus behind the past twenty years of reforms came from many quarters: those who were dissatisfied with the instability and confusion of the Cultural Revolution; those who desired democracy, intellectual freedom and a cultural opening; those who wanted to rebuild the legitimacy of the Party's rule;[18] and those who wanted to rise out of poverty and achieve a better material life, who gave the whole movement its popular appeal. When these various aspirations converged in the late 1970s, the stage for reform was set. As that grand curtain was slowly raised, it looked

---

[16] The 'future' here is not fifty, a hundred, or several hundred years, but five, ten or twenty. Longer time-spans in speaking of the future, no matter how impressive they may sound, are meaningless.

[17] For the pessimism of the new rich, see Li Qiang's fascinating description in 'Dangdai Zhongguo shehui de sige liyi qunti' (Four Groups of Beneficiaries in Contemporary Chinese Society). The complete text of this article was first circulated on the Internet, and was later published in considerably edited form in *Xueshujie*, No 3, 2000.

[18] From the 1950s through to the 1970s, the political legitimacy of CCP rule was largely based on Mao Zedong Thought, whose myth of revolution derived from the notion of 'proletarian dictatorship' was generally believed by the masses. This myth was shattered by a series of events during the Cultural Revolution, including the mysterious death of Lin Biao in 1971, the campaign against Deng Xiaoping in 1976, and especially the suppression of the April Fifth Movement on Tiananmen Square of that year. Thus after the Gang of Four was put down, the CCP needed to re-establish a legal mandate for its rule. The important Third Plenum of the Eleventh Central Committee of the CCP, launched in 1979, announced that 'emancipation of thought' would be the 'basic path for the Party in the New Era', and that the focus of its work would shift from 'class struggle' (revolution) to 'economic construction' ('earning a decent living' – *xiao kang*), in a clear attempt to find a new basis of legitimacy for its rule.

as if the people were as one, every member of society participating in the will to change it. But actually, in a country like China with a highly centralized system of power, the various forces behind calls for reform were differently situated on the social hierarchy, and their goals were far from common, some even being mutually opposed.

By the end of the eighties, it was already very clear that there were two main forces behind reform in the Party. One sought a move towards socialist democracy and the other a Western-style market economy, yet both were ousted from the ranks of the rulers in quick succession.[19] In the past ten years the voices of those in the scholarly community who had supported these two factions have been silenced along with them.[20] As for the public, its aspirations for political reform were already severely curtailed by government officials in the late seventies. The Xidan Democracy Wall incident of late 1978 signified the formal beginning of this kind of suppression. So when the ideological and political changes sought by the party reformers and the scholarly community met with repeated setbacks, public attention naturally turned to economic reform, almost exclusively focusing on improving the material welfare of the individual. In the 1990s there was a climate of disappointment, apathy and even dread of politics and public life, and a narrow utilitarian mentality – 'after all, the country isn't doing too well, so I'd better earn some extra money!' – permeated every level of society.

On the other hand, when protests spread from Tiananmen Square throughout the entire country in the spring of 1989, one communist party after another was tottering in Eastern Europe – seeming to confirm Mao Zedong's dark prediction of the mid-1950s that if the ruling party in a socialist country embarked on political reform, it would lead to the collapse of its political power, and the fall of all associated with it. In China, it was because those who accepted this axiom gained the upper hand at the top levels of the government and Party, that machine-gun fire crackled in the final hours of June 3, 1989, and tanks rumbled towards the student tents

---

[19] The first was led by Hu Yaobang, whose primary focus was reform of the political system and cultural openness, with no intention of embracing capitalism wholesale. The second was represented by Zhao Ziyang and his economic advisers, who wanted to use comparatively radical methods to establish a capitalist market prior to reforming other aspects of society.

[20] After the mid-1950s, every cultural worker became a 'government cadre', and an intellectual world that had previously been independent of the political system disappeared. Nor has China really had an intellectual community independent of the state since that time. From the late 1970s onwards, with a loosening of government cultural policies, a growing number of intellectuals have attempted to express their own opinions, gradually converging into an important force for reform. However, the vast majority of these individuals still belong to government organizations, forming a rather unique intellectual world 'within the system'. Even today, because the state continues to control all methods and organs of cultural dissemination, including educational and research institutions, it is still difficult – despite the emergence of a handful of freelancers or independent directors – for an intellectual world to form outside the system.

on Tiananmen Square. Once officials at every level heeded this warning, debates over 'internal party reforms' to save socialism ceased, and all factions closed ranks around the principle of utility. The entire ruling class immediately welcomed Deng Xiaoping's call in 1992 for renewed market reform. At its core this new round of reform of the 1990s differed greatly from the contract-based land reform ('household responsibility system') of the early 1980s, and still more so from the political and cultural reforms envisaged by the 'ideological emancipation movement' of the same period. The direction of reform had clearly changed, and so each social factor it interacted with changed greatly as well.

In the 1990s, reform seemed merely to mean the creation of an economic system whose only standard would be profit. All it now aimed for was efficiency, competition and wealth, and all it promised was improvement of material welfare. Nothing else – not political democracy, environmental care, ethical norms, cultural education – lay within its scope.[21] In the 1990s, any resistance to this new cycle of top-down reform was muted: the gunshots of 1989 still rang loudly enough to curtail any social opinion critical of government initiatives. Public enthusiasm for demanding or questioning reforms of a cultural or political character faded away. When people rolled up their activist banners and set up their mah-jong tables instead, turning to private concerns of clothing, food, housing and transportation, a new reform with the aroma of money was widely welcomed. Once it was made clear that reform affected only economic processes, and power became a great material resource, officials jettisoned the tentative attitude they had towards reform in the 1980s, and eagerly plunged into the market economy.[22] Market reform promoted in these circumstances made the sudden ascent of a new rich class only natural.

Once this type of reform pushed society onto the twisted path of 'efficiency', anything that was not easily converted into cash – poetry, love, philosophy, conscience, dignity, or solving Goldbach's Conjecture,[23] popu-

---

[21] The belief that China should first pursue economic development and temporarily ignore all else was by no means confined to government officials. It was widely held by other social classes, including many intellectuals. Li Zehou's notion that China's progress could be divided into a sequence of five steps was typical of the time. The general reasoning was that even if there was no prospect of reforming other social conditions, economic marketization could still be realized, and in the end would bring further benefits, including democracy, with it. Some thinkers were willing to support a form of political dictatorship, as long as it promoted marketization: theories of a positive 'new authoritarianism' were popular in the mid-1990s.

[22] For the changes in Chinese society from the 1980s through the 1990s, especially the abrupt break marked by June Fourth, see Wang Hui's penetrating analysis: '1989 shehui yudong, xin ziyouzhuyi jiqi piping' ('The Social Movement of 1989, the New Liberalism, and Its Detractors'), *Taiwan shehui kexue yanjiu*, Taibei 2000.

[23] Translator's note: In 1742 Christian Goldbach, a German schoolteacher, conjectured that every even number greater than 2 is the sum of two primes. In 1979 Chen Jingrun, a Chinese mathematician, proved the conjecture true, and became a symbol of modernization in China in the early 1980s.

lar national pursuits in the early 1980s – was written off, and all human balance lost. Government and individuals alike started to base their actions on calculations of short-term profit, making it very difficult to defend long-term interests. Efficiency is a criterion pertinent to both short- and long-term goals, requiring calculations specific to each. Once people forget there is a vast world beyond efficiency, they naturally focus only on the most immediate aspects of any economic decision. From each level of governmental planning, for a city, a rural district, or even larger areas, to specific plans by ordinary people for their families, children and private life, from the investment projects of business people and professionals, to hundreds of thousands of cases of corruption, in almost every corner of society we see the multiplication of short-term goals, and the way these gradually overwhelm and destroy any rational concern for the longer-term interests of individuals, organizations, and regions. [24]

The closure of factories and the growing number of unemployed, the undermining of education, the deterioration of the environment, the corruption of law enforcement, the crumbling of social trust, and the general decline of cultural and moral standards all combine to destroy public confidence in the ability of the government to hold society together.[25] These maladies feed off each other and threaten the entire fabric of life. What is truly worrying is that in many places in China today – not only in the countryside – these diseases are indeed interacting. The number of such regions is growing day by day.

To complicate matters further, the past century has seen the triumph of globalization over every aspect of human life. Since the collapse of the Communist Party in the Soviet Union and Eastern Europe, the substance of that globalization has become ever more uniform, as the power of capitalism expands around the world as never before. China today is caught in the whirlpool of this globalization. On the one hand, international capital urgently seeks to prise open the Chinese market, on the other domestic enthusiasm for modernization continues unabated. The government needs foreign capital to maintain continuous growth, so Chinese society is being

---

[24] If the official approach to policy-making in the 1980s was expressed in Zhao Ziyang's maxim of 'crossing the river one stone at a time' – a relatively measured and cautious stance, the continuous changes in basic economic policy since the mid-1990s demonstrate that the state has lost any clear plan for the nation. Policy-making has shifted from the realization of long-term plans to dealing with immediate problems. In these conditions, each level in the bureaucracy competes so hard to get instant results for its 'political record', that it has no compunction sacrificing the long-term interests of the area for which it is responsible.

[25] In China, where power is still highly centralized, and non-governmental civic organizations are virtually non-existent, a serious weakening in the government's ability to influence and mobilize society gives rise to clear side-effects. Fragmentation of a unifying social structure and the separation of its once coherently connected parts increases the likelihood of social unrest and instability.

obliged willy-nilly to 'join the world'.[26] Thus China's new cycle of reform in the 1990s necessarily went hand in hand with economic openness. From the Shenzhen to the Pudong Special Economic Zones, from service industries adopting Western management practices to branches of government competing to install Microsoft in their offices, or the PLA donning American-style uniforms, if anything has been carried over from the 1980s, it is the Open Door. Producing obvious changes in everyday life, this strongly encourages the optimistic view that the country is moving towards modernization. In south-eastern coastal cities like Guangzhou and Shanghai, where there are obvious improvements in the material welfare of many urban residents, this sentiment is quite widespread. As long as openness is not viewed as a paradise, and modernization is seen as a necessary process that brings both gains and losses,[27] we can say that China is not only being modernized, but is already halfway down the road of globalization.

But it is difficult to avoid thinking here of Krylov's fable of the cart pulled simultaneously in three different directions by a swan, a pike, and a cray-fish.[28] China is undergoing a number of completely different sorts of change at the same time. The sudden rise of 'power plus capital' consumes and pillages society ever more ruthlessly, causing a growing number of ordinary citizens to become victims of reform. The economic transitions to greater openness and modernization continue as before, but now under the growing pressures of globalization. The economy of some areas will show a marked improvement, while others deteriorate, even to insolvency. Such changes are interrelated, but do not all move the country in the same direction, indeed are often in conflict with each other. Their coexistence in contemporary China puts society at odds with itself, and pulls it to pieces. Are there other features of the current scene that can be viewed more optimistically? There are, but for the moment they remain less important.[29] What we can mainly see of China's future are the vicissitudes and collisions

---

[26] This has been a slogan of official propaganda since the mid-1980s, constantly reiterated in newspaper commentaries and speeches given by the leaders. It is revealing that the term 'world' here does not include China, nor does it embrace everything outside China: it refers to the West and Western-style economies alone.

[27] For example, economic development vs. environmental damage, readjustment of social structure vs. polarization of rich and poor, cultural diversity vs. moral crisis, and so on. It should be emphasized that such 'drawbacks' engendered by the 'advantages' of modernization are quite different in character from the rise of the new rich, or the ruin of a region, described in this essay. In the 1990s, modernization itself was often held responsible for the latter phenomena, which were believed to be the price society must pay to progress. Today's intellectual community should not continue to confuse these issues.

[28] The fable was often understood to refer to the Russian Imperial Council [ed].

[29] For example, in the past few years, the number of Internet subscribers in Chinese cities has rapidly increased: according to one estimate, it had passed ten million by 2000. Since Internet providers compete for customers, they offer a much more relaxed space for information and communication space than official publications. Although recent developments in this space have not all been favourable – its infiltration by the public security system and government capital increases daily – the growth of the Internet remains a positive change in China.

of these larger changes. The more uncertain it is which of them will prevail, the more opaque and indeterminate that future appears.

The confusion pervading every level of society today is a natural reaction to this lack of certainty. When set in sharp relief against this complex reality, the extraordinary persistence of intellectuals in thinking in terms of such dichotomies as traditional/modern, closed/open, conservative/reformer, market/planned, socialism/capitalism, communist/anti-communist, seems simple-minded. What do these explain of the landscape of contemporary China? It obviously is not a capitalist country, yet it is also clearly not a socialist society of the kind it used to be. It is nominally controlled by a Communist Party, but in reality the mighty CCP of 'revolutionary ideals' that once moulded, organized, and controlled society so tightly, disappeared long ago. It is still a totalitarian regime with a highly centralized system of power, but its rationale, operating principles and social base are changing; it is not overstating the case to say they are completely different from those of the Cultural Revolution. It is presiding over a market rather than a planned economy, but large areas of this market have little to do with a freely competitive capitalism. China is currently importing many Western technologies, management practices, cultural products and values, but it is doubtful that she will easily change systems to become a Western-style modern society like Korea or Japan; rather, she will probably become something unique, that we do not expect. It seems impossible to define contemporary China. In almost every respect she fails to fit existing theoretical models, whether familiar or novel. She seems to be an unwieldy behemoth, the most difficult and unprecedented case of social change in twentieth-century history.

Faced with this challenge, it seems urgent that contemporary cultural studies be expanded. For in the past twenty years, each great change in society, be it the rapid rise of the new rich, the increasing number of depressed regions, or the widening of the Open Door, has been not only an economic, political, or ecological phenomenon, but also a cultural one. For example, the explosion of the new rich not only signifies a transfer of wealth and a new power structure, it also means the rise of a new set of fashionable ideals encased in an entirely new ideology. The image of the 'successful man' (rarely woman) that first appeared in the media and its advertisements, spreading from the coastal and metropolitan regions throughout the nation, with his various accoutrements – lifestyle, values, personal history and philosophy – is one illustration of this.[30] Modern man lives in a cultural cage, his sense of reality shaped by tastes and preferences selected by what it

---

[30] The earliest discussion of the 'successful man' is in Cai Xiang's article 'Advertisement Utopia' ('Guanggao Wutuobang') in his *Shensheng huiyi*, Shanghai 1998. In the autumn of 1998, a group of literary critics and scholars in the humanities in Shanghai launched an ongoing discussion of these issues under the general topic, 'market ideology in contemporary China'.

lets through. The components of illusion that result are all too familiar: he sinks into asphyxiating quicksand while imagining that he is flying gracefully in a boundless heaven. The more existence is filtered by the media, the less significant the tangible elements of life become.

When virtual realities so easily unsettle people, can they still be called virtual? In this mixture of true and false, where the virtual and the actual interchange, how is culture to be distinguished from absence of culture? The popular image of the 'successful man', for example, does not depend on the existence of a large group of new rich, although strictly speaking, the social class of the new rich and the cultural markers of 'success' came into being together and go hand in hand: the latter forms part of the construction of the former. There are many difficulties in trying to compose a sober analysis of economic and political realities in China today: the vastness of the nation, the limited channels of communication, the government's monopolization of the methods of collecting and publishing statistics, and unreliable data of many sorts. These make all the more urgent what is a feasible task: to take the socio-cultural scene of the nineties – especially popular culture in the coastal and urban areas – as the starting-point for describing and understanding contemporary Chinese society, perhaps even diagnosing its nature and future.

In China this type of cultural study has started only recently, and remains in outline form: its full potential has yet to be determined. But if the above analysis is basically correct, Chinese cultural studies should in the first instance focus on a number of key questions. The most pressing of these is the new ideology that conceals or glosses the realities of our society today.[31] Since the nineties, what was originally an official Maoist ideology dating from the Cultural Revolution has lost its hold over the public and, except for a few empty phrases in the editorials of party newspapers and speeches by leaders, has essentially vanished from the scene. But the spiritual arena of a society cannot remain empty; if the old retreats, something new must take its place. What filled this void in China? The reformist idealism of the 1980s was discredited long ago by domestic and international events. The gloom generated by the June Fourth massacre was dispersed by the promise of further reforms in 1992. It was effectively at this time that a new 'thought' took shape.

Announcing that China was once again moving down the path of modernization, this ideology drew on the longings and ignorances of the eighties to explain that there was no longer any cause for mourning, but rather a reason for celebration. Appealing to the common aspiration to rise

---

[31] This and other references to 'ideology' in this essay are to be understood in the sense theorized by Herbert Marcuse, as a set of ideas and concepts that do not exactly match reality, yet explain relatively systematically history, society, the meaning of life and of the future, and are accepted to varying degrees, by the majority in a given society.

out of poverty, it suggested that anything other than immediate material wealth was useless, the mere fabrication of a cultural elite who should just 'fuck off'.[32] Strenuously lauding a 'market economy with Chinese characteristics', it touted the ensuing arrangements as the last word in rational progress and development. Proclaiming that everyone was working together to achieve a 'decent living' (*xiao kang*), and all had a chance of success, it worked especially to minimize the profound differences between classes and regions, and within politics and culture in China. Deploying a range of 'modernizing' buzzwords – 'market', 'popular', 'consumer era' – it made every effort to distance itself from the empty shell of the old ideology, whose strength it intentionally exaggerated, so that it could side with the 'folk', or those on the 'margins', or describe itself as 'avant garde' or 'alternative'. But it very carefully avoided every issue that might displease those in power: intellectual freedom, civil rights, the protection of the average citizen's livelihood, the responsibilities of the state to society, the plunder of society by new systems of 'power plus capital'.

It is difficult, in all honesty, to know how best to characterize this new 'thought' since it hardly qualifies as a system, jumbling together, as it does, paradoxical propositions that are impossible to validate. Even though it pervades the majority of advertisements, it is not merely a capitalist product. It features so insistently in the media that it could be a set of official slogans,[33] but there is no clear evidence that it was ever intentionally designed by the government. It has no generally recognized spokesmen, and though it often surfaces in cultural and theoretical debates, no one is willing to stand up and take credit for it. But it is precisely this sort of ideology, of indeterminate origin and indistinct contours, that feeds the appetite of influential powers in China – and not just the government.

Its effect is to limit the public's perception of national problems, encouraging a petty concern with personal consumption in people blind to the damage and suffering around them. This ideology can even placate those without power or influence, whose feelings of despair and impotence are cultivated into apathy – if every day is fraught with tension, you might as well take a sedative to fool yourself for a bit. The new 'thought' covered over the chaotic, grim realities of the nineties, and served at least temporarily to relieve anxieties. It is little wonder it could emerge and spread so easily

---

[32] In the early 1990s, it was fashionable to adopt a deliberately boorish tone to mock and disparage those who concerned themselves with the fate of a humanistic spirit (*renwen jingshen*) and public affairs. Some of Wang Shuo's works offer obvious examples. There were a number of complicated motives behind these sarcasms, but one aspect of the fad embodied (or participated in) the formation of what I have been calling the 'new thought'.

[33] To this day, the entire Chinese media still belong to the state, so for the most part the opinions that find expression are those the government considers advantageous, or at the very least, harmless. This is especially true of television and radio, where it is virtually impossible to articulate ideas beyond the scope of official permission.

in China – green lights all the way – where ideological channels are otherwise so restricted and closely monitored, filling hundreds of thousands of minds, and shaping everyday sentiments, fantasies and judgements. Even Internet chat rooms now produce group after group of devotees. This is the most popular and influential way of looking at the world – at least in the cities – today.

The more one understands the operations of various political and economic powers behind this new ideology, and the ways it responds to and constructs mass desires and public imagination, stifling any social awareness of crises, the more cultural studies should take the new 'thought' as its most important object of criticism. Such criticism should eschew simplistic accusations for a careful description and thorough analysis of the phenomenon. For example, we need to identify those aspects of reality the ideology evades, simplifies or conceals, and those which it exaggerates, embellishes or fabricates. In doing so, we can provoke the kind of authentic response to the stimulus of life that is at present numbed, and help people comprehend and call into question the influences at work on them.

Special attention should also be paid to the ways in which this ideology enriches itself from economic and cultural exchanges between China and other countries, as restricted by the current pattern of globalization, and to the warm relationships between the new 'thought', state power and the new rich. Another important area for research is the complex relationship between the new ideology and the official ideology of the Cultural Revolution, and the ways in which the former has been able to draw on the widespread social disgust towards the latter to create a unique dual identity, as a mainstream ideology that simultaneously poses as a bold heterodoxy. This dual identity allows it at once to whitewash existing reality and to inhibit any other outlook that might question it. Here we would also need to clarify the extent to which the intellectual community itself has in some respects become an unwitting assistant of the new ideology,[34] and what critical resources the last two decades of literature, art and theory have bequeathed us to resist it. This type of housecleaning and self-reflection can help remedy the misconception that all is lost, encourage intellectuals to assume their responsibilities towards society, and recover the spirit to fight its evils.

Today the new ideology has seeped into every pore of society. Cultural studies must track its progress, without being inhibited by the borders placed between disciplines. Above all, cultural studies must not, in the name

---

[34] Take, for example, the conviction that human history follows fixed rules, and that it is therefore fully possible for China to duplicate the history of Euro-American modernization. This notion was not only one of the key theoretical arguments of the appeals made for modernization by intellectuals in the 1980s, but remains a commonly held belief today, when it forms a major prop of the new 'thought'.

of becoming modern, let itself be trapped by the compartmentalization of life and regulation of knowledge operative in increasingly complex academic-administrative systems, which are themselves one of the factors nurturing the new ideology.[35] Not only must we consider literature, music, painting, sculpture, and film. We must also pay special attention to commercial advertisements, magazines, popular music, soap operas, newspapers, TV shows, window displays and public decorations. We need to look not simply at concrete cultural products, but also at abstract theoretical discourses, and the relationship between these two dissimilar cultural activities. Paper, canvas, screen; buildings, publishers, government bureaux; bars, dance halls, and coffee shops – they should all be our province. Where necessary, each must be placed in its social context: cultural studies in China should neither rigidly adhere to existing disciplinary confines, nor strive to become a new discipline itself. Its aim should be simply to grapple with the more disturbing questions of contemporary life in China, in conditions of globalization, and perhaps to suggest some timely and vigorous responses to them.

Human history possesses no immovable laws. To adapt Lu Xun's words, what kind of 'momentous era' might China be entering? The answer is best sought in the contemporary culture that is the texture of life for millions of ordinary Chinese. Its vulgar, crass, dark features will not last forever. But they will require the light of a better culture to be dispelled. It is worth fighting for that. Perhaps seventy years ago, when Lu Xun wondered about China's future, he secretly harboured this same hope.

Translated by Robin Visser

---

[35] This point requires careful discussion, for which there is no space here. It is enough to note: 1) that the growing specialization of social systems strengthens the superficial perception that China is successfully 'aligning itself with the world'; and more importantly, 2) that virtually all domains of social existence are increasingly based on a 'specialization of labour', and so separated from each other (and this type of separation has an economic rationale). But the more thoroughgoing the separation, the harder it is for those who grow up in this type of structure to develop a broad and unconstrained intellectual outlook, and the easier it is for them to be drawn to a simple, clear, and specious popular ideology.

13

Refusing to Forget

Qian Liqun

The twentieth century was a period of unprecedented historical turbulence, for China and the world. Two World Wars, followed by the Korean and Vietnam Wars, and the Arab–Israeli conflict; the collapse of colonial empires, and the rise of newly independent nations in the 'Third World'; the emergence, crisis, and collapse of the international communist movement – all of these upheavals violently shook and transformed the world. In each of them, with the exception of the First World War and the Arab–Israeli conflict, China was in the firing-line. The country and its people (including its intellectuals) paid a heavy price for that, making tremendous sacrifices and suffering unimaginable hardships. The result was a uniquely Chinese experience. This experience had two principal aspects: the transformation of a semi-feudal, semi-colonial, late-developing society into an independent nation-state, in the course of a long struggle against autocratic rule from within, and oppression and invasion from without; and then the exploration of a distinctive road to modernization, the experiment of a so-called 'Chinese form of socialism'. Both of these had the West as a frame of reference. The first embodied resistance to Western colonialism and imperialism; the second at once borrowed from Western models, and criticized and departed from them. Of course, contemporary Asian nations – Japan, India, Korea – represented an even more important frame of reference, because of the similarity of their predicaments and aspirations. But if the common influences and borrowings among these nations are apparent, the differences in their modern history are also very clear. The Chinese experience of the last century was thus both intimately connected to that of the West and other Asian nations, and yet also a markedly 'alternative' path with its own special value and character, carved out by the Chinese people's century-long struggle to 'walk their own road'. In the process of doing so, there emerged a series of distinctively modern Chinese thinkers – politicians, strategists, and writers – of whom three of the most important, in my view, were Sun Yat-sen, Lu Xun, and Mao Zedong. We could say that China's experience of the twentieth century is encapsulated in their thoughts and works. Regardless of how they are judged, they remain 'relics' that cannot be overlooked or bypassed, crucial to the study and understanding of contemporary China.

However, as one who has lived through much of this period, I cannot but face the reality that, although it has won national independence, united its people, and initiated economic reforms, China has still to free itself from its political, economic and cultural backwardness. The sacrifices outweigh the returns, by a large margin. Reflecting on the bloody struggles of the last century, and the countless people who sacrificed their lives in them, Chinese intellectuals with a sense of historical responsibility can only feel grief and the need to rethink the experience of the last century, and its lessons for the Chinese people. There lie not only heroic or happy recollections, but also memories of humiliation and suffering, including such unbearable traumas as the Anti-Rightist Movement, the Great Leap Forward, the Cultural Revolution, and the 'massacre of 1989'. In this history, good and evil cannot easily be separated from one another: they are inextricably intertwined, and so induce very complex emotions, sometimes even a feeling of utter helplessness. Thus, although few deny the importance of reflecting on the experience of the past century, the subject is like a hot coal that nobody wants or dares to touch.

In the past twenty years, even though there have been many impressive advances in various fields of Chinese thought and scholarship, attempts to broach this topic have been rare: it is even regarded as taboo. In my view, this is a dereliction of responsibility on the part of the Chinese intellectual community. There is a historical debt here that must be repaid.

So we must ask: how did this 'forgetting' of history happen? Rulers have always understood the importance of accounts and assessments of the past for the legitimacy of their rule. In China they have unfailingly sought to monopolize the right to investigate our history. In 1976, after the end of the Cultural Revolution, those in power hastily and abruptly issued a document entitled 'Resolution on a Few Historical Problems', as a 'conclusive account' of events that could not be altered, questioned, or discussed. In effect, a circular by the ruling party attempted to 'end' any study of the past, even 'end' history itself. Afterwards, every resort of power was used to ban the collection, research or publication of historical materials, to enforce amnesia. In China's imperial past, there were many 'revisions' of historical annals that wantonly destroyed or expurgated ancient books, to blot out the violence of history. The approach today is even more direct and thorough: historical memory is erased at its root, by permitting no records from the start, nothing that could enter into a significant narrative.

Once all is forgotten, no painful lessons can remain, and history will become 'permeated with light'. Courageous resistance will no longer be visible, the legacy of pioneers and vanguards will be obliterated, and the past again becomes a smattering of spiritual ruins. This kind of enforced amnesia has proved very effective in contemporary China. Since people cannot live forever in their memories anyway, a prohibition on them allows the stench of blood to fade away, dissolving in the mundane concerns of everyday life. The younger generation already knows nothing of the killings just ten years ago, let alone the cruelties of the Cultural Revolution thirty years ago, or tragedies of the Anti-Rightist campaign forty years earlier. Faced with these blank pages in our historical narrative, they can only accept the official versions of the past, with no chance of forming any independent judgement of them.

Chinese academics have tried hard to develop between the cracks in this structure. In recent years, a good many memoirs, and a few scholarly articles and books on the Anti-Rightist campaign or the Cultural Revolution have appeared, all signs of the struggle to recover historical memory. But study of the Chinese experience of the twentieth century has not been actively pursued. For that, there are – in my experience – two reasons. Firstly, some Chinese intellectuals are unable to free themselves from dichotomies: that is, a tendency either to accept or to reject an idea completely. This mode of thinking is not conducive to sorting out the complexities of China's twentieth-century experience. Even more importantly, in the past twenty years, and especially since the 1990s, two opposite attitudes have become widespread in Chinese academic circles: the belief that China's problems stem from its 'break with tradition' and that their remedy lies in a 'return to Confucianism'; and the belief that, on the contrary, the crux of China's problems has been its rejection of Western, especially American, thought and culture, and that progress can only be achieved by 'taking the Anglo-American road'.

What the twin fixations on either ancient China or the modern West neglect is precisely 'modern' – twentieth-century – 'China'. Even discussions of modern Chinese literature and scholarship lean heavily towards those figures who were primarily oriented either to traditional or occidental culture. The result is that writers and thinkers who based themselves upon actual changes occurring in Chinese society, and took the need for solutions to its problems as the motor-force of their ideas, have paradoxically been displaced from the horizons of today's research. It is no accident that in recent years Sun Yat-sen has been neglected and Mao Zedong forgotten, while attacks on Lu Xun have multiplied.

In fact, the atmosphere since the 1990s has been very inhospitable to critical reflection on the experience of the past. Mainstream ideology consists of surface advocacy of the need to 'insist on Marxism' (even 'develop Marxism'), and substantive diffusion of 'utilitarianism' and 'hedonism' (consumerism). A divorce between outer and inner imperatives is the defining feature of this system. The outward show of 'insisting' is absolutely necessary for the legitimacy of those in power. On the one hand, it functions to silence independent intellectuals, and stem any critique of past or present at source; on the other, it serves as a form of ideological control and a way to manipulate the masses. What this new obscurantism generates is popular scepticism and apathy towards all politics and propaganda, which everyone treats as a charade. Everyone, from those in positions of power to middle and elementary school students, becomes used to telling tall tales, engaging in empty and superficial talk, and lying. This has become a game, with its own rules and regulations, played by all. Everyone speaks false words, lies to others and willingly allows others to lie to them. If anyone breaks these rules and tells the truth, he is regarded as 'an enemy of the people.'

This is precisely what those in power need to maintain stability: a time without critical reflection, theory, or belief. Only utilitarian hedonism and consumerism can fill the vacuum left by people's lack of faith, and these are just the values that the mainstream ideology, controlling the media and colluding with commercial culture, purveys to ordinary people. A bombardment of advertisements and frenzied variety shows masquerade as stability, diverting popular attention to unbridled consumption and 'pleasure in the present', and suppressing all spiritual pursuits or capacity for reflection. It is this *fin de siècle* revelry that drowns out the anguished cries of suffering from the oppressed and humiliated, and the voices of critical and independent reason. In the midst of such frantic celebrations, it is not surprising that the grim side of China's experience over the past century should be forgotten.

We must confront this national forgetting. What it means is that the lessons of history have not been learnt, that the ideas and practices that led to errors have not been seriously scrutinized or dispelled. The tragedies of history can then repeat themselves in unanticipated forms at unanticipated moments. The truly valuable lessons of China's experience will also fall victim to a collective amnesia, breaking any connexion with the best legacies of the past. People will not be able to build upon the critical achievements of their predecessors, but be doomed again and again to start all over from square one. This has been a pattern in modern Chinese thought, and is one of the reasons why it has so often stagnated at a low level. What lurks behind the present façade is a crisis in national culture that no intellectual with a conscience can view with indifference.

Lu Xun

The fate of Lu Xun is emblematic in this regard. In the 1980s he was the main inspiration for a new generation of enlightenment intellectuals. At that time, the most influential mottoes in Chinese debates inside and outside the universities were calls to 'return to May Fourth' and 'return to Lu Xun'. But after the storm that stunned the world on June Fourth, Lu Xun suddenly fell out of favour.

- The conservatives now in vogue look upon May Fourth as an evil origin of the Cultural Revolution, and Lu Xun's thought as a synonym for despotism.
- When a sudden fever for 'national studies' (*guoxue re*) arose, masters of 'neo-Confucianism' and advocates of a 'New National Essence' naturally saw Lu Xun as the chief culprit of a break with tradition – in the eyes of some, even a 'traitor' to China.
- The 'belated stars' of postmodernism, Chinese-style, regard knowledge as an accomplice of power, and rationality as a kind of crime: in bidding farewell to Lu Xun they are only being consistent.
- Those who look at the May Fourth generation through a post-colonial lens treat its attempts to reform national character, and Lu Xun's portrait of Ah-Q,[1] as little more than pandering to Western cultural hegemony.
- Liberals who champion tolerance, and show off their gentlemanly deportment, naturally cannot tolerate the 'intolerant' and 'narrow-minded' Lu Xun, who in their eyes collaborated with totalitarianism.

Here, then, is a striking cultural phenomenon. Chinese literary and academic circles of the past decade have been dominated by every possible -ism: yet no matter what -ism was adopted, almost without exception 'criticizing Lu Xun' was felt to be a necessary step to promote it. On closer scrutiny, it can be seen that these various doctrines were either 'new uses of an old recipe' – that is, a recycling of some traditional notions – or the latest 'import' from the West. In effect, they highlight the unusual nature, and distinctive value, of Lu Xun's thought. For his thoughts are genuinely modern, and uniquely Chinese, not a retailing of Western conceptions. This is where his originality lies. As he himself said early on,

> Those who admire what is ancient, return to antiquity! Those who want to leave the secular world behind, quickly leave! Those who want to rise to heaven, quickly ascend! Spirits that want to shed the human body, quickly depart! This world is the abode of those who embrace the present and hold fast to the earth ('Random Thought', vol. 3, p. 49).

Lu Xun himself was just such a writer and thinker, who embraced the present and held fast to the earth. His roots were firmly planted in the ground of twentieth-century China. He was intimately tied to the Chinese people who live and struggle in this land. His attention was focused on their problems, and his reflections were always firmly based on the realities of their country.

But in no way was his thought narrow or self-enclosed. When he first emerged on the Chinese intellectual and literary scene in the early twentieth

---

[1] Lu Xun (1881–1936), *Lu Xun quanji* (Complete Works of Lu Xun), Beijing 1981, vol. 1, pp. 487–527. Hereafter, references to Lu Xun are given by volume number and page number in the text.

century, he had already set out his mission: 'not to lag behind trends of thought in the world outside; not to relinquish long-standing cultural impulses within; to appropriate what we may, while preserving what is best, for the creation of a new way of thinking' ('On Cultural Extremes', vol. 1, p. 56). What he had understood was the problem that all late-comer nations must confront in constructing a modern culture: what to make of indigenous traditions, and imports from other nations round the world? This remains a global issue today. Lu Xun's approach was very tolerant and open. He was later to promote the notion of 'raptism' (the ethic of taking from others, or *nalai zhuyi*, 'Raptism', vol. 6, pp. 38–41), which proved very influential. But the most striking feature of his programme is that learning from the outside world and preserving impulses of tradition were not ends in themselves, but means to create what was most essential: 'a new way of thinking'. What Lu Xun sought was a set of novel ideas, values and principles that would improve the condition of the Chinese people. We might say this was the strategic objective that he laid out for the construction of a modern Chinese national culture. In my view, this is a task that has still to be completed.

On closer inspection, Lu Xun's tolerant attitude towards both Chinese traditional culture and the world – including Western – culture was based upon his conviction that 'in the chain of evolution, everything is intermediate' ('Postscript to *Grave*', vol. 1, pp. 285–260). As he saw it, intermediacy and finitude are the universal mode of existence of all the myriad things of this world. In this light, he thought all forms of culture – whether of China, other Asian nations, or the West – were 'extremes': that is imperfect, incomplete, fallible, transient, limited. Any complete or perfect culture lay forever beyond the horizon, an ideal that could be pursued (a pursuit that could inspire major cultural achievements) but not attained. In confronting the partiality of all human cultures, Lu Xun fundamentally destroyed all cultural myths. This was a position that broke with the Sinocentrism which attributed a sacred superiority to Chinese traditional culture – an outlook with very deep roots that has continually obstructed progressive reforms in China, and can spring up again at the first opportunity. At the same time, Lu Xun also broke with the Eurocentrism that gave Western culture a sense of superiority, and a claim to universality, that were to have a tremendous impact on many Chinese intellectuals.

That Lu Xun at the outset of his intellectual development should already have questioned Eurocentrism is remarkable. At the same time, it was his conviction of the partial and defective nature of every culture that made him tolerant of all of them, East or West, each with their own distinctive values. He anticipated a multi-cultural universe, in which different cultures would borrow from, as well as reject and compete with others, on a level playing field; in which intermingling and fusion, yet also uniqueness and independence would be equally possible.

Thus when Lu Xun was confronted at the beginning of the twentieth century with the historical question of how to construct a modern Chinese civilization (what today would be called China's path to modernity), he did not favour the simple route, adopted by many of his contemporaries, of wholesale importation of Western models. Instead, he adopted a critical, and inevitably complex, even contradictory attitude towards the West. In such essays as 'On Cultural Extremes', 'On the History of Science', and 'On Destroying Evil' (vol. 1, pp. 25–35, 44–57; vol. 8, pp. 23–34), he situated some basic themes of Western industrial civilization – 'materialism', 'science', 'reason', 'democracy', and 'social equality' – historically, in the development of science and of society. On the one hand, he affirmed the contribution of these values to the progress of Western society. Since they were lacking in China's traditional society and culture, he argued, they served as great landmarks for it. On the other hand, Lu Xun pointed out that behind such landmarks lurked an equally great crisis. For if the pursuit of material progress developed into a worship of materialism, 'people's soul and spirit will be eroded day by day; their reason, will and feeling will be unbearably coarsened; they will attend to the objective material world only, and uncritically discard the life of the mind that inheres in any subjectivity'. The consequences would be grave, as 'people blinded by the desire for material goods would cause the gradual decline of society, and eventually bring progress itself to a halt' (vol. 1, p. 53).

In similar fashion, 'if science is made into a religion', 'shrines are erected to reason', and 'the world worships only scientific knowledge', life will wither and become desolate, as the finer emotions fade, deeper insights vanish and science itself dies or loses its value (vol. 1, p. 35). Since, Lu Xun believed, 'scientific discoveries are the outcome of forces beyond the control of science', reason and unreason, science and faith were at once contradictory, yet mutually constitutive of each other (vol. 1, p. 29). Lu Xun offered a further word of caution. If democracy ever became worship of the masses, a historical cycle would repeat itself. 'In ancient times, it was the individual who governed the masses; now the masses could tyrannize the individual.' (vol. 8, p. 26). In such conditions, the essence of despotism and rule by violence would remain unchanged.

So too, if social equality were to 'make everyone under heaven uniform', compressing all the different 'customs, conventions, moralities, religions, tastes, fashions, and languages' into a single mould, the result would merely be to 'plane down those that stand out, without raising those that are inferior', ensuring that 'society will inevitably degenerate to a lower level than in the past' (vol. 1, pp. 50–51). We see here a consistent feature of Lu Xun's thought: he never considers only one thesis from a single perspective, isolated from others, but always also explores its antithesis. His thinking was instinctively dialectical, moving between opposites – science and faith, reason and unreason, material and spiritual, masses and individuals, equality and distinction, democracy of the majority and freedom of the minority.

Yet he never simplified the relationship between these pairs to make crude, black and white, distinctions. He would never adopt a position without questioning it, nor would he reject one without finding in it something valuable. This discursive to and fro makes his judgements highly tentative. But he never sought dubious syntheses, or concealed the quandaries and contradictions that arose in his work. His wavering between points reflected the extent to which he internalized the tensions between opposites into a kind of spiritual agony. In his eventual conception of China's path to modernity, taking Chinese nationalism as his point of departure, he stressed the importance of 'building a nation' (*liguo*) – that is, a modern nation-state that would be united, independent, democratic, strong and prosperous. Yet he also emphasized that this state must be a 'nation of people' (*renguo*), that had the 'development of the individual' (*liren*) as its premise and basis. In turn, what this meant was 'honouring individual character and raising its spirits'. Lu Xun declared that one cannot simply 'take wealth, scientific technology or government by the masses as civilization', but must instead take 'spiritual freedom' as the marker for modern Chinese civilization (vol. 1, pp. 44–57). Who could doubt the importance of defining this goal (or more precisely, ideal) for China's modernization?

Lu Xun's idea of 'individual spiritual freedom' contains a double-edged critique here. For it is aimed both at the despotism of traditional Chinese civilization, and at the negative aspects of Western industrial civilization that he noted. He described the former as 'a semi-paralysis generated from within' and the latter as 'a new illness transmitted from without', referring to them as 'two plagues', a diagnosis with far-reaching implications (vol. 1, p. 57). For modern Chinese intellectuals have always harboured the same dual fear and consternation, a heavy psychological burden affecting the way they have thought about the choices before China. The significance of Lu Xun lies not in any prescription for solving these contradictions, but in his relentless exposure of the evils of his day, his confrontation with their cultural consequences, and his struggle against the despair surrounding him.

Lu Xun closely observed the predicament of the Chinese people of his time, once remarking that 'the spirits of the Chinese masses are reflected in my essays' ('Epilogue', vol. 5, p. 403). Those texts offer an encyclopaedia of modern Chinese society, politics and culture, vividly depicting the psychological traits and the conventions, norms, sentiments, and customs of our people – and most valuable of all, with a deep empathy with them. The 'philosophy of life' at work in his writing sets Lu Xun apart from other Chinese thinkers of the period.[2] For on the one hand, he was acutely concerned with the historical and cultural realities of the situation in which

---

[2] Qian Liqun, 'Zuowei sixiangjia de Lu Xun' (Lu Xun the Thinker), *Zoujin dangdai de Lu Xun* (Approaches to a contemporary Lu Xun), Beijing 1999, pp. 63–82.

the Chinese people found themselves. On the other, in *Wild Grass* (vol. 2, pp. 159–225) and other works, he explored ontological predicaments of human existence, in a characteristic spirit of 'resistance amid despair'. To this day, Lu Xun is alive in China's problems. Intellectuals who are disturbed by them cannot escape his shadow. When people are satisfied with the status quo, however, and pursue only the lightness of being, they ought to leave Lu Xun behind and try to forget him. This is Lu Xun's fate.

Mao Zedong

No discussion of twentieth-century China can avoid the dominating presence of Mao Zedong. The two main chapters of China's modern experience, the winning of independence and the creation of a unitary state, and the experiment of 'a Chinese form of socialism', are inextricably tied to his name. But Mao is also, of course, the most controversial historical figure in modern China. Critical assessments of him not only vary according to people's personal experiences in the so-called 'Mao era', but also express attitudes towards current realities and the choices at present facing China. How to view Mao is still a highly sensitive and emotional issue.

In his later years, Mao often remarked that 'my heart is in the same place as Lu Xun's'. There were, of course, the tactical motives of a politician behind Mao's claim, but there was also an element of truth in it.[3] For in my view Mao Zedong and Lu Xun did have a number of traits in common: they both possessed 'a restless soul' and an impulse towards incessant destruction and (re)creation. Lu Xun said that 'true intellectuals' were critics who are 'never satisfied with society,' and this certainly included himself ('Regarding the Intellectual Class', vol. 8, pp. 187–193); as for Mao, he was just the type Lu Xun described as the 'everlasting revolutionary' ('On the Anniversary of the Death of Sun Yat-Sen', vol. 7, pp. 293–294). Lu Xun also emphasized that 'the real intellectual class' can always 'feel the suffering of the ordinary people, and speak straightforwardly for them' ('Regarding the Intellectual Class'). He was himself an 'artist who protests, rails and fights' for those who have been insulted and injured' ('Written Deep into the Night', vol. 6, pp. 499–510); while Mao had what can be regarded as an even deeper 'common people complex', believing that he was a champion of the interests of workers and poor peasants. Even more importantly, perhaps, both were firmly rooted in the piece of land called China, and its problems were always foremost in their thoughts.

But Mao Zedong also differed from Lu Xun in two fundamental respects: his 'sage complex' and his 'emperor complex'. Legend has it that during the

---

[3] The highly complex question of Mao's relationship to Lu Xun is beyond the scope of this paper; I hope to deal with it elsewhere.

Great Proletarian Cultural Revolution, when Lin Biao offered Mao four titles: great mentor, great leader, great commander, and great helmsman, Mao was only interested in 'great mentor', happily accepting this term. It was just this notion of 'mentor' that Lu Xun found repulsive ('Mentor', vol. 3, pp. 55–56). In his early years, Mao made a solemn vow: he did not simply want to be a 'hero', to make his name as a great politician, military strategist and thinker; even more than all that, he wanted to be a 'sage', to surpass all his other achievements by spreading 'universal truth'. He wanted his thought to influence his contemporaries as well as generations to come, as a missionary called to transform human souls and purify earthly existence.[4] Most assessments of Mao dwell on the earlier part of his career – that is, his achievements as an outstanding political leader, military strategist, and social thinker of the Third World. Here even his most strident critics acknowledge his contributions to the struggle against domestic feudatories and imperialist invasion, the establishment of the People's Republic of China, and the founding of a modern nation-state.

In my view, this part of his legacy and its reflection in his thought (especially such military and political maxims as 'use the weak to attack the strong, the small to attack the large, the native to attack the foreign') is an important element in the Chinese experience of the past century. Its influence on China and the Third World is not to be underestimated. But in Mao's own eyes, it was only the 'first step in the long march' towards his ultimate goal. As he says in his well-known poem 'Snow' – 'All have passed away – only today are there men of great spirit' – what he was really after was a spiritual transformation of humanity, a form of collective existence that would release 'a higher morality purified of baser tastes'.[5] This was an important element in the ambitious socialist experiment on which he embarked so impatiently after the establishment of the People's Republic of China, and it was one of his principal motivations in launching the Cultural Revolution seventeen years later. In his famous 'May Seventh Directive' of 1966,[6] he emphasized that the goal of the Cultural Revolution was to make the whole country into a 'one vast school' of his thought. That is where the slogan of a 'revolution in the inner depths of the soul' came from, which became extraordinarily popular in the later years of the GPCR.

Of course, what this conception led to was a 'thought reform' that lasted nearly thirty years in China, reaching its peak during the Cultural

---

[4] See 'A Study of Physical Education', April 1, 1917, and the letter to Li Jinxi of August 23, 1917, *Mao Zedong zaoqi wengao*, Changsha 1990, and in Stuart Schram, ed, *Mao's Road to Power, Revolutionary Writings*, vol. 1, Armonk 1992, pp. 113–127 and 130–136 [ed].

[5] Mao, 'Snow', see Robert Payne, *Mao Tse-tung*, New York 1950, p. 229; 'Jinian Bai Qiu'en' (In Memory of Norman Bethune), *Selected Works of Mao Zedong*, Beijing, vol. 2, pp. 659–660, 1991 [ed].

[6] 'Wuqi zhishi,' quoted for the first time by an official editorial in *The People's Daily* on August 1, 1966.

Revolution, which was in reality an increasingly strict form of thought control and intellectual tyranny, with consequences of the utmost gravity. For what it meant was nothing less than an attempt to transform human nature. This is what made its failure inevitable. Before he died, Mao finally admitted: 'Lu Xun was a Chinese sage of the highest calibre. Not I.'[7] If we were to judge wisdom by influence, the remark would be inaccurate. Lu Xun's impact was primarily on intellectuals and students; his influence on ordinary people was limited. Mao, on the other hand, affected everyone who lived through his rule, and his posthumous influence extends to the present. Chinese national characteristics were actually altered by Mao. To this day, observers of mainland ways of thinking and behaving, even of orating, notice traces of his legacy.

So far as his other complex was concerned, Mao himself was not shy in speaking of it. His candid admission that he thought himself the 'First Emperor of Qin plus Marx' is unlikely to have been a mere joke. The most common explanation for his 'emperor complex' is that it was a predictable consequence of the 'modern peasant rebellion' he led. Lu Xun is supposed to have referred facetiously to Mao as 'a lord of the mountain' (*shan daiwang*).[8] In his view, all peasant rebels had historically wanted to 'satisfy their own itch to be emperor' – he once remarked that rebellion is China's most profitable business ('Three Souls of Academia', vol. 3, pp. 206–210). But such quips only skim the surface of the problem. To view the Chinese revolution led by Mao as just another peasant insurrection is an oversimplification.

The real problem here lay in the choice of a path for China's modernization. Faced with oppression and invasion by Western colonial or imperial powers, late-developing nations all bore the scars of a sense of national crisis and humiliation – the feeling that 'the backward deserve to be beaten'. This produced a general urge to catch up and overtake the oppressor powers. That drive was especially strong in Mao: he made it the guiding principle and goal of the construction of the People's Republic of China. Spurred by it, he launched the Great Leap Forward, which in the end achieved the opposite of what was intended, causing widespread famine. But in its early stages, it had the full support of the people, including intellectuals. For the urge to 'overtake' was shared by the Chinese masses, who desperately wanted to escape their own poverty and backwardness. Mao called on them to 'seize the day, seize the hour' (*zhi zheng zhaoxi*). But how was this to be done? Mao believed it could only be accomplished by exercising full state power to organize the whole population, with the aim of mobilizing its abilities, and unifying theory and practice in order to 'achieve great things'

---

[7] Mao's speech at the Wuhan Military District of November 1971, quoted from Chen Jin, *Wenren Mao Zedong*, (Mao Zedong the Literary Scholar), Shanghai 1997.

[8] Quoted in Yi Yan, *Mao Zedong yu Lu Xun* (Mao Zedong and Lu Xun), Shijiazhuang 1998.

in modernizing the nation. This conception was basic to Mao's thought, and he eventually discovered such a form of semi-military organization in the People's Communes.

Here, in effect, was a combination of the Qin Emperor's centralization of power with a Soviet-style single-party system (what Mao understood as Marxism) that sought national strength and wealth in a totalitarian political regime, pursuing a statist path to modernization. Such statism required the sacrifice of individual autonomy and freedom, and the absolute submission of each to the supposed benefit of all in the construction of the nation-state. This was a road leading in the opposite direction to that proposed by Lu Xun, which had sought to found the nation on the development of the individual. There were thus two completely different blueprints for Chinese modernity in the twentieth-century. But the statist road to modernization under an 'enlightened autocracy' has always been dominant. The Western-ization Movement (*yangwu yundong*) led by Zeng Guofan, Li Hongzhang and others had already paved the way for it in the nineteenth century. It is clear how attractive this path has often been to strongly nationalist intellec-tuals in late-developing nations.

In the first half of the twentieth century, many Chinese thinkers – among them Lu Xun and the early Mao – were highly critical of traditional autocratic rule, as well as of the ills of Western modernity. In the years when he was fighting against the single-party dictatorship of the KMT, Mao identified his cause with Western principles of democracy and freedom.[9] But once the United States imposed a diplomatic and economic blockade on China, after the establishment of the People's Republic, Mao's experiment in a Chinese-style socialism increasingly sought a non-Western path to modernization. Fear of the maladies of Western modernity, and alarm at Western designs to transform China gradually into a capitalist society, led to a wholesale rejection of democracy, freedom, and other Western values, and the embracing of 'equality' as the main value system. The central goal of social progress became the elimination of the three great disparities: between physical and mental labour, between city and countryside, and between industrial and agricultural worlds. The aim was an ideal society completely free of 'bourgeois right', based on absolute economic and political equality, in which the abolition of the social division of labour would realize the full potential of every human being. The blueprint Mao designed for the Chinese people was clearly utopian, and efforts to realize the dream were far from successful. This was the equality foretold by Lu Xun: the bid to eradicate all disparities levelled those who stood out without substantially raising those below, leading only to regression. Even as attempts to

---

[9] Mao, 'Da lutoushe jizhe ganbei'er wen' (Reply to a Reuters reporter), *Mao Zedong wenji* (Collection of Mao's Writings), vol. 4, Beijing 1996.

eliminate social inequalities achieved a certain limited success, they inadvertently manufactured a different kind of inequality.

The reason why Mao was so self-assured that he could describe himself as a successor to Qin Shi-Huangdi, the First Emperor, is that he believed that he represented the interests of the workers and peasants. These classes made up the huge majority of China's population and formed the foundation of Chinese society, yet in traditional Chinese civilization they had always been looked down upon, humiliated and oppressed. So when Mao and his comrades announced that they intended to overturn this hierarchy, they were full of a sense of historical justice, and received the support of socially conscious intellectuals. In the 1930s Lu Xun had expressed his ardent hope that an 'entirely new, unprecedented social system may emerge from this inferno, and hundreds of millions become masters of their own fate.' ('Preface to Lin Keduo's *Impression of the Soviet Union*', vol. 4, pp. 424–427). For Mao and his generation of Chinese revolutionaries, this vision was not mere propaganda, but a task they undertook very seriously. In what people refer to as the Mao Era, the social status of ordinary workers and peasants was raised, their economic conditions were improved, and state policies in culture, education, and health-care were all angled towards them. The entire system of Mao's one-party rule had a popular basis in the workers, peasants and lower social classes of China.

When Mao realized that the Party and State apparatus was gradually becoming bureacratized, and might crystallize into what he predicted would be a 'bureaucratic class' in stark opposition to the working class and the low- and middle-level peasants,[10] he launched the Cultural Revolution without hesitation, attempting to establish a new kind of totalitarian regime that would discard the Party bureaucrats and link the authoritarian sway of an imperial leader directly to the rule of the masses. He had originally coined the slogan that 'the upper classes are the most stupid, the lower classes the most intelligent' with the idea that the capital of knowledge which 'bourgeois intellectuals' were employing to usurp leadership from the proletariat should be expropriated from them. But now, taking it to extremes, the Cultural Revolution became obscurantist and hostile to culture itself.

Mao was unwilling to give up the one-party system, but at the same time there is no doubt that he intended to 'take an eye for an eye' in settling accounts with the past, to oppress the oppressor and humiliate the humiliator. Thus in attempting to liberate workers and peasants, he subjected another part of the population to violence and tyranny. As the Cultural Revolution proceeded, its ranks steadily expanded, from so-called landlords,

---

[10] Mao, 'Dui Chen Zhengren guanyu shejiao dundian qingkuang baogao de piyu he pizhu' (Comments on Chen Zhengren's report on the experiment of the socialist rural education movement), in *Jian'guo yilai Mao Zedong wengao*, vol. 11, Beijing 1996.

wealthy peasants, counter-revolutionaries, bad elements and rightists, to so-called 'bourgeois intellectuals', cadres considered 'capitalist-roaders', 'rich middle-level peasants with capitalist tendencies' and so forth. The spread of hereditary theories (*xuetong lun*) of class descent further implicated the offspring of all these groups, creating a kind of mutant version of a feudal hierarchy that generated new social inequalities.

In this kind of social structure, even the liberation of workers and peasants was strictly limited. This was especially true of the peasants, because Mao chose to industrialize China at the expense of the peasantry, who were tied to the land, and remained mired in abject poverty. It is sometimes said that Mao himself despaired over this. The iron logic of the engine he set in motion could not be controlled even by its inventor. The Cultural Revolution in which Mao invested his highest hopes – he expected it would enable workers and peasants to 'occupy all social fields' – was in the end buried by the explosive cheers of hundreds of millions of peasants when they were finally awarded leases for their plots in the early 1980s, after decades of having no rights at all to the land they tilled: a bitter irony.

Mao enacted a great historical tragedy on the stage of twentieth-century China. He was a combination of utopian and tyrant of a kind rarely seen in our country, and in his thought and practice the imagination of a genius and its fatal consequences were inextricably intertwined. What he left to posterity is a complicated yet rich legacy, a fruit hard to consume, but impossible to discard. After his death, people tended to forget him, as they understandably sought to escape his shadow and move on in a new direction. But in the end they found that Mao's place in modern China could not – and shall not – be forgotten. The one-party state he established has been passed down, and further developed into new forms. Elements of his way of thinking and acting, even of speaking, continue to influence his successors, as well as ordinary people. His shade lingers in all corners of contemporary Chinese society.

Of course, his romantic imagination and ideals have been jettisoned. China has entered a utilitarian age. Moreover the social foundations of the totalitarian system he established are being steadily transformed. That which he most dreaded and tried to his utmost to prevent – 'capitalism' – has spread throughout today's China. Lu Xun's two plagues are more than ever realities that we face in the new century: on the one hand, the 'ills from within', including the unbroken dictatorial legacy (albeit in new forms) that Mao himself inherited and passed on; and on the other, the 'ills from without', the negative features of Western industrial civilization. Today the general perception is that Chinese society has become acutely polarized. The ideal of social equality has been completely discarded, and the whole society is now tilted towards the 'new rich'. The price of this social development has been paid by workers and peasants, who have once again fallen into the pit of the overlooked, the humiliated, and the abjectly poor.

Standards of social morality have declined alarmingly, plunging below even the basest levels.

It is in these conditions that people have again started to pay attention to the legacy of Mao. Yet, as we have stressed, Mao's powerful imagination, and his bold experiments in searching for a non-Western path to modernization that could avoid the maladies of the West, were inextricably tied to a new kind of despotism which had disastrous consequences, that still linger in Chinese society. It is extremely difficult to disentangle this fact from his legacy. Many Chinese intellectuals continue to be traumatized by painful memories of the Maoist period. They view the history of Mao's reign as a catalogue of crimes, and would rather completely forget and discard it. On the other hand, younger scholars with no personal experience of that time, but fiercely critical of the realities of today's China, idealize Mao's legacy, deliberately avoiding or even denying their idol's failings and the calamities he caused. As for China's lower classes, they have long regarded Mao's thought as a spiritual banner in their struggles. The need for an evaluation of his heritage that is both objective and critical has become urgent. Every Chinese intellectual with the sense of historical responsibility is called to take up this task.

Heretical spirits

Uniformity of opinion, thought, and action was mandatory under Mao's rule. But there were special circumstances, for example during the 'Hundred Flowers' interlude of 1956–1957 or during the Cultural Revolution itself, in which independent thinking could develop – unorthodox not only in its substance, also its mode of transmission, making use of big character posters posted in public spaces, or secret circulation of handwritten copies. The authors of such texts were subjected to different sorts of persecution, and often paid with their lives for their ideas, which were condemned to oblivion. This is a part of Chinese tradition. Lu Xun long ago commented that the reason why

> there are more heroes in other countries than in China is among other things because the punishments of other countries have never been so cruel as those of China. I researched in early European records on the torture and murder of Jesus's disciples, and the cruelty of their persecution in no way matches that of China. Those who did not succumb in the face of death were called saints. There are also Chinese youths who do not succumb in the face of death, but their names are kept secret, and are never disclosed . . . Consequently, promising and resolute fighters are extirpated; waverers degenerate; at this rate, there will be no good people left in China. If China meets its downfall, it is those who enact such

policies that will be responsible' ('Letter to Cao Juren', June 18, 1933, vol. 12, pp. 183–185).

In this whole history, what was forced to be forgotten were not only specific thoughts, but also the tradition of an inner world of resistance and independent reflection. This is the gravest and deepest wound inflicted on the Chinese national spirit. In the last few years, Chinese academic circles have struggled in difficult circumstances to recover, publish, and research the work of the independent thinkers of the twentieth century. An important motive for doing so is to continue the tradition of 'intellectual fighters', as Lu Xun called them.[11] The links between independent thinkers under Mao and Lu Xun himself are quite obvious.

It is striking, however, that those regarded as heretics often drew their inspiration from Marxism and even Mao's own thought. The most important 'rightist' thinker of 1957, Tan Tianrong, who led the democratic movement among students at Peking University, publicly stated that all of his critical ideas and opinions were based on the famous declaration of Engels in *Ludwig Feuerbach and the End of the Classical German Philosophy*:

[we] do not recognize any type of outside authority, religion, view of nature, social or state system – everything must be criticized mercilessly, everything must stand before the jury of reason, either to start proving the reason for its existence, or relinquish its right to exist. Critical reflection and rationality become the only measuring stick for the existence of all things.[12]

Likewise, independent-minded youth during the Cultural Revolution typically referred to themselves as 'Maoists'.[13] As one participant recollected later on, in that time people understood Mao's thought according to their differing class interests, and its ambiguity permitted this. On the one hand, in keeping with his principle of 'continuous revolution', from the start of the GPCR he proclaimed that 'it is right to rebel', calling on people (especially unencumbered youths) to destroy the bureaucratic system he was dissatisfied with, in order to protect what he regarded as the interests of

---

[11] Qian Liqun, ' "Jingshenjie zhanshi" puxi de zijue chengjie' (Conscious continuation of a line of intellectual fighters), *Burong mosha de sixiang yichan: chongdu Beida ji xiaowai 'youpai' yanlun* (An ineradicable intellectual legacy: re-reading 'Rightist' opinions in and beyond Peking University), Shantou 1999.

[12] Quoted in 'Di er zhu ducao' (The second poisonous weed), in Niu Han and Deng Jiuping, eds, *Yuan shang cao: jiyi zhong de fanyou yundong* (Grass on the plains: memoirs of the Anti-Rightist Campaign), Beijing 1998.

[13] Yibing, 'Guanyu jianli Mao Zedong xiaozu de jianyi' (Suggestions Regarding the Formation of a Mao Zedong Thought Group), in Song Yongyi and Sun Dajin, eds, *Wenhua da geming he ta de yiduan sichao* (Heterodox Thoughts during the Cultural Revolution), Hong Kong 1997.

workers and peasants. On the other hand, he was basically unwilling to reject the centralized system of one-party rule he had established. Indeed, we might even say that his motivation for unleashing the Cultural Revolution was precisely to strengthen that system. For whether he was willing to admit it or not, he had a vested interest in centralized rule. The call to 'rebel' was, after all, conditional; the absolute truth and authority of Mao's thought and the so-called 'proletarian headquarters' was not to be questioned.

Yet the process he set in motion developed into something Mao could not control. The slogan that 'it is right to rebel', the call to 'doubt everything', the principle that 'truth is in the hands of the few, protect the minority', struck a great blow at the norms in force before the Cultural Revolution, which included such maxims as 'be an obedient instrument of the Party', and 'to oppose the leaders of the Party is to oppose the Party itself.' The effect was to make restive or sensitive spirits – many of them oppressed by the previous system – question the myth of the Party that had been carefully cultivated over time. This was how the independent thinkers of the Cultural Revolution emerged. They called themselves 'Maoists' because they had been awakened by Mao. But when they turned a critical gaze towards past and present, putting his revolutionary logic to work, they all in the end rebelled against Mao himself and his reliance on the centralized system. This was something that Mao could not tolerate. These young rebels saw their mission as salvaging what was 'most vibrant, lively, and fundamental' in Mao's thought from those in power who monopolized it.[14] They did not realize that this was bound to subvert its conservative sides, contradicting not only Mao himself, but also the dictatorship that he wanted to preserve. So these independent thinkers were mercilessly suppressed. Repression in turn radicalized their resistance.

Thus almost all the independent thinkers of the Cultural Revolution underwent the same sort of 'break-out': from blind faith to increasing scepticism, and finally criticism of Mao's thought. What new sources of critical thinking emerged subsequently? One of the independent minds of those years suggests two main strands in the later thinking of the active youth of the sixties and seventies, both initially coming from within Marxism and then bifurcating. The first found its way from Marx through Hegel back to the Enlightenment and French Revolution, and from that starting-point developed an independent path towards modern Western constitutional democracy and human rights. The second followed the thought of Marx and Lenin to trace out the original aspirations of the Paris Commune and the October Revolution, and then worked its way forward through the history of the labour movement, rediscovering Bernstein, Kautsky, Trotsky,

---

[14] Ibid.

Bukharin and Luxemburg, to the reformist currents in the Soviet Union and Eastern Europe whose 'revisionism' Mao had denounced, and subsequent Eurocommunists like Berlinguer and Carrillo, ending up – perhaps without much conscious intent – as a strain of social democratic thought.[15]

The point to emphasize is that when those independent spirits who were active in the latter part of the Cultural Revolution sensed that new transformations of Chinese society were at hand, they fought for a new Enlightenment, in which they could express their hopes and expectations, without denying their original debts to Lu Xun and Mao. Their debates are recorded in a volume of the letters and diaries of a group of these thinkers published in the year 2000.[16] In it we read that their purpose was to make people conscious of their role in society, no longer leading a blind existence; that if workers are not awakened, and cannot determine their own fate, they will have no role in the management of social production, and continue to be manipulated and controlled by others. This is a line of thought that descends from Mao's 'Notes on a Textbook of Political Economy', which had a profound influence on independent spirits during the Cultural Revolution.[17]

The subsequent chapters of China's Reform Era did not follow or develop in the direction these thinkers hoped it would. In fact, they have gone the opposite way. Perhaps just because of this, the ideas and hopes of an earlier time take on all the greater significance today. As the Chinese people take stock of their situation at the threshold of the new century, the sum of China's experiences in the past century – of all its many thoughts and goals, successes and failures – is not to be forgotten.

Translated by Eileen Cheng

---

[15] Lanzi, *Bentu de dihuo: yige sixiang piaoliu zhe de jingshen licheng* (Fire flaring up from below: the spiritual journey of a wanderer in the world of thought), unpublished manuscript.

[16] Lu Shuning, *Jie hui can bian* (Fragmented pages from burned ashes), Beijing 2002.

[17] Mao, *Du Zhengzhi jingji xue jiaokeshu biji*. Translated in English as *A Critique of Soviet Economics*, New York 1977. The textbook in question was Stalin's *Economic Problems of Socialism in the USSR* [ed].

PART IV

14

A Dialogue on the Future of China

Wang Dan, Li Minqi, Wang Chaohua
Moderator: Leo Ou-fan Lee

How do you think the June Fourth Movement of 1989 will be remembered – as another May 4, 1919, the threshold of a period of general political awakening and turbulence, or instead as a Chinese version of 1848 or 1968 in Europe: a last spontaneous explosion of idealistic revolt, followed by a headlong pursuit of material consumption, and complacent institutional stabilization – the very opposite of the spirit of the explosion?

Wang Dan   I think the June Fourth Movement can be seen in either way, according to the time-frame we take. If we look at its background, it was more like a political awakening, that started with the intellectual ferment of the preceding year, when hopes were already stirred among academic circles that major changes were possible in China. On the other hand, if we view the movement as it developed, it is clear that it was a cultural rebellion by young people in an atmosphere of euphoria and revelry. The actual reality was a mixture of these elements.

Li Minqi   I believe that the mainstream analysis of the democratic movement of 1989 has typically failed to take into account the relations between different social classes in China at the time – especially the tensions between intellectuals and students on the one hand, and urban workers on the other. These were critical for its ultimate failure. For the communist regime that emerged in China after the 1949 revolution had a contradictory character. It was not the working class but a privileged bureaucracy that controlled political and economic power: in Marxist terms, New China remained an exploitative society. But the PRC was not just an oppressive regime. It was the product of a genuine social revolution that mobilized broad layers of the people. So to some extent it had to reflect their material interests and values. Urban workers gained real socio-economic rights – to employment, food, health-care, education and housing. In a more limited way, peasants benefited too. But the problem was that this combination was unstable.

Theoretically, two solutions were possible. One was a deepening of the revolution, allowing workers to win effective control over political and economic power. The other was a consolidation of the rule of the bureaucracy, allowing a new privileged class to deprive workers of their economic and social rights, along a path of outright capitalist development. It was the second process that actually took place.

In the eighties, workers' rights were steadily eroded as the bureaucracy started to impose 'scientific management' in state-owned factories – in effect, capitalist-style work-discipline – and to break the 'iron rice-bowl' of secure employment. Naturally, this resulted in growing resentment and discontent in the big cities. But this could find no political outlet. For the Maoist ideology of the Cultural Revolution had been discredited, and no alternative vision of socialism was available. In practice, the Chinese working class was unable to act as an independent force in defence of its own interests. Instead, from the mid-1980s onwards there developed an enthusiastic consensus among Chinese intellectuals in favour of free-market capitalism: leftist voices were virtually unheard of. The result was that popular discontent found expression in a democratic movement led not by ordinary working people, but by intellectuals and students committed to a system quite foreign to them. Of course, this made any active and effective mobilization of the great mass of urban workers ultimately impossible. But without their participation, the movement was doomed to failure.

Wang Chaohua   Surely the question is rather about how future history will remember the movement of 1989? So we have to consider what has actually happened in China since. From this perspective, I would be inclined to admit – unhappily – that June Fourth looks less similar to May Fourth than to the 1848 revolutions and the 1968 student revolts in Europe. For however we define the nature of the conflicts in 1989, we can hardly deny that their aftermath has been a strengthening of the existing political regime and a widespread turn away from ideal questions to a pursuit of consumerism. This amounts to a kind of compromise between material betterment and political oppression. This is the basic trend of the whole society.

Wang Dan   I stand by what I have said, but I would make a distinction between the process and the result of '89. The movement itself can indeed be compared with May Fourth, as both a political awakening and a social revolt. But I agree with Chaohua that its effects have been more like those of 1968 in Europe. We have to register both aspects.

Li Minqi   I believe the failure of the 1989 democratic movement actually paved the way for capitalist development in China. To unleash a full-blown capitalism in China, workers had to be deprived of the extensive social and economic rights they enjoyed after the 1949 revolution. The problem was that they would not accept this voluntarily, but lacked the political organiz-ation and ideological confidence to impose any other direction. Meanwhile there was another force, intellectuals and students, who were capable of acting in their own interests. They agreed with the government on the economic future of the country – both wanted capitalism – but disagreed on the distribution of political power. Although the aims of the intellectuals were actually against the interests of the workers, the urban masses had little choice but to rally to the democratic movement led by them, which was after all directed against their present – as opposed to potential – oppressors.

Popular participation in the revolt did threaten to undermine the project of capitalist development. But the failure of the movement ensured that for a long time the Chinese working class would not be able to act as a collective political force, independently or otherwise. In the nineties scat-tered labour protests have continued, but broad political opposition to capitalist reform is not on the agenda. In this sense, the outcome of the June Fourth Movement has been not unlike that of the 1848 revolutions in Europe. In France, the uprisings in Paris eventually led to the establishment of the Second Empire. The Bonapartist regime, claiming to be a state above all classes, went on to lay the foundations for capitalist prosperity in France. In fact, we could actually extend the comparison, since we know that in reality the principal social basis of Bonapartism lay in the French peasantry. So too, at least in the initial stages of capitalist reform in the eighties, the Chinese peasants were the main social support of the Deng regime. In 1989 the peasantry played no role in the democratic movement, and their neutrality was a critical factor in its defeat. It will be interesting to see whether the current Chinese regime will go the way of the Second Empire, which was eventually replaced by a stable bourgeois democracy under the Third Republic, or will break down in some quite different way.

Wang Chaohua   I agree with your comments on the role of the peasantry. But your account of the situation of the working class is much too simple. Official ideology at that time was still very uncertain and confused over the issues of urban economic reform, the future of state enterprises, and the social status of the working class. There was no complete ideological conversion to capitalism by the CCP. So the working class inevitably lacked a clear orientation. Workers tended to swing between the legacy of a residual Maoism and the thoroughgoing liberalism advocated by students and intellectuals. They did not yet feel that official ideology wholly failed to represent them, and they were still unsure whether the intellectuals' ideology could represent them better. I believe the main body of the urban working class was caught between these impulses. In 1989, it acted mainly in support of the students – who were not in their eyes, or indeed in reality, the same as the intellectuals. Only rarely did workers attempt to voice their own demands.

Li Minqi   It is true that the official ideology of the CCP in the 1980s was not yet free of Maoist residues – it was still in the transition to a fully developed capitalist outlook. But already the changes were far-reaching. The economic reform had handed greatly increased powers to the managers of the state-owned enterprises, stripping workers of much of the informal control they had once exercised over the labour process, and introducing Taylorist methods instead. Changes in health-care, in housing, and wage contracts were all helping to develop capitalist-style economic relations. The direction of development was clear. When Milton Friedman extolled the free market and full-steam-ahead privatization to Zhao Ziyang as General Secretary of the CCP, Zhao had not a word of objection. Other party leaders might differ from Zhao on specific points, but no one seriously challenged the basic direction of reforms set by Deng Xiaoping.

Wang Chaohua   The authorities were indeed trying to float various ideas and put into practice market-oriented policies. But urban residents and workers were resistant to many of these proposals. They were suspicious of moves to dismantle housing benefits and public health-care, and they could use the formal ideological commitments of the regime – its traditional socialist ideology – as a resource in resisting them. The very point you insist on, that the outlook of intellectuals didn't well represent the interests of the working class, ensured that the consciousness of workers swung between the two poles. Workers were unwilling to discard the whole legacy of the People's Republic in favour of the liberal agenda advocated by intellectuals. That is why they kept arguing in the All-China Federation of Trade Unions over whether they should give up their – theoretical – status as the 'masters' of state and society.

Wang Dan   I disagree with the view that a contradiction between workers and students was a significant reason for the failure of the June Fourth Movement. This idea lacks any basis. I have never seen any evidence for tensions between the student headquarters in Tiananmen Square and the Autonomous Association of Workers that could have affected the move-ment. There's no reason to think that the political proposals of the students and intellectuals were in conflict with workers' interests. They were inspired by a liberalism that would have created a social environment beneficial to all social strata. Actually, there could be no opposition between the two forces, because the workers didn't have any definite proposals of their own. During the late eighties, intellectual and student groups already had clear ideas about the reforms that Chinese society needed, which included draft programmes published in periodicals like the *World Economic Herald*, covering the reconstruction of the state as well. These were the product of stable groupings of reformers. But among workers you can't even find one such group in the whole movement of '89. Of course, outfits like the

Autonomous Association of Workers surfaced, and even the All-China Federation of Trade Unions discussed the situation. But there was not a single mature programme or organization. In the absence of any form of such organization, discussion of the relations between students and workers in '89, as if there were an important dynamic at work between them, lacks all reality.

Li Minqi Intellectuals perform mental rather than physical labour, which makes it easy for them to articulate their own material interests. Workers are typically manual labourers, trapped in oppressive conditions that make it much more difficult for them to explain their viewpoint in a systematic way. But this does not mean they lack interests which are different from those of other social classes, and have no immediate demands or desires based on them. Historically, progressive intellectuals have often played a role in helping to bring these demands to theoretical expression. In 1989, however, there was no longer any progressive segment of the intelligentsia in China, distinct from the pro-capitalist mainstream, capable of developing ideas or proposals in the interests of working people.

Do you believe the fatal outcome of the movement of 1989 was more or less inevitable, or do you think with hindsight it could have been avoided? If so, how?

Wang Dan Circumstantially, I think the outcome was inevitable, since by the end the biggest argument in the movement was simply over the question: should the students withdraw from Tiananmen Square? What would happen if we withdrew? What would happen if we didn't withdraw? Historically, one can't make hypothetical projections in such cases. Even if the students had withdrawn from the square, we don't have enough evidence to know whether the result would have been more peaceful or the conflict even sharper. Once Zhao Ziyang lost power, the authorities' attitude towards the students was clear-cut – an eventual showdown with the government was inevitable. How could we have changed that? At best, we might have reduced the intensity of conflict and altered the timing of the outcome.

Li Minqi My opinion is just the opposite. Circumstantially, the immediate upshot was probably avoidable, but if we consider the entire historical context, the defeat of the movement was inevitable. To understand this, we need to consider the situation of Chinese intellectuals at the time. Traditionally, they belonged to the highest layers of society. But after the 1949 revolution, they lost most of their inherited privileges, and in the Cultural Revolution they suffered greatly. In a general sense, any Chinese intellectual – the same was true in the Soviet Union or Eastern Europe – could understand that they would be better off in a capitalist than in a state-socialist society. The same was true for Soviet and East European intellectuals. So it is not surprising that in the late eighties most intellectuals championed a capitalist path for China. But since we know that intellectuals can, under certain historical conditions, transcend their own immediate interests and try to analyse society from a wider standpoint, this in itself isn't a sufficient explanation of the role they played in '89. Here we have to remember the particular history of the PRC, in which they had been the primary victims of successive Maoist 'campaigns', and learnt to be afraid of any mass mobilization. This was a historical burden under which a whole generation of Chinese intellectuals laboured.

Under Deng, however, the rulers of the country needed to free themselves from the inhibitions of their Marxist past and equip themselves with modern bourgeois ideology. This objective necessity was especially urgent in the field of economics. So a subtle, though still fragile, symbiosis started to develop between rulers and intellectuals. Both wanted to see capitalist development. But the intellectuals were unhappy with their political position, and wanted greater power, so they began to demand more liberty and democracy. But although they needed a certain level of democratic movement to win political concessions from the government, they never sought an active mobilization of the working class. This was their limit, and the movement they led suffered from it. The intellectuals were not ready to take resolute measures to win the democratic struggle, and the workers – lacking a political force or vision of their own – were not in a position to push them to a more consistent strategy. In this sense the failure of the movement was predictable.

Wang Chaohua   My own view differs from both of yours. I believe that circumstantially the movement could potentially have led to alternative outcomes. This is a conviction based on my personal experience, as Wang Dan knows. The hunger-strike that escalated the conflict with the government in mid-May was not inevitable. Indeed, it was never approved or voted by the Beijing Autonomous Students Union. It was a personal initiative of one group of leaders, opposed by others. Had a different line been adopted at that moment, the outcome of the Movement could have been less disastrous. This does not mean – here I differ from Li Minqi – that a straightforward success was conceivable either. He considers just two possibilities: the disastrous actual result, and a hypothetical triumphant outcome of the democracy movement in '89, depending on whether or not the workers were adequately mobilized. But I always believed there was another possibility: neither a total success nor a complete disaster, but a political compromise. This possibility was not at all out of reach. Why was it not realized, nor any other alternative outcome? In my view one significant reason was an over-optimism among intellectuals.

At the end of the eighties, the rulers of China had not yet completed a transition from the exercise of political power to the acquisition of economic capital. There were still many internal conflicts within the official ideological sphere, as capitalist-oriented developments gathered pace. So workers could continue to feel their position had some protection in a nominally socialist regime, and the likelihood that they could be strongly mobilized against it was rather slim. On the other hand, a compromise between the rulers and intellectuals was not impossible, even if the likelihood was against it. By the late eighties, intellectuals had been the main driving force of the whole reform period, while the authorities were often hesitant and divided. But this made the intellectuals overconfident, so that when the crisis came they had little inclination to stop midway. The result was inevitably disaster.

Wang Dan   I will answer both of you. Li Minqi has said that Chinese intellectuals wanted to recover their privileged position in society. But if we consider the actual character of the Movement in '89, its main body was made up of students. It was they who took the final decisions on most critical issues, such as the launching of the hunger-strike. The question of whether or not to withdraw from the square still lay in the hands of students. In fact, the Union of Intellectuals eventually urged the students to pull out of the square, but their proposal was rejected by the hunger-strikers. It was students who determined the issue. So let's look at their role in the Movement. What were their aims? Were they – or the intellectuals – pursuing power or freedom? These are two different things. If they were seeking power, then it was no doubt a political mistake on their part not to mobilize the workers. But they made no attempt to do so. What this shows is that, on the contrary, the intellectuals were not intentionally trying to gain back a privileged position. The students, for their part, did not have a strong power-political consciousness or even orientation. They were young people rebelling against a dictatorial culture. They wanted an atmosphere of freedom, in which they could say and do what they wanted within the confines of the law. This was the kind of life experience that mattered to them. It never occurred to them to mobilize workers or form secret organizations. They didn't even want to think about practical strategies. Why didn't students combine with workers? Just because this was a pure student movement – that's the proof of it.

Nor do I agree with Wang Chaohua's remarks. There were many key turning-points in the whole Movement – the marches, the dialogue with the authorities, the hunger-strike, the debate over whether we should withdraw from the square, etc. But when we discuss these issues today, no matter how much we might like to rethink the process, we can never get beyond mere conjecture. Even if we hadn't suggested a hunger-strike, we couldn't have prevented other people from launching one. At that moment the situation was such that if one person went on a hunger-strike, one hundred would join, and if one hundred joined, a thousand more would join. There is an emotional dynamic in all such mass movements. The decision whether or not to call a hunger-strike was only a tactical issue, for there was an unstoppable force pushing the movement to a confrontation with the authorities. We can't say that if we had not launched a hunger-strike the later sequence of events could have been averted. No one can claim this so absolutely.

In fact, there was never a single leadership of the Movement anyway. Originally, the decisive role was played by the Autonomous Association of University Students. Later, central power shifted to the headquarters in the square. Then, outside the square, there developed the Patriotic Assembly of All Professions in the Capital in Defence of the Constitution, which came to include both an Autonomous Workers' Association and an Autonomous Citizens' Association. If we look at the other key question posed by the outcome of the Movement, the decision to stay in Tiananmen to the end, the square headquarters and the Patriotic Assembly had different opinions about it, and this was an important reason why we did not withdraw. Actually, according to my memory, the square headquarters was willing to consider a withdrawal, but it was the whole body of students occupying Tiananmen who voted against doing so. In my heart I don't believe that at that moment they wanted to keep their distance from workers. They acted from spontaneous emotion. They didn't make any social calculation.

Li Minqi   I agree that an ideology need not find a clear expression in every situation, and that the students were often unconscious of the logic of their position. I well remember our outlook, which I shared, at the time. But the explicit social ideal of many of the intellectuals was to build capitalism. If you were a worker in '89, and were asked to join the democratic movement, why would you want to do so?

Wang Chaohua   You insist that the problem was the unwillingness of intellectuals and students to mobilize workers. Actually, if we move our focus away from the square, we can see that many students did go out to factories and attempt to arouse workers. This was particularly true in Shanghai. But they had little success. In part, this was because the students themselves were not well organized; their associations had virtually no practical control over voluntary actions of this kind. However, there was another side to the problem too. Some workers did organize themselves in the Autonomous Workers' Association led by Han Dongfang, yet they too found it very difficult to mobilize the great mass of the working class. You should ask yourself why this was so. When in 1990 I watched a videotape of the workers' debate in the All-China Federation of Trade Unions, I was struck by the fact that a central issue puzzling them at the time was whether or not they should hold a strike. This was a very perplexing idea for many of them, which they could accept only after long, painful debate. Why? Because they were still to some extent under the spell of a belief in 'collective' ownership of the means of production in a workers' republic. So they kept asking: 'Aren't we the masters of our state? How can we strike against our own state?' You could see their confusion.

How long do you think the present regime will last? How do you envisage the most probable ways it could end?

Wang Dan My personal guess is that within five to eight years Chinese society will undergo a big change. How will this transformation occur? One possibility is a peaceful extinction of the communist dictatorship, as progressive groups within the Party unite with democratic forces outside it to form a new political front capable of gradually taking power. This would be a more stable path. But it is also possible that the present regime will stubbornly cling to power, intensifying its suppression of the social contradictions in the country. That will unleash major instability, which could even lead to fighting between local warlords. I think either scenario is conceivable. Today, the decisive power is still in the hands of the government. But we can be sure China will be transformed within less than a decade. The basis for this judgement is that Chinese society itself is swiftly changing, no matter what the government does. No political authority can halt this process. The critical question is how the change will happen.

Li Minqi I am not that optimistic, or should I say pessimistic? My own view is that in the nineties China entered a period of rapid capitalist development, that has brought a stage of relative prosperity and stability to the country. While the economy is currently in recession, I believe this is a cyclical rather than structural setback, and will be overcome. Of course, this doesn't mean the current regime can last forever. One important result of capitalist development is to increase the size of the working class. In the private sector, the labour force is growing rapidly, and its ability to organize and struggle is improving. In the state sector, on the other hand, workers have been losing their traditional rights and their position is being reduced to the condition of the workers in the capitalist sector. As their experiences converge, the two are likely to join forces in common battles. This development is going to have a fundamental impact on the future of Chinese society. In 1989 the Chinese working class was too small and weak to push the democratic movement forward, and the peasants gave it no support. The situation will be different in the years to come. For the first time in Chinese history the modern working class will soon make up a majority of the population. This is going to make a decisive contribution to the victory of democracy in the future.

For Wang Dan, it is very important whether the current regime meets its end peacefully or violently. I'm not so worried about this. What I care about more is whether China achieves democracy under capitalism or under an alternative social system. We need to remember that China has joined the world capitalist system as a backward late industrializer. Its position in the world market is not only inferior to advanced capitalist economies such as the United States, Japan or Europe, but also to such newly industrialized capitalist economies as South Korea or Taiwan. The development of Chinese capitalism relies heavily on ruthless exploitation of large numbers of cheap workers. This requires a very specific politico-economic institutional framework. In the West, the historic strength of the labour movement forced the bourgeoisie to make major concessions to the working class, including political democracy and the welfare state. In many countries, universal suffrage itself was won by workers' struggle. Eventually, a relatively stable class compromise was achieved. But in the case of China, where capitalism depends so much on abundant cheap labour, is there any comparable room for the Chinese bourgeoisie to make similar concessions – to grant political democracy or social welfare – and at the same time maintain competitiveness in the world market and a rapid rate of accumulation? It seems rather questionable.

Wang Chaohua   In my view the regime can be relatively optimistic. If its opponents are realists, they should be pessimistic. For my instinct is that the status quo could last for another twenty years, or even longer. Since 1992, the PRC has entered a phase where it can sustain a broad capitalist development through continuous self-adjustments. On this point, my view is not very different from that of Li Minqi. But if we consider the kind of social and political changes such an economic path will most likely bring, I'm of quite another mind. Let me take three main issues. Firstly, although the working class will surely increase in size, we have to remember how low the level of urbanization has been in twentieth-century China, in any comparative sense. This continues to be true even today, and will persist into the foreseeable future. We cannot imagine that the working class will quickly become a majority of the nation.

Secondly, as rural migration to the towns proceeds, a modern multinational capitalism is invading China, and bringing huge disparities into the urban workforce itself. The gap in income and life-conditions between white-collar and blue-collar workers, which is already significant, is likely to increase greatly, splitting the working class even as it multiplies in numbers. So I am very doubtful about your assumption that there will be a highly disciplined, homogeneous industrial working class in China. This strikes me as old-fashioned. From what I can see in the United States, or other Third World countries, it is more probable there will be big social and regional divisions in it. Thirdly, China cannot possibly repeat the pattern of industrialization in countries like Britain, where the population became highly concentrated in a few industrial zones, centred on big cities like London or Manchester – still less the even more centralized pattern of recent developers like South Korea, with the huge predominance of Seoul. The process will inevitably be quite dispersed in China, and may turn out to be more one of generally spreading commercialization than industrialization. We shouldn't forget what the global environment for China's capitalist development at the beginning of the twenty-first century will be like.

In such a perspective, political changes may come about neither through a renewed movement for democracy, nor as the outcome of a sudden revolution, but perhaps as a gradual corrosion of the centre by various factors and forces in the provinces. Could any of these stand for an alternative to capitalism? Only if there were articulated oppositional ideologies, considered or accepted by some of China's intellectual elite. For that purpose a simple 'socialist' discourse is unlikely to be enough, since any such alternative would have to be able to explain how it differed from the experiments of Maoism. Only then could it gain circulation, or hope to capture the imagination of the masses. Of course, it is true that China today still contains fertile soil for the reception of socialist ideas – significant groups that are certainly susceptible to them, which cannot be explained by analogies from the history of capitalist development in the West. For even now the legacy of the communist experience of the past four or five decades is still not dead.

Wang Dan Let me explain what I meant by predicting a basic change in China within five to eight years, or otherwise you might think me too optimistic. If we ask, how long CCP rule will last, we need to distinguish between two different kinds of ending – disintegration, and evolution into something different. I feel there is a good chance of the latter, which would involve economic changes of a kind we should discuss later. For the moment, what I want to point out is something else. Both of you speak of the future as if it were exclusively a matter of rational social analysis. But shouldn't we consider the possibility of sudden contingencies in the process of historical development? In the past, as we know, a mistake in the translation of a telegram could cause a war between two countries that might alter the entire political configuration of Europe. In China, the accident of Hu Yaobang's death set off a huge mass movement, which no one anticipated. So mightn't another unexpected event upset the path of development prescribed by the political establishment? We can't discount the possibility. In the PRC today there are no rules governing relations among the different social strata; no rules to guide leading groups in handling social contradictions. In these conditions, if an accident erupts, the different forces in play might not be able to reach a rational solution, opening up the possibility of a major change. Moreover, in the present situation, where social contradictions are very tense, the possibility of a sudden accidental crisis is increasing. That is why I do not give the current regime more than five to eight years of life.

Li Minqi   Wang Chaohua has pointed out that there could be a division between white-collar and blue-collar worker in China. But I don't think this phenomenon can by itself explain why there has so far been no revolution against capitalism in the West. It is the ability of the Western ruling classes to reach a compromise with their working classes by building political democracy and a welfare state that is more relevant. If we look at the late twentieth century, how far has the development of the labour movement repeated the pattern of the nineteenth century? The experience of Korea or Brazil provides a clear enough answer. In both countries, the working class played a crucial role in democratization. As for China, we might see a more complete development of capitalist relations of production in our own country than in any other Third World nation. For China had a relatively thorough social revolution and complete agrarian reform, which eliminated any trace of pre-capitalist exploiter classes. The development of the working class may therefore also reach a higher level. This doesn't mean there are no differences within the working class, for example, between employees of transnational corporations and workers in state-owned enterprises. But they are all subject to the oppression and exploitation of capital, they share a common social position, and material interests. This will make it possible for them under certain conditions to act as a united force.

What do you regard as the best immediate strategies for promoting democratization in China?

Wang Dan   For a century China has been trying out various institutions, including many borrowed from Western political systems. But what our country lacks is a public sphere independent both of the government of the day and of competing interest groups. Such a public sphere could keep direct material conflicts and the ensuing social instability at bay. That is my point of view, though I realize it may seem a narrow one. I hope there will be an independent intelligentsia in China, in possession not only of political and economic but also moral resources, without which there can't be a real opposition in society. Its institutional position should be completely independent. Even if a relatively democratic government should appear in China, this kind of group would still be necessary as a counterweight to it. Critical journals and publishing houses are vital here. Such an intellectual force might have different kinds of connections with the authorities of the hour, even getting involved in politics as a means to influence its outcomes. But as a social power it should not only act as a political balance, it should also check tendencies towards cultural hegemony and resist any interest group that might threaten civic liberties. That's my basic idea.

Li Minqi   Chinese intellectuals by themselves won't be able to bring the democratic movement to victory, largely because of their instinctive fear of the working class. In this sense, the future of democracy in China depends on whether urban workers can turn themselves into a powerful political force with their own standpoint – that is, something very different from what they were in 1989. It must find out its own political interest and an ideology appropriate to it. I think this is the key to the success of democracy in China. But for this to happen, at least a section of the intelligentsia would have to adopt their standpoint, and help them develop an alternative social programme. The question here is the same as that raised by Wang Chaohua: is it possible for people from an elite background to identify themselves with the interests of a popular class? At the moment, the intellectual mainstream in China is undoubtedly pro-capitalist. But there have been some changes since the end of the 1980s. There is now a certain space for the left, and small groups of radical intellectuals are emerging, as the development of capitalism develops its contradictions as well. In one way or another these are likely to be reflected more strongly in the next generation, who will be freed from the burden of the historical memory under which their elders still suffer. Being less marked by the ideological and psychological scars of the state socialist era, they are more likely to observe and interpret society, and its contradictions, in a sober and objective manner.

Wang Chaohua   I believe the most effective strategy to promote democratic change in China must be a combination of two sets of demands. The first set is based on the principle of human rights, especially freedom of speech and assembly, guaranteed civic liberties. We should do everything in our power, using every ounce of our strength, to press home this essential principle as the aim of our political work. Many different specific issues can be taken up and argued through on the basis of a general conception of human rights. The second fundamental principle is social justice. China is certainly changing rapidly, but what kind of society is it changing into? Is our ultimate goal simply to make China richer? Is it a faster growth rate or greater efficiency? I believe our intellectuals should commit themselves very explicitly to a society that is juster for all its members, one that is fairer and more equal than what we witness today. It is only by this yardstick that we should be discussing efficiency or development. It is by firmly sticking to these two principles that we can serve the cause of Chinese democracy best.

Is it realistic to pin most hopes for the future of democracy in China on an emerging middle class?

Wang Dan   At present, I don't put much hope in them. The middle class that has recently appeared in China has mostly gained its property by taking advantage of loopholes in the system, from which they have benefited greatly – indeed through which they obtained their current positions. He Qinglian has shown the way state properties were divided up by these people. They secretly acquired assets through their power, then cut their official connexions, took off their red hats and changed the property into their own private firms. Such a stratum is more interested in maintaining the existing order. If society were transformed into a true free-market system, their methods of profiteering would be blocked. In fact, I doubt there is a real middle class in China, and if one does exist, I don't think it can move in a liberal direction.

Li Minqi   Maybe we should first clarify the concept of 'middle class'? It's often very confusing in the context of contemporary China, where people sometimes refer to the emerging private capitalist stratum as a 'middle class', while at other times the term is used to mean professionals and intellectuals. The second definition appears to be more consistent with usage in other countries.

Wang Chaohua   The reason why there is increasing interest in this issue in Western Sinology is closely related to the model of capitalist development in Europe in the seventeenth and eighteenth centuries, and in particular to Habermas's study of the conditions of a public sphere that eventually made democracy possible there, and the way these conditions have decayed in today's post-industrialist world. So I assume the question refers mainly to the role of a bourgeois stratum whose members own capital, rather than to intellectuals who perform mental labour. The historic bourgeoisie of early modern Europe is not the same kind of force as the middle-income class in America today, buying cars and houses. Questions about the role of the middle class in the emergence of democracy in developing countries like China usually have the former in mind. In this sense I think Wang Dan has good reason to identify an emerging middle class with bureaucratic capitalists in China, who convert public assets into private capital. In fact, this group does not confine itself to turning public property into private wealth inside China. It often transfers the proceeds to secret bank accounts abroad.

Li Minqi   Personally, I doubt whether the private capitalist class can make any substantial contribution to the democratic movement in China. This class has a dual nature. To a certain extent it is opposed to the bureaucratic capitalist class: there are contradictions and conflicts between the two. In this sense the private capitalist class seeks to share in political power, from which it is still relatively excluded. But the existing dictatorship, by repressing the workers, helps private capital to exploit labour. This is naturally in the interest of private entrepreneurs. If the workers had more political rights, and were free to organize unions and undertake collective bargaining, it would be against the interest of these capitalists. So we must always remember this dual character when we try to assess the potential role of the private capitalist class in the democratic movement.

Wang Chaohua   I certainly don't think that we should pin our main hopes for a future democracy in China on this stratum. On the other hand, if we look at the question in a comparative perspective, remembering West-European experience, we cannot deny that the emergence of a middle class in China might make some contribution to the formation of a democracy in the country. We must assume that an ideal operational environment for capitalist entrepreneurs requires highly codified legal protection, and unambiguously defined property rights. If instead of talking about current experience in China, we think of an abstract model, then we can say that private entrepreneurs need clear-cut property rights, defended by the law, to prosper. These are basic conditions for the existence of this particular class.

In this regard, although there is a lot of talk both inside and outside China about an emergent 'middle class', private entrepreneurs in today's China are not unlike the workers Li Minqi describes. They have not yet been able to articulate a consistent ideology, or to find their own political channels and agencies. This class remains an object of speculation, not a subject that can make its own voice heard or form its own political organization. In current conditions, it is still very difficult – if not impossible – for this class to transform itself from a 'self-existing' to a 'self-acting' class. At any rate, that is my understanding of the matter. If we take this into consideration, we shall not pin all our hopes for a future democracy in China on it.

Li Minqi   Historically it has not been unusual for clearly defined private property to coexist with political dictatorship, so even a very moderate hope for a progressive middle class in China might prove unrealistic. In China the government is now conducting so-called village-level elections in the countryside. Private capitalists often play a big role in these elections. In some cases, they are also prominent in the elections to local and provincial people's assemblies. In this way they have some access to political power.

Wang Chaohua   These political gains are mostly linked in various ways to bureaucratic connexions and intrigues. They're not enough to define this group as a 'self-acting class'.

Li Minqi   Well, I admit that. I wouldn't myself say that private capitalists are a class for itself yet in China.

How far should Chinese dissidents cooperate with foreign governments? Is it appropriate for them to criticize the domestic or foreign policies of other countries, or should they only speak of topics relating to China?

Wang Dan I think we should clarify the concept of dissident. In my view, there are two types of dissident. The first are intellectuals who resist dictatorship. It doesn't matter what kind of regime it is. I don't have any personal resentment against the Communist Party. What I resent is its dictatorial methods. I'm a dissident because of my beliefs. But there is another kind of dissident – political opponents of the current regime, who want to replace it. This type is very different. They believe their political ideas best represent the interests of the country. They have definite tactical orientations and clear expectations of political success. For us there is no such expectation. No matter what the situation, we will remain dissidents. So for us there can be no question of cooperating with foreign governments. Personally speaking, I have no contact with the American political mainstream. But the second type of dissident should cooperate with foreign governments because they have to think about China's position in the future international system, as they hope to govern China tomorrow. They also sometimes criticize the foreign policy of Western countries – Wei Jinsheng is an example. In my view, this is a mistake. They should speak only about Chinese affairs. Their role is to act like a future shadow cabinet. To criticize the policies of a foreign government is improper from a strategic standpoint, because each country has its own independent interests, which should be respected.

Li Minqi I have nothing to say.

Wang Chaohua My personal choice is very similar to Wang Dan's, but I wouldn't make the same criticism of the second type of dissidents. For me, there is no question of cooperating with foreign governments. To be an independent intellectual is to think in a principled way about human rights and social justice, and if you are thinking independently, you will naturally be able to criticize anything you believe deserves criticism.

What kind of constitutional structure should a democratic China aim for? Do you favour a Russo-American style of presidency, or Euro-Japanese form of parliamentary government? Have you any electoral systems in mind? What degree of federal devolution would you regard as desirable?

Wang Dan Since I identify myself as an independent intellectual, this question is not within the range of my interests. I hope that no matter what kind of constitutional system China adopts, it will embody the two concepts of freedom and justice. As long as it does not violate these, I will support it. But if it opposes them I will criticize it. Otherwise, I don't care what kind of system it is.

Li Minqi   I think we should care. Within the basic framework of capitalism, a European-type parliamentary system is a relatively more rational political arrangement. If we believe in the goal of freedom and equity, the European pattern is closer to it. The American system is based on the division of power between the three branches of government, which historically was set up to concentrate influence in the propertied class, and to guard against a popular majority having a direct impact on policy-making. This concern finds clear expression in the Federalist Papers that laid the theoretical basis for the US Constitution. The Russian Constitution is the fruit of Yeltsin's armed bombardment of parliament. It is deliberately designed to weaken the legislature, and to give the President virtually unlimited power. It has nothing to do with democracy.

Wang Chaohua   I too would prefer a parliamentary system for China. At the moment, I wonder if Taiwan mightn't offer the most relevant experience for us. Its constitution seems to be a mixture, neither fully European nor American in inspiration. It does have a directly elected president, but in practice the development of the system – also the voting rules – seem to give strong balancing powers to the parliament. The institutional result seems quite unstable, as the position of the premier has become increasingly independent of the presidency in recent years.

Li Minqi   Could this be compared with France?

Wang Chaohua   Perhaps it could. However, the peculiar position of Taiwan has created a situation that I don't think exists anywhere else. The KMT has kept a monopoly of the Presidency, based on its control of the armed forces, huge wealth and media resources. When there is any cross-straits tension, this power-complex tends to benefit as voters seek stability. In other conditions, the government can easily be affected by electoral pressures.

Li Minqi   In both Taiwan and Korea, presidents are elected by relative rather than absolute majorities. This allows the candidate of the ruling party to take the presidency with only a minority – say, one-third – of the total votes cast.

What economic system would you advocate for a democratic China? Which foreign countries would come closest to it?

Wang Chaohua   It is hard for me to point out a clearly defined economic system that I would want to advocate forcefully in China. The most important issue is for us to insist that all the members of our society have an equal say in the ongoing transition away from a so-called socialist – actually state-controlled – ownership system. Everyone should have the right to learn of the consequences of each possible option, and to make their own choice on the basis of full information about them. People with different proposals and beliefs should be given the same opportunities to explain their ideas to others. These are the conditions under which ordinary citizens, without much specialized knowledge of economics – I am one of them – could have a chance to arrive at their own decision as to what would be best for the country, and to try to rally others to support their choice.

In broad terms, I believe a democratic China should enable the great majority of its people to share its social and economic achievements. If someone could point out a convincing road to this goal, I'd be happy to follow. The Cultural Revolution in China pursued the aim of social equality, but it did so by driving members of society towards a common austerity, pushing anyone who enjoyed better living conditions down to a lower and poorer level. This kind of egalitarianism is incompatible with a healthy society, and created yet more social problems and conflicts. I do think this kind of practice must be reformed.

If I'm asked which existing economic system in the world could be closer to the ideal conditions I've just mentioned, I would tend to put quite a lot of weight on cultural factors. So I would tend to look at Taiwan, as a Chinese society that could suggest some directions for the mainland in the future. I was quite impressed by its rural cooperatives, which seem to be fairly genuine collective enterprises. Even in the industrial sector, the proliferation of small and medium firms in Taiwan, which forms a big contrast with the pattern in South Korea, indicates the importance of the family as a socio-economic unit there. I think elements of both social justice and connectedness of societal members are embedded in these local-collective and family-based enterprises, in a way that is more readily visible to people who have grown up in a Chinese cultural environment. Such economic forms may be easier for our people to accept, if they care about social justice and social cohesion.

Li Minqi I agree with Wang Chaohua that in the process of economic transition every member of society should have access to the relevant information and the right to express different opinions about alternative economic systems. Unfortunately that is far from the case in China today. But this should not prevent us from working for an economic system that combines greater equity and efficiency. Since the beginning of capitalism, human beings have been grappling with the problem of how on the one hand the forces of production and civilization could be rapidly developed, and on the other hand the majority of people could benefit from this development. In China, as in the former Soviet Union and Eastern Europe, a revolution made in the name of socialism failed to fulfil this expectation. But this should not prevent us from continuing the search for the answer to the question. It is a basic tenet of Marxism that every mode of production is the appropriate form for the development of the forces of production only under certain historical conditions. Since these conditions change over time, no mode of production can remain the same forever. Capitalism is no exception.

The experiences of certain capitalist economies in the post-war era are particularly relevant here. If we look at East Asia, we see that in Japan, Taiwan and South Korea the government has played a crucial role in resource allocation, especially in capital investment. The government provided cheap capital to cutting-edge sectors, encouraged export-orientation, and directed flows of investment through the banking system. The very rapid growth that resulted from this pattern challenged the orthodox belief that a free market is the optimal mechanism for resource allocation and economic development. Of course, these were no ideal societies. The close collaboration of the government with big capitalists was not only incompatible with equity, but eventually also injured efficiency, as we see in today's regional economic crisis. But let us imagine that the East Asian systems were not based on collaboration between the government and big capital, but were under the democratic control of the majority of its citizens. Wouldn't that be a preferable choice?

A second experience that we need to think about is the typical structure of German and Japanese, compared with American corporations. In the American system, which approximates to a pure classical version of capitalism, the corporate owners have near absolute power over the firm, while the workers are little more than wage-labourers, without any participation in management or any profit-sharing. Moreover, in conditions of a highly flexible labour market, it is relatively easy for the corporations to lay off workers. The German and Japanese pattern is quite different. Under their system, workers share in profits, participate in management, and enjoy considerable job security. But if we compare the economic results of the two types of structure, we see that throughout most of the post-war years Germany and Japan had faster rates of growth of labour productivity and higher levels of investment than the United States. The mainstream ideology argues that one cannot have both equity and efficiency, and that economic efficiency requires the sacrifice of equity. But the two experiences I have outlined are inconsistent with this view. They suggest that more equity may bring about higher efficiency.

If we consider the current Chinese economic system, we observe that despite many market-oriented reforms, the state remains a central actor in resource allocation – still more so than in Japan, South Korea and Taiwan. Shouldn't we try to preserve state economic intervention, but democratize it, so that the majority of the people determine the direction of social investment? That might yield a relatively rational arrangement. As for our state-owned enterprises, we know that they used to have certain features not unlike aspects of German and Japanese firms: workers had job security and some informal power in the process of production. Since the onset of the reform era, however, workers' rights have been steadily eroded, while managers' prerogatives have greatly increased. This has a strong negative impact on labour incentives. According to one investigation by the All-China Federation of Trade Unions, workers' incentives in state-owned enterprises have now fallen to their lowest point since the reform started. Naturally productivity has suffered. If we want to improve the economic performance of state-owned enterprises, we shouldn't be trying simply to define ever-clearer property rights. We should also be trying to improve workers' incentives, by giving them more say in management, and a bigger stake in profits.

Wang Chaohua   When you bracket Taiwan together with South Korea and Japan, I think you are overlooking one difference between them. In launching its so-called economic 'miracle', the government in Taiwan subsidized a lot of capital investment in big state-owned industrial enterprises. These are quite different in structure from the *chaebol* in South Korea or the *keiretsu* in Japan. Private entrepreneurs and big capitalist enterprises occupy a weaker position relative to big state-owned firms in Taiwan. This example does tend to show that it's not impossible to stimulate development via 'state-owned' firms as leading industrial agents.

On the other hand, it might be true that in the early years of the PRC, working-class commitment – linked to improved social status and economic benefits – contributed to some high-efficiency growth. But I doubt whether a decline in workers' initiative in state-owned enterprises started only after Deng's reforms were launched. Loss of worker enthusiasm was very visible in China by the latter years of the Cultural Revolution, I would say since 1972 or 73. Have the reforms so much worsened the situation?

Li Minqi   I didn't say workers had higher incentives in the Cultural Revolution. In fact, in the initial stage of Deng's rule, some of the reform measures did help to improve labour incentives. But since the mid-1980s, job security and other social rights have been progressively undermined, contributing to a crisis of productivity in state enterprises.

Wang Dan   In my view, if we want to reach an ideal system, we should respect two principles. Firstly, there should be a free-market system in China based on private property. For the normal functioning of any society, it is clearly essential to have private property; just as a free market is necessary for an efficient economy that can satisfy basic material needs. Secondly, however, there should be a social safety net, that guarantees a degree of justice in the overall structure of society. My ideal is a free-market economy of this kind.

Do you think bankrupt state industries should be closed down today, as the IMF recommends?

Wang Chaohua This opinion is not just that of the IMF. It is held by a considerable number of economists in China. The question isn't so easy to answer, because it's not always clear what has driven many state-owned firms to bankruptcy. It seems likely that the reasons are rather different in the nineties than in the eighties. In the last decade there has been a qualitative change in the process. In the eighties, the reforms sought to solve certain problems arising from lack of workers' commitment to the performance of the enterprise. In the nineties, many state-owned enterprises had a chance to rejuvenate themselves under less rigid directives from the centre. But now the propagation of free-market ideology has closed down other options for them. Their assets were often simply transferred – legally or illegally – to the managers who happened to be in charge of them at the time. With this unchecked personal power in the hands of managers, who have not hesitated to appropriate public assets, more and more firms are sliding towards bankruptcy, leaving their workers to shoulder the costs of liquidation – i.e. wholesale dismissals. In cases like these, the government has a clear responsibility for the fate of these workers and their firms.

There is a further problem in China today. This arises when the government seeks to modernize certain industrial sectors, such as the textile or coal industry, under environmental pressures. Typically, these sectors are at least two epochs behind average international development, making them highly vulnerable to an open-market prospect under reform guidelines. When such sectors need to be comprehensively updated, I believe the state as the central social organ must shoulder the costs involved, from the accumulated wealth in its coffers. It's not acceptable to see the state shifting the costs of its own previous policies onto workers who had no responsibility for them.

Li Minqi I think a related problem is the declining efficiency of state-owned enterprises, reflected in deteriorating financial indicators throughout the nineties. Here we must not ignore the unfavourable institutional context with which such enterprises are confronted. The effective tax rate charged on state-owned enterprises is much higher than on non-state-owned enterprises. The situation used to be that all the capital of these firms was provided by the state. But since the mid-1980s, this has generally ceased to be the case. Moreover, the capital that was earlier invested by the state has since been redefined as loans made by the state. This change means that state-owned enterprises now have to pay interest on loans as well as tax on profits to the state: they are charged twice by the same owner.

Secondly, there is the problem which Wang Chaohua has just talked about – that is, the increasingly unchecked power of managers in these firms. This has encouraged the rapid spread of corruption and loss of public assets. Thirdly, as I've already said, the reform has undermined the social and economic rights the workers used to enjoy, damaging labour incentives. If we take all these factors into account, it seems evident that privatization is not the only way to solve the problems of state-owned enterprises. Nor is it the best way or the most equitable way. If the workers had more say in management and more of a stake in these firms, they would be more motivated to improve productivity. If the managers were more subject to control from the workforce, there would be less corruption and plundering of public assets. If there was also a fairer fiscal framework for them, there is no reason why state-owned enterprises could not become much more efficient.

Wang Dan   If a state enterprise has a lot of bank debts and falls into insolvency, obviously it should be closed. But there is an issue of justice here. By that I mean compensation. If you suddenly shut down a lot of enterprises without considering this, it will cause social instability. There are two aspects to compensation. The first concerns employment. Workers who have been laid off should have a chance of finding jobs elsewhere. Here I disagree with Li Minqi. It is privatization that would create these jobs. The government's resistance to wide-scale privatization is blocking people from finding alternative employment in the free market. This is the first injustice.

The second aspect of compensation is a question of money. Here too there is much injustice. For example, in the province of Liaoning the first ten months of 1997 saw a strange situation. The economic plight of state enterprises was among the worst in the country, yet the nominal rate of growth of the province was among the fastest in the country. How could this be? I think one of the reasons was the miserable compensation workers received when their state firms were closed down. Each worker dismissed was given only 100–200 RMB per month. This is absolutely unfair to workers who have laboured in an enterprise for many years. In Western countries, if firms go bankrupt they give workers extremely high compensation. But when Chinese state enterprises shut down they give workers very little compensation in order to ensure the growth of GNP. This is very unjust. If this practice continues, it will certainly lead to social conflict.

Li Minqi   You believe that in the West, if an enterprise fails, its workers receive high compensations? I am very surprised. Nor do I quite understand how massive privatization could help to solve the problem of unemployment.

Wang Chaohua   I took Wang Dan to mean that the creation of new private firms, not the selling of bankrupt state firms, would create new employment opportunities. That doesn't seem unreasonable.

Li Minqi   But it's not as if the development of this kind of private enterprise is prohibited in China. It's actually encouraged.

Wang Dan   No, there are major limitations on China's privatization programme. For example, the PRC has only one bank, Minsheng Bank, that specifically provides loans to private enterprises. When other banks provide loans to private firms, they are much more restrictive than when they lend to state enterprises. This is a big problem, because the development of a flourishing private sector depends on the availability of credit.

Li Minqi   So far as I know, if state banks are reluctant to offer large loans to private enterprises, it is not because they are private, but because they are mostly small firms. Since it is usually riskier to lend to small companies, these enterprises tend to have less access to loans. This is not an ideological discrimination.

Wang Dan   In the economic transformation of East-European countries various bureaux were specifically set up by the government to support the development of small and medium enterprises. This has not been done in China. Therefore I say that the Chinese government still does not accept the private sector that the country needs.

Do you regard mass unemployment as economically inevitable in China? If not, what policies would you support to fight it?

Wang Chaohua   I believe that large-scale unemployment today is closely related to current reform policies. To say it is a problem left by earlier socialist experiments is to simplify the issue. The management of state-owned firms in the nineties is not a consequence of the so-called 'iron rice-bowl' of the fifties or sixties. If so many workers are losing their jobs today, it is mainly because the policies of reform were not fully examined, its main principles were not exposed to public discussion, and state-owned enterprises were not given a sufficient range of options. It is China's policy-makers themselves who brought about today's large-scale unemployment. Therefore, I do not think it is entirely inevitable. In fact some state-owned enterprises have made serious efforts to rejuvenate themselves, as we can see from recent experiments in Wuhan. It isn't the case that there have been no local initiatives to sustain public employment in a cost-effective way. Encouraging workers' participation in economic management, and protecting workers' rights in local administration, will contribute to them.

Li Minqi   I largely agree. Even within the framework of the existing regime, large-scale unemployment is not unavoidable. The government could undertake a more active fiscal policy, expand public investment, and provide support to workers who are laid off. This would increase effective demand and lower the rate of unemployment. Some people argue that any further increase in the public deficit would only result in inflation. I disagree. The primary problem of the Chinese economy today is inadequate aggregate demand and underutilization of capacity. The present rate of capacity utilization is only about 50 per cent. In these conditions, an increase in the deficit would help to reduce unemployment, rather than unleash inflation.

How far do you think privatization of the Chinese economy should go?

Wang Chaohua   I think China's major industrial sectors should remain state-owned, but private enterprise be allowed to develop wherever necessary at local or regional level. The system of national economic planning needs to be thoroughly reviewed and readjusted. In the localities there should be no discrimination against or suppression of private firms: local monopolies should be firmly opposed, particularly where they are linked to political control.

Li Minqi   Since the beginning of the reform, the share of the public sector has been diminishing. Now state-owned enterprises and state-controlled stock-holding concerns together account for less than one-third of China's industrial product. The following division of labour has taken shape. High-tech industries have basically been taken over by transnational corporations. Labour-intensive small and middle enterprises are basically either private, or so-called township and village enterprises. Many of these TVEs are *de facto* private firms. State-owned enterprises now are concentrated in certain heavy industries that require large capital investment and provide basic inputs like raw materials and energy to the rest of the economy. In the immediate future, the private sector may continue to expand and the state sector to diminish. But given the current division of labour, it is not very likely that foreign or domestic private enterprises can replace state-owned enterprises in those industries where they are still dominant today – either because these sectors are not profitable, or because private firms do not yet possess the capital or know-how to enter them. So the share of state industry may fall to around a quarter of GDP in the near future, but is unlikely to drop much further after that. If the Chinese people had a chance of democratic choice between alternative socio-economic systems, the existing state-owned enterprises could be transformed by expanding workers' rights and powers within them. Meanwhile, a democratic government should also encourage the development of cooperative enterprises.

Wang Dan   I will consider the problem of privatization from a political angle. In the future, when China undergoes a democratic transformation, a new political order should take economic measures to integrate different interest groups. Firstly, land should be privatized to satisfy the rural population. This would make people feel that here was a government with new policies. Secondly, housing should be privatized to give urban residents a feeling of security. Both of these privatizations should be gratis, in other words with no charge to the beneficiaries. Thirdly, it is very important to get rid of the need to apply for permission to establish enterprises. China should be exactly like the West, where all you have to do is register a firm. I differ from Wang Chaohua and Li Minqi in that I want to promote privatization and reduce state enterprise at all levels.

Li Minqi   At present Chinese peasants exercise *de facto* private control of the land they cultivate. So when you speak of the privatization of the soil, you are essentially referring to the freedom to buy and sell it. Are you quite sure peasants would welcome a free market in land, in which they might lose their plots?

Wang Dan   That's why I said this should be considered from a political angle, because there is in fact a kind of private property in land now. Under the current policy, contracts from the government run for 30 years or are even permanent. So it virtually amounts to individual ownership. However, in order to give people a feeling of security, a new government should write private property in land into the Constitution, settling the question once and for all. This is a political priority, to give the public a sense of stability and certainty. But it would also promote economic efficiency and help to develop the forces of production in the countryside.

Wang Chaohua   I'm very doubtful about privatization of land. On the other hand, Wang Dan has touched on another kind of problem, which is the legal protection of personal belongings. This issue was one of the driving forces for reform in the late 1970s. It didn't so much go back to the collectivization of agriculture in the fifties, as to the trauma of the Cultural Revolution. The question now is how far redressing its excesses should take us right back to the situation under Nationalist rule. Whatever our answer, there is certainly a need for juridical clarity and certainty. We must ensure that in China individual rights and assets are not casually infringed upon by political power.

Li Minqi   Why don't we consider the historical experience of Russia? The rural communes in Russia in the nineteenth century were very similar to the family contract system in our country. On paper, land was owned by the village community, but peasant families had *de facto* private control of land. In the 1860s, Russia abolished serfdom and later introduced other reforms, allowing free buying and selling of land. The result was to break up the communes, and sharpen conflict between the state and the peasantry.

Wang Dan   If we accept that land is a type of commodity, we must allow it to be bought and sold freely. I admit that privatization of the soil will increase inequality, which might intensify social contradictions in the countryside. But we have to weigh the pros and cons of any policy. If we don't privatize, it would go against the nature of commodities. Nationalization of land in a planned economy inevitably leads to problems. There is plenty of room to develop a regulatory system to make adjustments after land is privatized. Comparatively speaking, the results of privatization might not be as bad as failing to privatize.

Wang Chaohua   I don't agree with the privatization of land. If we look back at the reform process in China, we can see it became an opportunity for redistributing resources on a grand scale, with a lot of corruption. The actual effect of land privatization would probably in practice be just the opposite of what you expect.

Wang Dan   The point is that the political environment would be different. Do you really think there is no way to control the damage and reduce it to a minimum?

Wang Chaohua   Privatization is a revalidation of the property rights of different members of society. How do you choose which rights to legitimate, and on what grounds? Certain lived continuities cannot be randomly cut off, or you introduce general confusion, as we can see in Eastern Europe. Where do we find the source of legitimate agrarian rights in China? Is it in the Cultural Revolution, the land-reform of the fifties, the KMT distribution, or do we go all the way back to the Qing Dynasty?

Wang Dan   Certainly, in the process of privatization, inheritance should be recognized. This principle has two implications. People may pass on what they possess now, and they may inherit property of their ancestors. There are technical ways to deal with the problems posed by the application of this principle. The political problems are another matter. The tensions that have arisen in dividing up state enterprises have been due to corruption. But this is a question of the political system, which we want to change.

Wang Chaohua   That does not dispose of the ideological difficulty no one can get around. Why did the land reform of the fifties not lead to any big commotion over property rights? Essentially because the political and the economic ideologies of the revolutionary regime worked in tandem. Why do the current reforms invite such controversy? Because the political and economic doctrines of the government are at such variance with each other. If we throw open the issue of landownership, it will create even greater confusion. Deng Xiaoping granted the present thirty-year contracts. Why should a new government respect his measures?

Wang Dan An open and transparent division of the land into individual units would solve this problem.

Li Minqi Just for your information – land in the Chinese countryside is technically not owned by the state, but by the village community. Some people argue that it would be better to replace the fictions of this 'collective' property with state ownership.

Wang Dan The whole expression 'state-owned land' is wrong. We lived on this land for countless generations, why does it belong to the state?

Li Minqi If we are talking about a dictatorial state, your argument may make sense. But if we are talking about a democracy, why can't the state own the land on behalf of the whole people?

What range of social inequalities would you think acceptable in China?

Wang Chaohua This is indeed a tricky question. I tend to view it in a comparative perspective. Among the initial pressures for reform in China were critical reflections on the 'absolute' equality that was preached during the Cultural Revolution, when the official way to break up all social, cultural, political and economic privileges was to send people down to the countryside to share the mire and poverty of peasant life. This is certainly not an experiment China should have to undergo again. It follows that a certain degree of inequality will be inevitable in the process as we search for a better society. If we look around us, I would say that in this respect Taiwan offers a somewhat better example than Hong Kong.

Li Minqi I agree that China doesn't need another Cultural Revolution, forcing people to accept a certain form of economic organization by coercive means. However, I believe, as I've said, that equity and efficiency can actually reinforce each other. It's perfectly possible for a new democratic China to have less inequality than we now observe in most capitalist countries.

Wang Dan I have nothing to say about this question.

Does Hong Kong offer an attractive model of a future Chinese society to you? Do you think its economic regime should be broadly reproduced in a post-communist China? Would you commend its fiscal structure to your compatriots?

Wang Chaohua   I tend to compare Hong Kong with Taiwan, and find I usually prefer Taiwan. It is closer to the mainland both as a model of development and as a living Chinese society. It would also be easier to emulate, if any such need arises.

Li Minqi   Hong Kong's political system is basically a product of British colonial rule, updated by a deal between the Chinese bureaucracy and Hong Kong's millionaires. It is strongly weighted towards the interests of the local capitalist class, and excludes any real participation by workers. Economically, the enclave follows a traditional policy of laissez-faire, in which the state scarcely intervenes at all in the market. I don't think this pattern is relevant for China, whether China takes a capitalist or socialist road. If we want any reasonable degree of social equity, if we want to improve our country's position in the world system, to develop our technological capability, or to check the inherent instabilities of the market, substantial state intervention is inevitable. So far as public finances are concerned, Hong Kong is often praised for its zero deficits. But under modern conditions, in fact ever since the Great Depression, this kind of ultra-conservative fiscal policy is outdated. For a big country like China, the purpose of fiscal policy should not be to maintain a mechanical balance between revenues and expenditures, but to promote economic development in the interest of the majority of the population.

Wang Dan   Hong Kong is very attractive to me. I also think it's a model for China. Of course, we don't want to copy Hong Kong completely. But I admire many features of this society. One of its virtues is to be multicultural. Because of its location as a margin, no culture has an exclusive monopoly in Hong Kong – all kinds of cultures can develop there. It is also a highly efficient society, very different in this respect not only from the mainland but also Taiwan. You have only to look at the way their journalists operate to see that. Another positive feature of Hong Kong is its press freedom, which has made a deep impression on me. Up to 1997, at least, there was a professionalism and liberty of expression in the media seldom seen else-where. Mainland journalists should learn from this. Last but not least, Hong Kong enjoys a special position between East and West. It's not totally Eastern and it's not totally Western. Later on, when the mainland adjusts it own cultural stance, it also should take up a position between East and West – inheriting some things from the East and adopting others from the West, in order to learn from both sides, as Hong Kong has done. That will make our society livelier. So to sum up: what I feel can be learnt from Hong Kong are multiculturalism, efficiency, freedom of the press and balance between East and West.

Leo Lee If we are going to discuss the Hong Kong model, it would be better to let people from Hong Kong speak for themselves. They might feel the big issue right now is the legal system, or the special Anti-Corruption unit, which they think is a Hong Kong invention. Another local specialty is complete economic laissez-faire, although recently the government has had to intervene a bit. Culturally, of course, there is no elite sphere. Commercialism is in command and intellectuals don't get any respect. That is roughly the Hong Kong model.

Wang Chaohua I think there is a certain connexion between the colonial legacy that Li Minqi emphasized, and the features of Hong Kong life that Wang Dan has talked about. It is the link between these two that makes any reproduction of the Hong Kong model virtually impossible elsewhere, even in post-hand-back Hong Kong itself. A crucial feature of the model was that, up to nearly the last moment, the Chinese population in Hong Kong – if we except a handful of lawyers and tycoons – played no political role in the government of the territory. Hong Kong was a British colony, which did not even have the representative institutions usually granted to other British colonies. You could call it an external dictatorship. Its administrative and legislative authorities were imposed from abroad. This was what made possible its extreme laissez-faire policies. In practice, this meant that so long as you were law-abiding, the authorities didn't care what you did. I believe this political structure was partly responsible for the lack of any cultural elite that Professor Lee has just mentioned. When there is no possibility for a cultural elite to play any political role, its resources for maintaining a privileged social status are sharply limited. In this respect, Hong Kong was very different from mainland China, whether under the Qing, the Nationalists or the Communists, where there was always a circulation between cultural and political power.

Li Minqi But if people just passively obey the law, doesn't this kind of civic consciousness inhibit them from taking any active part in political life?

Wang Chaohua Today the situation has changed. This model becomes unviable once there is a local administration running the affairs of the territory. If we imagine that all sixty seats in the current legislature were directly elected – at present, only twenty are – there would be a dense web of connexions between the legislators and their constituents, and representatives would have to speak for their electors, and care about the various questions raised by civil groups in their districts. All these issues would at once be no longer the same as those that faced the colonial governor. Every issue would be an acute local-political question. That's why I said the familiar Hong Kong model can't even be copied in Hong Kong itself, after colonial rule has come to an end. Now its political culture will be much more closely related to local society, and we'll see a change in people's lack of interest in public affairs.

Do you regard the fast growth in China of a mass commercial culture, based on US or HK models, as basically a threat or as a comfort to the government? Does it function mainly as a critical stimulant, or as inexpensive opiate?

Wang Chaohua   The two external influences are distinct. In Hong Kong, where the colonial structure excluded any democratic self-government case, commercial mass culture undoubtedly played a certain role in stimulating public opinion, and provided considerable room for freedom of expression. One consequence was that by the eighties Hong Kong society could respond promptly to the political developments in the mainland. Of course this culture did not permit the same degree of critical reflection on political affairs in Hong Kong or in Britain. There was a big contrast with Taiwan in this respect. The Hong Kong cinema never produced anything approaching the historical self-awareness we find in a film like Hou Xiao Xien's *City of Sadness*, or the Taiwanese New Wave generally. But in a more commercial way, the Hong Kong media and entertainment industry did create an environment that could respond in a timely way to crises in the mainland. Its freedom and its limitations were all part of the same colonial experience, based on a lack of any direct political power for the majority of the population. This too can't be reproduced anywhere else today.

Now if we look at the mainland, I think the dichotomy in the question we are asked is too simple. Mass commercial culture, whether influenced by Hong Kong or Hollywood, doesn't represent a threat to the authorities. But they can't control the development of this culture either. In the nineties, we are currently witnessing another 'cultural fever'. There is a lot of ferment in publishing and academic circles. It would be hard to describe all of this as 'critically stimulating public opinion', but it may not be merely cultural opium either. I tend to see a certain room between the two extreme poles, though in China it does not yet amount to a 'public sphere' such as we might imagine in the West. The main problem is that the room between the two poles in China today is a silently negotiated space, without legitimate legal protection. You have to be an inside-player in order to know how to manoeuvre within it. For example, there are freelance writers and journalists active in China today, who may run a daring journal in Guangdong. When it is closed by the authorities, they might launch another magazine in Beijing, or later in Shenzhen. In this sense, the situation is actually quite favourable for critical discussions among intellectuals.

Li Minqi   Yes, but are such freelance authors part of a mass commercial culture, or are these two different issues? What you are talking about is the space in which certain intellectual journals can be produced, raising some 'daring' or not-that-'daring' questions. What does this have to do with mass culture?

Wang Chaohua   The phenomena are related, because if we ask how it's possible to launch new journals swiftly when old ones are closed down, part of the answer is that commercial development offers a basis for such nimble moves. Take a television programme like *Eastern Time and Space* put out by CCTV – would you term it a product of mass commercial culture or official political culture? This kind of venture utilizes a developing commercial environment to try to express something new. In this sense, the current mass culture does to some extent reduce the political control of the authorities. In the peculiar environment of mainland China, since many social issues of popular concern may not be easily discussed because of political controls, in a paradoxical way they can become hot items commercially in the television ratings. So as mass culture spreads in China, the 'space' it creates is not only filled with mere entertainment or consumerism. It allows for the introduction of delicate political topics, which otherwise would fall under official prohibition. So we can't say that commercial culture just spreads political apathy, though it surely also does this.

Li Minqi   Here we are talking about the new commercial culture, and we are asked whether it has contributed to apolitical and apathetic attitudes among the mass of the population. I wouldn't deny that it affords some space for other kinds of production, but if we consider the bulk of its own output, we can hardly deny that it is pretty stultifying. However, we should be careful here. What we customarily refer to as 'mass' commercial culture in China is restricted for the most part to upper and middle strata. The majority of the population is little influenced by it. The situation is quite different from the United States and Hong Kong, where the whole population is really saturated with it.

Wang Dan   In my view, the wave of commercial culture that developed in the nineties was to a certain extent encouraged and promoted by the government. It is one of the phenomena that appeared after 1989. If we recall our first question, we can say the deeper social significance of '89 can be seen in the rise of this commercial culture. From then on, the Communist Party has depended on an expanding commercial culture to neutralize the negative image of its political suppression among the population. But the wave of commercialism has now become a threat to its own power. The government's original plan was to promote a commercial culture and hope that it would become a kind of opiate. However, I don't think that it has resulted in political indifference. Rather it has released an independent social space, in which more and more unpredictable forms will emerge, either created by the common people or mediated by commercial influence. Take for example, Cui Jian's songs, Zhang Yimou's movies, and Wang Shuo's novels. All three demystify the existing power from different aspects. They are almost the same as the protests in '89. Their role is to deconstruct despotism. These things can spread to the whole country through commercial culture. *Eastern Time and Space*, which Wang Chaohua mentioned, is a good example because without the existence of commercial culture it could never have gained such importance. Television shows like *Telling the Truth* ('Shihua shishua') are also the product of this commercial culture. They are not a threat to the regime now, but they will become one. In another ten years, when the rulers look back on the reasons for their fall, they will realize they made a mistake at the beginning. The government thought it was only promoting commercial culture, but this force creates a political and social space within which forms destructive of its authority are being created. If commercial culture did not exist there would have been no possibility of this after 1989. The government is digging its own grave.

Li Minqi What's not clear to me is why this kind of development is a threat to the government, or deconstructs its authority. If you think it provides some independent space, what if people have become so independent within it that they cease to be interested in politics any more? Why would that be bad for the government? Why is this not just a smarter form of control?

Wang Dan You keep talking about political indifference. But if we consult political science, we see that indifference is inevitable in a democracy. Look at the number of people who bother to vote in the United States today. The totalitarian regime constantly used its power to mobilize people and launch political campaigns. If common people become politically indifferent, it is impossible to mobilize them. The regime will find it has lost its resources. So I don't think political indifference is a bad thing.

Li Minqi I disagree. The political campaigns you are speaking of were phenomena of Maoist China and Stalinist Russia. But they are not a general feature shared by every dictatorship. Historically it has been more usual for political apathy to coexist with tyranny. It's perfectly possible for us to have political apathy as well as political dictatorship.

Wang Dan The basis for political mobilization in China and the Soviet Union was lack of political indifference. When everyone was politically enthusiastic, like during the Cultural Revolution, these regimes were at the height of their power. With the erosion of beliefs caused by commercial culture, there comes spreading political indifference. This becomes a kind of threat to the system.

Do you think popular nationalism is a strong force in the PRC today, or one that is exaggerated? If fairly strong, how far do you regard its mentality as benign?

Li Minqi   I don't have much to say on this topic, though I did pay some attention to it when the famous book *China Can Say No* was being widely discussed. Nationalism is a phenomenon which tends to emerge with the development of capitalism. With rapid economic growth and increasing prosperity in China, the ruling class has become more confident of itself, and more middle-class intellectuals are willing to identify with the existing regime. The rise of nationalism reflects the self-assurance of this new Chinese capitalism. But I don't think Chinese nationalism has become strong enough to incorporate all social classes, or to suppress the consciousness of contradictions between them. It is by and large restricted to a section of the intelligentsia. In the past, nationalism played a progressive, anti-imperialist role in China. But today it's different. While it's still difficult to decide how far it is virtual or real, it's clear that under certain conditions it could become dangerous. For example, many people now believe that China should use military force to resolve conflicts with neighbouring countries.

Wang Dan   Chinese nationalism has become a hot topic, but I think it is exaggerated by foreigners. I don't think it really has that big an influence. Take, for example, Clinton's experience at Peking University. We all know that the many provocative questions put to him at his first public meeting were prearranged. These students were carefully selected by the Party. But when Clinton donated books in front of the Peking University Library, the atmosphere was totally different. It was vividly described by friends of mine. His reception was a very, very sincere welcome. This contrast tells us a lot. The fact is that nationalism in China today has a political background. It has nothing to do with academic discussions. Nationalism has appeared because the government wants to distract people's attention from the loss of credibility of communism. They want to see if nationalism will release them from the pressures of domestic dissatisfaction. That is why they promote it.

In my view nationalism is a negative phenomenon, with dangerous implications for China's future. As we face the twenty-first century, there are two big trends. The first is the need to redefine some currently accepted concepts, including the ideas of state and nation, and even sovereignty. This is connected with the new importance of human rights. The second trend is the number of international conflicts caused by national claims. This nation wants to be independent, that nation wants to be independent. China faces a big transformation in the near future, which I hope can be smooth. Personally I don't think we should encourage the growth of nationalist emotions, which may bring more hidden problems to the future of the country.

Wang Chaohua   I believe that Chinese nationalism now has considerable potential. But, if I may borrow Li Minqi's phrase about the working class, I would say that nationalism has not yet found an organized focus or an integrated voice. It has not yet been able to join up with other forces, or project any coherent policies. So although we can observe emotional reactions to various issues in different groups or areas of the country, so far these have found no systematic expression. The government utilizes it in a very instrumental way in its foreign policy. It manipulates nationalist sentiment on some issues and completely ignores it on others. This is also true of domestic debates among intellectuals.

As for the question whether nationalism is benign or not, I'm reminded of an essay by Zhang Xudong in the journal *Dushu* in 1997. He introduced Gellner's argument for the positive function of nationalism in developing or late-industrializing countries in the twentieth century, particularly in Eastern Europe. In this respect, we do see some trends in China encouraging major industrial sectors to develop state-owned national industries. There is also a so-called New Left emerging in today's China that would like to resist the expansion of multinational corporations in the country. Still, the problem of ambiguity remains. For example, to what extent would we feel a national monopoly controlled by power-holders in the state is tolerable – at what point would we judge it intolerable and foreign participation preferable? The current, still rather inarticulate, nationalism confronts more complicated issues than the nationalism of the 1950s. Bearing this in mind, I would say that Chinese nationalism today is not entirely calamitous.

Do you think the categories Right, Left and Centre have relevant meaning in China today? If so, how would you identify each? If not, what do you regard as more appropriate categories of analysis?

Li Minqi   I think the concepts of Right, Left, and Centre do remain pertinent to ideological differences in China today. However, it is also important to remember that for a long time now these terms have been used in ambiguous or confusing ways. Since the eighties, both ruling politicians and mainstream intellectuals have typically divided the field of political opinion into two camps, 'conservatives' and 'reformers'. In this usage, conservatives are often referred to as 'leftists' – a term that then becomes virtually a synonym for reactionaries. This kind of characterization suits the established order, and the majority of conformist intellectuals. For them, there are only two ideological lines. One represents modernization and progress – that is, the speedy introduction of a free market and private property in all domains. The other is conservative, and includes both those in the Communist Party who want to maintain the old regime's planned economy, and any independent critics of capitalism. The conservatives represent yesterday and have no hope. Naturally, this schema has given rise to a lot of confusion.

This situation needs to be changed. The concepts of Left, Centre and Right should be used in ways more consistent with their original meaning and their place in modern world history. With the development of capitalism in China, different social classes are more clearly taking shape. In future, intellectuals themselves will be increasingly divided between rival groups reflecting sympathies with opposing social classes. We can then say that a rightist is one who advocates capitalist development, whether he or she supports political democracy or dictatorship, while a leftist is one who takes a critical view of capitalism and responds to the needs and interests of the working class. A Chinese Left is still in its infancy. For the moment, it is mainly occupied with introducing the latest progressive ideas from the West into our culture. However, when we have a new generation of Chinese intellectuals, whose minds reflect the contradictions of capitalist development, we can expect a new situation. What about the Centre? The term is perhaps best used for those who favour privatization and capitalism in China, but object to the way power-holders have appropriated so much private wealth for themselves. They want a 'juster' privatization that would be more respectful of the rights of ordinary people. This is what some theorists in the West call 'clean-path capitalism'. I think this outlook is utopian and unrealistic – it ignores the whole history of primitive accumulation across the world. But it definitely has some resonance among Chinese intellectuals now.

Wang Dan I do not use the categories Left, Centre and Right. The meaning of these terms has changed so many times that they have become completely confused. If I want to differentiate groups involved in active political discussion, I would classify them in four types. The largest group are liberals, who form the majority of Chinese intellectuals. They can be subdivided into three branches. The first are what I would call pure liberals – principled individual thinkers, who are completely independent of the state, like Zhu Xueqin and Liu Junning. The second I would dub constitutionalists. These include people who were in the system but later expelled from it, as well as others who were outside the system but wanted to get into it, for example Chen Ziming and Wang Juntao. The third branch could be termed theoreticists (*wuxu pai*): they are heterodox Marxists of an older generation, for example Wang Ruoshui and Yu Guangyuan. Together pure liberals, constitutionalists and theoreticists form one camp, the liberal bloc. The second group are nationalists, people like Sheng Hong and Hu Angang, who put forward views like those we have discussed. The third group are populists, such as Han Shaogong or Qin Hui. Most people don't see them in this way, but I think culturally they should be called populists. They try to identify local resources and popular traditions in rural society which would assist modernization. They take a great interest in the peasantry. The fourth group includes people like Cui Zhiyuan in MIT or Rong Jingben who works at the Central Translation Bureau, and the group that produces the journal *Comparative Economic Systems Research* (*Jingji Tizhi Bijiao Yanjiu*). They are usually called neo-conservatives. I'm not sure if this is very accurate, but let's go ahead and use the term. So I divide the groups into liberals, nationalists, populists and neo-conservatives. As far as I know, there are no real socialists or communists because if we talk about the authorities, the CCP, I don't think they have any real ideology. They might be called pragmatists, I suppose, but they don't form an intellectual school.

Wang Chaohua   In my view, this question is related to the complex interactions between Western intellectuals, generally from the Left, and Chinese intellectuals, and the efforts of Chinese intellectuals to explore various Western traditions of thought. We cannot simply say that the categories of Left, Right and Centre are meaningless in China. On the other hand, it is no easy task to apply them. What criteria are to be used for their definition? Li Minqi classifies positions according to economic questions only: capitalism versus socialism, private enterprise and a free market versus collective ownership and planning. I believe that this approach, dividing people just by preference of socio-economic system, is too simple in today's China. Take me, for example. I am strongly for the individual right of every citizen to their own personal property, which requires legal protection of a kind the PRC has never given. On the other hand, I am by no means against all forms of public ownership, and I object to current one-sided proposals to amend the Constitution of the PRC, put forward by certain power-holders at the National People's Congress, which would legalize privatization in a way that will certainly harm considerable numbers of our fellow citizens. We must uphold basic liberal freedoms that the Chinese people have never so far enjoyed, while at the same criticizing the hypocrisies of Western capitalist practice. This is the sense in which I would call myself a leftist, but I am aware that among those who use these categories – unlike Wang Dan – I would often be considered a centrist.

Wang Dan   Daniel Bell said some people are Rightist culturally, Leftist economically and Centrist politically. This is one possibility. That's why I reject the divisions between Left, Right and Centre, since one person can occupy all three positions at the same time.

Li Minqi   That seems like an evasion. The central issue in Chinese politics is whether our country should take the path of capitalist development or work out some alternative. Should we adopt a social and economic system that basically favours a minority of the rich and powerful, or should we instead try to create one that reflects the interests of the majority of ordinary people? We can't dodge this question. Wang Dan has advocated the privatization of land.

Wang Chaohua   But does Wang Dan's support for land privatization fall under your category of measures that favour only the interests of a wealthy minority? Does he himself accept that it would have such consequences? You didn't stop at 'capitalism' or 'socialism'. Your definition is highly value-added.

Li Minqi   Most Chinese economists now support such privatization. They make no secret of its possible effects on social equity. But they still insist that privatization is exactly what they want.

Wang Chaohua   That's another question. Personally, I think the socio-economic consequences of wholesale privatization of land would be disastrous for the majority of China's population, and so I'm against it. But Wang Dan could perfectly well say he expected the opposite from it – he would scarcely be advocating land-privatization on the grounds that it would be damaging to the majority of the population.

Wang Dan   Maybe Li Minqi has read more academic books, since he is studying economics at university, but the rest of us read Milton Friedman's books and know that he declares the system of private property is good.

Li Minqi   I did not say those who favour privatization think it to be harmful. Those who believe in capitalism certainly say capitalism is good.

Wang Chaohua   I suspect that the categories of Left, Right and Centre will soon become all but inevitable in China. Then we will be forced to clarify the difference between their meaning in the China of the twenty-first century and the uses of 'Rightist' in the fifties or 'Leftist' in the Cultural Revolution of the sixties and seventies. What sorts of connexions between economic issues and political questions will take shape in this spectrum in the future? Li Minqi seems to hold that economic programmes are the sole criterion for distingushing Right, Centre and Left in China.

Wang Dan   But what about political systems – for example single-party or multi-party? Isn't that an important criterion too?

Li Minqi   In advanced capitalist countries, not a single leftist party is against the multi-party system. Thus, nobody uses the multi-party system as a criterion to distinguish Left and Right. It's not that I want to use the economic order alone as a criterion, but the question of what kind of system China is going to adopt is the basic key to a consistent classification. Actually, my way of identifying Right and Left is common to every country.

Wang Chaohua   You believe the criterion you uphold is universally accepted today. It distributes people according to their opinion about the economic system China should develop. So far as I can see, this still reduces everything to a single question. But there are many political issues in the present that don't fit so easily into this framework.

Do you think China should accept the independence of Taiwan as an independent state, more or less as Germany has accepted the separate existence of Austria? If so, would you extend the same principle to – say – Guangdong, if the local population decided its language, size and wealth entitled it to its own separate state?

Li Minqi   I have nothing to say about this question.

Wang Dan   Nor me. I haven't studied this issue.[1]

Wang Chaohua   The status of Taiwan is a problem left by China's modern history. We can say that Taiwan has inseparable connexions with the mainland, but it is also dependent on the protection of the United States. However, what is undeniable is that in the past 15 years Taiwan has achieved a relatively high level of democracy. Without the efforts of the Taiwanese people, this democracy would have been impossible. Certainly Chiang Ching-Kuo opened up the Nationalist dictatorship, and Lee Teng-Hui has shown electoral skills, but had there not been the Democratic Progressive Party and a brave popular struggle against the KMT, neither of these conservative politicians would have awarded freedoms to the population of Taiwan. Left to itself, the KMT would never voluntarily have given up power. Against this background of Taiwan's history, to refuse the island the possibility of becoming independent amounts to directly denying the rights of the Taiwanese people. In my view, this would contradict the legitimate stance the CCP took when it supported the Taiwanese popular uprising of February 28, 1947 against the brutal rule of Chiang Kai-Shek's governor, and violate the principles on which the PRC was founded. The People's Republic was not established just to recover traditional territory. The PLA's mission was to liberate regions in keeping with the legitimate rights of local self-determination. Therefore the PRC should respect these rights in Taiwan today. If Taiwan voted in referendum to reunite with the mainland, the PRC would surely accept that as the choice of the Taiwanese people. If it voted for independence, the mainland should accept that outcome too. Meanwhile, as a first step the PRC should cease to threaten to use force to recover Taiwan.

The critical issue here is political. Those who base the case for Taiwanese

---

[1] Wang Dan has since chosen to do his doctoral research on Taiwanese intellectual history in the period of democratization [ed].

independence on claims about the special character of Taiwanese society or language have a very weak argument. Historically, as the centre of a civilizational complex, China treated neighbouring regions not according to their degree of linguistic similarity or difference to its own culture, but according to the compatibility of their socio-political systems with its empire. Where local systems could be structurally subordinated to the centre, language differences were subdued as an issue. This explains why Guangdong, where Cantonese is no less distant from Mandarin than the version of Fujian dialect spoken in Taiwan, shows no sign of wanting to break away from the PRC, which is firmly in control of the province. Similarly, if we compare the situation in Tibet and Xinjiang, we can find an informative contrast. In Xinjiang, although the Uighur and Han languages were completely different (there are other ethnic and linguistic groups in the area as well), for a long time the basic political structures were highly dependent on a central government external to the region. The situation was much the same with the various khans and lords in Inner and Outer Mongolia. Typically they were not autonomous enough to dispense with resources and support coming from outside the region. By contrast, the political and institutional structures of Tibetan society were highly independent of the Han world. So when the PLA overthrew the feudal system there, and the CCP sent its cadres out to mobilize 'class struggle' for 'land reform' and other theoretically progressive changes, the character of Tibetan society was deeply damaged, leaving lasting problems to this day, which there is no prospect of overcoming under Han domination.

What is your view of the Chinese war with Vietnam in 1979?

Li Minqi   I have nothing to say on this question.

Wang Dan   I don't know anything about it. I was only ten years old at the time.

Wang Chaohua   Although I am not very knowledgeable about the war with Vietnam, my impression is that it was launched to distract domestic attention, not unlike the Sino-Soviet border conflict of 1969. The war was the occasion for a huge propaganda campaign at home, as if it was a great national emergency. The CCP regime invested tremendous efforts in trying to mobilize public opinion behind nationalist slogans. Vietnam was portrayed as a 'regional hegemon' that needed to be taught a lesson by the Chinese. There was very little political argument in the official propaganda, unlike the heated polemics with the Soviet Union in the early 1960s or even in 1969. People just knew we were fighting. What was the background? One factor was that a young generation of military commanders had come to power, with the reorganization of the armed forces after the fall of Lin Biao and the Gang of Four. They saw an opportunity to assert themselves and acquire battlefield prestige. Hence there was a constant rotation of regiments to the front, so that as many troops as possible could gain experience of a real war.

What was the attack for? The war was not aimed at expanding territory, and the army was withdrawn from Vietnam when hostilities ceased. In this sense it looked similar to the Sino-Indian War of 1962, when the Chinese army advanced across the MacMahon line, overrunning a large area of land, but then withdrew completely behind its existing borders. In Vietnam, because there was no seizure of land, it might be more accurate to call the war an act of aggression, rather than an invasion.

Are there any issues on which you would have wished China to vote differently from the US or its allies in the Security Council?

Li Minqi   This is not a very comfortable question. But I believe the Chinese government should oppose the United States whenever it displays its imperialist armed force, imposing its hegemony on other countries.

Wang Dan   I think each country should vote according to its own national interests. If something is harmful to the Chinese State and nation, China should vote against it. I don't care how other countries vote.

Wang Chaohua   Since the visit of US President Nixon to the PRC in 1972, China's foreign policy has lost any basic principles. Earlier, whatever it sought to say or do was grounded on certain coherent principles, whatever we think of them. According to these, it selected its international partners and provided them with material assistance, when this was needed. Since the Nixon visit, there have been no principles in Chinese foreign policy at all. Without any firm compass, for many years Chinese diplomacy seemed very cautious. This caution was not just a question of uncertainty, it also had an unspoken sense of learning, as China watched other players to see how to obtain higher gains. If we look at the results, merely to ask how it should have voted differently from the US is not enough for me. Certainly I would have wished that it opposed the recent bombings of Iraq. But the PRC commits reprehensible acts of its own. For instance, two years ago China vetoed a Security Council resolution to send a peace-keeping force to Guatemala, where for three decades military governments had brutally suppressed native Indian populations and waged a civil war, and peace negotiations were extremely difficult. But because Taiwan was invited by the Guatemalan regime to take part in the peace-keeping plan, China blocked the scheme, delaying a UN-monitored truce between the army and the guerrillas. In this case, it would be very hard for us to say that China should vote for whatever is in its national interest, since the PRC certainly believes the recovery of Taiwan is in the country's interest.

Wang Dan   Of course, I wouldn't disagree with that.

Wang Chaohua   Looking ahead, though the Permanent Members of the Security Council are themselves a Big Power club, a democratic China holding a seat there should make every effort to ensure that international relations are based on the pursuit of peace, justice, and equality among UN members.

The Chinese government and the Chinese opposition paradoxically often express a common admiration for the United States. What head of state other than Jiang Zemin has ever urged his nation's whole youth to see a Hollywood film, as a high moral duty? Are you ever puzzled by this? Do you have any serious reservations about American culture or society yourself?

Li Minqi   I feel no surprise that both the Chinese government and the opposition admire American culture. I've explained that the growth of large-scale commercial culture does not necessarily hurt the current regime. For myself, as a Marxist, I naturally have serious reservations about American popular culture.

Wang Dan   I'm sceptical about the premise of this question. I feel it's a joke to speak of the Chinese government's or Jiang Zemin's admiration for America. I don't think Jiang really urged everyone to watch a Hollywood movie as a moral duty. He is a politician who likes to perform; he's an amateur actor. He also has strategic motives, and a taste for Americana. All of this is very utilitarian. We should not base any evaluation on it. The opposition's admiration for America also needs to be analysed a bit further. You can find some criticisms of the US among certain opposition figures. For example, Wei Jinsheng quite often criticizes the American government. But it's true the general attitude is one of admiration. But how deep is their understanding of America or American culture? I doubt it has much depth – it is rather like that of the Chinese government. It cannot be regarded as real admiration or a real desire. As for myself, since I have only been a short time in the US, my understanding of American culture is limited and I have no criticisms to make of it.

Wang Chaohua   In my view, we can indeed observe a widespread admiration for American culture among Chinese dissident groups, the Chinese authorities and the general population in China. But the attitudes of these three forces need to be differentiated. What attracts each of them in the spectacle of the United States is not at all the same. The government is primarily concerned with the US as a great power, which it would also like to be. It therefore seeks to cooperate with the American government over most issues, with the exception of a few particularly sensitive questions like Taiwan. The general population is more entranced by the glamorous image of America projected by the mass media, which in all kinds of ways take their inspiration from the US. Here the impact of commercial culture is very clear. On the other hand, among Chinese dissidents, or intellectuals more generally, it is conceptions of liberal democracy and human rights that are typically associated with the American example. These ideas have European origins long before the US existed, in the Renaissance and the Enlightenment. But the United States was the first example of a political system based on them that was directly created by institutional design, rather than through a slow development greatly conditioned by older traditions. Of course, the abstract principles and the concrete practices of the American order are not the same. As Qin Hui says, we must distinguish between abstract and empirical freedoms. The empirical freedoms of US society are limited by the severe hypocrisies of American capitalism. But we still need shared general concepts of abstract freedom, to be able to distinguish between hypocritical practices and genuine mistakes. Without them, we can't even speak of the hypocrisies.

Li Minqi The abstract principles you talk about were developed by Enlightenment thinkers exactly in response to the social needs of the propertied class.

Wang Chaohua We need to ask against whom the idea of protecting property arose. It was not an idea initially conceived as a safeguard against the masses. It was directed mainly against monarchical regimes and the aristocracy.

Li Minqi No, it was not aimed at feudal lords. The US Constitution was designed to protect creditors' interests against the interests of farmers who were then the majority of the population.

Wang Chaohua You are talking about the specific design of the US Constitution, whereas I was talking about the origin of such ideas.

Li Minqi Historically, the ideas of Montesquieu and others were closely related to the question of how best to protect the interests of the propertied classes to which they belonged. What you call abstract freedom is actually not that abstract. It reflects concrete interests.

Leo Lee All of you are trying to raise this question to an ideological level. But the question is about contemporary American culture. You have not expressed your opinion about *Titanic*, or the President of the PRC's commendation of it.

Wang Dan   Jiang Zemin was just performing a show. 'Everyone should watch it to raise their moral level' [imitating Jiang].

Wang Chaohua   This is similar to the way all Western politicians nowadays are talking about family values. It is quite ideologically instrumental. In this case, we may well talk about commercial culture being a political opiate.

Wang Dan   No, Jiang's promotion of *Titanic* has no ideological meaning. It was simply personal – he wanted to show off, as a politician who is open-minded, with an understanding and a taste for things from the West. He could have arbitrarily picked up any movie.

Wang Chaohua   Then why didn't he pick, say, *Schindler's List*? Why did he choose particularly *Titanic*? There must have been some element in the film that resonated in him, or which he thought he could use for his own purposes of moral propaganda. In this case, it was not family values that he was promoting. Jiang talked about the 'gentleman's value' of sacrificing oneself for others. The subtext was: look, even the Americans are advocating such values, so Chinese youth should surely do so.

Wang Dan   In fact, the fundamental theme of *Titanic* is not about moral values at all, it's about romantic love. That's why I said he didn't understand the film, he was just performing. Any movie would have done as well.

Leo Lee At this point I want to say something. Do you know that President Jiang said that he loved three movies above all others in his life? One was *Gone with the Wind*. The second was a Broadway musical called *Green Bank on a Spring Morning*. The third one was *A Song to Remember*, about Chopin. All three were produced in the thirties and forties. So you could say that this was part of his personal experience as a young man watching movies in Shanghai at that time, when these films caused a sensation. All were about love. More importantly, however, they were all very well made. Why? Because most directors at that time came from Europe. Hollywood then was very different from Hollywood today, in technique, forms of expression and content. Jiang, by connecting *Titanic* with this type of movie, showed his ignorance of the cinema. For the leader of a country to talk carelessly about this kind of issue is a bit of joke. If a US President exhorted all Americans to see a movie for uplift, he would become a laughing stock. There would be a thousand cartoons ridiculing him. Of course, you could say Jiang also considers himself a human being, and might simply be trying to say that he loves movies. Or that he wants to show his appreciation of films in the same way that he likes to show that he understands German and English. Actually, *Titanic* has a quite different significance. It is a story about Western modernity, high technology and money at the beginning of the twentieth century; then the ship crashed and sank. This is the symbolic meaning of the movie. But nobody in China discussed it. The film won its audiences as high-tech entertainment.

Wang Dan   What attracts people are those amazing spectacles, which are vextremely beautiful. The whole sky is full of stars and people are fascinated.

February 21, 1999

Postscript

What is your view of the bombing of the Chinese embassy in Belgrade by the United States? How do you interpret official and popular responses in China to NATO's war in Yugoslavia?

Li Minqi   The attack on Yugoslavia is an imperialist war without legal or moral justification. NATO's 'humanitarian mission' has already killed over a thousand civilians, and made many more homeless and jobless. The American bombing of the Chinese embassy was only one of these crimes. Whether or not it was premeditated is a secondary issue, although all serious technical analyses suggest how difficult it would have been to make such a mistake. The main point is that the bombing of the embassy simply demonstrated how crazy and barbaric NATO's war has become.

An unintended consequence of it has been to educate the Chinese people in a brutal, but effective, way. Ten years ago, Chinese students celebrated the Statue of Liberty, symbol of Western bourgeois democracy. Today they are burning the American flag in the streets. The anti-imperialist demonstrations in the big Chinese cities mark a sea-change in outlook. A new generation of students and intellectuals has begun to understand the limits of 'freedom of the press' in the West – as they see the way Western media have served as propaganda outlets for the war, suppressing alternative voices – and has started to question the nature of the political system in whose name it is being fought. For the first time in many years, socialist terms and ideas can be heard again. This is a very encouraging development. Meanwhile, liberal intellectuals used to glorifying everything from the West are in serious disarray. Those who have chosen to echo the mainstream media in the West have shown their complete indifference to the feelings and wishes of ordinary people in China. Their influence on the newest generation of students has consequently been greatly undermined, if not yet altogether discredited.

Wang Dan   The first large-scale student movement in a decade exploded in a score of Chinese cities, starting on May 8, in protest against the bombing of the Chinese embassy in Belgrade by NATO. I supported this, for two reasons. Firstly, patriotic passion is a valuable force in itself. It was just this passion that students brought onto the streets of the country in 1989. As Chinese, we ought to uphold the honour of our country and the dignity of our nation. Secondly, it is a positive sign that, after ten years of silence, college students are once again speaking to society. In the 1990s, the mercenary calculations of a commercialized society overwhelmed ideal-istic social concerns among Chinese youth. Consequently, the traditional role of students as a klaxon of public issues virtually disappeared. I hope what we now see is a new beginning, which will revive among a younger generation of students the spirit of personal responsibility for the fate of the nation ['the concern of everyone for the prosperity and ruin of all under heaven' – moral imperative from Ming times].

However, as the high-tide of this student movement recedes, we also need to reflect calmly, and make three distinctions. Firstly, we need to distinguish patriotism from nationalism. Patriotism is a virtue, whereas nationalism – once it becomes emotional – may not be to the long-term advantage of the country. There were some excessive actions in this latest student movement, such as setting fire to the American embassy or consular buildings, assaulting foreign journalists, and so forth. Although these were not the main trend, they showed the danger of too emotive a protest. The student movement should stick to the principles of peace, reason and non-violence. Secondly, we need to distinguish between the country and the state. We love China because we are the people of China, not because we are subjects of the Chinese government. So, when we give expression to our patriotic passion, we still need to think for ourselves. For example, when Japan repeatedly challenged China's claim to the Diaoyu islands, or mobs viciously attacked the Chinese minority in Indonesia, the PRC authorities twice refused to grant Beijing students permission to hold protest rallies. Obviously, political purposes other than defending national dignity were behind this double standard.

Thirdly, we need to distinguish conjunctural reactions from long-term strategies. We strongly condemn the bombing of our embassy by NATO member states, but we must not extend this to a rejection of everything Western or American. If the current conjunctural reaction were to be perpetuated as the basis of a long-term strategy for China, the country would revert to a bygone 'Closed-Door era'. History has shown that, without opening its doors to the outside world, China cannot become a strong power.

Wang Chaohua   I believe that NATO's air strike against Yugoslavia is illegal. This is an invasion of a sovereign state whose government was – not perfectly, but in a rough way – democratically elected. Such armed intervention in the affairs of another country by big powers implies a revival of a colonial outlook in new forms. NATO justifies its actions on the grounds that the sovereignty of the 'nation-state' should today give way to 'universal' values. Meanwhile, not a single NATO state has given up its own national security apparatus, or shared its wealth with those who are suffering the consequences of frightful inter-state wars in Africa or financial crises in Asia. Instead, NATO wages war against the Serb nation in Europe, dropping cluster bombs on residential areas and shattering the country's infrastructure, plunging an entire people into misery, in the name of helping the Kosovans, whose life has also deteriorated since the air attacks started.

Many Chinese were sceptical about the US-led intervention in the Balkans from the start. When five American 'smart' missiles hit the PRC embassy in Belgrade, it would have been unimaginable if the Chinese people – with their own memories of Western colonial arrogance – had not reacted spontaneously and strongly. It would also be surprising if they had easily accepted official explanations that it was a mistake by the CIA, without any sign of a thorough investigation of the operation. At the same time, the Chinese government is heavily handicapped in its response to the attack by its economic dependence on the flow of inward Western investment. Beyond a pro forma appeal to the United Nations, whose impotence in the Balkans was made clear from the outset, the PRC took no serious diplomatic measures to disturb the course of the war. Its only gesture was to break off talks with the US about human rights – as if refusing to discuss its own violations of them in China, rather than indicting American violations of them in Yugoslavia, was an intelligent response to the bombing.

May 31, 1999

Translated by Xiaoping Cong
Joel Andreas
Li Minqi
Wang Chaohua

Selected Glossary

'An-gang xianfa'   '鞍钢宪法'
'baijin wenxue'   '拜金文学'
Bian Wu   卞悟
' "Bu daode" de jingjixue'   "不道德"的经济学

Cai Xiang   蔡翔
Cai Yuanpei   蔡元培
Cao Jinqing   曹锦清
Cao Weidong   曹卫东
Chen Duxiu   陈独秀
Chen Jingrun   陈景润
Chen Pingyuan   陈平原
Chen Xiaoming   陈晓明
Chen Yangu   陈燕谷
Chen Yinke   陈寅恪
Chen Yuan   陈原
Chen Ziming   陈子明
Cheng Xiaonong   程晓农
'chi huangliang'   吃皇粮
Chiang Ching-kuo   蒋经国
Chiang Kai-shek   蒋介石
Cui Jian   崔健
Cui Zhiyuan (Cui Zhi-yuan)   崔之元
cun   村

Dai Jinhua   戴锦华
dang zheng fenli   党政分离
Daqing   大庆
dazhong wenhua   大众文化
Deng Lijun   邓丽君
Deng Liqun   邓力群
Deng Xiaoping   邓小平

Ding Ling   丁玲
diyu minzhu   地域民主
Dong Xiuyu   董秀玉
Dongfang   *东方*
Dongfang shikong   东方时空
duli zhi jingshen, ziyou zhi sixiang
独立之精神，自由之思想
'Duobi chonggao'   '躲避崇高'
Dushu   *读书*

Ershi yi shiji   *二十一世纪*
Fan Gang   樊钢
Fan Wenlan   范文澜
Fang Lizhi   方励之
fang quan rang li   放权让利
fanshipai   凡是派
Fei Xiaotong   费孝通
fen zao chifan   分灶吃饭
Fengfu de tongku   *丰富的痛苦*
Gan Yang   甘阳
Gaobie geming   *告别革命*
Ge Fei   格非
Gonggong luncong   *公共论丛*
gongren shi qiye de zhurenweng
工人是企业的主人翁
gongxiao hezuo she   供销合作社
Gu Zhun   顾准
guanliqu   管理区
Guo Moruo   郭沫若
Guo qin lun   *过秦论*
guogu   国故
guoxue   国学

guoxue re 国学热

Han Deqiang 韩德强
Han Dongfang 韩东方
Han Shaogong 韩少功
Han Yuhai 韩毓海
He Qinglian 何清涟
He shang 河殇
He Weifang 贺卫方
He Zuoxiu 何祚庥
hei wu lei 黑五类
Hou Xiao Xien (Hou Hsiao-Hsien) 侯孝贤
Hu Angang 胡鞍钢

Hu Jintao 胡锦涛
Hu Qiaomu 胡乔木
Hu Shih 胡适
Hu Yaobang 胡耀邦
Hua Guofeng 华国锋
Huang Ziping 黄子平
Huang Zongxi 黄宗羲
Huanghe bian shang de Zhongguo 黄河边上的中国
Ji Weidong 季卫东
Jia Yi (Chia Yi) 贾谊
Jiang Zemin 江泽民
jiangfen fei 降分费
jiaoyu chanyehua 教育产业化
Jin Guantao 金观涛
Jin Yan 金雁
Jing Ke 荆柯
Jingji tizhi bijiao yanjiu 经济体制比较研究
jingshi 经世
jingxue 经学
jiu xue xin zhi 旧学新知
kuozhao 扩招

Lankao 兰考
Lao Tse (Lao Zi) 老子
Lee Teng-Hui 李登辉
Li Changping 李昌平
Li Gongpu 李公朴

Li Honglin 李洪林
Li Hongzhang 李鸿章
Li Lanqing 李岚清
Li Minqi 李民骐
Li Peilin 李培林
Li Peng 李鹏
Li Qiang 李强
Li Ruihuan 李瑞环
Li Shenzhi 李慎之
li tu bu li xiang 离土不离乡
Li Tuo 李陀
Li Xiaojiang 李小江
Li Yining 厉以宁
Li Zehou 李泽厚
lianchan chengbao zeren zhi
    (lianchan chengbao zhi) 联产承包责任制
Liang Qichao 梁启超
Liang Shuming (Liang Shu-ming) 梁漱溟
liguo 立国
lilun wuxu hui 理论务虚会
Lin Biao 林彪
liren 立人
Liu Junning 刘军宁
Liu Qingfeng 刘青峰
Liu Xiaofeng 刘小枫
Liu Zaifu 刘再复
Lu Chunlin 陆春林
Lu Shan 陆山
Lu Xun 鲁迅
Lu Xun quanji 鲁迅全集
Lun Zhongyang-difang guanxi 论中央地方关系

mai duan gongling 买断工龄
malie zhuyi laotaitai 马列主义老太太
Manhadun de Zhongguo nuren
                  曼哈顿的中国女人
Mao Dun 茅盾
Mao Zedong 毛泽东
min ban jiaoshi 民办教师
Min Bao 民报
Ming-pao 明报

minjian shehui　民间社会

minjian wenhua　民间文化

Minzhu Zhougguo　民主中国

'nalai zhuyi'　'拿来主义'

Nanfang zhoumo　南方周末

nu gong zhi　奴工制

Pengzhuang　碰撞

Qian Liqun　钱理群

Qian Mu　钱穆

qiang guo ruo min　强国弱民

Qiangguo, fumin, minzhu, wending

　　　　强国，富民，民主，稳定

Qiansha chuang xia　茜纱窗下

Qin Hui　秦晖

Qin Shi-Huangdi　秦始皇帝

Qipan xiang　棋盘乡

Qu Qiubai　瞿秋白

queru　阙如

qun　群

Ren Jiantao　任剑涛

renguo　人国

rentou fei　人头费

renwen jingshen　人文精神

Renwen jingshen xunsi lu　人文精神寻思录

Rong Jingben　荣敬本

Ru Zhijuan　茹志娟

'Sanbajie you gan'　'三八节有感'

shan daiwang　山大王

Shang Yang　商鞅

Shanghai wenxue　上海文学

Shangjun shu　商君书

shehui　社会

Shen Changwen　沈昌文

Sheng Hong　盛洪

shi dafu　士大夫

'Shihua shishuo'　'实话实说'

Shijie　视界

shishiqiushi　实事求是

Shuwu　书屋

sifa suo　司法所

Sima Guang　司马光

Sima Qian　司马迁

Su Shaozhi　苏绍智

Su Wen　苏文

Su Xiaokang　苏晓康

Sun Liping　孙立平

Sun Yat-sen　孙逸仙（孙中山）

Sun Zi　孙子（兵法）

Tan Tianrong　谭天荣

Tang Yijie　汤一介

Tianya　天涯

Tongmenghui　同盟会

Tu Wei-ming　杜维明

wan yan shu　万言书

Wang Anyi　王安忆

Wang Chaohua　王超华

Wang Dan　王丹

Wang Dingding　汪丁丁

Wang Guowei　王国维

Wang Hui　汪晖

Wang Juntao　王军涛

Wang Lixiong　王力雄

Wang Meng　王蒙

Wang Ruoshui　王若水

Wang Shaoguang　王绍光

Wang Shouchang　王守常

Wang Shuo　王朔

Wang Xiaobo　王小波

Wang Xiaodong　王小东

Wang Xiaoming　王晓明

Wang Yan　王焱

Wang Yi　王怡

Wang Yuanhua　王元化

wanzhu wenxue　顽主文学

Wei Guoqing　韦国清

Wei Jingsheng　魏京生

Wen Jiabao　温家宝

Wen Tiejun　温铁军

Wen Yiduo   闻一多

Wo xiang zongli shuo shihua   我向总理说实话

Wu Guoguang   吴国光

Wu Jinglian   吴敬琏

'Wuqi zhishi'   '五七指示'

wuxu pai   务虚派

xi xue dong jian   西学东渐

xiagang   下岗

xian   县

Xiandaihua de xianjing   现代化的陷阱

xiang   乡

xiao pizi   小痞子

Xiao Xuehui   肖雪慧

xiaokang   小康

xing she xing zi   姓社姓资

xinxinkuku jishi nian, yizhao huidao jiefang qian
                    辛辛苦苦几十年，一朝回到解放前

xixue   西学

Xu Ben   徐贲

Xu Jilin   许纪霖

Xu Weicheng   徐惟诚

Xu Youyu   徐友渔

xue zai minjian   学在民间

Xueren   学人

xueshu shi   学术史

xueshu suibi   学术随笔

xuetong lun   血统论

'Xuezhe de renjian qinghuai'   '学者的人间情怀'

yan da   严打

Yan Fu   严复

Yan Jiaqi   严家其

Yang Fan   杨帆

Yang Jisheng   杨继盛

yangwu yundong   洋务运动

Yao Yilin   姚依林

yi zi dai lao   以资代劳

ying shi jiaoyu   应试教育

Yu Guangyuan   于光远

Yu Hua   余华

Yu Ying-shih   余英时

Yuan Shikai   袁世凯

zanzhu fei   赞助费

Zeng Guofan   曾国藩

zhaiji fei   宅基费

Zhang Chengzhi   张承志

Zhang Rulun   张汝伦

Zhang Shuguang   张曙光

Zhang Taiyan   章太炎

Zhang Weiying   张维迎

Zhang Xudong   张旭东

Zhang Yimou   张艺谋

Zhang Yiwu   张颐武

Zhanlüe yu guanli   战略与管理

Zhao Yiheng   赵毅衡

Zhao Ziyang   赵紫阳

zhen   镇

Zheng Yongnian   郑永年

zhenli biaozhun   真理标准

zhi zheng zhaoxi   只争朝夕

zhishi fenzi   知识分子

zhiyong   致用

Zhongguo de xianjing   中国的陷阱

Zhongguo jin sanbai nian xueshu shi
                    中国近三百年学术史

Zhongshan   钟山

Zhou Enlai   周恩来

Zhou Lisan   周立三

Zhou Litai   周立太

Zhou Qiren   周其仁

Zhou Yang   周扬

Zhu Rongji   朱镕基

Zhu Wei   朱伟

Zhu Xi   朱熹

Zhu Xueqin   朱学勤

Zhuang (nationality)   壮

ziliudi fei   自留地费

zu miao gongchan   族庙公产

Contributors

Wang Hui is Professor of Humanities at Tsinghua University and co-editor of *Dushu* (Readings). Of his many works, the most recent are *Zhongguo xiandai sixiang de qiyuan* (The Rise of Modern Chinese Thought) (2002) and *China's New Order: Society, Politics, and Economy in Transition*, edited by Theodore Huters (2003).

Zhu Xueqin is Professor of History at Shanghai University. His major works include *Daode lixiang guo de fumie: Cong Lusuo dao Luobosibi'er* (The demise of the Republic of Virtue: from Rousseau to Robespierre) (1994) and *Shuzhai li de geming* (Revolution inside a study) (1999).

Chen Pingyuan is Professor of Chinese Literature at Peking University. His major works include *Qiangu wenren xiake meng* (The Literati's Chivalric Dreams: Narrative Models of Chinese Knight-Errant Literature) (1991), *Zhongguo xiandai xueshu shi de jianli: Yi Zhang Taiyan, Hu Shizhi wei zhongxin* (The establishment of modern scholarship in China: A case study centered on Zhang Taiyan and Hu Shih) (1998).

Qin Hui is Professor of History at Tsinghua University. His most recent works include *Si wu ya, xing you zhi* (Thinking without limits, walking with care) (2002), and *Jingji zhuangui yu shehui gongzheng* (Economic transition and social fairness), co-authored with Jin Yan (2002).

He Qinglian is teaching at City University of New York, Staten. Her major works are *Xiandaihua de xianjing* (Modernization's Pitfall) (1998) and *Women rengran zai yangwang xingkong* (We are still watching the starry sky), Guilin, 2001.

Wang Yi is a lecturer at the Law School at Chengdu University, Sichuan. He hosted influential Internet forums in China, and writes widely for leading intellectual journals, such as *Dushu* and *Shuwu*. His writings are collected in *Zaiman e de huoche* (A train loaded with geese) (2001) and *Fucong de jianghu* (Obedient water margin) (2003).

Li Changping was a rural cadre and now is a researcher in Beijing. He gives a first-hand account of fighting against corruption in his best-selling book, *Wo xiang zongli shuo shihua* (Telling the Prime Minister the Truth) (2002).

Hu Angang is Professor in the School of Public Policy and Management at Tsinghua University. His most recent works include *The Chinese Economy in Crisis: State Capacity and Tax Reform*, co-authored with Shaoguang Wang (2001).

Xiao Xuehui is Professor of Ethics at Southwest Nationality Academy, Sichuan. Her major works include *Yuzhou liangzhi – xin lunli wenhua shiye* (Conscience and universe: A new cultural perspective on ethics) (1998).

Wang Anyi is a writer whose works have been widely translated into other languages, including, in English, *Lapse of Time* (short story collection, 1988) and *Baotown* (1989). Her latest novels include *Chang hen ge* (Song of eternal sorrow) (1996) and *Shang zhong honglian xia zhong ou* (Crimson flower above and lotus roots below) (2000).

Gan Yang is a research fellow at the Centre of Asian Studies at the University of Hong Kong. His major works include *We Are Creating Tradition* (1989) and *Reflections on Liberalism* (1997).

Wang Xiaoming is Professor of Cultural Studies at Shanghai University, and Professor of Chinese Literature at East China Normal University. His most recent works include *Wang Xiaoming zixuan ji* (Self selection of Wang Xiaoming) (1997) and *Ban zhang lian de shenhua* (Myth of half-face) (2003).

Qian Liqun was Professor of Chinese Literature at Peking University until his retirement in 2002. His recent works include *1948: Tiandi xuanhuang* (1948: Heaven and earth in turmoil) (1998), and *Fanguan yu chonggou: Wenxueshi de yanjiu yu xiezuo* (Reflecting and Reconstructing: The writing of literary history) (2000).

Wang Dan is a Ph.D. student in Chinese studies at Harvard University. A top leader of the student movement in Beijing 1989, he was jailed for four years, released in 1993, and re-imprisoned for subversion in 1995, before being exiled to the US in the spring of 1998. He writes widely in Chinese language media and has published a collection of poems written in prison.

Li Minqi teaches economics at York University, Canada. A graduate student at Peking University in 1990, he was arrested and jailed for two years for publicly commemorating the first anniversary of the military crackdown in Beijing. He earned his Ph.D in economics from the University of Massachusetts, Amherst.

Wang Chaohua is a Ph.D candidate in modern Chinese literature at the University of California, Los Angeles. A student in the Graduate School at the Chinese Academy of Social Sciences in 1989, she was active in the pro-democracy movement that year. She arrived in the US in 1990.

Index